ABOUT ISLAND PRESS

Island Press is the only nonprofit organization in the United States whose principal purpose is the publication of books on environmental issues and natural resource management. We provide solutions-oriented information to professionals, public officials, business and community leaders, and concerned citizens who are shaping responses to environmental problems.

In 2004, Island Press celebrates its twentieth anniversary as the leading provider of timely and practical books that take a multidisciplinary approach to critical environmental concerns. Our growing list of titles reflects our commitment to bringing the best of an expanding body of literature to the environmental community throughout North America and the world.

Support for Island Press is provided by the Agua Fund, Brainerd Foundation, Geraldine R. Dodge Foundation, Doris Duke Charitable Foundation, Educational Foundation of America, The Ford Foundation, The George Gund Foundation, The William and Flora Hewlett Foundation, Henry Luce Foundation, The John D. and Catherine T. MacArthur Foundation, The Andrew W. Mellon Foundation, The Curtis and Edith Munson Foundation, National Environmental Trust, The New-Land Foundation, Oak Foundation, The Overbrook Foundation, The David and Lucile Packard Foundation, The Pew Charitable Trusts, The Rockefeller Foundation, The Winslow Foundation, and other generous donors.

The opinions expressed in this book are those of the author(s) and do not necessarily reflect the views of these foundations.

Native to Nowhere

NATIVE TO NOWHERE

SUSTAINING HOME AND COMMUNITY IN A GLOBAL AGE

TIMOTHY BEATLEY

⬤ **ISLAND**PRESS | WASHINGTON • COVELO • LONDON

ISLAND PRESS is a trademark of The Center for Resource Economics.

Library of Congress Cataloging-in-Publication data.

Beatley, Timothy, 1957-
  Native to nowhere : sustaining home and community in a global age / Timothy Beatley.
    p. cm.
  Includes bibliographical references and index.
  ISBN 1-55963-914-8 (cloth : alk. paper) — ISBN 1-55963-453-7 (pbk. : alk. paper)
  1. Community life. 2. Neighborhood. 3. Home. 4. Identity (Psychology) 5. Socialization. 6. Quality of life. I. Title.
  HM761.B4 2004
  307—dc22   2004012080

British Cataloguing-in-Publication data available.

Printed on recycled, acid-free paper

Design by Kathleen Szawiola

Photographs by Tim Beatley, except where noted.

Manufactured in the United States of America
10 9 8 7 6 5 4 3 2 1

To my daughter, Carolena, in the hope that she will have a green and healthy city in which to live and flourish.

Contents

Preface and Acknowledgments

This book has grown from nearly eight years of work visiting and attempting to understand many innovative local sustainability projects and communities. It is born from the strong belief that any real solution to our current environmental and sustainability challenges will by necessity be *local*. Designing, redesigning, and building communities that work for residents, that respect and strengthen unique qualities of place, and that acknowledge extralocal connections and obligations must be at the core of any future global environmental strategy.

Much of *Native to Nowhere* builds closely on my earlier work. In particular, the European cases and observations build on *Green Urbanism* (2000), in which I examined thirty cities and sustainability initiatives in twelve European communities. New European cases and cities take advantage of the extensive travel and fieldwork I have done since *Green Urbanism* was published. In particular, the discussions to follow draw from my recent field visits to Sweden, Finland, Italy, Germany, Spain, Belgium, the United Kingdom, the Netherlands, and several former eastern bloc countries, including Poland and Lithuania.

This European work began for me with a year's residence in the Netherlands, in the beautiful city of Leiden, and the experience and timeless lessons of this city continue to influence my work. Following this residence, Leiden has continued as my family's adopted home for summers and academic breaks, and continues to teach us many things. My debt to this city is great and is reflected in many ways in *Native to Nowhere*.

The book also builds on *The Ecology of Place* (1997), essentially an examination of local sustainability practices in the United States. In addition,

I have benefited from extensive recent visits to a number of U.S. and Canadian cities and regions, which have inspired and informed much of what follows. In particular, visits to and time spent in Vancouver, Chicago, Cleveland, Seattle, Tucson, and New York City have all been important to the thinking herein.

There are many people and organizations in these European and North American cities to which I owe a debt of thanks; really, too many to give an accurate reporting here. As usual, Heather Boyer of Island Press provided great editorial advice and guidance.

Special thanks go to my patient and understanding family. My wife, Anneke, in particular deserves my gratitude for her tremendous loving support and great personal enthusiasm for the subjects of this book. She has served as an essential sounding board, another set of eyes for interpreting European and American cities and landscapes, and a fount of good advice and valuable insights.

In the four years since the publication of *Green Urbanism* my most significant life change has been the birth of our daughter, Carolena. She has changed my perspective on the world, and on cities in particular, in profound and unimaginable ways. She has given me not only her spirit, energy, and laughter, but also her penetrating child's perspective on place. I have had the great fortune to view the world and its cities, towns, communities, and landscapes through her fresh eyes. I have become convinced that planners, especially, have much to learn from the young, and my daughter has repeatedly demonstrated the bounty of insights that emerge when one listens and acknowledges the place of the young in our lives and communities. If there is any hope that we can create livable and sustainable cities in the future, it is because we believe the dreams and spirit of our young.

In the end, I have benefited from many people in writing this book—colleagues, friends, family—and I thank them all. Any mistakes, misinterpretations, and faulty reasoning present here are, of course, mine entirely.

Sustaining Place in the Global Age

A couple sitting next to me at a Starbucks in Falls Church, Virginia, was admiring the music being piped in and asked the Starbucks employee behind the counter who the musician was. You might have thought they were asking for an explanation of Fermi's Paradox. The flustered young man behind the counter confessed that he did not know who it was and really had no easy way to find out because the music was mixed and programmed in Seattle and sent to Starbucks stores across the country.

Starbucks's need to so firmly control the musical ambiance of their stores is a small thing, to be sure, but a telling window into the many ways in which global companies influence the texture and quality of people's lives. Whether by intention or not, the cumulative cuts at our unique places, the places we call home, the local realm, are real and insidious. Starbucks stores seem to be on every corner of every major city.

There are, of course, many advantages and benefits of our global era. We have a wide range of products and goods from around the world. We enjoy fruits, vegetables, and other agricultural products in the dead of winter, and we owe many jobs and much income to global trade and commerce. There is much to be positive about, as proponents of globalization are quick to point out.

And, certainly, I like Starbucks coffee. When I'm on trips, even short distances from my home, I'm pleasantly relieved when I discover a Starbucks. I know what to expect.

But the proliferation of mind-numbing sameness is an alarming trend. As the march of globalization continues, it manifests across the continent in places that look and feel alike. In shopping malls that carry the same stores, and in commercial strips that have the same fast-food franchises, there is a stifling sense of sameness to the new suburban and exurban landscapes we inhabit. The mall of America replaces Main Street. Starbucks replaces the corner coffee shop. There is little sense of the historical background and unique histories of the places where we live, and even less real understanding of the ecological heritage and natural landscapes upon which we rely. The rise of an Internet culture of virtual places may, for many at least, represent a replacement for actual places.

That we need particular and unique places is a central tenet of this book. We need places that provide healthy living environments and also nourish the soul—distinctive places worthy of our loyalty and commitment, places where

Figure 1.1 | Sprawling land use patterns seem designed primarily to support the lives of automobiles, not people.

we feel at home, places that inspire and uplift and stimulate us and that provide social and environmental sustenance.

The growing uniformity and anonymity of contemporary settlement patterns begets an attitude that they are disposable and interchangeable. One is just like another. Without intimate contact with real places, there is little chance that the loss of environments and the practice of unsustainable patterns of consumption and resource exploitation will be reversed. Perhaps now more than ever, in the face of global economic and social forces, the march of sameness, and the reckless treatment of landscapes and environment, we need the solace and support of places. Now more than ever we need to revisit what it means to be *native* to where we live, to recommit to place.

The Value of Real Places

At the heart of this book is the belief that reconnecting to people and landscapes at the local level and having a better understanding of the built and natural surroundings in which we live will result in better, more enjoyable, healthier, and more fulfilling lives. Meaningful lives require unique and particular places.

Certainly, part of our current crisis of place is the crisis of community. We are clearly a social species, though that would be difficult to discern from the many forces and impulses driving us (literally) apart. We can experience emotionally rich and gratifying lives only through deep personal interactions with other human beings. The evidence of our need for others, of our need for close and direct personal contact, is considerable. We know, for instance, that individuals with more extensive social networks and friendship patterns are actually healthier, and that such networks and relationships are essential for surviving the buffeting waves of life (e.g., Trafford, 2000).

There is a compelling and growing literature that demonstrates the critical emotional value of friendships and social networks, which in turn translate into improvements in health. For example, Karen Weihs, a professor of psychiatry at George Washington University, has shown the value of friendship networks in women diagnosed with breast cancer. In a seven-year study, she found that women with larger networks of friends were more likely to have survived the cancer (Weihs, 2001; see also Mann, 2001; Elias, 2001). Lisa Berkman, an epidemiologist from Yale, found similar results in looking at longevity for those who have suffered heart attacks. People with extensive social support networks lived much longer than those with little support (Berkman, 1995; see also Frasure-Smith et al., 2000). Having more extensive social networks has been associated with reduced deaths from accidents and suicide, with reducing the onset of dementia, and with slowing down the progression of diseases such as HIV (Kawachi et al., 1996; Leserman, 2001; Brummett et al., 2001).

Loneliness, then, is now understood as a major risk factor, and as an increasingly large number of both the young and the old find themselves living alone, the emotional and health-enhancing values of place are ever more essential. Genuine and strong places must now be expected to do much of the "heavy lifting" in building a healthy, happy society.

Places can facilitate social interaction, to be sure—through urban form that permits walking, an abundance of "third places" (other than work or home) for socializing, investments in pedestrian and bicycle infrastructure, inspirational architecture and interesting design; and through sponsoring or convening many public events, from parades to place celebrations—and as a result they are likely to bring about better health and enjoyment through greater levels of physical activity on the part of their inhabitants. Overly sedentary lifestyles and bad food choices have resulted in an "obesity epidemic" (Centers for Disease Control, 2002; Jackson, 2003). Large numbers of Americans (almost 70 percent) are simply not getting the requisite physical activity—a recommended thirty minutes or 10,000 steps per day—to keep them healthy and to stave off many types of illness and disease (Centers for Disease Control, 2002). The benefits of daily physical activity are also emotional and mental, as exercise generates endorphins, the body's natural painkillers, and has positive effects on mood and outlook. A reinvigorated local realm has the potential to profoundly improve public health in this way, while making possible more enjoyable, meaningful lives.

Direct involvement in our communities and neighborhoods is another element in a meaningful, healthy life and will often yield tremendous enjoyment and personal satisfaction. Strong communities can do much to facilitate this participation and make it easy and enticing. Volunteering and other types of community involvement are not only essential to building a sense of commitment to place but also yield many personal benefits, deepen our lives, and give meaning to what we do (e.g., Miles et al., 1998). Participating in civic activities of various kinds builds place bonds and place commitments, strengthens local democracy, and is good for our health and emotional well-being (Victoria Population Health Survey, 2001).

Places that provide the spaces, reasons, and opportunities for people to come together, to share their passions, hopes, and troubles, will be healthier, stronger places and places where people trust and care about each other. And the more involved and engaged we are, the more likely we are to care about our communities and to be committed to working on their behalf in the future. It is a virtuous circle that real places understand and actively cultivate.

In one of the first national studies of *social capital,* the social networks and shared norms that serve to bind us together, prepared by the Saguaro Seminar at the Kennedy School at Harvard, some interesting conclusions were reached about positive relationships between community connectedness and personal happiness. Controlling for income and education levels, the study found that the extent of community social connectedness and trust were highly associated with the greater personal happiness reported by

Figure 1.2 | The march of sameness: the typical depressing commercial strip with chain stores, fast food restaurants, a sea of parking, and many opportunities to buy the same kinds of products.

respondents (Sagara Seminar, undated). Being connected to others and to a broader community will (help to) make us happy.

Place helps overcome anonymity. Real places, real communities where people know each other and have deep connections to and understanding of each other, are in turn much more likely to be caring places. Homelessness, poverty, inadequate health care, to name a few of our more pressing contemporary challenges, are easy to ignore in lives lived in isolation, in cars and cul-de-sacs. We don't see these people, and we don't grasp the seriousness and reality of these problems; the people and issues are abstract and remote, and consequently we don't care about them. Real communities offer the great promise of nurturing an ethic of care and responsibility. It is more difficult to ignore community needs, individual and family suffering, when they are attached to recognizable names and faces.

Good and real places have the power to make us happy, or at least to lay the critical foundations for personal happiness, over the full course of our lives. There has been considerable research in recent years about what it takes to ensure health and happiness as we age, and again, not surprisingly, physical activity and mental and social engagement have been found to be critical. Even modest regular physical activity has tremendous health benefits, including prevention of stroke and osteoporosis. Hartman-Stein and Potkanowicz (2003) in their review of the research conclude that "regular physical activity in our daily lives is the greatest weapon we have against the on-set of age-related disease and disability." Considerable research, moreover, demonstrates that cognitive health and happiness require mental exercise as well as social participation and engagement. What some have called a "sense of embeddedness," or feeling a part of a community or social network, appears to extend longevity in older people (Greene, 2000). These studies suggest the central importance of strong neighborhoods and communities, and the benefits of volunteering and of participation and engagement in the social and political life of place.

Genuine communities challenge prevailing assumptions about happiness in the modern age. Much conventional thinking still seems to hold that material objects and material consumption holds the secret to personal happiness. "Bigger and more" and "faster and more convenient" are key descriptors for much of our current community design and planning: bigger cars, bigger homes, more and faster technological gadgets, longer distances and land-scapes to travel through in our pursuit of the accoutrements of modern American life. Yet, perhaps most of us know the truth of the expression "money can't buy happiness," and a growing body of research confirms this. A study published in the *Journal of Personality and Social Psychology* con-cludes that the most important factors in determining personal satisfaction are a sense of autonomy, competence, relatedness ("feeling that you have reg-ular intimate contact with people who care about you rather than feeling lonely and uncared for"), and self-esteem. Not making the list were influence, luxury, or money, many of the things that we typically (and falsely) associate with a happy life (Sheldon et al., 2001).

Reconnecting to place is about taking control of our lives. Much of our frustration today is a function of our feelings of having little or no control over the events and dynamics that shape and affect us, whether military ac-tion in Iraq or an economic downturn or the morning traffic congestion in which we find ourselves stuck. Commitments to place are about taking charge, about proactively participating in the creation of one's own life, while at the same time seeking to connect to others.

It may be difficult to affect or influence the broader economic and social forces, but commitments to and participation at the level of place offers the possibility of real change, of making important differences in the feel and quality of one's own life and the lives of others in the community. And as the stories and examples in this book show, the methods of personal engagement are myriad: creating public art, gardening, mentoring a child, shopping at a community food store, and strolling in one's own neighborhood, for example.

An agenda of strong and vital places has a tremendous potential to build greater resilience into our communities and individual lives in many ways, from place-based energy systems that strengthen the economy, protect the lo-cal (and global) environment, and contribute to uniqueness of place, to green forms of infrastructure that provide essential services while celebrating and protecting important place qualities.

If happiness is at least in part about the richness of experience, exposure to a vitality and variety of voices and perspectives is essential. Bigness and the growing corporate consolidation in our society and in our communities fur-ther diminish place and uniqueness of place. For example, the recent changes in Federal Communication Commission rules allowing greater corporate ownership of local media, and the general trends in this direction, threaten the expression of many diverse and locally unique voices. It is already common practice for many seemingly local television and radio broadcasts—the weather, the state and local news—to originate hundreds of miles away in the studios of large, centralized news organizations. It is not just that the stores and cafés of the future will look alike and carry the same fare, but, perhaps even more profound, that the voice and message from media may increasingly have a singular content. In this way, sameness in place strikes at the very heart of our democracy.

Local communities have it within their power to provide safe harbor for and actively cultivate these unique local voices and talents, to the enjoyment of many. Local-oriented media, community radio and television, can be an important element in strengthening communities and emphasizing the uniqueness of place, providing a partial antidote to sameness. Creative community media centers, such as the one in Grand Rapids, Michigan, provide local media training and cover local music, artists, community events, and much more.

The challenges of growing centralization and consolidation in our society, which manifest in a marked shift away from a neighborhood and community orientation, are considerable indeed. As supermarkets have become larger, many smaller neighborhood groceries have closed. To reach the supermarket, one needs a car, often making it harder for the less affluent members of the community to reach them (Sustainable Food Center, undated). Small pharmacies, bakeries, and clothing stores have fallen to the one-stop shopping of *supercenters,* now getting ever larger. Movie theaters have also gotten larger, with an ever-rising number of screens to choose from. The Daly City Megaplex, in the San Francisco Bay Area, for instance, has an amazing twenty screens—"megaplex mania" reads a recent *San Francisco Chronicle* headline (Meyer, 2003). At the same time, many small neighborhood theaters have bitten the dust (an estimated three dozen over the last twenty years). Communities have resisted these changes, and organizations like the San Francisco Neighborhood Theater Foundation have formed to battle their loss, with some degree of success (Adams, 2002). Some of the new megaplexes are in downtown locations (such as San Mateo's twelve-screen

Century Theater), but many are not; they are for the most part large chains with little connection to the communities in which they are situated.

Genuine places have the potential to be profoundly more interesting and stimulating. Part of the essential stimulants of life is exposure to diversity of people, perspectives, and experiences. While we are being increasingly isolated, segmented, and sorted—by income, age, and ethnicity—we lose much of what makes our existence interesting. Part of what makes life interesting is the challenge of being confronted with different ideas, images, and perspectives that expand our thinking and force us to contemplate and process many things. The antidote in part to boring lives is the design and planning of unique places, the learning about the particular and special aspects of our home-place, the nurturing of and bringing to the surface the many different localized voices and talents in our midst.

The Nature of Place, the Places of Nature

We are social creatures, to be sure, but we are also creatures that need contact with nature and other forms of life. The natural environments in which our communities and neighborhoods have been built, and the proximity to and visceral connections with the natural world, are equally important elements of good and nourishing places. Meaningful and happy lives require connections with nature, and real places provide the contact with nature and our physical surroundings that are also necessary. E. O. Wilson, Harvard entomologist and authority on biodiversity, and others have argued persuasively that desire for connections to nature are hardwired, the result of centuries of evolution, really coevolution, of humans with their natural environments (Wilson, 1984; Kellert and Wilson, 1992). We need contact with nature—this is not an optional extra, it is essential to our well-being and to our emotional health, to a deep sense of who we are.

There are discernible and demonstrable physiological and emotional benefits from exposure to nature (Frumkin, 2001). Research shows we are calm and healthier when we own pets, and we are more relaxed looking at scenes of greenery and nature (Baker, 2002). Studies show that watching fish in aquariums reduces stress for patients about to undergo oral surgery (Katcher et al., 1984). Flowers and plants in the workplace have been found to enhance creative problem solving and productivity (Texas A&M University, undated). A classic study of patients with heart disease found increased longevity for those with pets (Friedman and Thomas, 1995). Natural gardens in hospitals have been shown to reduce stress and improve recovery of patients while also benefiting health care workers and the families of patients (e.g., see Cooper-Marcus and Barnes, 1999, 1985; Ulrich, 1983, 2002). Nancy Wells, a psychologist at Cornell University, has found that greenness and nature enhance the cognitive functioning in children (Wells, 2000).

Studies of nursing homes that are following the principle of the Eden Alternative, an effort to green and humanize nursing homes, found considerable positive benefits for the residents (better health, fewer behavior incidents) as well as reduced staff absenteeism. Presence of trees and greenspaces has been shown to reduce aggression and violence and to lessen mental fatigue (Kuo and Sullivan, 2001).

Health and well-being are positively affected by nature in many other ways, of course. Trees, urban forests, community gardens, and green rooftops serve to moderate urban temperatures, reduce air pollutants, and help control stormwater runoff. Such community greening techniques also reduce water and energy consumption (and thus indirectly the toxic emissions of power plant pollutants such as mercury). These benefits are in addition to the aesthetic and quality-of-life improvements that result from the important green elements of place.

In so many places today, and in so many ways, though, we turn our backs on the amazing natural (and cultural) heritage of the places where we live and the life-enhancing power they hold. The deepest ways in which our communities and regions are special and unique are typically ignored when making our most important public (and personal) decisions. The visual splendor of our home-place is often underappreciated, though profoundly important to our mental health. In many ways and on many levels the natural beauty of place is a comforting, uplifting, calming, steadying force, which gives many of us joy and pleasure. The market values that attach to views of Central Park in New York City or the Front Range of the Rocky Mountains, albeit both dramatic examples, support the premise that much is gained and enjoyed.

We develop subdivisions, commercial strip malls, and office complexes that ignore the intrinsic defining physical features and qualities of place. We ignore the topography, the existing vegetation patterns, the native flora and fauna, and the natural breezes and microclimatic conditions that are so important in shaping and defining a location. In my own community, it seems so odd that most development literally turns its back on the foothills and green verdant backdrops of Monticello and Carter's Mountain; what exerts a magnetic pull are the streets and traffic and the standard conventions of developing that seem impossible to break away from.

The status and condition of local biodiversity—the diversity and abundance of biological life in all its forms—whether judged in terms of individual species or broader ecosystem functions, is dismal and largely tied to the march of suburban and exurban sprawl. Sonoran desert is gobbled up by master-planned communities on the edge of cities (and beyond); salmon watersheds in the Northwest are deforested, paved over, and sent a toxic mix of urban runoff; the habitats of the Chesapeake Bay are disappearing in the face of second-home and residential growth. These habitats and natural systems are an absolutely essential component of what makes a place special and unique.

A significant pathway to greater meaning in our lives and greater commitment to place is understanding and knowing the landscapes, creatures, and people who live there. As Terry Tempest Williams has so eloquently said, ". . . if we don't know the names of things, if we don't know pronghorn antelope, if we don't know blacktail jackrabbit, if we don't know sage, pinyon, juniper, then I think we are living a life without specificity, and then our lives become abstractions. Then we enter a place of true desolation." (London, 1995)

Places to Help Us Overcome Lost Connections

An agenda of rebuilding and restoring strong unique places is largely about overcoming a variety of lost connections. Residents in American communities today have lost, for instance, much of their visceral connectedness to the seasons and rhythms of nature. And our "supply lines" are increasingly distant and abstract. Food arrives from far away—traveling an astounding 1,400 miles on average—and we lose all possible understanding of its source, how it was produced, who produced it, or the health of the lands and landscape that generated this generous bounty (Spector, 2000). We take no responsibility for how food is produced—for the energy used, the pesticides employed, the soil erosion created, and the habitat destroyed in the process of producing the matter that nourishes our bodies and often makes us happy.

Many of the natural processes and cycles that sustain us, and that might provide visceral connections to place, are often hidden away from us, thanks to modern engineering and the tendency toward leveling and paving. Stormwater is a good case in point. Our usual attitude is to see it as a problem to be overcome, something to contain, guide, and eliminate as quickly as possible from our urban and suburban neighborhoods. This attitude is changing in some communities, as a growing appreciation of how such things as rain gardens and stream day-lighting (uncovering and bringing to the surface streams and creeks that were formerly buried) can actually help to re-establish connections with our hydrological cycle and watersheds.

Another lost connection is intertemporal, that between generations and age groups. Symptomatic again of the physically isolating built form, active and intimate contact between generations is limited today. Connecting generations provides many important benefits—for the young, a visceral and genuine sense of history and the past, as well as specific knowledge, stories, and insights about what the community was like in an earlier time. The essential histories that define a place, moreover, are not just the built form or natural landscapes; they are the meanings and particular human histories that personalize them. Every community has a rich history and many compelling and special stories to tell about its past and the former residents who lived, married, raised families, started businesses, and undertook community and civic projects. Today there are few opportunities to learn this intimate history from those who lived it. On the other hand, older citizens benefit tremendously from the incredible energy, skills, insights, and optimism of the young. These intergenerational connections are part of what provides a sense of tangible grounding to place and a sense of the continuity of life that provides meaning.

As much as anything, our current disconnect with our natural environment and broader ecological home seems a function of a kind of disinterest or inattentiveness. Perhaps because we have less essential need to understand how our environment works in order to survive (we have others who grow the food and worry about frost, who think about and warn of impending dangerous weather, who deliver to us water, warmth, and light), we have forgotten how to pay close attention to these things. This is dramatically evident in the purchasing of a home where the greatest amount of attention is given to such things as the kind of countertops in the kitchen, the number of bathrooms and fireplaces, and the square footage of the unit. A prospective homebuyer is much less likely to be concerned about or ask about such place-connecting things as where the parcel drains to, where in the local watershed the home lies, from which direction the prevailing winds blow, and the extent to which native trees, plants, and wildlife can be found on the site.

There are, of course, many benefits to be had from restoring these lost connections: flavorful local food, beautiful landscapes of native plants and flowers, homes that use less energy because they have been sited to take advantage of unique local microclimates, the fascination and wonder to be found in understanding the hydrology, ecology, and celestial position of one's point in the universe, and of course the many new personal and potentially satisfying relationships that result (e.g., personally knowing the farmers who grow the vegetables you eat). These things should not be underestimated when accounting for what creates meaning in life.

Restored connections also provide critical ethical insights and capacities. A meaningful life is one that acknowledges duties and obligations and commitments beyond one's own narrow self-interest. "Doing the right thing" is commonly difficult because of the disconnect between personal actions and behaviors and the result or effects of those actions and choices. Restoring lost connections highlights these choices, helps point to their ethical implications, and provides guidance about how more responsible actions might be taken. "Owning" the impacts of one's energy consumption or food choices, for instance, in turn leads to the possibility of alternative place-strengthening choices—for example, buying locally produced food or supporting local renewable energy production. And we are almost never held accountable for the full cost of our extravagant choices, whether in terms of the environmental damage from excessive fossil fuel dependence, or the social costs of fleeing cities, or the long-term ecological damage done by our sprawling land use patterns. Without restoring these connections, the external and very large costs associated with our place-destructive ways are mostly hidden (though not unknown) and not factored into most of the choices and decisions we make. A meaningful life is a principled life, and without attending to these many lost connections, living a meaningful life is difficult or nearly impossible.

Economic Arguments for Place

Emphasizing the local and striving to create and maintain distinctive places also makes good economic sense. Today there is much understandable angst about the high cost of living, and especially the high cost of housing. At the civic or governmental level, the push continues to be in the direction of tightening belts and reducing budgets, finding ways to creatively do more with less. An emphasis on local, place-based strategies is frequently the most cost-effective way as well, and indeed most of the place-strengthening ideas presented in this book are strongly defensible on the grounds of economy. We know that community-diminishing sprawl and socially isolating systems of highways and cars are expensive. Actions to strengthen place can at the same time reduce the costs of fire, police, and other public services, and infrastructure investments such as sewer, water, and roads. Containing sprawl has been shown by some studies to cut infrastructure costs by nearly half (Sierra Club, 2000; 10,000 Friends of Pennsylvania, 2000).

Distinctive places, places that nurture and grow their unique qualities, that highlight and restore their natural environments, will in turn be places where people want to be and where businesses want to locate. Mayor Richard Daley's impressive greening efforts in Chicago are in part about being more environmentally responsible and in part about enhancing quality of life in that city, but largely about doing things that will make the city more attractive and economically competitive. Extensive tree-planting, brownfields redevelopment, improving bicycle facilities, installing green rooftops—these and many other place-strengthening actions have certainly paid dividends as people are returning to this city to live and businesses are locating here, motivated by this emerging "good address" (including, for example, the coup of enticing the Boeing Company to relocate their headquarters from Seattle).

The new attention being given to the role of the emergence of the "creative class" provides further support for many of the place-creating and place-strengthening ideas advocated here. Richard Florida's recent important work provides a complementary set of arguments for investing in places and nurturing their special qualities. Florida argues that members of this creative class, so important as drivers of innovation and growth, are especially attracted to cities with lots of lifestyle amenities (e.g., cafés, music, art galleries, nightlife, active outdoor recreation), cities that value diversity and provide diverse experiences, that are open, tolerant, and stimulating (Florida, 2002).

A place-strengthening agenda suggests real change in our economic development strategies and in looking beyond what is perhaps conventional or easy. Companies like Wal-Mart, BestBuy, and Home Depot, to name a few, have little reason to shepherd over or care about the quality of the environments in which their stores are located. Their primary concern is making money; perhaps we should expect little more than this. It's not their job to think about communities—it's ours. But we seem today ever more accepting of the mistaken premise that what will generate corporate profits will make us all (and our places) better off. We must tend over our places if we want to preserve their special qualities and the essential ways in which they help us to be grounded and human.

Smaller, locally owned businesses, it turns out, make good fiscal sense at the same time they help strengthen the community and contribute to its uniqueness and distinctiveness. A study of the public costs of different forms of growth in Barnstable, Massachusetts, prepared by Tischer Associates, is telling. When tax revenue and public costs, especially road maintenance and public safety costs, were taken into account, big box commercial was found to be a net loser—costing $468 per 1,000 square feet. Fast-food chains were the most fiscally costly—with a net cost to the community of a whopping $5,168 per 1,000 square feet (Mitchell, 2003). Specialty retail, on the other hand, generates a net profit for communities. A study by Austin, Texas–based Civic Economics found that the multiplier effect was dramatically greater for locally owned stores (Civic Economics, 2002). For a big box store, only $13 in additional local economic activity is produced, compared with more than three times that for locally owned stores (stores that buy local goods, pay local accountants, etc.). In Austin, plans for a Borders bookstore (and with considerable local subsidies) were scrapped in part when this analysis showed such a definite comparative economic benefit from local stores such as BookPeople and Waterloo Records. These stores, for a variety of reasons, are more likely to contribute to strengthening places—stocking local writers and artists, for instance, and recirculating more of the community's income and resources.

Many of the specific place-strengthening programs, policies, and projects described in the following chapters typically generate many more benefits than costs, even when judged in relatively short time frames. Designing schools to, for instance, maximize the presence of daylight not only enhances student performance and helps create healthier learning environments, but also saves energy and pays for itself almost immediately. A recent analysis of several dozen green-certified building projects in California concluded that while the green investments added on average less that 2 percent to the construction costs of the buildings, they yielded energy and cost savings of ten times this initial investment over a (relatively short) ten-year period (Kats, 2003).

Taking actions to strengthen and build upon the unique and special qualities of place will pay economic returns to a community, no question. Designation of historic districts, for example, has been found to raise property values in these areas (National Trust for Historic Preservation, 2002). Investments in parks and open space clearly increase property values as well (and have often generated additional tax revenues sufficient to pay for them in a short period), enhance the economic attractiveness of a city, and produce a host of valuable environmental and social benefits, from retaining and managing stormwater to stimulating walking and physical activity (see the report "A Healthier America? It's a Walk in the Park," prepared by Paul Sherer of the Trust for Public Land, 2003, for a good summary of the research and experience to date on this).

So, it appears that strengthening and renewing the special qualities of place and investing in environment and place amenities—all things that will lead to vibrant, sustainable places—will also amount to a very good economic development strategy.

Rebuilding Place

Although there are undoubtedly many ways in which long-term planetary health will require global strategies, the rubber hits the road (and the effluent reaches the stream) in actual places. Protecting and restoring the environment will be in no small measure about specific people caring for and actively working on behalf of real places. As the many place-building, community-building stories told in this book demonstrate, there is tremendous potential and promise for local actions and initiatives. From tree planting and habitat restoration to local renewable energy production, to building homes and neighborhoods in harmony and closer connection with nature and biodiversity, much can and must happen at the local level.

It is a key premise of this book, then, that we fundamentally *need* places, and in this increasingly global epoch this need is more critical than ever before. We need meaningful places to improve the quality of our lives and the depth and meaning of our personal and interpersonal relationships. Indeed, the planet needs such places for its very sustenance and survival and for that of its many generations of humans and other abundant life voyagers. Sustaining *place* helps us create *sustainable* places. Appreciating and protecting our landscapes, our biological diversity, and our built heritage will necessarily lead us down the path to a more sustainable society. Because of the sustainability challenges we face today, we will need to be more conscious and cautious about what we are losing through mindless, excessive consumption, resource extraction, and ecosystem destruction. Strong connections and commitments to place will help to inoculate against indifference to landscape and environmental effects and impacts, wherever they occur.

Strengthening place and rebuilding commitments to the local realm will not be easy, and we will have to overcome some difficult cultural, social, and economic obstacles. The busy ways we lead our lives and the extent to which we are increasingly disconnected physically and emotionally from our physical, biological, and geocultural contexts are much of the problem. Urban sprawl and car-dependent landscapes mean that Americans spend an inordinate amount of time in these vehicles of detachment.

The trade-offs we are making today, that we are willing to accept, are not ones that we will be happy with in the long term, and are not likely to be seen as favorable by our descendants who will inhabit our communities in the future. We have larger houses and homes with many more amenities (remarkably, about 18 percent of our new homes are equipped with three-car or larger garages for instance). The spreading out of our communities, and the additional driving we must then do, leaves little time to enjoy our environment, our families, or our communities. Aldo Leopold (1947) talked of these trade-offs more than sixty years ago:

> Our grandfathers were less well-housed, well-fed, well-clothed than we are. The strivings by which they bettered their lot are also those which deprived us of [passenger] pigeons. Perhaps we now grieve because we are not sure, in our hearts, that we have gained by the exchange. The gadgets of industry bring us more comforts than the pigeons did, but do they add as much to the glory of the spring? (p. 109)

Our diminished level of social engagement and public and political involvement are now widely appreciated, thanks in part to Robert Putnam's work, notably the seminal study *Bowling Alone* (2001). As Putnam and others have documented, we are less likely today to participate in a social club or to write a letter or otherwise participate in local politics or governance than were our counterparts a generation ago (Putnam, 2001; Putnam and Feldstein, 2003).

There are many reasons that help explain our aversion to and difficulty in developing solid and specific place affections. Given the transient nature of modern North American life, it is perhaps not surprising that we fail to develop this intimate knowledge of place—why should we? We're likely to be living in another house, neighborhood, or community very shortly. American homeowners, according to the U.S. Census Bureau, will likely live in their homes only six years on average before moving. A remarkably small percentage of Americans—9.7 percent of heads of households—have lived in their homes thirty years or longer (Rich, 2003).

Cultural trends suggest that Americans are increasingly reverting to the private realm, eschewing many of the traditional public or civil patterns that help to cement community bonds. As homes have gotten larger and time more precious, home and work occupy much of our waking existence. Home entertainment centers replace going to the movies, a visit to Amazon.com replaces time spent in the public library, time shuttled around in (ever larger) cars replaces the neighborhood stroll or a relaxed lunch at a café.

Our busy American lifestyles certainly make it challenging to commit in real and genuine ways to the places in which we live. Americans continue to work long hours, compared with most other Western industrialized nations, and the necessity of two-income earners in the household adds to the stress. Expectations about lifestyle and material needs further aggravate these stresses. Juliet Schor has effectively documented these stresses in her books *The Overworked American* (1993) and *The Overspent American* (1999). Americans, it seems, work harder and longer, often to support increasingly higher levels of consumption and personal debt, in a kind of overwhelming spiral of stress and anxiety.

The hectic pace of American life reinforces stultifying uniformity in our communities. Fast-food franchises and chain stores cater to car-oriented convenience. Locally owned and operated smaller stores have a difficult time surviving in the face of superstores. Few Americans are willing (or able), however, to make multiple stops and take the extra time needed to visit the local bakery or florist or hardware store, where they exist at all. A significant obstacle, then, to creating community and strengthening commitment to place is simply the increasingly harried and hurried pace of American life.

For many Americans, place has become primarily a matter of consumption, a commercial transaction. Choosing and purchasing one's house is primarily and essentially an economic investment decision, more a matter of economic return than about joining and becoming part of a community. The aspects of house and home that grab our attention—a house's curb appeal, the affluence of the neighborhood, the perceived security, the appliances and accoutrements of the house itself—are either investment considerations or aspects of very individualistic consumption choices. And it seems that often these concerns about protecting the investment value of our homes in turn drive a variety of restrictions, constraints, and ordinances that further represent obstacles to creating distinctive, sustainable places. Prohibitions on the placement of photovoltaics on rooftops in residential neighborhoods, for example, or preventing homeowners from converting their industrial turfgrass lawns into natural habitats or gardens for growing food, are examples of actions taken (essentially) to protect private property values.

With minimal civic involvement, little time or inclination to know one's neighbors or one's community, it is perhaps not surprising that there is considerable fear and anxiety about "others." Both a product of our current culture and a considerable obstacle itself to strengthening place and community, this fear often keeps us apart. We fear the unexpected knock at the door, and we worry that reaching out to others, including our immediate neighbors, will unleash unknown risks.

Another major place obstacle is the pervasive sense that there is not much to be done, not much that can be done, that the forces of sameness and disconnection are inexorable and beyond meaningful change. Many of the forces negatively affecting places—whether by diminishing their natural or built heritage, undermining their local economies, or separating and isolating people—are market forces. Not only are citizens and communities not always able to see or understand the nature of these changes, we are preconditioned to give them deference, when they are economic or market in origin.

Advances in technology, while improving our lives in many ways, have also had community-distancing impacts. They further contribute for many of us to the black hole of time loss that we devote to our jobs. Computers, the Internet, cellular phones, and e-mail have improved communication, but along with this improvement has emerged the unfortunate expectation of instant or very quick responses to messages sent.

Media of various kinds tend to absorb large amounts of our time and attention, making community and place commitments difficult or tenuous. And the patterns start early. A 1999 study sponsored by the Kaiser Family Foundation found that children spend an average thirty-eight hours per week consuming media in one form or another, from watching television to surfing the Internet, to listening to music or playing computer games. For typical kids, this is the equivalent of a full-time job. The study even identifies a category of children as "heavy" media users, consuming more than ten hours per day; about one in six children fall into this group (Kaiser Family Foundation, 1999). No wonder children grow up with little understanding or enjoyment of the landscapes, nature, and unique qualities of place.

Americans, moreover, spend almost 90 percent of their time indoors, itself a remarkable form of disconnection both from the natural world and from social and community interaction. A scant 7 percent of our day is spent outside—its little wonder we don't know much about our neighbors (human and nonhuman) or our neighborhoods (built and natural) (Klepeis et al., 2002).

Opportunities to Recommit to Place

Sense of place, or emotional connection to place, is a challenging concept to articulate, but one more important then we often understand. Yet, most of us know what this means in a deep visceral way. The placelessness of many of the American settings I have lived in or visited has been brought home to me while living off and on in recent years in the Netherlands. Residing in the old Dutch city of Leiden, one is continually presented with visual and other stimuli that convey a definite sense of being somewhere in particular. It is undoubtedly part and parcel of living in a city whose physical form and building stock reflect centuries of gradual organic growth. And much of it was certainly uniquely Dutch—the canals and houseboats, the narrow homes and businesses with steeply pitched roofs, each a different size and with different architectural details, and the sights and sounds of bicycles and ancient clock towers. The presence of significant visual landmarks is important also, such as the looming spires of the city's three major churches, the city hall,

Figure 1.3 | The city of Leiden in the Netherlands has nurtured and strengthened its already strong sense of place, including its built heritage, its sounds, and the exquisitely walkable nature of its streets and spaces.

and other prominent public buildings. Leiden offers abundant civic spaces; pedestrian-friendly, walkable streetscapes; and a scale and pace that value slower human watching and interacting.

To be sure, there are many American communities where similar distinctive place qualities exist, resulting either by accident or by design, or by some combination of both. Washington, D.C., has special and endearing qualities: the baroque and charming elements of its grid and street system, for which L'Enfant deserves much credit, and its monumental character and low-rise streetscapes. New Orleans, Santa Fe, and Boston also have many impressive qualities, the outcome of a particular mix of culture, history, architecture, climate, and landscape that give them a special feel. These qualities are to be celebrated and nurtured. They serve to ground us and connect us to actual people and environments. They engender fondness and concern and care for place.

The horrific events of September 11, 2001, have made recommitments to place even more pressing. In the hours and days closely following the tragedy, the support functions of communities were essential, and the role of the physical and civic spaces in these communities as places to grieve, to hug and hold hands, to share common experiences and emotions and anxieties about the future, absolutely critical. Our common values and commitments and our shared bonds found expression, as in the end they only could, in the parks, plazas, and streets of the places where we actually live. It is hard to see where these unifying, affirmational functions and activities would have occurred otherwise. Moreover, the events of September 11 have clearly demonstrated the need for community resiliency and have given added support for many of the elements of more sustainable cities and regions (e.g., safe and renewable forms of energy, a robust and diverse transport system).

Recent polling by the research firm Roper ASW detects a trend toward "local area nesting," suggesting individuals and families are spending more time closer to home, are more physically present in their neighborhoods, and have a greater sense of wanting relationships with neighbors and community. As chief operating officer of this research firm, Ed Keller, is quoted in the *Washington Post*, "Americans are going out seeking connections to people they value" (Stepp, 2003, p. c2). We are perhaps poised for a resurgence of community and place; the conditions are ripe, and the many examples and stories contained in this book give hope that it is possible.

Being *native to somewhere* means working toward the creation of *real* places, places that are genuine and authentic, not replicas or copies of developments and communities across the region or across the continent. Partly, this is a matter of how a place feels to us, whether it elicits a sense of being special or distinctive, even if not in clear or tangible ways. But it is also about qualities that are more easily verified or counted or observed: are there fewer chain stores, more diversity in architecture and physical form; is the indigenous landscape and nature present; are the vagaries and peculiarities of place—its history, climate, culture, and the like—made visible and present in a place? And, of course, places must be healthy and sustainable and beautiful, qualities that are for the most part incredibly reinforcing in nature. There is much work to be done at the collective or policy level, and much thinking as well about how individual actions and responsibilities can strengthen place.

What, more specifically, does a community look like that is truly striving to be native to its location on Earth, and where its inhabitants are deeply rooted in and committed to it? Although they overlap, the following are some of the most important attributes or qualities of a genuine community:

- Recognizes and emphasizes the unique qualities of the community; values complexity, richness, and layering of history, environment, and architecture; strengthens, nurtures, and highlights this diversity and distinctiveness.
- Understands the natural environments, ecosystems, and landscapes in which the community is situated, and strives to protect, nurture, and restore them (even in dense cities) and to bring nature into intimate contact with residents.
- Understands and celebrates its unique histories of both built and natural environments; makes these histories visible and alive and prescient to inhabitants.
- Fosters artistic impulses to build unique community character and instills a sense of ownership in those who create and enjoy the art.
- Seeks to emphasize locally owned businesses and products, and seeks to harness local entrepreneurship and ingenuity in the solving of local problems (while not disconnected from the global marketplace).

- Values and encourages engagement and participation; works to replace individual passivity and apathy with active concern and engagement.
- Is designed to facilitate active lives and lifestyles, foster social interaction and development of deep community and interpersonal ties and commitments, and minimize dependence on the automobile.
- Strives for social inclusiveness and revels in and nurtures diversity of many kinds, including ethnic, age, gender, and income.

The chapters to follow were written largely out of a concern about both the quality of the places we are designing, planning, and stewarding, and the unsustainable levels of resource use, consumption, and destruction, both global and local. It is a key supposition that inextricable connections exist between sustainability, livability and health, a strong sense of community, and a commitment to place. Many of the most sustainable dimensions, whether commitment to renewable energy or greenspace protection, will in turn contribute to a community's unique character and thereby engender greater affection for and commitments to place by its residents. Place and place connections to both nature and other people are essential for happy, meaningful human lives. Good places—distinctive, genuine places—create the context in which place affections and commitments will occur. More sustainable places, place design, and patterns of development will create the essential opportunities for community building and place commitments.

Working toward the *placing* or *re-placing* of our planet, to *becoming native again,* to returning to old principles of place as well as exploring the potential of new ideas and technologies for strengthening and sustaining places, must be a primary task in the years ahead for planners and citizens alike. It can be done, and I believe we can make progress in fundamentally strengthening our commitments to place as a means to creating a more sustainable world.

Place Basics: Concepts, Research, Literature

Our daily lives are not played out in an intellectual realm or virtual world, but rather in very real and tangible places—environments, neighborhoods, cities. We arise each day to sights, sounds, textures, and encounters with climate and flora and fauna, often very specific to the places we live. This chapter identifies and isolates some of those important aspects of place that shape us and that we in turn shape, and it summarizes the main thinking and literature about place and good place building.

There is a long history of scholarship, research, and writing about place. And although what follows is by no means a comprehensive summary or survey, it is an attempt to acknowledge this extensive and rich body of thinking. The fresh ideas and thinking in this book are built on the solid foundations laid by many others.

To begin, there is a common distinction in the literature between "spaces" and "places." Spaces are generic and nonspecific; places are "immediate, known and lived in. We move through spaces, we stop in and are directly involved with places" (Yencken, 1995, p. 11). Places have significance and meaning to us; our memories are wrapped up with them. Places are those spaces and environments (built or natural) imbued with personal and cultural meanings. Environmental psychologists Setha Low and Irwin Altman (1992) define place in this way:

> Place . . . refers to space that has been given meaning through personal, group, or cultural processes. . . . [p]laces may vary in several ways—scale or size and scope, tangible versus symbolic, known and experienced versus unknown or not experienced. (p. 5)

Thus, familiarity and knowledge of space and environment transform it into place. As the philosopher Yi Fu Tuan (1977) says, "What begins as undifferentiated space becomes place as we get to know it better and endow it with value" (p. 6). "When space feels thoroughly familiar to us, it has become place" (p. 73).

Much of the place literature supports the notion that creation of place is a dynamic or an ongoing process. It is not something that starts or ends at a specific point. Even places we think we know quite well may feel different with the passage of time and with the development pressures and demographic changes that accompany it.

Many things influence what a place feels like, its place qualities. The unique qualities of places are the cumulative result of the many sensory impressions we experience when being there. We often tend to emphasize the visual experiences, of course. We see the buildings and human-built environment, the natural landscapes, and the ways in which humans (and nonhumans) interact with these environments. But, of course, our other senses are also very much involved. Sounds are crucial—one thinks of the sounds of the street vendors when walking along the Rambla, the main pedestrian street in Barcelona, Spain, or the unique sounds of Venice, Italy, a result of the absence of cars, and the noise of pushcarts being pulled up and down bridge-steps in that city. We hear places as much as see them.

Smells often provide the most vivid memories and recollections of place. The distinctive smells of place are many, and one recognizes them though we may not always be able to isolate or disentangle the (usually) delightful sensory mix. Smell is highly underrated as a sense and an important way we experience places. It is commonly said that humans are actually capable of distinguishing 10,000 different smells, though our language and ability to describe and articulate them is woefully underdeveloped. The fish market vendors at the market in Leiden, the fragrant smells of vegetables and herbs—melons, tomatoes, basil, zucchini—are some of the most enjoyable aspects of shopping at community farmers markets, to be sure (a pleasant contrast to the antiseptic, smell-free atmospheres of most large grocery stores). There are many seasonal smells that characterize our place memories—the smells of falling leaves in autumn along the Eastern U.S., the smell of snow, the smells (and other sensations) of summer thunderstorms. There are many food smells that we experience in cities—the aroma of Cajun food in New Orleans, bakeries in Paris, the numerous food smells of Chinatown in San Francisco. City smells, though not always entirely pleasant (car exhausts, garbage waiting to be collected) are also place-defining. Burning charcoal in Caribbean cities like Kingston, Jamaica or Port-au-Prince, Haiti, are defining smells in these places.

These spaces with imbued personal and social meaning can take many physical forms. They can be largely natural environments—national parks and scenic landscapes—or built environments such as cities, towns, or rural

Figure 2.1 | Venetian *campi,* or small squares, each have their own special quality and flavor, and serve important civic and social functions for the surrounding neighborhood. Campo San Luca, shown here, is one of the most delightful.

agricultural landscapes. They can be large (New York City or the Florida Everglades) or rather small and confined (Natural Bridge in Virginia, or an urban courtyard or urban space, such as the Plaza in Santa Fe).

An interesting or unique neighborhood has its own quality of place, a function of its buildings, people, and environment, but it is also shaped by, and in turn helps to shape, the broader town and region in which it lies. The Plaza in Santa Fe is itself a significant and important place, yet together with other buildings, neighborhoods, and city features make up the place of Santa Fe, which itself is embedded in a rich landscape mosaic comprising a distinctive New Mexican place. The delightful small plaza spaces of Venice, Italy— the *campi*, as they are called—each have their own unique and special qualities. They are places, at a certain neighborhood scale, that build together with special qualities of water, wind, bridges, and architecture to create the special feeling and experience of Venice the city.

Increasingly, it seems, and perhaps paralleling the immense mobility and travel now enjoyed by those living in industrialized northern nations, the places that are significant to us and that have meaning are many and diverse. We may enjoy an attachment to our place of birth or homeland, to where we presently live (or have lived), or to many other places imbued with some degree of specialness or sacredness to us. This modern phenomenon of multiple place experiences is both a vice and a virtue. On the negative side, our tendency to be "place grazers" may serve to diffuse or dilute the commitments we feel to any one specific place. This is one primary problem associated with the high degree to which Americans tend to move around. We know many places casually but few in much depth or particularity.

On the other hand, a variety of place commitments are helpful and healthy, even to those places we visit infrequently. Two examples are Yosemite and New York City, a natural environment and a built environment. Both places instill tremendous pride, affection, and loyalty to many people, and both might be aptly characterized as sacred places. Both places hold important place affections for me, even though I do not live in or near them—they are place affections borne of periodic visits and the memories of the experiences there.

Many types of place bonds develop over one's life, some from religious or cultural importance, others from important personal events or tragedies.

University of Utah environmental psychologist Setha Low (1992) speaks of the importance, for example, of "pilgrimage" in creating place bonds: "Pilgrimage to a place, the desire to visit a place, and participation in a celebratory event such as a parade or festival is a special kind of place attachment, in that the experience of the place, although intense, is usually transient, but the idea of the place and its religious, spiritual, or sociopolitical importance lingers on for years" (p. 173).

There is a considerable literature on the notion of sacred places and the importance of such places in our spiritual and cultural lives. Native Americans and other native peoples have attached special values to unique or distinctive natural places—a mountaintop, a sequoia grove, a coastline. Tragic events forge special bonds with the places affected—for example, the September 11 terrorist attacks on the World Trade Towers site. Ground Zero has become a sacred site, creating special duties to design and build in ways that are respectful of this importance.

The Language of Place

There is indeed a language of place—different terms and terminology, some popular, others more professional or specialized—by which we talk about places. The significance of places to us can be and is spoken of in many different ways. *Sense of place* is one common way, a term I have already employed.

As David Hummon, a sociologist at Holy Cross College (1992), observes,

Sense of place involves a personal *orientation* toward place, in which one's understandings of place and one's feeling about place become fused in the context of environmental meaning. (p. 262)

One's sense of place involves both a subjective and an objective perspective. Objectively, there are many place qualities, such as landscapes, buildings, and community features; subjectively, we judge and assess the meaning and personal value of these objective qualities. The literature offers a number of ideas and cases demonstrating actions that can be taken to make or strengthen a sense of place. These include public art projects, distinctive pedestrian environments, landscapes using native species, parks and gardens, and gateway projects that strengthen a sense of entering a new and different place, among many others (Winikoff, 1995). Much of this book discusses these different ideas.

Place *attachment*, or emotional commitments to place, is another way we relate. Places that have significance or special meaning to us also engender special considerations in our actions and behaviors. Place attachment can be described as a "positive emotional bond" and "the emotional linkage of an individual to a particular environment" (Mesch and Manor, 1998, pp. 504–505).

Community *rootedness* is another way of talking about place attachments. To what degree do residents actually feel a part of a place or community? Are they in a familiar place, one that feels comfortable and nurturing, one where they feel like "insiders"? Place attachment and commitment and place rootedness are important in part because they can serve to shape personal choices and behavior. It is hoped that residents with greater levels of attachments and rootedness are more willing to take the many actions essential to conserving and improving places. Few individuals will care about sustaining places if they have no attachment or rootedness.

Home is an important word in our place language. For most Americans, home connotes a structure or building, usually a single-family house, but of course the word has a broader, more expansive meaning. It is a place that we like very much or love, that makes us feel secure and cozy, where we enjoy being, that replenishes, refreshes, reinvigorates us, to which we have significant attachments. *Coming home* is a good thing—these are places that reassure us, provide shelter and safety, where there is rest and nourishment. These are places that are familiar to us. Our larger home, beyond the narrow notion of our house, including our streets, our neighborhoods, our communities, similarly provides us with comfort, sustenance, and reassurance and equally warrants our care and commitment.

Some authors argue passionately for the need to define our home in an even broader, more biophysically appropriate or logical way. Our home is the *watershed* we live in or the *bioregion* we occupy, however that might be defined. Bioregionalism has been brilliantly defended and argued for by individuals like the writer Kirkpatrick Sale and the naturalist Gary Snyder (Sale,

1985; Snyder, 1982). Landscape architect Rob Thayer (2003) defines a bioregion, what he calls a "LifePlace," in the following way:

> . . . a unique region definable by natural (rather than political) boundaries with a geographic, climatic, hydrological, and ecological character capable of supporting human and non-human living communities. Bioregions can be variously defined by the geography of watersheds, similar plant and animal ecosystems, and related, identifiable landforms (e.g., particular mountain ranges, prairies, or coastal zones) and by unique human cultures that grow from natural limits and potentials of the region. (p. 3)

Supporters of bioregionalism argue that efforts to reorganize our thinking and lives around discernible bioregions will itself facilitate place commitments. If we begin to see ourselves as embedded in the Cuyahoga bioregion or the Mt. Shasta bioregion, we may further develop a strong sense of regional and place dimension to our language, thinking, and lives, and this will make it easier to live more sustainable, place-based lives.

In this book I often use "home" in this more expansive way, in a broader ecological and geographic sense consistent with the lifeplace and bioregion/ definitions tendered by Sale, Thayer, and others. Our "home" is our lifeterritory—the communities, landscapes, and bioregions that we occupy and depend upon for our emotional and physical existence.

In planning for sustainable communities, much importance is placed on how to encourage or facilitate or strengthen these commitments to place. Research helps us understand the many sources from which we derive our emotional commitments to place, including genealogical and family ties to place, religious or cosmological attachments, pilgrimages to places of personal importance, and narratives or the telling of stories that connect people and communities to the land (Low, 1992). Age (the older the person, the greater the attachment), homeownership, and length of residence are all positively related to place attachments. Longevity of residence in a community, which results in greater social ties and more extensive personal memories of place, has been found to correlate highly with place attachments (Hummon, 1992).

In a study of Calvert County, Maryland, by University of Maryland researchers Sagoff and Wasserman, through a series of focus group sessions, found distinct differences between older residents and more recent residents. Older residents were seen to have a "richly nuanced sense of place," born of personal histories and hardship, whereas newer residents were found to have "a thin, relatively under-developed sense of Calvert County as a place, they saw the county as a place of pleasant scenery and relaxation from the rigors of work and the commute, but also as a place of isolation and sometimes burden" (Sagoff and Wasserman, undated). Perceptions of place will also vary by race, and in the study the researchers found that for African Americans the county's place history was "polluted by segregation and racism." Consequently, this group appeared less interested in preservation and more supportive of future development.

Desirable natural and physical qualities of community are also important in strengthening place attachments. The distinctive natural qualities of South Carolina's Low Country, for example—its bays, marshes, palmettos, and tremendous natural beauty—has much to do with place affections. Views of the Rockies in Denver, spectacular visual connections to the bay in San Francisco or to Diamond Head in Honolulu, are extremely important natural and physical elements of these places—they make them different and special to us and uplift us emotionally and spiritually.

It is, of course, much more than just the physical environment, the buildings and landscapes, that are important to us; it is the social qualities and characteristics of the places, as well. Considerable research explores the impact of social networks and personal relationships on commitments to place. Perhaps not surprisingly, the more extensive the neighborhood social and familial ties, the greater are the expressed commitments to place. A place survey by sociologists Gustavo Mesch and Orit Manor (1998) came to this conclusion: "The larger the number of friends living in the neighborhoods and the closer the relationship with neighbors, the greater the pride residents took in their neighborhood. The more satisfied individuals were with the neighborhood physical and social characteristics, the more likely was attachment to place" (p. 515).

Places are important to us because we have family or close friends living there, and because we value the closeness, familiarity, comfort, and support that are derived from these social and familial connections. It is sometimes difficult to disentangle our affection for a city or region from the social and personal connections we have there. A street recalls friends we knew there, a hospital recalls illness or tragedy (or perhaps the elation and beauty of the birth of a child), specific cities are home to grandparents, adult siblings, close friends. The geographical and social are intimately bound together.

Places where we have spent time, where we have grown up, where we formed opinions of the world, where relationships have developed, are all important because of these patterns. Landscapes and places are embedded with memories, and the nature of these memories affect how we value and treat places. History, personal and collective, is an important dimension then in place building and in forging place commitments. Battlefields involve a solemnity that makes them important collectively and, sometimes, individually. The house and neighborhood where one grew up often imbues them with special, valuable memories. They can consequently be the basis for place attachments.

We live on a coinhabited planet, and the communities and landscape where we dwell are home to other forms of life. Our source of place and our commitments to these places are formed in part through these relationships to others. Personal stories and recollections are common of time spent watching wildlife, climbing trees, experiencing in some direct way the biodiversity of place. The interaction of the human and natural environments is a special and important relationship. There is growing recognition that nonhuman species influence our perceptions of place and, indeed, are shaping these human places in important ways.

Native peoples often conceptualize lands and landscapes in terms of their "sacredness," that is, the extent to which they are especially important for religious or historic reasons. Native Americans have identified a number of environmental features as sacred. Increasingly, the notion of sacred places has taken on a more secular meaning—places that are of special value, emotionally or spiritually. Battlefields may take on this label for some; special geological features or spectacular elements of natural beauty such as coastlines may be viewed as sacred to others.

Another contemporary reality is that a place, or places, can no longer be viewed as a discrete or separate thing. Our modern notion of place must acknowledge the *connectedness* between places. This connectedness is physical, social, and temporal. Physically, places are connected in many ways. Communities lie in complexly intersecting physical and ecological spaces—

watersheds, aquifers, airsheds, viewsheds. What happens in one community may affect other communities hundreds or thousands of miles away.

The notion of an ecological footprint, popularized by William Rees, a planning professor at the University of British Columbia, is one tool for understanding and appreciating these place interconnections. It is a quantitative expression of the land base needed to support a human population and its consumption habits and a powerful measure of place sustainability (Wackernagel and Rees, 1994). About 25 acres of land is required to provide the average North American with food, energy, and other needs. When the aggregate footprint of a city or town is calculated, the land impact can be immense. A recent ecological footprint study done for London shows that the city's population, for instance, requires a land area nearly 300 times the actual size of the city (Best Food Forward, 2002). London depends on the resources and life support provided by many other places, some quite far away.

The rise in bioregional literature and thinking further reflects the importance of connecting place with the ways in which we live our lives (e.g., Thayer, 2003). Bioregionalism believes in the primary importance of reestablishing deep place connections and awareness. Described simply by some as "living a rooted life," it "means you are aware of the ecology, economy, and culture of the place where you live, and are committed to making choices that enhance them" (Great River Earth Institute, undated).

Few, if any, places can be accurately characterized as the proverbial island (even, and especially, islands!). These place relationships are often described in urban–rural terms. Cities and rural areas do themselves each represent places worthy of appreciation and protection, perhaps based on quite different physical, architectural, or landscape qualities, but they also seem to be connected. Water, food, and resources may derive from the surrounding countryside as many as hundreds of miles away in an increasingly globalized world, and employment and recreational community patterns may represent similar connections. Modern concepts of place must, as a result, acknowledge these interconnections.

The connections are social and cultural, as well. Immigrants to a new country typically maintain family and personal connections to their country of birth. Indeed, partly because of technologies of air travel and communications, international families maintaining strong connections and bonds to places outside their immediate residence are increasingly common.

There has been considerable attention in the professional planning literature to strategies and ideas for strengthening sense of place, and for creating or building new places. Protecting sense of place is often about protecting the special or unique historic qualities of the community, as well as preserving the natural landscapes and characteristics of such communities. Urban design guidelines, historic preservation initiatives, Main Street programs, and land conservation initiatives are frequently supported on the basis of strengthening a sense of place. Sameness and a homogenization of the landscape is the often criticized outcome of sprawl (e.g., Moe and Wilkie, 1997).

Place knowledge is yet another way we commonly talk about this issue. The extent (or lack) of knowledge about a place is often viewed as a proxy for the extent of commitments and the placeless existence many of us lead today. Our paucity of specific place-based knowledge is especially accentuated when considering the natural environment. Many surveys of geographical knowledge suggest that our specific understanding of the places in which we live—their natural and biophysical conditions and characteristics, and their history and built heritage—is limited to nil (e.g., National Geographic Society, undated; Jones, 2001).[1] Learning about place seems a low priority in our consumption-oriented society; where we're working harder and longer, commuting farther, all to buy the things that we are interested in learning about—the play station, the Navigator, the latest bargains in cellular phones. Residents commonly have scant knowledge of the ecosystems and landscapes in which they live. Most would have difficulty naming a species of butterfly or native wildflower or snake, and would not recognize such if (when) they present themselves in the flesh. Even recognition of common species of songbirds or native trees is limited. And, no wonder. Little emphasis or value is placed on knowing such things, either within the community or through conventional educational institutions. The irony is that children are able to recognize a Burger King logo at a distance of half a mile but would have trouble identifying even a common species of dragonfly or damselfly. It seems knowledge of our broader ecological community, as Aldo Leopold conceived of it, is quite limited indeed.

Figure 2.2 | The main street of Franklin, Virginia. Despite devastating flooding from Hurricane Floyd in 1999, the city has worked hard to strengthen and enhance its charming downtown. Recent efforts have focused on encouraging new housing above shops.

Diminished engagement or involvement in politics (especially local politics) influences place as well. And many writers and commentators have made the connection between a declining civic realm and a diminished and deteriorating place. William Shutkin (2000) of MIT observes that much developed or built landscape reflects an "atrophied civic life," as does the way in which we treat the natural environments to which we have been entrusted:

> Civic expression goes beyond architecture to land use and environment itself. . . . Contaminated urban land, suburban sprawl, polluted rivers, drained wetlands, regional smog, acid rain, clear cutting and endangered species: these are some of the adverse and interrelated physical effects of development that ultimately are a reflection of the civic health and consciousness of communities. (p. 46)

In Shutkin's view, such outcomes and physical conditions reflect an "impersonal, indifferent, and rootless society" (p. 76). "Similarly, place can nurture public memory, the sense of civic identity, which empowers citizens and inspires them to contribute to civic life" (p. 49). There is power in place, to be sure, in its promise for binding us together politically and interpersonally.

Place Qualities: What Do We Like About Places?

The physical and natural context of places, as determinants or influences on sense of place and place quality, are undeniable. J. H. Crawford, in his book *Carfree Cities* (2002), talks of the importance of making *magical* places. To Crawford, such places are marked by "human scale, rich detail, beautiful setting, harmonious sounds and evocative scents. They require an appreciative public to come alive: people involve themselves in the magic helping to sustain it" (p. 288). Creating magical places, soulful places, distinctive and genuine and inspiring places, is the charge and challenge, and it is a difficult one today.

Distinctiveness is one feature of place consistently valued in literature and in planning practice. No place can be considered special or unique if it looks, feels, and functions the same as every other place in the world. Other words and sentiments are often used to express feelings of placelessness. Gertrude Stein is famously quoted as saying about Oakland, California, that there is no there *there*. Joel Garreau (1992) and others have talked of "soulless" cities and communities. Urban designer Kevin Lynch (1972) has argued convincingly in support of the values of *place diversity* and *identity*: "Places should have a clear perceptual identity: recognizable, memorable, vivid, engaging of attention, differentiated from other locations" (p. 225).

Lynch's classic study *The Image of the City* (1960) identified in systematic fashion the key building blocks of a distinct place. The visual qualities or "imageability" of a place, to Lynch, derives from the arrangement of five main building blocks: paths, edges, districts, nodes, and landmarks. Paths are the movement corridors, the ways that we pass through places, and how we experience them, whereas edges create boundaries and breaks that help distinguish, differentiate, and organize space. Districts, perhaps a commercial area or ethnic neighborhood, share common qualities, and nodes are important junctions or foci. Landmarks, of course, are of various sorts and critical to creating recognizable, unique place. A large church, a civic structure such as city hall or a courthouse, a prominent theater, and other "point-references" help to build familiarity, orient residents and visitors, and build strong physical (and social) identity. Lynch (1960) cites the Duomo, in Florence, Italy, as an example of a distinct landmark, at once orienting and symbolic. Together, these essential elements "must be patterned together to provide a satisfying form" (p. 83).

Another useful way of thinking about the determinant of unique and special places is to identify the place "assets" that exist and upon which a strengthening of a sense of place can take place. Place assets are of many kinds. Some are, of course, essentially beyond control, such as the topography of a place, its climate and natural beauty, although of course there are many actions that can be taken to protect, nurture, and promote greater appreciation of and connection to these environmental assets. Historic buildings, charming streetscapes, and the cultural flavor and ethnic mix of a place are other kinds of important place assets, as are all manner of amenities, from restaurants to art galleries to outdoor recreation facilities and opportunities. These are assets that, as Richard Florida (2002) demonstrates in his research, can serve to attract the so-called creative class and can be so important in driving local economy.

Residential or community satisfaction, although separate and distinct from commitment to place, does appear to be related. Access to basic human needs in a community, such as abundant natural lighting, fresh air, and stimulating parks, and outdoor environments, for instance, is essential to creating good places (e.g., see Hiss's discussion of this in *The Experience of Place*, 1990). Inspiring and beautiful architecture is important to many. A diversity or distinctiveness to the buildings and architecture of a place is a common plea in good place building.

Creating "legible" places is an often expressed goal. Legibility can be understood as the ability to understand the pattern of a place, to know and find one's way around. Urban designer and planner Kevin Lynch (1971) talks of both spatial and temporal legibility—the former, understanding the physical cues and spatial elements that guide and orient one; the latter, involving the elements of place that "orient its inhabitants to the past, to the present with

Figure 2.3 | Distinctive and beautiful architecture is an essential element of place. Ghent, Belgium, seen here, exemplifies the importance of inspiring architecture and urban design, in this case evolving over several hundred years.

its cyclical rhythms, and even to the future, with its hopes and dangers." Places must be meaningful, as well; they must have both practical utility and emotional and aspirational importance.

There is considerable academic and policy research and writing about the design and planning qualities of a good place. These qualities include mixed uses and walkability, communities and cities with clear boundaries, extensive open space, parks and nature. The New Urbanism movement in the United States, especially in the last two decades, has been a vocal proponent of more compact, walkable neighborhoods and urban design, based on the traditional design qualities of small American cities and towns, circa 1900 or 1920 (e.g., see Katz; Congress for the New Urbanism, 1998). Gridded street patterns, narrower streets with sidewalks and trees, on-street parking and alleys behind homes, and porches and picket fences are common signature elements of New Urbanist communities (e.g., for review of New Urbanist principles, see Congress for the New Urbanism, 2000, or www.cnu.org).

Sociologist William Whyte's seminal observational work *The Social Life of Small Urban Spaces* (1980) provides significant insights into public and community spaces that people like and are attracted to and that, on many levels, can be said to *work*. Through his Street Life Project and the extensive use of time-lapse photography, he extracted many key design and planning insights. Whyte's analysis highlighted the importance of such essential features as adequate sitting space (including ledges, benches, and movable chairs, ideally), sun, trees, and water (people like them, and are attracted by them), and wind (people seek spaces that shield them from cold winds).

Sun access should be protected, Whyte believed, and where urban spaces did not get sufficient sun, it might be possible to bounce the sun into these spaces off of the surfaces of surrounding buildings. Whyte's discussion of water conveys the desirability of this element in cities—not just to see, but to learn, feel, and even experience by immersing one's feet and hands in it. "It is not right," Whyte notes, "to put water before people and then keep them away from it. But this is what is happening across the country" (p. 48).

Perhaps Whyte's most important insight about places may be the most obvious—that we seek out and want to be in places where there are other people. We cluster together, and seek out sitting spots and spaces where others are not far away. Fundamentally, Whyte and other proponents of public spaces regale them as serving important community building and social enhancing goals. These are the places where we come together as a community, where we hold rallies and parades, and where we celebrate both the festive and the somber. They have much to do with creating a distinctive sense of place and affectionate attachment to place.

Few individuals have had as much influence on the architecture and planning academics about place and what makes a good place as urban critic Jane Jacobs. With no formal planning or design training, she expounded classic and enduring principles of good urbanism, most clearly and importantly articulated in her *Death and Life of Great American Cities* (1961). In many ways she caused a reconceptualizing of cities—the seemingly messy and chaotic nature of life in places like New York were not bad or negative qualities but quite positive indeed. These are the qualities essential to vital urban life and a creative market economy. Jacobs believed in the importance of urban densities, the mixing of primary uses (and was very critical of efforts by planners to "sort" uses), a diversity of housing types, and the need to protect and preserve historic buildings and neighborhoods. Her vision of active, vibrant streets and street life is perhaps her greatest legacy. Streets were the real public spaces in the city, the essential social glue binding a city and its residents, places for socializing and for raising children, and places where people and activity provide a natural kind of collective security (her famous adage "eyes on the street"). Her contributions to our understanding of real places have been immense.

British urban designer John Montgomery argues, along with Jane Jacobs, that economic activities and "transactions" are the real life of cities, and the heart of what makes a "successful" place (Montgomery, 1995). And, what is needed to allow and encourage these interactions is a highly mixed and diverse set of land uses and activities. Many observers of places and place making have of course bemoaned the tendency of contemporary planning, especially in the United States to separate and isolate different uses and activities. Having a "variety of building types" is also equally important: "a mixture of uses, blocks, building sizes, ages and conditions, types and adaptability" (Montgomery, 1995, p. 147).

Walkable or pedestrian-friendly communities are highly valued in the place literature. A walkable community requires a form and street pattern, as Montgomery notes, that is highly "permeable":

> People need to be able to move around places with relative ease, crossing roads, seeing around corners, being tempted down the "side streets of disorder" as well as sticking to the "avenues of order." Permeability is the capacity to move into and through an area. (Montgomery, 1995, pp. 147–148)

Urban environments and communities that provide rich and stimulating experiences are important. Enjoyable, desirable places are places that stimulate our senses, that promote what Tony Hiss (1990) calls "simultaneous perception," and that allow us to, at once, appreciate and draw in many dif-

Figure 2.4 | The Grand Canal, Venice, Italy. Few places evoke the majesty and visual beauty of this special interplay of buildings, water, boats, and the movement of people and goods.

ferent sensations and stimuli. For Hiss, this kind of perception "seems calmer, more like a clear, deep, reflective lake" (p. 3). And the places that encourage simultaneous perception, like Grand Central Station in New York City, can "amplify our perceptive real, allowing us to notice aspects of our mental activity that are normally veiled," and can as a result "give us a mental lift" (p. 27).

Perhaps more than any other designer, Christopher Alexander has shaped our understanding of what makes good places, and the elements of communities that respond to timeless human needs. His classic *A Pattern Language* (1977) remains a fount of insights into good place building. Along with several colleagues, Alexander provides a comprehensive set of guidelines or "patterns" from the scale of regions and towns down to buildings and construction, that reflect established principles of good place building. Alexander identifies each pattern he believes "describes a deep and inescapable property of a well-formed environment" (p. xiv).[2]

Urban planner Sidney Brower (1990) reviewed and summarized the findings of some thirty-six studies about the qualities associated with neighborhood satisfaction. Although the findings depend on the preferred living environment (city, suburb, size of community), and some qualities are often at odds with each other, some consistent qualities do seem to emerge. Neighborhood maintenance and appearance, safety and tranquility, friendliness, and community amenities (recreation, restaurants, shopping, etc.) are most important to people.

Surveys of the public about what makes up a good place may, of course, differ from what planners, community leaders, and community institutions hold to be important values. This is a major tension today in community planning and place building. Brower's survey of the literature about neighborhood qualities suggests that many respondents in these kinds of studies value "ethnic, religious and income homogeneity," although urban respondents all appear to value diversity more. Yet, the goal of diverse neighborhoods and communities is established and widely accepted in planning and design. Planners and architects believe in the critical importance, and fairness, of diversity and social opportunity in any concept of a good place.

Disagreement exists today about how best to grow cities, and there is concern that large-scale building and development, often focused on converting large, previously undeveloped areas to new urban and suburban uses, will do little to create unique special places. Many believe (as do I) that cities, towns, and villages that grow slowly over a relatively long period of time (or even grow quickly through hundreds or thousands of small building and renewal projects) have an historical texture and rich design complexity that places built largely at once do not have. Older centers of European cities like Leiden or Copenhagen, for instance, have a charm and flavor and level of historical detail typically lacking in new towns or in major new growth districts in these cities. But the approaches are not mutually exclusive, of course, and efforts can be made in the design and planning to stimulate diversity, to make historical connections, and to incorporate livability and sustainability features (e.g., good cycling facilities) that may compensate for the feelings of newness and sameness that many of these places may exude.

The Importance of Nature in Place Making

Arguably, good places, places we love, respond to and acknowledge our basic human needs. Although no consensus exists about the full panoply of physical and biophysical human needs, some fairly clear indications are provided by the literature and research. In only very recent human history have we, as a species, begun to spend the majority of our days indoors, toiling and living in the midst of artificial lighting and mechanical ventilation.

There appears, as well, a hardwired need for direct contact with nature and other forms of life. E. O. Wilson speaks of this in terms of *biophilia,* or our innate need to connect with other living organisms. What strikes some as an academic notion is demonstrated daily around the United States and the world, as humans show their fascination with and concern about other forms of life. The demonstrated therapeutic value of contact with animals, even domestic pets, shows our biophilic physiological and emotional needs (Frumkin, 2001). With the reintroduction of peregrine falcons in the early 1980s, crowds in New York City huddled around street-level TV screens that projected pictures of nesting falcons on their ledged perches. There are now sixteen pairs of nesting peregrine falcons in the city, providing tremendous enjoyment and satisfaction to residents lucky enough to see them.

We biologically need full-spectrum natural sunlight, the ability to see sky and stars, and access to the natural elements. Other elements of landscape that humans appear innately to prefer include vistas, open space, "legible" landscapes (landscapes that are readable and make finding one's way possible), and landscapes with winding paths that hold mystery for us (see Hiss, 1990).

There is no question that urban residents prefer living in neighborhoods that are "greener." And, to a considerable degree, the marketplace recognizes the value of these green features in the form of higher rents and property values. Studies show that home lots containing trees have a higher market value than lots without them (Benotto, 2002). Visual preference surveys, which have been used extensively around the United States, especially by architect/planner Anton Nelessen, equally demonstrate the value, at least in the visual realm, of trees and tree-lined streets. Rated consistently high in visual

Figure 2.5 | Urban forests contribute much to communities: beauty, connections to landscapes and nature, essential natural services. This is the large Eilenriede forest in the center of Hannover, Germany.

preference surveys are streets with generous sidewalks, on-street parking, and a row of mature trees. A recent study of the economic value of greenspace in London further demonstrates the strong impact such factors have on market values (Greater London Authority, 2003).

Trees and greenspace in the urban environment have been found to produce soothing and therapeutic benefits (see Frumkin, 2001, for a good overview of the research). These effects may even translate into significant medically and physiologically restorative qualities. Roger Ulrich, a researcher at Texas A&M, has done some of the most important work documenting these therapeutic qualities. In perhaps his most famous study, Ulrich (1983) sought to test the impact that views of trees from hospital rooms have on the recovery of surgical patients. Comparing recovery time for patients with rooms with tree views against those with windows looking out on a brick wall, he found that patients in the rooms with views of trees recovered from surgery faster, needed fewer drugs, and had fewer postsurgical complications.

Ulrich's theoretical approach is typically characterized as one founded on notions of stress reduction—that natural environments reduce stress, with accompanying psychological and physical benefits. Others have emphasized the concept of "directed attention" and the role nature plays in recovery from fatigue and the ability to focus attention. Undoubtedly, both dynamics are present and both sets of benefits occur (Kaplan, 1995). Rachel Kaplan in early research (1973) has demonstrated the therapeutic benefits of urban gardening as one example. Sometimes described in terms of restorative benefits, the main idea is the ability of these natural qualities and activities to elicit feelings of fascination and to replenish our natural energies.[3]

Studies suggest that homes with views of trees and natural environments will have a positive psychological effect on children. Nancy Wells, a professor at Cornell's College of Human Ecology, conducted a study of the cognitive functioning of children aged 7–12 years in low-income families. In this longitudinal study, children were evaluated when living in poor housing conditions with little access to nature, and then later when their housing circumstance had improved to include views of trees and natural settings. Exposure to nature in these different home environments was evaluated through the use of a ten-point naturalness scale, evaluating the extent to which views of nature are present from different areas of the house. Parents were given a standardized set of questions aimed at judging the cognitive attention-focusing ability of their children. The results show a strong correlation between naturalness of the home and cognitive functioning. Professor Wells (2000) concludes that these effects are "profound": "Children who experienced the most improvement (increase) in the natural elements or restorative characteristics of their home tended to have the greatest ability to direct their attention several months after moving to the new home" (p. 790).

Phil Leather and his colleagues at the University of Nottingham in the United Kingdom (1998) found that sunlight penetration and window views of nature in the workplace were positively associated with job satisfaction and well-being, and negatively associated with intention to quit. Based on a sample of 100 workers at a wine operation in southern Europe, the study demonstrates what seems intuitive: that workers with windows and workspaces providing more natural sunlight and views of trees and the natural environment will be happier, and happier in their jobs.

Applied psychologists Hartig, Mang, and Evans (1991) have shown through several experimental and quasi-experimental studies the restorative value of natural environments and the ability of exposure to nature, even urban parks, to reduce mental fatigue. In this study, participants who recreated in nature (backpackers) performed better on a proofreading test than those who did not have a similar nature vacation. Follow-up with participants over time suggests that nature experiences may have longer-term restorative value, or "proactive effects, preparing people to better cope with the stress and strain of daily life" (p. 15).

While backpacking in a remote wilderness is one way to achieve these elements, University of Michigan psychologist Stephen Kaplan (1995) and others acknowledge that many of these qualities can be present in urban environments and through experiences much closer to where most people live: "The sense of being away does not require that the setting be distant. Natural environments that are easily accessible thus offer an important resource for resting one's directed attention" (p. 174). Those restorative qualities can be achieved through careful design of small urban spaces, through connected trails and pathways that maximize these experiences in urban setting, for example.

The enjoyment many people get from bird watching, often in urban environments, is indicative of the recreational and therapeutic benefits and personal enjoyment of wildlife viewing. We tend to think that true wildlife experiences can only happen in remote national parks, yet cities represent important habitats for a rich array of wildlife and biodiversity. Enhancing this urban biodiversity, restoring it where possible, and expanding opportunities for urbanites to gain direct exposure becomes an important strategy for strengthening place, and for reducing urban stress.

A recent study comparing play patterns in public housing projects that have trees and vegetation, to play patterns in projects without these features, provides compelling support for the socializing and developmental benefits provided by nature and natural features. Children's play in green housing projects was substantially higher, and presence of and exposure to adults also significantly greater (Taylor et al., 1998). The authors, a group of environmental psychologists at the University of Illinois Urbana-Champaign, Professors Andres Faber Taylor, Angela Wiley, Frances E. Kuo, and William Sullivan conclude with an admonition to the design disciplines about the importance of incorporating natural features, especially trees: "We hope these findings, along with future research, will encourage city planners and designers to include more trees and grass in public housing developments. Doing so is likely to have a number of positive consequences that benefit children, their families, and their communities" (p. 23).

Nature and Its Capacity to Strengthen Place and Build Community

Nature and the natural features of cities help to actively strengthen community in several ways. First, greening urban environments can create important preconditions for socializing behavior. Presence of trees and vegetation create more appealing places in which to meet, socialize, and interact with other community residents. As community gardens in New York City and elsewhere demonstrate, these natural areas are extremely attractive and vitally important places in which to hold community events, meetings, and celebrations. These forms of urban nature not only provide the physical spaces in which these community-strengthening activities can occur but, as cited earlier, likely serve to enhance the attractiveness of participating. Where a political rally or food drive or civic event can occur in park and forest settings, as opposed to say an auditorium, greater attendance and participation are likely.

The various programs and initiatives designed to enhance, restore, and expand green qualities in communities can themselves be important processes for building and strengthening community. Andrew Light (2000), a philosophy professor at New York University, has argued that ecological restoration has "inherent democratic potential" in its possibility of involving large numbers of citizens and volunteers working in a largely equal way to pursue collective goals. Restorative work is not by definition participative or democratic (e.g., consider the scale and tasks associated with the new Everglades restoration project), but it can be. And, natural restoration in an urban setting tends to be small-scale and decentralized, the result of many good people acting together to make a difference and to improve their community.

There is much anecdotal evidence, moreover, that such forms of direct personal action and participating directly in the improvement of one's community has a commitment-strengthening function. Tree planting parties, urban stream cleanup and restoration functions, and other similar initiatives typically amount to a kind of "ecological barn raising" and can make a large difference in the public life of a community.

Considerable and convincing research suggests, then, that access to trees and nature has profound therapeutic, life-enhancing, and community-building qualities. Although access to nature is perhaps easier in rural and natural settings, there is an increasing importance, as discussed further in Chapter 5, to design and manage cities in ways that maximize opportunities for interaction with nature. Cities can and must become more natural and ecological, and doing so will respond to basic human needs.

Place Ethics

An important body of thinking and writing focuses on the value and normative dimensions of place, a recognition that there are fundamental ethical dimensions to the ways in which we treat places—how we use and affect natural and cultural space, and the human and nonhuman lives that occupy and depend on these spaces. We might refer to this broad but important component of the literature and theory as *place ethics*.

What is the extent of our place obligations? What do we owe places? How ought we treat places and the people and things that occupy them? Elsewhere I have argued for the importance of the concept of the *moral community* (Beatley 1994), and in particular the question of three ethical dimensions—temporal, spatial, and biological. Do we have obligations to future generations (temporal), duties beyond our immediate community or jurisdictional borders (spatial), and duties to forms of life other than our own (biological)? There is now a growing body of literature largely in environmental ethics that seeks to address these questions (e.g., see Nash, 1989).

The normative impact of public design and planning, and the powerful effects of the designed qualities of our cities and communities, is a point often made in the literature. Sidney Brower (1990), a professor of planning at the University of Maryland, for instance, talks of the important civilizing function of communal spaces in a neighborhood: "The neighborhood center represents, however, not only a spatial but also a social focus; it is the symbolic center of the neighborhoods. The design of the center celebrates community; it is pleasurable and spiritually uplifting. This is desirable because good design has both educational and social value; it teaches taste and refinement, and it has a civilizing influence, reducing the likelihood of conflict" (p. 75).

Bioregionalism is often argued for on ethical or moral grounds. Among the personal actions that a bioregional or place-based ethic suggests are, where at all possible, consuming locally, supporting locally owned businesses, buying products that minimize environmental impacts (locally and globally), supporting green companies and businesses, investing and banking locally, and being actively engaged in local politics and in the social life of one's community. So much of the essence of bioregionalism is about developing and nurturing a far greater consciousness of the local and regional ecology and working on its behalf. And, very important, making an effort to understand the connections between one's life choices and lifestyle, and the condition and quality and health of that ecology—that is, where does the electricity come from to power your home, and what are the environmental impacts created through producing and delivering this power, where does the water come from, where does the household waste end up, what happens to the stormwater running off your yard (and what happens to the fertilizer or herbicides applied to it?)? Understanding these connections is a key premise of bioregional living, and then taking tangible actions to sustain and nurture and commit to place is the next step.

Place-based living, it can be argued, is in direct contrast to our typical modern globalized lives. Place-based living or bioregional perspective suggests that it is indeed extremely important to know where our food is grown, for instance, and the impacts on the environment involved in growing it. Place-based living holds that individual consumers ought to take responsibility for the consequences of these consumption choices.

Globalized lives allow us to be anonymous—our consumption and its impacts are anonymous, hard to know or understand, and consequently absent of any corresponding duties or responsibilities. Our high petroleum consumption results in great ecological damage, yet we feel little direct responsibility because we typically lack specific information about these impacts and are not able to discern or understand a direct cause and effect.

An ethic of place demands of us, then, not only actions locally and bioregionally to protect and restore and nurture, but to be accountable for the destruction and impacts outside of where we live. We are concerned about and responsible for our place effects, wherever they might manifest.

There is considerable diversity of opinion about the need to disconnect completely from the global economy in order to achieve a truly bioregional society and a truly harmonious relationship between land and community. Bioregionalists like Kirkpatrick Sale argue essentially for economic self-sufficiency for bioregions. Many others argue for movement in direction of local self-sufficiency, reducing the amount and flow of goods and materials coming in from far distant lands, and favoring locally produced food and other products where possible, but accepting the inevitability of the global economy. At the heart of this philosophy is the sense that by bringing production and consumption closer together there will be greater awareness (and, it is hoped, efforts and ability to minimize) of the ecological and social impacts of such consumption.

A new kind of political ethic is also suggested. A call for *civic environmentalism* has been made by a number of recent authors. Civic environmentalism suggests the need to move beyond top-down laws and programs, on the one hand, and the NIMBY-ism (Not in My Backyard) that typically characterizes much contemporary local politics. The virtue of broad-based community organizations and coalitions that look across issues and focus on the "whole" and the long term is emphasized (John, 1994).

The discussions that follow in this book also emphasize the important—indeed, fused—relationships between sustainability and place. Creating sustainable communities and cities, advocated by many (e.g., Newman and Kenworthy, 1999) must necessarily happen in a place and in a locality; it is by definition place-based.

Conclusions

Place is an essential element in all human existence and living; all lives are lived in relation to actual, physical places, and thinking about what constitutes a good and healthy place is an important undertaking, to be sure.

There is a rich and abundant literature on place and place making, and on the qualities and conditions that make up a good place. Much can be learned from this extensive past research, scholarship, and writing. We know that there are many ways of defining and thinking about place, but at the core they represent the spaces, landscapes, and environments to which we attach meaning. Meaningful places are essential for meaningful lives. The meanings we attach to places are influenced by many factors, and any effort at creating sustainable places must acknowledge these influences and, where possible, bring them to the surface. Among the place qualities that emerge as important are exposure to nature and the natural environment (e.g., trees, water, wildlife).

Notes

1. Phone interviews by the National Geographic Society asking questions about rivers concludes that Americans have a low "River IQ," and "lack knowledge of even the most basic river facts." A little less than half the respondents (44%) could not define the term *watershed,* and exhibited a limited understanding of the threats to rivers and water quality (Jones, 2001).

2. At the town building scale, for instance, these include "city-country fingers" (every urbanite should be within a half-hour bicycle ride of the countryside): diverse cities with a "mosaic of subcultures" encouraging a "vast mosaic of small and different subcultures, each with its own spatial territory, and each with the power to create its own distinct life style" (Alexander et al., 1977, p. 50); "scattered work" where there is no separation between work and living environments.

3. More specifically, several qualities have been associated with maximizing the restorative qualities of nature. These include being away, fascination, extent, and compatibility (Kaplan, 1995).

Place Strengthening
through History and Heritage

Much that is distinctive or special about a place is a function of its unique history, the heritage of its built environment, and the natural and ecological conditions in which this built form coevolves over time. History and heritage help in fundamental ways to define a place. As the stories in this chapter tell, history can be used to strengthen place and place commitments, as well as to enhance, in essential ways, the quality of life. Saving historical buildings and landscapes also makes sense from a sustainability perspective.

The history of a community and region can be thought of as an important *place asset*, essential for nurturing connections between people and environment and place, and providing intertemporal connections—essential connections between the current inhabitants and the people who came before and those who will come along in the future. Historical connections, and having a sense of the people and events that have shaped the communities in which we live, are critical in making places meaningful to us, in casting the collections of buildings as home rather than just empty vessels for sleep and work. The more we understand about the beginnings and evolution of a place, the greater importance that place will assume in our lives. These are connections we need for our sense of groundedness and are requisite elements in building commitments to place.

The history and heritage of a place are typically assets in an economic sense, as well, in that they can be effectively used to strengthen the special nature and feeling of a place, and in turn its economic appeal and attractiveness. John Nau III, chairman of the Federal Advisory Council of Historic Preservation, makes an eloquent case for the importance of preservation efforts in strengthening a locality's overall attractiveness and economy. Historical preservation is an "essential component" to a city's success: ". . . preserving your past and putting its tangible assets to new purposes . . . will go a long way toward creating the kind of dynamic and livable community that will help resolve problems associated with a flat economy, a population plateau, a stagnant tax base, a withering inner city, insufficient opportunities for recreation, culture, tourism, and an urban environment that does not entice people to want to work and live in a community" (Nau, 2002). Specifically addressing the potential benefits for Cleveland, Ohio, Nau speaks of the many local benefits that preserving history and heritage provides at once:

> Historic Preservation positively addresses all of these issues; it can benefit a community economically, culturally, socially, environmentally, and educationally. By taking advantage of existing assets—historic buildings, courthouses and battlefields—in adaptive reuses, communities can achieve economic diversity.

Preserving and strengthening a community's history and its important historic buildings and landscapes can, moreover, in many important ways reduce its ecological impacts and can advance the goals of sustainability. In many European and American cities, renewing and reinvigorating older neighborhoods and buildings is an important way to reduce, for example, development of new greenfield sites and land-consumptive (and auto-dependent) development. Preservation of an older structure, such as a warehouse, a factory building, or a church, represents the preserving of the embodied energy of that structure—the energy needed to produce the materials that go into the building, to transport them, and to actually construct the building. Preserving historic buildings and landscapes, then, is often a community sustainability strategy, as well.

The history and heritage of a place can be imparted to its residents and visitors in many ways. More attention in public schools to teaching about the history of a community would be welcome, as would teaching about the major events in the past that shaped the community in important ways (e.g., floods, fires) and the civic leaders who helped steer and steward a place. Local newspapers and media might spend more time on the subject, perhaps more fully acknowledging the past contributions of leaders when they die or writing stories about the history of particular neighborhoods or buildings as a regular feature. Celebrating important historical events and commemorating those events in a variety of ways certainly helps. Making place history as transparent and visible as possible is an important strategy, whether through murals depicting history on the sides of buildings or through walking tours and historic trails or by simply leaving historic elements uncovered and visible (e.g., when renovating older structures or replacing urban infrastructure). The history and heritage of a place can and should be a major starting point in creating places that we have and want to be a part of.

Confronting the Industrial Past and Building on Its History

In many cities and regions, heavy industry has given way to new economic impulses, economics based more on services and information, for instance, yet the remnants of the important industrial past become monuments and historical assets. In this way, an authentic place is one that acknowledges, uncovers, and actively seeks to make sense of all of its past, and to accept even those dimensions of its history that may be uncomfortable or unattractive—they are all strands in forming a real place.

Redeveloping contaminated urban sites, and the design of new buildings and landscapes, can be used as opportunities to reconnect to the history of the site and to its past industrial and other uses. It is increasingly argued that sustainable cities and communities must look for opportunities to reuse or redevelop these abandoned industrial sites, commonly referred to as *brownfields,* before allowing undeveloped land at urban fringe to be developed. Extensive brownfield initiatives have been under way at both federal and local levels in the United States, as well as in many European cities, with significant new financial investments and incentives provided to encourage brownfield redevelopment.

The opportunities to strengthen the uniqueness of place are great, indeed, and brownfield sites should be seen as assets and opportunities rather than liabilities. Many examples help make this point, of course, and the new Glass Museum on a contaminated waterfront site in Tacoma, Washington, is a good one. The museum is an important cultural center for Tacoma, and one of the first projects in attempting to reconnect residents to the city's long inaccessible waterfront. Its design incorporates, for instance, a dramatic vertical cone, harkening back to the wood-burning conical stacks of the industries that once existed there (Fortner, 2001). Creatively, the cone now contains a 200-seat auditorium. A major site cleanup was required, including excavation and disposal of contaminated soils.

A number of other communities and regions worldwide have creatively confronted their grimy, industrial pasts, turning liabilities and former negative conditions of place into aspects of pride—exercises in place building. Perhaps the most significant and creative effort to acknowledge, preserve,

Figure 3.1 | The former gasometer in Oberhausen, Germany, has been converted into vertical artscape and a cultural center.

and adaptively reuse industrial landscape can be seen in the Ruhr Valley of northwestern Germany, an industrial area of former coal mines and steel plants. In 1989, the state of North Rhine–Westphalia initiated a unique project—the International Building Exhibition (IBA) Emscher Park—to highlight this industrial heritage and sponsor building projects and development schemes that would creatively restore, renew, and reuse these landscapes.

The result is a wild mix of creative projects—some 120 in all—that celebrate this industrial heritage. A unique example is the reuse of the large gasometer (a tank used to store gas) in Oberhausen, Germany, in the Ruhr Valley. This 110-meter-high structure (about 360 feet) has now become a cultural as well as a visual landmark. It regularly hosts art exhibits and installations of various kinds. American artist Bill Viola recently utilized the vast interior spaces of the building to put on a provocative multiple-screen video show called "The Six Angels of the New Millennium." The dramatic, slow-motion photography, combined with basal sounds, made the gasometer the perfect venue. This project shows that building on the history of a city may also present unusual opportunities to expand the cultural and artistic life of a place and to enhance quality of living.

Landscape Park Duisberg-Nord, Germany

The Landscape Park Duisburg-Nord, is another project funded under the Emscher initiative and a dramatic case of renewal and reuse. Here, under an inspired design by landscape architect Peter Latz, an immense park has been crafted around and among industrial ruins. Doorways are carved out of concrete walls of ore pits, opening to lovely gardens; tall foundation walls have become sites for climbing and repelling; the superstructure of a blast furnace has become a network of walkways and ladders for visitors to climb and explore. An obsolete industrial landscape is now a bustling park that at once reuses scarce land and creates a symbolic and visual connection to the region's important industrial past. This example, and the many other Emscher Park projects, also illustrates the importance of building on the unique and particular histories of place and creatively utilizing them as strategies for overcoming the sameness that exists in so many other regions and communities.

Figure 3.2 | Landscape Park in Duisburg-Nord, Germany. Designed by noted landscape architect Peter Latz, this unique park creatively reuses the industrial landscape of this former steel mill.

The Landscape Park has become an important public park and civic space for residents of Duisburg. As Steinglass (2000) notes in a story about it in *Metropolis* magazine:

> By all accounts the landscape park has contributed immeasurably to the cultural welfare of Duisburg. The park draws outdoor classical music concerts and auto trade fairs, and it hosts the local Turkish community's annual festival. . . . Duisburg–Nord is just one of dozens of similar projects sponsored by the IBA: sculpture parks on slag heaps; factories converted into industry museums; land-art projects in wheat fields. The Ruhr's defunct factories were once regarded as gargantuan eyesores; now lit up to advantage at night by fashionable theater lighting designers, they're seen as spectacular monumental architecture. (p. 131)

Water plays an important role in the design of the park. Much of the elaborate design has the intention of purifying water as well as making it an elemental feature of this landscape restorative project. One visually prominent feature is a large windmill that pulls water up from the canal running through the site and sends it, oxygenated and via elevated aqueducts, to the gardens and green spots in the park, before being returned to the canal, much the cleaner as a result.

A relatively large park, some 570 acres, the Landscape Park Duisburg-Nord benefits from proximity to an urban population. Some arrive by car (there is parking), but many get to the park by public transit, by way of several nearby tram lines. There is about everything that you could want here—fields for dog runs; places for children to climb, play, and explore; a café; a demonstration environmental farm; and a petting zoo.

Westerpark Gasfabriek, Amsterdam

The ongoing redevelopment and reuse of the Westerpark Gasfabriek in Amsterdam is another marvelous example of a city seizing on the unique opportunities of its changing industry and economy. A heavily contaminated site in the Westerpark district, a fairly short walk from the center of Amsterdam, this used to be the site of the city's coal gasification, where the gas needed to power the city's streetlamps was produced. With the arrival of natural gas, the plant became obsolete and closed in the late 1960s.

Perhaps a reflection of the times, the city's original concept was to tear down the nineteen historic buildings on the site, and start afresh. Largely for lack of funding from the national government, this demolition plan stalled; once control over the site passed to the district government (Westerpark Stadsdeel), new concepts emerged. And thankfully so, as the site consisted of some impressive structures and, although having no legal protection, had considerable architectural and historic merit. Included among these remaining structures was a large gas tank, the so-called gashouder, where the gas was actually stored.

Crafting a vision and process for restoring, cleaning up, and reusing this site was daunting, but Westerpark district went about it in some creative ways. They realized that the long-term reuse and cleanup would take many years, and that a strategy and method for securing short-term uses was needed. The district essentially moved forward on these two fronts at the same time. In the end, a private management company was given control over short-term leases for the buildings, while cleanup and longer-term redevelopment occurred. A variety of interesting short-term uses have taken place in these buildings now for a number of years. From offices of the Circus Soleil to cafés and nightclubs to a movie house, a number of public events and performances have occurred there. This is a site that has not lain dormant as a sterile construction site, but has already forged a place in the minds of Amsterdamers as an emerging center of cultural activities. A number of large events, including operas, have been held in the gashouder.

Much of the long-term vision for the site comes from the creative master plan prepared by American landscape architect Kathryn Gustafson. She won a competition held in the early 1990s, with a creative fusing of the industrial site with the preexisting Westerpark neighborhood park to the east of the site. The Gustafson plan ties together the many disparate pieces of the site, including the original, more formal neighborhood park to the east. Gustafson's overall theme is change, reflected in the structure and elements of the park and, especially, it seems, in the evolution of what a park looks like and how it functions. The restored, former industrial elements include newer ideas about what a park should include: for example, connections to a rural

Figure 3.3 | At the Westerpark Gasfabriek, a large brownfield site is being converted to a major new cultural center for the city of Amsterdam. This café is housed in one of the many historic buildings being reused.

polder, wetlands and aquatic pools where there once stood smaller gas-holders, and school gardens.

The park plan manages to satisfy many cultural and recreational needs; there will be sports fields and events fields, an artists' village, and a market square, with these spaces connected and tied together through a central axis and a canal promenade. It is easy to imagine how the Westerpark Gasfabriek, though not yet finished, will become the epicenter for the arts in Amsterdam and a prime destination on weekends and evenings.

American Efforts at Reconnecting to Industrial Pasts

Many American cities have similar opportunities to creatively reuse and highlight their industrial pasts. In New York City, the Bronx River Alliance is spearheading a new river greenway that would creatively convert an abandoned cement plant into a waterfront park. In Pittsburgh, a new park along the Monongahela River, Nine Mile Run, is being forged out an area of massive slagheaps, an industrial-scarred landscape left over from the city's steel era. Stream restoration, pedestrian trails, and new housing are all underway there (see APA, 2002).

In Cleveland, what to do with Whiskey Island, a place of salt mines and terminus point for iron ore pellets, used to fuel the steel industry there remains a major issue. While still in private hands, momentum exists to buy the land (probably the City of Cleveland) and convert it to a park, as an element of the city's larger ambitious waterfront plan. This is an excellent idea, given the ecology of the island, and the interesting place history lessons it could convey.

Some of the most visually dramatic industrial remnants on Whiskey Island, until recently, have been the four Hulett Iron Ore Unloaders, massive 10-story high structures of vertical and horizontal arms that lifted coal from Lake Erie boats arriving at the Port of Cleveland. Built in 1912, and designed by a native of Cleveland (George Hullet) there had to have been threats made in the past by the Cleveland/Cuyahoga Port Authority to tear them down. Several local groups, notably Friends of Whiskey Island, and the Friends of Hulett Ore Unloaders, campaigned timelessly to preserve the unloaders (including the staging of a "clandestine lighting" of the unloaders in 1999, by

the so-called "Huletteers," see the dramatic photo at www.citizensvision
.org). While Cleveland City and Cuyahoga County jostle over who should
buy the land (and also who will be able to pay for its acquisition, see Gill,
2003), the idea of preserving Whiskey Island as a significant place-enhancing
landscape and landmark is simply undeniable. In 2002 the Port Authority
scrapped two of the four unloaders, and in a compromise dismantled the
other two, to be reassembled (and preserved) somewhere else. Funds still
need to be raised, but a decision is near concerning where to place the reassembled behemoths. When they are they will be a dramatic, interesting and
educational living piece of Cleveland's industrial history. Cities like Cleveland are smart to see such a step as a critical investment in its distinctiveness
and specialness and in strengthening the overall quality of life there.

Historic Fragments and Textures

Cities are also faced with preserving not only single buildings or heritage
sites, but linear heritage features that bisect and intermingle with the living

Figure 3.4 | The Telus Building in
Vancouver, British Columbia, has
been renovated and redesigned to
use substantially less energy,
through the addition of a double-
glazed glass skin. The choice was
made to renovate and update this
older building rather than build a
new structure.

spaces. One of the most intriguing examples of place building are the efforts in New York City to protect and restore the High Line—a 1930s elevated freight rail line that travels about a mile and a half through the West Side of Manhattan, from Washington Street north to 34th street, nearly to the Hudson River. Opened in 1934, the use of the line for freight traffic ended in 1980. What to do with this industrial and transportation remnant has occupied considerable discussion and debate on the West Side.

Advocates for preservation of the High Line imagine a "one-of-a-kind grand, public promenade" (see www.thehighline.org). Joshua David and Robert Hammond together created Friends of the High Line (FHL) in 1999, a 503(c)(3) nonprofit, to build support for preserving the line, and have worked tirelessly on behalf of this issue. Their tactics are both legal and political. Legally, they have petitioned the Surface Transportation Board to reconsider its 1992 conditional demolition permit, and appealed to the New York Supreme Court, and won, to invalidate on procedural grounds a demolition plan.

Politically, they have worked hard to garner support among Chelsea residents and business owners. The politics of protecting this line have not always been easy. The city's mayor at the time, Rudy Guiliani, did not support the project and had difficulty seeing the virtues of saving the line. Though neither David nor Hammond is a lawyer, having a legal background would have been helpful in this case. Much of the wrangling over the High Line has been in the courts. A demolition agreement reached in the final days of the Guiliani administration was contested by FHL and thrown out by the courts.

Many writers, both residents and visitors, have speculated about what it would be like to have such a community resource. Eugene Patron (2002) talks about how walking along the elevated line would be "the urban equivalent of exploring the Costa Rican rain forest on a trail suspended up in the trees. Even familiar scenery can turn exotic if seen from a new perspective. We can trek the High Line through both the concrete jungle and the Emerald City" (p. 13).

But not everyone in the city supports preserving the High Line, and considerable controversy has been generated by this bold proposal. The Chelsea Property Owners Association is the principal opponent; it supports demolishing the structure and using the space for development. They see the High

Line as an eyesore and argue that the structure is unsafe and structurally unsound. Friends of the High Line swiftly counter that the structure is indeed sound (the freight rail company CSX, current owner of the High Line, concurs, noting that the structure was designed to support at once two fully loaded freight trains), and that the economic advantages to surrounding property owners of proximity to a new elevated park and greenway would be extensive. High Line supporters, moreover, envision the ability to build and develop extensively around the structure, and perhaps creatively design new buildings in ways that allow access to the promenade or otherwise take advantage of it as a development resource.

One of the dynamics arising from efforts to preserve this kind of urban historical texture is the stories from the past, the historical detail, that almost *must* be told. While gazing at the High Line from ground level, I heard its history from Josh David: The elevated freight line was a badly needed response to the public safety and neighborhood disruption posed by the street-level line. Fast-moving freight trains were the cause of numerous deaths on the West Side, despite the presence of a "Tenth Street Cowboy," a rider on horseback who alerted pedestrians to the dangers of approaching trains. The elevated track, a result of the West Side Improvement project, was opened in 1934.

One is struck, in both the High Line and the Duisberg-Nord Landscape Park, by how quickly and beautifully nature reclaims such spaces and interweaves natural elements with the industrial and human made. Patron (2002) notes that "nature has remade" the High Line. "Dozens of plants, mosses, birds, and small mammals have created an ecosystem of their own on the track bed. Theirs is a narrative that is as much a part of the High Line story as was the boxcars" (p. 16). A journalist writing in the *Wall Street Journal* describes it as an "elevated Eden," where "[a] swath of Manhattan [has] gone to seed, reverting to a kind of native prairie: knee-high grasses, white and yellow wildflowers, a miracle born of neglect" (Connors, 2002).

The current administration of Mayor Bloomberg has been highly supportive of preserving the High Line, and the prognosis for the future now seems very good. In Spring 2004, FHL held a design competition for what the future High Line might look like. Some 52 entries were submitted, from which FHL has selected four. A final masterplan to guide its redevelopment is expected in Spring 2005 (Perez, 2004).

Urbanscapes as Historical Stage

Artifacts from the past, other than buildings per se, can be creatively worked back into the urban environment; reminding us of these events and history while adding intriguing texture to community landscapes. Downtown Vancouver has built a glass structure, part of a large community center, to house and showcase Engine 374—a steam locomotive that in 1887 traveled the newly opened transcontinental railroad, linking Vancouver to the provinces to the east. Repairing and restoring the engine itself happened through a community process, with individuals purchasing for $20 (Canadian) a heritage brick with their name on it as a way of raising the necessary funds.

Today, the engine is a tourist attraction and a source of pride. The locomotive rests on a small section of track and is rolled out of the glass enclosure for special events and outdoor receptions. The community center building itself sits on the site of a railway turntable, or roundhouse. A "heritage yard" has been created around the turntable, adding important civic and public space to this part of the city.

Restoring and rebuilding the historic fabric of a community can further strengthen its distinctiveness, its historically unique qualities, the important elements of organic evolution that every community contains. There are many positive examples of this at both large and small scales. Numerous communities have discovered the historic "gems" that are often overlooked or underappreciated.

Places with a distinctive feel are often communities that have made a conscious effort to preserve at least some of the layers of history that manifest in big ways (historic buildings) but often in many smaller ways. This patina of a place's history is composed of so many things, functional and artistic, ordinary as well as designed objects, that give visitors and residents alike a sense of temporal connectedness, small insights into what the past of the place was like. These potential elements are many: manhole covers, tree grates, lampposts, sidewalks and tilework, and of course elements of natural environment

Figure 3.5 | Engine 374, an historic steam locomotive, rolled out in downtown Vancouver. (Photo compliments of Maurice Jassak, Image West Marketing, Vancouver)

such as older trees and hedgerows, that have historic significance. We may sometimes overlook these smaller place-enhancing features, but they are cumulatively important, to be sure. Older manhole covers that remain add a degree of character and visible memory to a neighborhood, and several cities have undertaken efforts to ensure that they are protected and preserved.

There are some 600,000 manhole covers in New York City, and even a Society for the Preservation of New York City Manhole Covers formed to educate and work on behalf of their protection. A New York photographer, Diana Stuart, has catalogued and researched many of these in her excellent book *Design Underfoot* tracing unique designs back to the mostly local foundries that produced them. She also gives manhole cover tours that are now attracting considerable attention. Some cities like Los Angeles have given landmark status to their manhole covers, and a number of other cities where efforts are underway to promote greater awareness of them and to design the next generation of them (see chapter 8).

The cumulative effects of preserving the historical fragments of a neighborhood or city are considerable indeed and worth the cost, technical difficulties, and political opposition that will be sparked in some quarters. In the Georgetown neighborhood of Washington, D.C., an interesting battle has been raging over what to do with the remaining remnant tracks of the Cabin John-Green Echo Trolley line. Portions of O and P streets there still contain the steel tracks installed in the mid-1890s, part of what was one of the few so-called "conduit" style systems, where the electric lines powering the cars were placed underground rather than overhead. Many current nearby residents don't like the remnant tracks much, and argue they are hazardous to both pedestrians and drivers. The D.C. Department of Transportation would like to remove them when they undertake major utility work in the area, and believe putting them back would be too expensive. Others in the community see them as an important link to a previous era, and they do seem a very valuable element of community character and charm. I agree.

Driving on the Georgetown tracks requires one to slow down, a good result for lots of reasons, and they almost cry out for some explanation of their purpose, origin, and history. While a compromise is in the works (as of press) that will likely preserve some portion of the tracks, the Georgetown case shows the importance of worrying over and seeking to preserve the seemingly smaller pieces of the urban fabric that give insight, provide historical context, and special meaning to places. These tracks seem a small community element, to be sure, but add much to the textured and layered meanings and history of this place. Saving even small remnants becomes an important place-making act.

Various other street features offer opportunities for connecting with a community's past. Freiburg, Germany, that beautiful city carefully reconstructed following the severe bombing of World War II, is a case in point. Here, sidewalks are adorned with circular pebble mosaics, an ancient practice in this city, each indicating the nature of a shop or business found there. A unique system of small waterways is also found throughout the historic center. Dating back to the thirteenth century, the network of *bachle* diverted water from the Driesan River into the city (Beatley, 2000). It adds immensely to the special feel of Freiburg, and planning officials there have sought out every chance to add to and expand this system. A recent example includes a circular channel and a series of interesting sculptures built by a department store, as a condi-

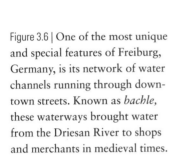

Figure 3.6 | One of the most unique and special features of Freiburg, Germany, is its network of water channels running through downtown streets. Known as *bachle,* these waterways brought water from the Driesan River to shops and merchants in medieval times.

tion of receiving approval to expand its building. Now public buildings and projects also tie in and expand this network of water channels.

Freiburg's good work in pedestrianizing most of its center, and investing in the stonework, seating, and other amenities of its historic district has paid off in many ways. This is not only a place of palpable antiquity; it is also a delightful place to visit, shop, and live. Moreover, there is no feeling of sameness here. Freiburg has taken full advantage of its special qualities of place, the historically unique elements of its built and physical environment, to nurture a special place indeed.

Enhancing the Presence of History and Heritage in Communities

Finding creative ways to highlight the history of a community, and to incorporate it into the built environment, becomes an important challenge. A number of ways, such as using murals, sculptures, and outdoor art, offer great potential. (For a more extensive discussion and additional examples, see Chapter 7, "Place Building through Art and Celebration.")

The history of a place, its important events and people, can be made visible in many creative ways. Many cities have encouraged or allowed mural painting of community events and historical eras (see the discussion of Chemainus, British Columbia, for instance, in Chapter 7). Plaques and signage at key points is helpful. Communities impacted by major natural disasters, such as floods and earthquakes, can find visually dramatic ways to depict these events in the public realm—signage showing the line of flooding (of say the 1992 Mississippi floods) makes the extent of damage and fear and hardship experienced by residents palpable (and educates in turn about the natural forces and vagaries of living along a river).

Asheville, North Carolina, has creatively encouraged residents and visitors to learn about its history in this way. In the early 1990s, it created the Asheville Urban Trail, a 1.7-mile-long trail that runs through the heart of the city. With thirty "stations" or stopping points along the way where one can learn about the history of the city, often through a piece of contemporary art, Asheville has been described as a "living, historic walking town . . . a museum without walls that illustrates and highlights the city's heritage" (www.ci.asheville.nc.us/parks/urban.html). Designed by volunteers and funded through private donations, the Asheville Urban Trail is, at once, a marvelous way to teach about history and to get people outside and physically active, and a nice way to instill civic pride. The trail is both a public art project and a way to promote the learning of local history. Both guided tours (on Saturdays) and self-guided tours are available. The trail is punctuated by pink granite markers with logos indicating one of the five historic periods into which the stops are divided, beginning with the frontier period.

History and Sustainability

There are many ways in which place history and sustainability are reinforcing agendas. Reusing and recycling older buildings is not only a significant place-strengthening strategy, but it can also provide marvelous opportunities to reduce energy and resource consumption. We know that one immediate savings is reaped in the form of embodied energy—every brick left standing is one less that requires energy to fire (and to transport and put into place).

It is also possible for us to preserve and extend the longevity of older buildings in our communities, at the same time that they are reconfigured to use dramatically less resources and energy. Many good examples of such community retrofits exist. The Telus Building in Vancouver is a great case in point. An older 1940s structure, home to Canada's Telecommunication Company on Robson Street in the heart of Vancouver, the building has been restored and renewed with architectural and technological updates. Indeed, preserving and reusing the building was a stated charge given by the Telus Company; tearing the structure down was not viewed as acceptable. A number of retrofit elements were included, but most dramatic was the installation of a new double-glazed glass skin on the south façade, resulting in a "triple-skinned" structure. The new façade layer creates a 1-meter-thick (slightly more than 3 feet) buffer, providing insulation in the winter and ventilation in the summer. During summer months, motorized dampers on top and bottom allow natural ventilation, with help from photovoltaic-powered fans. During winter months, the dampers are closed. A new heat recovery system, utilizing waste heat, is another important energy element in the building's upgrading. The structure uses some 30 percent less energy now, and will save an estimated 54,000 metric tons of greenhouse gas emissions over a seventy-five-year period (Busby and Associates Architects, undated). Updating the old building instead of building a new structure also saved an estimated 16,000 tons of demolition waste from going to local landfills.

Much of the task of preserving the history of places, moreover, is about repopulating them, about bringing people and vitality back to them. While sprawl consumes rural land and natural resources, we abandon many older places. Cities such as Philadelphia have large numbers of abandoned structures (15,000 according to the National Trust Report, 2000) and large numbers of vacant lots, both of which represent opportunities not only to accommodate housing and population growth but to reinvigorate older neighborhoods and repair the damages done to older places.

Repopulating such urban neighborhoods and using and reusing abandoned properties is a sound place-making strategy, and one that builds on the history and texture of a place. And there are an increasing number of tools and successful programs that can be utilized. Providing financial support for renovation and redevelopment is one option.

Preserving and reusing historic buildings and landscapes, a practice that promotes sustainability through material recycling and maintaining the embodied energy of these buildings, is another key ingredient. Creative examples abound. In Amsterdam, late-nineteenth-century grain silos have recently been converted into apartments and offices. The grain silos are historic buildings and, as a result of their preservation and reuse, will remain prominent landmarks in Amsterdam. They have, more recently, served to stimulate and anchor additional (and creative) residential redevelopment along the water. In 2002, a highly interesting addition to Amsterdam housing was completed, a few meters away, along the water, in the form of an MVRDV-designed ten-story building of flats. Designed with interesting lines and color, the new building is clearly a modern addition. The two structures together nicely show the new and the old, and the ability to blend and balance these different temporal reference points all within a single view.

Reusing historic buildings often means preserving structures and facilities that have a palpably unique and special character to them. In Turku, Finland, amidst an area of rebuilt and restored warehouses and other industrial buildings along the Aura River, sits the renovated 1912 rope factory (Koysitehdas). When built it was purported to be the longest building in Nordic countries and today has been masterly reconfigured and given marvelous new life as the home of the Turku Conservatory and the Turku Music Academy. In this long structure is now housed a variety of artistic and musical endeavors: it includes concert halls (including the 350-seat Sigyn Concert Hall), classrooms and teaching spaces, and a café and cafeteria. It is an important community venue for music and dance concerts, and situated along a very enjoyable and immensely walkable riverfront district. The structure is distinctive, to be sure, and an important element of that city's history and a very creative melding of new and old. Such developments at once strengthen the historic core, conserve land and resources, and build a unique sense of place.

Many older cities are implementing programs to underwrite the renovation and revitalization of older neighborhoods and structures. In the United States, cities like Baltimore and Philadelphia offer financial incentives, such as low-interest second mortgages, in targeted neighborhoods (e.g., see Langdon, 2003). Boston's Historic HomeWorks program will provide matching grants to homeowners (up to $4,000); the home must be at least fifty years old, and the repairs must respect the "original architectural integrity" of the structure. State and local government tax credits for renovation of historic property make a big difference as well.

Reducing the regulatory and other burdens to restoring, rebuilding, and renovating is another important strategy. New Jersey's adoption in 1998 of a new and separate Rehabilitation Subcode, the first in the country, has helped in that state. The code offers greater flexibility in dealing with older buildings and is already credited with reducing payment costs and significantly increasing (41 percent in the first year) rehabilitation activity in New Jersey.

Delicately Balancing Preservation and Modernity

Bungalows in Chicago

The existing building stock in a city can represent both an important historic and cultural resource and an essential element of sustainable place building. Appreciating, protecting, and restoring older homes is a great way to strengthen place and capitalize on the distinctiveness of community. In Chicago, an important form of housing is the bungalow—small one-and-a-half-story homes built in the arts and crafts style between 1910 and 1940. In Chicago, Illinois, these homes—some 80,000 of them (or about one-third of the city's single-family housing stock)—represent a special part of the history of the city's built form. They were built in neighborhoods surrounding the city in what has become known as the "bungalow belt." Bungalows are sited on small lots—typically, 100 feet deep and perhaps 25 to 35 feet wide. Many of the neighborhoods are still very walkable, have commercial areas not very far away, and represent highly sustainable living environments. They were an affordable housing option for many Chicagoans, the first home they were able to purchase.

The unique Historic Chicago Bungalow Initiative came into existence in 2000. A partnership between the City of Chicago, the Historic Chicago Bungalow Association, the Chicago Architecture Foundation, and local banks, its goals are to educate and promote awareness of this special housing type and to provide financial and technical assistance to those interested in buying and rehabilitating these homes. The Bungalow Association has certified some 2,700 bungalows so far, with owners receiving a medallion and qualifying for special financial assistance and expedited permitting (Newberg, 2003).

Supporting the renovation and public appreciation of this housing style makes good sense in many ways: it builds new understanding of local history, promotes a sustainable housing and lifestyle option, and builds upon and strengthens a unique local quality or condition. A major aspect of this initiative is marketing—conveying to owners, and potential owners, how special and significant the bungalows are to the history of Chicago.

The financial incentives, moreover, are substantial. For purchases, these include a grant (if below an income threshold) equal to 4 percent of the mortgage amount, below market interest rates, and vouchers for energy improvements. Vouchers and matching grants are also available for rehabilitation, as is free architectural assistance and expedited permit review. In November 2002, eligibility for the financial incentives was expanded. The initiative has also prepared a set of design guidelines for renovating and a series of public education events, including an exhibit and lecture series about bungalows, a

Figure 3.7 | There are 80,000 bungalows like this one in Chicago. The Historic Chicago Bungalow Initiative seeks to spur new appreciation of this special housing type and a rejuvenation of the neighborhoods in which these homes are found.

new book about bungalows, and tours of the bungalow belt (on the "bunga-lows bus"), which have been sold out.

The Historic Chicago Bungalow Initiative understands that certain changes and upgrades to these homes may be necessary to suit more contem-porary housing needs. Increasing the size of the home with a back addition, or extending the upstairs ceiling to provide more space, is commonly done by new owners. The Historic Chicago Bungalow Association (HCBA) realizes that these changes will, for many Chicagoans, make the bungalow a more at-tractive option. Consequently, the design guidelines prepared by HCBA pro-vide advice about how to make the improvements while also preserving the overall architectural qualities of the home (e.g., maintaining the same roof pitches, setting back second-floor additions a minimum distance from front façades; Historic Chicago Bungalow Association, undated).

The HCBA has become a sort of cheerleader in the process, helping to "generate enthusiasm" for this housing type. The bungalow serves as a kind of historical glue that binds people and neighborhoods together. In the pro-gram's short life span, it has already provided owners and neighborhoods "a source of pride and a role in the shared history of Chicago" (Newberg, 2003, p. 66).

Waterscapes and New Buildings in Germany

Herbert Dreiseitl's masterful waterscape interventions in many older Ger-man villages and towns are important examples of how historic cities can be enlivened and reinvigorated, introducing new perspectives and new modern layers to a place. His design for the German village of Gummersbach, for in-stance, has reclaimed a dangerous and undervisited center-city space and given it new life and vibrancy. In Hannoversch-Munden, Dreiseitl's water-work has transformed a dead car and bus parking area into a new public plaza.

In many ways, the history and natural heritage of a place can give impor-tant cues for designers. Dreiseitl's design for the jagged watercourses at the Mont-Cenis Academy at Herne, Germany, builds, as he explains, on the in-dustrial landscape of cracks and fissures. He designs new intentional "cracks" where water moves, connecting visually and emotionally with the

pattern of land subsidence and degradation resulting from the heavy industrial character of the Ruhr. This waterway zigzags like cracks and fissures,
harkening back to the mining landscape, down the giant steps and entrance
way to the main building. When completed, it will be a dramatic visual statement about connections to the past, as well as an amenity for residents of the
250 new flats in this neighborhood. The cracks and fissures are visceral, jar-
ring, but aesthetically interesting reminders of Herne's mining past.

New buildings and construction, sensitive to a city's history, can be instrumental in strengthening public understanding of that history. In Freiburg,
Germany, a new and relatively tall building was permitted on the site of one
of the city's old gates and entrances into the town. The tall structure, obviously modern, is viewed by Freiburg planners as an important new visual
landmark and reference point that marks an important historic entrance to
the center city. Modern design and building can, in many cases, serve to
strengthen the historic fabric of a place.

The main building of the Mont-Cenis Academy is a highly modern
structure—a solar greenhouse within which smaller buildings are arranged—
but pays tribute to that history in a number of ways, utilitarian and aesthetic.
Utilitarian is the adjoining Mont-Cenis energy park that collects the natural
gas emanating from the mines and uses it as a fuel to generate both electricity
and heat. The plant is located along a major walking path and displays information about this process and the techniques of electrical production. Several
mine shafts have been incorporated into this new neighborhood, each
marked by vertical mining sculptures.

Perhaps most dramatic is a kind of sculpture garden in the adjoining park
made up of foundation pillars and other remnants of the industrial buildings
once found there. One publication refers to this as "a meadow covering the
old industrial remainders" (EMC 1998, pp. 8–9). It's a special industrial garden, a place that speaks to the future by acknowledging the past.

Many cities, like Freiburg, have sought to ensure that there are sufficient
numbers of people living in their historic centers, recognizing the many benefits of maintaining a safe, economical, and sustainable location. In Freiburg,
the conversion of flats to offices or shops is now forbidden, and other historic
cities in Germany and elsewhere have followed suit.

Figure 3.8 | The Mont-Cenis Academy in Herne, Germany, is located on the site of former coal mines. Here, children enjoy playing in a unique industrial sculpture garden.

New Master Plans and Urban Improvements in Italy

Many other older cities have equally risen to the creative challenge of nurturing their heritage without forgoing contemporary and sustainable living spaces. Venice presents one especially interesting case of an historic city struggling with questions of how to protect its historic essence while grappling with extreme tourism pressures that undermine those qualities, as well as how to maintain and improve the quality of life for those who call Venice home. The pressures and changes over time have been dramatic—annually some 10–12 million tourists visit the historic center of Venice. At the same time, as hotels expand and part-time residents are able to outbid for housing, the number of full-time residents of the city has declined (from about 175,000 in the 1950s to about 60,000 today). Many workers, unable to find affordable housing in the city, commute into the city each day. Whether Venice is a city for tourists, for merchants depending on these visitors, or for those who live there (increasingly older people) is an open question.

Venice is famously conservative when it comes to architectural and development proposals. Yet, when the lagoon and municipality are considered as a whole, there have been remarkably creative and forward-thinking planning and project proposals that are highly modern. Adopted in 1996, a new master plan for the city puts forth a bold concept for tying the region together and for thinking of Venice in a more holistic way.

At the heart of the plan is the notion of a broader and larger city, Venice as a kind of bipolar city. What was the area of the ancient city of Venice becomes a new pole, with Mestre and *terra ferma* (the mainland), the other pole. The city also includes the interior islands (e.g., Burano, Murano), the Lido (barrier islands), and the industrial area of Porto Marglera, the shore of the Pellestrini, and, of course, Mestre. Under the plan, distances diminish, and the spatial connectedness between these poles is strengthened. The plan envisions a number of projects—some still in planning, many already under way—to begin to implement this new bipolar vision. The pieces include the "reindustrialization" of Porto Marglera, the site of Europe's largest chemical plant. Under the new plan, the bridge traversing the lagoon, connecting Mestre and the ancient city, will constitute the key internal linkage between the two poles. The bridge will eventually be reserved for movement by residents of the cities, and for movement of goods between them. Tourist movement will someday, under the new plan, be diverted to other, mostly new, movement corridors. Envisioned are three new massive terminals (Fusina, Tesera, and P. Sabbioni) that will take tourists into the city by boat from points to the north, south, and west. Also planned is an underground rail system that will move tourists from the mainland to the old city. The new plan seeks both to solve current accessibility problems (the main bridge must sometimes be closed at peak visitation times, when on some days 150,000 or more visitors enter the city) and to give a high degree of accessibility to new areas of the city. Even the city's unique boat transport system, the Vaporetti, is viewed as being slow and an impediment to attracting new businesses to the city, although it is clearly part of the charm of the city. Other new projects include a Frank Gehry–designed airport gateway and convention center, a new bridge spanning the Grand Canal, and a new cruise ship terminal.

Preserving the history of a city will also require that there are sufficient economic, social, and other reasons to ensure the current viability of such places. They are not museums, but require committed residents and a living present. The Venice plan envisions substantial new housing, as well, mostly within compact existing settlements on the mainland and on the islands of the Laguna. Renovation of historic buildings and conversion of abandoned schools to housing are some of the ideas embraced in this plan (Venezia Commune, 1996).

Other Italian cities have made similar impressive strides at balancing history and modernity. The efforts at restoring and reinvigorating the center-city district of Pomposa, in Modena, Italy, are instructive. A number of programs have been undertaken, and perhaps the most interesting realization here is that rejuvenation—real rejuvenation—requires more than physical improvements. A number of physical changes have been made to the district, including the dramatic and significant step of pulling up asphalt and restoring the natural stone paving of the district (and its historic feel), while at the same time deftly working in stone swaths to make it easy for bicyclists and walkers.

A new program of urban improvements—from new street lighting and furniture to creative new neighborhood signs and banners—is another part of this initiative, intended to strengthen a sense of identity and distinctiveness for the district. A series of vertical Plexiglas lights are under consideration and will certainly enliven these visual aspects of Pomposa. Modena, though, has gone further, providing financial subsidies to help the establishment of small businesses. It also held a competition and solicited proposals for new businesses in Pomposa. The city received some 100 proposals and has been able to fund 40, giving grants of up to EU 7,500 (euros) (about US$9,000) each, over a two-year period. The emphasis on funding small businesses, in essence a kind of neighborhood-specific, microcredit approach, is extremely promising. And, Modena officials feel that many of the other business ideas not funded will, in fact, find ways of moving forward.

Urban Successes in the United States

Many American cities, of course, have done exemplary work in balancing preservation and development, and in committing to save and build upon the history and heritage of their built environments. American successes are considerable, including efforts at preserving the Art Deco of Miami Beach, and the preservation and creative reuse of tobacco warehouses in southern cities

like Durham, North Carolina, where availability of federal, state, and even local historic tax credits has made a real difference. The preservation and reuse
of the Presidio and Alcatraz prison in the San Francisco Bay Area are good examples of recognizing and building upon important historical and place assets. Efforts are under way in Tampa, Florida, to declare as landmarks its
(many) remaining former cigar factory buildings and to promote and encourage their reuse, an important aspect of the history of that city (Froelich, 2003).

Combinations of tax incentives, new code restrictions (that ensure protection of building façades and architectural details), and public investments in
infrastructure (pedestrian amenities, public transit) that enhance overall attractiveness of historic districts have had dramatic effects in many American
cities. Dallas adopted, in 2000, a preservation ordinance providing stronger
protections for its historic buildings, creating a preservation fund and utilizing property tax abatement to encourage reinvestment. Considerable success
in that city can be seen in the adaptive reuse of historically important buildings like the Majestic Theatre (Costello et al., undated).

A major downtown renaissance can be seen in Denver, Colorado, based to
a large degree on the character and charm of its historic structures. Denver is
an American city with much to be proud of. The rejuvenation of its downtown, especially LoDo, its lower downtown, is a positive story of what is possible through a mix of public and private sector actions. In an area comprising
twenty-three blocks of former warehouses and commercial structures, reinvestment was helped along by the designation of a LoDo historic district in
1988, making available new financial resources (e.g., tax credits) and design
guidelines to protect the exterior qualities and feel of the district. Much of the
success of LoDo must be attributed, however, to the power of positive examples, as redevelopment projects like the Wynkoop Brewery showed what was
possible. Here, a now wildly popular eatery and bar has reinhabited and
reused a former warehouse, helping to set in motion a period of redevelopment and re-appreciation of this historic district (and incidentally a public career for the Brewery's owner and present mayor of Denver, John
Hickenlooper).

The redevelopment of the Denver Dry Goods store has been one of the
most powerful examples of how the historic integrity of this district could be
preserved at the same time that new sustainable uses and activities can be

accommodated. A joint redevelopment project of the Denver Urban Renewal Authority and the Affordable Housing Development Corporation, the multistory structure has been reconfigured to accommodate a mix of housing on the upper floors (some market rate condos and apartments, and some subsidized), and retail and office uses on the ground floor. Important green aspects were included in its redevelopment, including tying into the downtown's centralized steam heat system and installing energy-efficient windows and an evaporative cooling system.

The Dry Goods Building shows the kind of obstacles faced with this sort of redevelopment: concerns expressed by lenders about the unproven mixing of market and affordable housing and the mix of uses envisioned. The project has been a financial success and has certainly demonstrated that building onto the special history and feel and pedestrian nature of such districts makes economic sense. It has resulted in considerable spin-off development (renovation and redevelopment of some twenty other buildings in a sixteen-block area, as reported in Horizon Solutions, 2003).

Denver has taken other admirable steps, as well. An innovative program called Preservation in the Schools, spearheaded by the organization Historic Denver, Inc., encourages students in these historic schools to research and learn about their history, "creating video histories, interviewing alumni and neighbors, creating scale models and computer renderings, hosting tours and identifying historic landscaping" (National Trust for Historic Preservation, 2000). Such a strategy of making preservation and place history a key element of a school curriculum is a terrific idea for place strengthening.

Conclusions

The history of a community is one of its most important assets, and an essential basis of its uniqueness. Each place will have its own special historic assets—buildings, ecological features, landscapes—and recognizing these assets and organizing planning efforts around them is an essential place-building strategy. Making the history of a community real and transparent to its citizens, and looking for creative design and planning solutions that acknowledge and express this history, is key. These solutions and strategies can take the form of building preservation and adaptive reuse (e.g., grain silos to houses), protecting and reusing historically significant infrastructure and place qualities (e.g., the High Line), and telling the history of a community through murals and monuments, among others. Building on the historic fabric that every community has can do much to enhance its distinctiveness, to nurture a sense of the uniqueness and specialness of that place, and as a result to bring about new place commitment.

Tackling Sprawl: Community Design, Sustainability, and Place

Sprawl is one of the most serious threats to creating and maintaining genuine places. Excessively low-density, scattered forms of development are the bane of American (and a growing number of European) communities. At best, these prevailing development patterns generally disregard place; at worst, they are actively destructive of place. Typically, important landscapes and ecological features are destroyed, and existing historic elements of the built environment are ignored or replaced. The resulting urban or suburban forms are difficult to love: they are mind-numbingly uniform and sterile, designed around the private spaces of cars, and generally serve to separate and isolate people, both from themselves and from nature.

Much of our society's large ecological footprint, moreover, owes to these prevailing wasteful land use patterns. Car-dependent sprawl means high consumption of energy and high emissions of greenhouse gases and other pollutants. Sprawl generally equates to loss of natural habitat and a major threat to biodiversity around the world. For these many reasons, the goal and vision of creating real and sustainable places requires a head-on tackling of the problems of sprawl.

Sprawl is also a major culprit in the unaffordability and inequity of American communities today. Sprawl can substantially raise the costs of infra-

Figure 4.1 | Typical sprawl—low density, auto-dependent, land and energy consumptive—represents a serious challenge to creating genuine, sustainable places.

structure and services (e.g., higher costs for roads, schools) and, in turn, the cost of private housing (Clarion Associates, undated). A more spread out development pattern requires more roadway footage, water and sewer pipes, and makes everything from policing to fire protection to snow removal more difficult and costly. With the rise of Vehicle Miles Traveled, and the growing dependence on automobiles, sprawl makes mobility for much of the population more difficult and expensive. Urban disinvestments and the sharp income and social segregation found in many cities are exacerbated by such sprawl patterns.

Building on the fabric of existing cities and towns and respecting the history and culture of the area presents the greatest opportunity of strengthening sense of place and bringing about an organic built form that creates the feel of history, historic continuity, and diversity that helps to make places special and enduring.

Ideas and Strategies for Overcoming Sprawl

The planning responses to urban sprawl in Europe and North America are many and varied, with varying degrees of success. Europe can cite a number

TABLE 4.1 | Recommendations for Combating Sprawl

1. Reinvest in neglected communities and promote more housing opportunities.
2. Rehabilitate abandoned properties.
3. Encourage new development or redevelopment in already built-up areas.
4. Create and nurture thriving, mixed-use centers of activity.
5. Support growth management strategies.
6. Craft transportation policies that complement smarter growth.

SOURCE: Ewing, Pendall, and Chen, 2002.

of successful efforts at promoting compactness, and the United States has many tools and initiatives under way, such as the use of urban growth boundaries, the transfer of development rights, and the establishment of greenbelts. A major point is that there are indeed many tools, measures, and strategies that can be employed to contain growth and to guide urbanization into areas within and adjacent to existing cities, to promote higher-density development, infill development, reurbanization, and development on brownfield (rather than greenfield) sites (see Table 4.1).

Alternatives to sprawl can offer many advantages, of course, in addition to strengthening place and avoiding the patterns of homogeneity that sprawl tends to bring about. Ecology and nature are conserved, public infrastructure costs are reduced, and the possibilities of a pedestrian, car-free lifestyle and the opportunities for social life are enhanced.

Many of the cities I am lucky enough to visit and study have positive stories of combating sprawl (to various degrees) and strengthening place. One city that inspires me, and a place which has been able to preserve and build upon its unique place qualities, at the same time advancing quality of life, is Vancouver, Canada. The efforts at avoiding a sprawl future are exemplary and multifaceted. Few areas have been as successful as the Vancouver region at protecting its environment and land base, while also promoting compact livable communities. The Livable Region Strategic Plan, the vision for regional Vancouver, was endorsed in 1996 by all municipalities in the region. It seeks both to attract people and activities to designated growth centers, and to prevent growth in its pure agricultural and natural areas. Its key goals are protecting the "green zone," building complete communities, achieving a compact metropolitan region, and increasing transportation choices.

The region's green zone, an area outside cities and urban growth areas, contains about 200,000 hectares of land, including an Agricultural Reserve of about 54,000 hectares (about 500,000 acres and 130,000 acres respectively). Gaining permission to build in the green zone is difficult, and development is steered into highly desirable development centers, clustered along the spine of the Skytrain. This has been highly successful, at least compared with most U.S. efforts at growth containment. Almost 70 percent of the population growth in the region does in fact occur in these regional modes, and although there is sprawl, its extent and impact are much reduced from what we see in a typical U.S. region. And a much higher percentage of housing is built in the form of denser, more compact multifamily housing (GVRD, 2001).

One of Vancouver's newest compact and high density developments, Concord Pacific Place, is a successful infill project that is green in its design and functioning, and shows the many virtues of this city's approach to growth. In this Concord Pacific Place development project, some 8,000 new residents will be housed on a little less than 100 acres of land. The amenities include

Figure 4.2 | Vancouver, British Columbia. Through an effective regional growth strategy, investments in transit, and the city's "living first" policy, Canada's Vancouver has become a highly walkable, livable city, with a strong sense of place.

access and proximity to the waterfront (and striking views), a series of parks, a continuous, high-quality bicycle and walking path along the seawall edge, a marina, new day care and elementary schools, and great access to shopping and restaurants. A former railroad roundhouse has been converted to a community center serving the neighborhood. Most impressive have been the efforts to tie this development area into the city, and to emphasize strongly the amenities of living in this place. The downtown's existing street pattern has been extended, and sidewalk and tree lines are maintained. The seawall trail is designed to allow both pedestrian traffic along a bricked pathway and faster bicycle and Rollerblade traffic on a parallel, adjacent asphalt trail. Even on a cold day, the number of people enjoying these spaces is high. A system of small (and colorful) water ferries shuttle people to and from several points along the waterfront, further adding to functionality of living there.

Remarkable, as well, are the price range and income diversity of the housing being built in Concord Pacific Place. Large numbers of relatively affordable flats are found in buildings adjacent to luxury high-end buildings. Although the income mixing does not apply within individual buildings, it does occur within the area of a few blocks. This is in considerable measure due to Vancouver's 20 percent affordable housing requirement. Vancouver also has an unusual requirement that a minimum number of these new units be designed to be family friendly, an effort to overcome the popular impression that center-city living is only for the young and for empty nesters. The Vancouver model includes a high level of planning control over new development, the application of detailed (and impressive) design guidelines, and the expectation that developers will pay for many of the amenities that are required.[1]

There are many European examples of cities, both new and old, that exemplify much greater compactness and density than even the best North American examples. Exemplary are Copenhagen, Stockholm, and Amsterdam in northern Europe, for instance, and Barcelona in the south. A variety of tools, techniques, and growth-containing strategies are in use in the best examples. Clustering high-density development along the spines of public transit (and, indeed, major investments in and commitments to public transit!); limiting the ability to develop outside of existing cities, towns, and designated development areas; and instituting generally stronger public planning and control of the land develop process are hallmarks of these cities. A greater willingness to acquire and bank land, to influence growth patterns, and to establish an urban development process in which the municipality typically takes an active initiating role are all helpful, of course.

European cities, moreover, are evolving in their strategies. London represents an interesting case in point. Its mayor, Ken Livingstone, has proposed a new spatial plan which seeks to promote more compact and intensified forms of growth in the future. (Greater London Authority [hereafter, GLA], 2002).

Figure 4.3 | The newly opened home of the Greater London Authority (London City Hall), designed by Norman Foster and Associates, at once represents a commitment to sustainability, distinctive architecture, and a reinvigorated central London.

There is a recognition that future population growth (the city is predicted to grow by 700,000 people over the next twenty years) can no longer happen in land-consumptive, resource-consumptive ways. In the words of the plan:

> London cannot continue to swallow more land, more natural resources, more scarce energy unchecked. Development needs to be focused where it will do least harm and most good. That is through intensive development on brownfield land, close to existing and new public transit facilities and services. In this way, London's greenbelt and other green spaces can be protected. Strategic spatial planning has to encourage and direct such development. (GLA, 2002, p. 2)

More specifically, the plan calls for directing future growth to large regeneration areas of East London and the Thames Gateway, more intense growth in central London, in town centers, and in identified Opportunity Areas. Major improvements in public transport are envisioned, and the mayor has implemented a congestion charge for cars coming into central London that has been touted as a success in easing congestion. This self-described "radical" vision for London also clearly accepts, indeed encourages, more growth in skyscrapers. Significant new green skyscrapers in London, buildings like the nearly completed Swiss Reinsurance building, promise both to change the look of London and to accommodate additional jobs and population on a smaller land base, resulting in a dramatically smaller environmental impact.

Now, to be sure, the conditions in Europe differ from those in the United States: there is an incentive structure that discourages sprawl (e.g., high gasoline prices, carbon taxes), a stronger planning system (e.g., Dutch right of first refusal to purchase in development areas), a different attitude about land and property rights (e.g., the Dutch view that there is no inherent right to develop farmland or rural land), and cultural differences (e.g., the desire to live compactly in Spanish cities as a matter of history and preference).

Building compact cities in the United States will require many things to be done at once: investments in transit, establishment of land use regimes and incentives structures that support higher densities, and investments in schools, day care, and cultural and other amenities that make living in such places the most attractive option. Adapting some of more proactive planning strategies and tools used by European cities seems sensible—for example, right of first refusal in the Netherlands (requires private landowners in designated growth zones to first offer to sell their land to the municipality), more detailed physical planning and design as in the Netherlands or Germany, greater willingness to publicly acquire and own land to manage growth patterns, among others.

Elsewhere, Rich Collins of the University of Virginia and I have argued that smart growth initiatives are likely to fail in the long run without confronting head-on many of these value issues (see Beatley and Collins, 2001, 2003). Perhaps the single most important cultural factor we need to confront is our prevailing sense of land and nature: there are several elements to this, but at the heart it is a fundamental view of land as essentially an economic commodity, free and abundant, and primarily of instrumental value. Other critical elements of our value and cultural backdrop are our suspicion of proactive government roles, our excessive individualism, our treatment of land and housing values as a primary source of personal and family wealth (in a society where one's basic health and living conditions are unusually subject to the vagaries of the marketplace), our excessive focus on work, and our lack of place knowledge and commitments to place, among many others. Success in promoting compact urban form will require efforts at more carefully understanding and then confronting directly some of these basic value and cultural underpinnings. This is no easy agenda.

Several additional points about future cities and future land use should be made. Compactness and compact cities and development patterns can happen in many ways and through urban form and land use configurations of many kinds. As creative as our architectural and design imaginations are, as different and diverse are the styles and feelings of our best buildings, so also ought our approaches to compactness be. Compact satellite communities, organized along transit lines, emerging high-rise development models of growth à la Vancouver, Canada, or Frankfurt, Germany, or compact developments where growth takes the form of attached housing clustered around car-free greenspaces, are all viable, place-sustaining strategies.

Green skyscrapers like the Commerzbank in Frankfurt further demonstrate the possibility and desirability of tall buildings in any scheme for compact urban forms. Frankfurt has a number of high-rise buildings, but their numbers and spacing and their design and orientation to the street, as in Vancouver, buffer any negative visual effects. Much of downtown Frankfurt

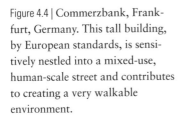

Figure 4.4 | Commerzbank, Frankfurt, Germany. This tall building, by European standards, is sensitively nestled into a mixed-use, human-scale street and contributes to creating a very walkable environment.

is in the form of six-story-high structures, with taller buildings flanked and thus tempered by these more moderately sized buildings. Buildings like the Commerzbank have done a good job respecting the scale and functioning of streets and, like many of the high-rises in Frankfurt, are stepped back, with significant public and pedestrian spaces accommodated.

Many U.S. and Canadian cities provide good (partial) examples of efforts to promote infill and development within existing urbanized cities. Denver, Colorado, has seen dramatic rejuvenation in its lower downtown. Austin, Texas, has been implementing a municipal smart growth program that offers substantial financial incentives, including reductions in capital facility fees, where development locates in older areas and preferred growth areas. Conscious public policy and clear planning priorities explain these successes, and state and provincial governments can play an important role. New Jersey has sought to make it easier to restore and reinhabit older buildings and urban neighborhoods by providing greater flexibility in meeting fire and safety standards. Maryland's statewide smart growth system seeks to encourage growth in already urbanized areas by limiting state expenditures for school, transportation, and other public investments to such locations. Elected in 2002, Maryland governor Robert L. Ehrlich appears committed to continued implementation of the core principles of the smart growth program created by his predecessor, Parris Glendening. In October 2003, Ehrlich issued his "Priority Places Strategy" executive order, which recommits to brownfields redevelopment, new investments in revitalizing existing communities, and reducing the regulatory obstacles to building in priority funding areas, mostly consistent, it appears, with the original smart growth ideals (Office of the Governor, 2003).[2]

Reducing Sameness in Community Building

New growth areas in communities, as well as redevelopment of older areas, can be designed in ways that resist sameness, and promote the fine-grained visual diversity that characterizes many Dutch and European cities. Much of what delights us in cities and towns is the variation in color, style, and architecture of buildings. It is a matter of seeing the city as an architectural palette, where creative design and stylistic differences are encouraged, and where the resulting differences deepen the experience of place.

The redevelopment of the eastern docklands in Amsterdam is one good example. In Java-eiland, a major portion of the docklands area, an overall design for the community (by town planner Sjoerd Soeters) delineates density, massing, and circulation for the district. Diversity and distinctiveness in the design of the actual buildings was encouraged through a restriction on the number of buildings that could be designed by a single architect (see Beatley, 2000). The result is a stimulating community where buildings have been designed by scores of different architects. This island district successfully balances connection to the past (a series of canals and building scale reminiscent of historic Amsterdam) with unique modern design (each of the pedestrian bridges crossing the canals offers a distinctive look and design). Java-eiland demonstrates that city building can occur in ways that create interesting and organically evolved places, and that also acknowledge and respect history and context, and thereby overcome sameness.

A strong emphasis in EVA-Lanxmeer, a new ecological neighborhood in Culemborg, Netherlands, has been to promote different architecture and creative design. In addition to the ecological goals and mission, the founders wanted a place to live that did not look like every other new development in

Figure 4.5 | Java-eiland is a new high-density, walkable neighborhood on the former site of Amsterdam's eastern docklands. It emphasizes distinctive architecture and is a highly pedestrian-oriented new urban quarter.

the Netherlands. The number of different architects with designs in this neighborhood is impressive, and a number of individual building lots have been designated for those interested in designing (often with an architect's help) and building their own homes. The distinctive design of these houses already demonstrates the value of this kind of policy and philosophy. For example, the Tempelman house is structured around a huge 40,000-liter storage tank and has two large solar hot water roof panels to supply it with hot water. Also, the visually striking Foresee house, designed by ecological architect Pijnenborgh, combines living and working, has a green roof, and includes an observation tower that may eventually house a small wind turbine.

One way to avoid sameness in retail architecture is to minimize the number of big box establishments. Big box retail is commonly defined as large retail establishments usually selling many different types of goods, and at least 25,000 square feet in size. Few local issues engender sharper and more extensive debate and controversy than battles over superstores, like Wal-Mart. Communities from Taos, New Mexico, to Chestertown, Maryland, recognize the potential negative impacts on their unique communities and have firmly resisted Wal-Mart. Taos decided a second time to uphold its Vision 2020 Master Plan, which limits commercial establishments to a size no greater than 80,000 square feet. Larger communities have imposed similar restrictions. Oakland, California, for instance, prohibits big box grocery stores larger than 100,000 square feet. Inglewood City, in Southern California, recently adopted an ordinance with the active support of the local union of grocery store workers, prohibiting stores of over 155,000 square feet in size (although this is still rather large!), or that sell more than 20,000 "non-taxable items" (Cleeland and Goldman, 2002).

Davis, California, limits the size of commercial establishments in an effort to prevent big box retail. Davis is working to have community commercial centers fairly evenly distributed throughout the town, within walking and bi-cycling distances of surrounding neighborhoods. While grocery stores are permitted, the size of any single store is limited through the town's zoning ordinance.

Communities have more regulatory power to resist chain store sameness and commercial homogeneity than they sometimes realize, and here, too, are important tools for strengthening place. Some coastal communities like Carmel, California, and Cannon Beach, Oregon, prohibit "formula" restaurants, that is, fast-food chains. It is also possible to require or work toward better integrating chain stores into the spaces of existing cities and towns in ways that contribute to urban and town vitality, rather than drain it away, as is the case in typical auto-dependent strip commercial locations.

Efforts at encouraging and protecting the existing small store flavor (and economy) can take other forms. Concerned about the gradual consolidation of smaller stores into large chain stores, Santa Monica, California, recently adopted an ordinance limiting the frontage size for stores along its popular Third Street Promenade. For new or expanded uses the ordinance restricts allowable frontage to 50 feet.

Communities don't have to accept big box developments as proposed, but can and should work to ensure that they blend in as best they can, and that their visual, environmental, and other impacts are minimized. Some communities are holding big box developments to stringent architectural design standards. Ft. Collins, Colorado, has been implementing an impressive set of design standards and guidelines for "large retail establishments" since 1995 (City of Ft. Collins, 1995). These stipulate a series of aesthetic and design requirements intended to reduce the visual and other negative impacts of large retail stores, and to incorporate features that enhance positive community and public values. Building façades and exterior walls must be "articulated," with "animating features" that break up the visual monotony of the buildings (e.g., awnings, windows, arcades), variations in roof lines are required, and limits are placed on exterior colors and building materials. Multiple entranceways are stipulated, as well as internal pedestrian walkways, and limits are placed on the amount of parking permitted between the structures and public streets (no more than 50 percent).

Under the Ft. Collins ordinance, at least two design elements must also be included that "contribute to the establishment or enhancement of community and public spaces" (such as a pedestrian plaza or water feature) (City of Ft. Collins, 1995, p. 14). Taken together, the standards impose a considerable obligation on big box developments to better fit into their communities, and to make (more of) a positive contribution to place making.

Greening the big box is another option. Though it may not reduce its economic and aesthetic impacts, it suggests the sensible principle that large retail establishments should have a special obligation to reduce the impacts of consumption. Madison, Wisconsin, is one of the first communities to take this tack. It is demanding that a proposed 130,000-square-foot Sam's Club be certified under the U.S. Green Building Council's LEED certification system. Under LEED (Leadership in Energy and Environmental Design), buildings receive points for the different green features they include, and if they reach certain point thresholds, they are certified as gold, silver, or platinum buildings (see www.usgvc.org). Wal-Mart is resisting, fearful of the precedent that such a move might set nationally.[3] Although green big box helps in reducing the impacts of these temples to consumption, such standards may do little, of course, to minimize the car trips generated by them and the economic impacts on locally owned businesses.

Steering Wal-Marts, Targets, and Home Depots into better, more appropriate locations is another possibility. Rather than promoting sprawl and taking public business and economic activity away from existing downtowns, these stores might serve to strengthen and shore up downtown economies. This has proven a hard sell and has been widely resisted by big box companies, particularly as they move toward even larger supercenters greater than 200,000 square feet. One of the few, and now often discussed, successful examples of this is the Wal-Mart located in downtown Rutland, Vermont. In the heart of anti-big-box country, what Wal-Mart was willing to accept in Vermont, after many years of battle and the efforts of then governor Howard Dean and others, it is unlikely to accept elsewhere. Nevertheless, the Rutland case is instructive. Here, a new Wal-Mart store located in a smaller than usual (78,000 square feet) building, formerly occupied by Kmart, near the center of a small downtown, with many small locally owned stores and restaurants. All reports suggest the store's positive impact in anchoring the downtown, serving to bring more shoppers and customers to these other stores.

Another recent positive example comes from Pasadena, California, where through intense lobbying by that city's manager, Target agreed to locate a multistory downtown site. Such place-strengthening locations don't easily fit the big box development formula, and many require special work to overcome their perceived limitations (wide "walk through" elevators solved for Target some of the main limitations of a multistory building; Beaumont, 1998).

What the Rutland and Pasadena cases suggest is that there are indeed alternatives to big boxes on sprawl-inducing suburban or exurban sites, but that substantial effort and work may be needed to bring them about. Actively working to support local businesses is another option, one typically requiring a more active local government role. Providing local subsidies and tax concessions (commonly used already to lure companies into a community) to allow important local businesses to survive and compete may be even more important that the classical use of local land use regulations or development restrictions. Burlington, Vermont, recently provided substantial financial start-up costs for a locally owned grocery store for an important downtown location. A much larger chain grocery store, Shaw's, was rejected in favor of the consumer-owned store, The Burlington City Market, which stocks many Vermont foods and goods.

The Burlington City Market is a food co-op, in which customers in the community become members by buying equity shares. Such establishments help build community, promote active community involvement and participation in governance, and generally deeper place commitments, as well as providing foods and other products, often at much lower prices. Unlike corporate chains, furthermore, a store like the Burlington City Market boosts a variety of mostly Vermont-originated products and goods, including, for example, bread from eighteen Vermont bread companies (see www.onionriver.org).

The People's Food Co-op in Portland, Oregon, is an excellent example of what the alternative to strip commercial and chain-based stores might look like. It demonstrates convincingly the promise and potential of locally based stores that provide healthy, responsible products, in this case healthy food, while at the same time promoting sustainability and building community. The Co-op is like other food co-ops in its operation: members buy shares, entitling them not only to consumer benefits but also to an active voice in the governance of the store. Some 2,050 members have joined the Co-op, paying the $180 cost of a share in the store. Membership gives an immediate discount of 4 percent for food purchases. Members are indeed involved in the life of the Co-op in many ways. Members are actively involved in making decisions for the store, decisions about everything from the kinds of food stocked to the design and operation of the structure itself. Members are encouraged to volunteer at the store, which earn them a 19 percent discount on purchases—a great way to reduce the cost of living and to provide meaningful community-creating employment. For full-time employees, the working conditions are even better—starting wages are always considerably higher than the minimum wage, and the staff are organized nonhierarchically in a "staff collective" (there are no bosses, but eighteen "co-managers"). Morale seems high among employees, and employee turnover is low.

The community-enhancing aspects of this model are several. The fact that members actually own this store means that they feel more personally invested in it, feel they have a stock in its success, and see it as a kind of small community within a larger community. There is a sense of trust about the store, perhaps a response to Enron-era skepticism about large, remote corporations. The philosophy is clearly different than that of a chain grocery. As Erica Simon of the Co-op explained, the goal is to provide the service to its members and community, not to maximize profits. Although the store certainly turns a profit, this is seen not as an end in itself but as a means of providing capital to do things. The store has been very successful on every level and seems to demonstrate that these kinds of noble goals can be practically realized. The store and its staff are active participants in the life of the neighborhood in which the store sits. When the store was recently expanded, permanent space for a farmers' market was provided. A bicycle delivery service for elder residents and shut-ins in the neighborhood has been established. The expansion itself became a participatory project with the construction actually done by several hundred members.

Such locally owned businesses can be designed and can operate in sustainable ways, as well. The green and sustainable features of the People's Co-op, for instance, are several. The food stocked is generally organic and, to the extent possible, locally produced. The recent expansion of the store, more than doubling its size, incorporated a number of impressive green and ecological features, including two separate green roofs, a rainwater collection system,

Figure 4.6 | People's Food Co-op, Portland, Oregon. This co-op grocery store shows the many advantages of locally owned stores, committed to the community and working hard to reduce their environmental footprints. A number of green building features have been incorporated into the Co-op's recent building expansion, including green rooftops, a rainwater collection system, and use of more environmentally sustainable building materials. (Photo by Erica Simon.)

the use of reclaimed building materials, sustainably harvested wood, a ground-sourced heat pump, and an interesting building material called *cob* (a mix of earth, sand, water, and straw). The building is very energy efficient, using about the same amount of energy while it more than doubled in size. The structure incorporates a "solar chimney" that draws air through the building and in this way provides natural cooling. The Co-op expresses its green ethic in its operation and management as well, such as through composting all food waste, using recycled paper, and other environmentally responsible measures.

Part of the task of creating strong places is to take a hard look at what is being financially supported or underwritten in the economic development process, what is being offered, and to what kinds of companies or businesses. The larger question remains: What kind of economic development incentive packages are available? Strengthening local uniqueness, and locally owned and controlled businesses, would seem a sensible goal, and taking away or denying economic aid for place-destructive activities a legitimate tact. It makes little sense to subsidize or underwrite chain stores or large corporate stores where local sales send a considerable amount of income and jobs out of the community. Subsidies, on the other land, for locally owned businesses are much more defensible and can serve to strengthen more sustainable, place-based economics.

Commercial establishments can do a much better job of fitting in and actually helping to strengthen existing neighborhoods and places. Columbus, Ohio, for instance, adopted an urban commercial overlay zone in 1999, with the goal of maintaining the historic quality and strengthening pedestrian characteristics of its older commercial streets. The city has designated about 14 linear miles of the overlay zone. Within these areas, new commercial establishments are subject to new standards. Although there is no minimum setback from the sidewalk, there is a maximum of 10 feet. Parking is to be in the rear or at the side of the building. At least 60 percent of the building façade must be clear window glass "permitting a view of the building's interior to a minimum depth of four feet" (City of Columbus, undated, p. 2). On sites such as North High Street, the overlay has already made a visible difference. Mixed-use developments and small commercial establishments are pulled snug to the sidewalk, with parking behind the buildings. The result is maintaining (or reestablishing) the pedestrian look, feel, and function of these older streets and making them once again interesting and inviting places to walk.

Form-based zoning codes take the Columbus idea even further, and show at once both the vagueness and the rigidity of conventional zoning. Form-based zoning seeks to replace sterile, avisual, legalistic zoning requirements with tangible physical design suggestions, expressed visually. In Arlington County, Virginia, a new form-based code has been created to guide development along the 3.5-mile length of Columbia Pike, a rundown commercial strip. Here, the result of public design charrettes, the new code stipulates building heights of three to six stories, trees and sidewalks, parking at the rear, and in general, painting a more precise picture of what the desired outcome should be. Housing over shops would be encouraged, not forbidden, as it often is in conventional zoning, and required on-site parking would be reduced. The option of developing under the conventional zoning is still there, but a strong incentive of faster permit approval is provided under the form-based code.

Overcoming the drab uniformity of fast-food franchises and at the same time strengthening local economy and making more sustainable connections with place and local landscapes ought to be part of what we aspire to. There are many good examples of locally owned restaurants and food shops that exhibit a strong place commitment and a green ethic. One of the best examples is Hot Lips Pizza, in Portland, Oregon. Its owner, David Yudkin, has made a name in that city for both the taste of the product—gourmet pizza—and his sense of responsibility to community and environment. His three shops sell pizza made with organic, locally grown ingredients, and his stores incorporate a variety of green and energy-saving elements. He employs energy-efficient ovens and, in one restaurant, has installed a clever heat-recovery system (recovering heat from the oven) that provides all the hot water needed for the store, and a pan washer that conserves and recycles rinse water (Northwest Energy Efficiency Alliance, 2002; Businesses for an Environmentally Sustainable Tomorrow (BEST), 2003). In June 2003, it was announced that Hot Lips would use dough made from sustainably grown wheat from farms in the region. The wheat is certified by the nonprofit organization Food Alliance, and is grown through a "direct seed" or no-till cropping system that conserves soil, provides wildlife habitat, and reduces the amount of energy consumed (Food Alliance, 2003). But most impressive are the efforts to connect with and support regional growers and to build local economy while supporting sustainable production. And most customers will attest that the pizza is very tasty!

Pedestrian Connectivity through Good Neighborhood Design

There is no question that conventional suburban growth patterns in the United States have severely limited the ability of residents to walk or ride bikes to perform errands or for recreation near their homes. The proliferation of cul-de-sacs (French for "bottom of the sack") has made distances for most trips longer, usually requiring the use of a car and generally reducing the connectedness of residential neighborhoods to each other and to the broader communities in which they are situated.

Emphasis on the vitality and life of streets, and on the pedestrian freedoms and joys in European cities such as Leiden can be seen in some emerging American examples. Olympia, Washington, adopted in 1995 a new set of public work standards (and included in its comprehensive plan) forbidding cul-de-sacs except in cases where "topographic constraints, wetlands, water bodies, or unusual property shapes" make them necessary (Climate Solutions, p. 8; Buntin, 2001). Maryland's Baltimore County and the City of Charlotte, North Carolina, have adopted similar standards (Buntin, 2001).

Community connectedness can happen in many other ways as well. Comprehensive greenways and greenways systems that permit movement and mobility between neighborhoods and different parts of a city and permit direct access and connection to natural systems are an important strategy. Chattanooga, Tennessee, for instance, has worked hard to create a greenway along its riverfront, connecting residents to this natural system and to each other. Milwaukee, Wisconsin, and Providence, Rhode Island, among others, have substantially expanded pedestrian and public spaces along their waterfronts. Rails-to-trails projects provide new connections for pedestrians and bicyclists on former rail rights-of-way.

Even existing suburban development patterns could be creatively retrofitted to provide greater pedestrian connectivity, as some neighborhoods have already done through connecting adjoining, underutilized backyard lots to create new community spaces (see, for instance, the N-Street co-housing project in Davis, California where the backyards of 16 homes are now connected as common green space, with a walkway, gardens, children's play spaces; see http://www.dcn.davis.ca.us/go/nstreet/).

Building onto and Strengthening the Existing Fabrics of Place

Sustainability requires greater efforts at utilizing scarce land resources more efficiently, and promoting more compact, infill development. Yet, this may also result in changed conditions, or the fear of changing conditions, in a neighborhood or district, especially when proposed infill projects threaten to consume forests and open lands that residents may have assumed would be there forever. Sustainable infill can occur, however, in creative, sensitive ways that respect neighborhood wishes and engage neighbors directly in designing such projects.

A positive example can be seen in a small infill project, Amherst Commons and Robinson Woods, undertaken in the Kellytown neighborhood of Charlottesville, Virginia. Here, an established neighborhood's fears about what development might bring, some forward-looking city leaders and university faculty, and an open-minded developer resulted in a collaborative process for exploring an infill design. The Neighborhood Association worked with the developer to develop a plan for the site that would not only protect important amenities but also allow a profitable use of the land. University students conducted essential research on the natural features and social history of the site, and developed different design options, presented at an all-day design charrette. Remarkable consensus developed around the proposals, which called for a housing configuration similar to the "family clusters" that had characterized the historic pattern of development in the area. As well, the plan called for protecting a large parcel of existing forested land, an important local amenity, and home designs that reflected the qualities of a compact, walkable traditional town street. The plan also called for the two portions of the development—Amherst Commons and Robinson Woods—to

Figure 4.7 | Robinson Woods, an infill development project in the Kellytown neighborhood of Charlottesville, Virginia, demonstrates convincingly that it is possible to sensitively site new housing in existing neighborhoods, creating pedestrian-friendly projects and a sense of community among the neighbors.

be accessible by separate entrances but connected by a pedestrian pathway to reduce through traffic. Preserving and integrating the historic buildings on the site was also an important element.

In all, the 10-acre site accommodates thirty-two new single-family homes in a way quite acceptable to existing residents. The Kellytown case shows how understanding and working with a neighborhood's sense of its own place, working to develop collaboratively a plan and vision for change, and listening and trying to incorporate amenities and changes that will be viewed as positives are key lessons (for a discussion of this case, see Vogel, 1998).

Mixing land uses in a community is another important strategy. Extreme separation and isolation of different uses and activities—megaschools on distant arterials, grocery and other shopping far away from residential neighborhoods, shopping areas surrounded by roads and a sea of parking—create insurmountable physical barriers to access by anything other than a car.

The challenge is to create more diverse, textured land use patterns in which people do have places they can walk to. It means citing neighborhood commercial areas, nearby offices and services, and schools that are within walking distance for most residents. Some have called this "access by proximity." Fundamentally rethinking and redefining facilities like schools as multiuse centers is another promising step. The new Millennium Primary School, part of the Regeneration of the Millennium Peninsula in London, for instance, is the site of other community services, including a community health center, a preschool, and a day care facility. Every school could and should be the center for many community services and activities, ideally close by and walkable for many residents. The Vancouver urban design guidelines that stipulate certain services and facilities (e.g., day care) within a certain distance of new development is a good start.

The Promise of New Urbanism

Perhaps what is needed is a new urban design sensibility that might draw from the traditions of place building in the United States. Neo-traditional development design—now called New Urbanism—is another potentially helpful strategy and trend in combating sprawl. Largely an architect- and developer-driven movement, the idea is to return to the traditional principles of town design and urban form found in American cities and towns circa 1920: more compact, organized around a grid street pattern, with homes closer to each other and closer to the streets, with narrower streets, back alleys, and porches and picket fences.

While a positive trend in the sense that New Urbanist projects represent somewhat higher density and more land-efficient forms of development, the practice to date has been only a modest improvement over conventional suburban sprawl. The projects are often sited on greenfield locations and are often very car-dependent. Although projects designed around New Urbanist principles still represent a relatively small percentage of new construction in the United States, the movement has picked up considerable momentum. The Congress for the New Urbanism (CNU) boasts some 2,300 members, mostly architects, planners, and developers, and the completion nationally of more than 210 New Urbanist projects (see www.cnu.org). The CNU and its members have been vocal proponents in defense and support of its ideas (for a succinct expression of what New Urbanists believe, see the "Charter of the New Urbanism," CNU, 1998).

Many legitimate criticisms have been leveled at New Urbanism (including those by this author): New Urbanist projects are often located in suburban and exurban locations, or greenfield sites, and are car-dependent, with little access to transit. There is an odd feeling of sterility and sameness to notable projects such as Celebration, in Orlando, Florida, and there are legitimate concerns about affordability and social diversity. And, for the most part, New Urbanist practice, despite its stated goals as a movement, has exhibited relatively little attention to ecology and sustainability.

There is no question, though, that New Urbanist principles can also be effectively coupled with ecological designs that better acknowledge and tie into local landscapes and biodiversity. The new community of Civano, outside Tucson, Arizona, does an excellent job of incorporating native plants and

Figure 4.8 | Highlands' Garden Village, Denver, Colorado. A 27-acre project jointly developed by the Jonathan Rose Company and the Perry Affordable Housing Company. It incorporates a number of green features, including energy-efficient homes, native vegetation, and car-sharing. (Photo compliments of Perry Affordable Housing Company.)

Figure 4.9 | A rendering of Glenwood Park, soon to be completed in a neighborhood in Atlanta, Georgia. It represents an impressive mixed-use, mixed-housing, highly walkable neighborhood. The design includes a large, oval green and a market square, which will serve as key focal points in the community. (Image compliments of Green Street Properties.)

landscaping throughout, helped by an on-site nursery that salvages and reuses plants and trees. The use of adobe and other local materials and building styles further reinforces those place connections. The use of recycled water, homes designed to use much less energy than a typical Arizona house, and a number of other green features add considerably to the value and appeal of New Urbanism in this case (see www.civano.com).

Although New Urbanist principles and projects are not a silver bullet, they do represent a step in the right direction, and there are increasingly more positive applications of these ideas, particularly in infill and in already-developed sites within existing urban areas. One of the best recent examples is Highlands' Garden Village in northwest Denver, Colorado. A collaborative development between Perry Affordable Housing Company and Jonathan Rose Companies LLC, this 27-acre project has many admirable, place-sensitive qualities often lacking in New Urbanist developments like Celebration. Like Civano, it incorporates a number of green features, including energy-efficient homes and the use of renewable energy. It has recycled parking lot asphalt, uses native vegetation, and protects wetlands and mature trees. Bus transit and car-sharing cars are available. Unlike Civano, though, it is located on an infill site, recycling a former amusement park. It not only includes a compact, gridded, walkable neighborhood, but creatively designs-in and preserves many of the historic features of the amusement park, including restoration of the historic Elitch Theater and original gardens. And home designs are based on historic architectural styles seen in Denver. The project provides a mix of uses, and a variety of housing types and styles, including co-housing, live-work studios, and apartments for seniors. In addition, 20 percent of the homes are set aside as affordable (e.g., see Chittum, 2003; Perry/Affordable Housing Development Company, undated).

New Urbanist design principles and sensibilities can certainly be focused on infill sites, within existing urban and suburban areas, where its potential is greatest. And there are many emerging positive examples of this, where New Urbanist design helps to strengthen and regenerate neighborhoods and provide greater cohesion and connectedness. Glenwood Park, a new development in Atlanta, Georgia, is an excellent example. A compact, mixed-use community with a town center, it seeks to promote walking and repairs an existing neighborhood. In Glenwood Park, public spaces are key elements, and there are two focal points—a large oval park and a village square. Restaurants and retail will be within a short walk, car traffic will be slowed and minimized, and streets will be narrowed (see http://glenwoodpark .com)—all on the site of the former Blue Circle concrete plant. Also, most of the single-family homes and townhouses will be certified as green under the Greater Atlanta Home Builders Association's Earth Craft rating system (see www.southface.org).

New Streets and Mobility Concepts

New Urbanists, despite the limitations of what has been built, have it right in trying to limit the speed and presence of cars. Real communities, communities in which people relate and connect in genuine ways, and communities to which people will express commitments, are much more likely where a life beyond the car is possible. There are many reasons, of course, to support communities where people have alternatives to the car—walking and bicycling are an important response to the growing rate of obesity and sedentary lifestyles, they reduce energy consumption and carbon emissions, and they take up less of our precious community space. And, I unabashedly argue that quality of life is simply better in such places.

Many urban design and community design strategies to curtail and slow down cars in our communities are available and in use. Doing anything to reduce traffic speed in neighborhoods and communities should be the goal, and research on pedestrian death and injury demonstrates the remarkable effect of this strategy. "Speed kills" has become a mantra of sorts, but has never been more true than when considering threats to pedestrians. Recent studies prepared for the National Highway Traffic Safety Administration came to these important conclusions: ". . . about 5% of pedestrians hit by a vehicle traveling 20 mph will die. The fatality rate jumps to 40% for cars traveling 30 mph, 80% for cars going 40 mph, and 100% for cars going 50 mph or faster" (Insurance Institute for Highway Safety, 2000b).

The carnage and personal and family effects of our auto-dependent society are astounding, and for the most part not appreciated. More than 40,000 Americans die in auto accidents each year, and many more are maimed or injured. A recent report by the Insurance Institute for Highway Safety (IIHS) cites a cumulative loss of life of more than 3 million since Americans began driving. Highway and road accidents are now the leading cause of death for Americans aged one to thirty-five. Yet, as the IIHS notes, these statistics are met with what amounts to a "collective shrug" and little sense of concern by most of the driving public, who believe that accidents will happen to others, and that their driving skills are superior to the other drivers on the road.

There are many reasons why these unsafe road and highway conditions exist. The IIHS points to inadequate funding of research in highway safety, lax and unenforced traffic laws, weak federal leadership, and even imbalance in coverage by the media (they are more likely to cover a small plane crash in which there are no fatalities, than a local highway accident). But much can be done and is possible at the community level. Jurisdictions that aggressively enforce traffic laws, that use red light camera systems, and that take numerous actions to calm traffic can create much safer communities.

Installing sidewalks, crosswalks, and pedestrian islands would be a good start in creating more walkable places. There are, of course, a variety of traffic-calming measures that can be undertaken, from traffic circles and

Figure 4.10 | Ghent, Belgium, demonstrates how pedestrians and bicyclists can be given priority, and the impact of cars moderated. New restrictions on cars in the city center have been combined with a series of underground parking garages and a system of signage that guides drivers to where available parking spaces can be found.

roundabouts, to curb extensions to speed humps and tables. Many American communities now have extensive (and positive) experience with these measures. Portland, Oregon, has led the way (more than 1,200 traffic-calming devices installed there), but even many smaller cities and towns are using them (Kilborn, 2002).

The design of local road systems can make a great difference in safety for children and elderly alike, both within cars and while walking. The widespread use of traffic circles on local surface roads in cities in Spain and the Netherlands is striking. As noted earlier, these circles work well to reduce speeds and to minimize the possibility of catastrophic impacts at road intersections.

Redesigning all roadways to fundamentally slow car traffic and increase safety (for those in cars as well as those walking or on bicycles) should be a priority. Evidence is pretty convincing, for example, that roundabouts are safer than conventional intersections. Research by the IIHS indicates that accidents and injuries go down dramatically at the same time that traffic delays are reduced—nearly a 40 percent reduction in crashes and a 76 percent reduction in injury-producing crashes. These intersections experienced a 90 percent reduction in fatal collisions or collisions involving "incapacitating injuries" (IIHS, 2000b). Other studies suggest significant reductions in traffic delays, as drivers do not have to stop at conventional lights and traffic always continues moving. Most important, though, the design of roundabouts makes it quite difficult for fatalities to occur:

> Roundabouts benefit from good geometry, exhibiting only a fraction of the troublesome crash patterns typical of right-angle intersections. . . . The speed depends on the intersection but generally remains at about 15 mph. At that speed, drivers and others on the road have more time to react, so there's a smaller chance of collision. When crashes do happen, most will be minor. (IIHS, 2000a, p. 3)

Would Americans be willing to tolerate a shift to traffic-calming strategies like roundabouts? Although initially against them, there is ample evidence that Americans, once they personally experience them and appreciate their virtues, will support them. Surveys of motorists in several states demonstrate fairly remarkable shifts in opinions, in favor of roundabouts once they've driven them (IIHS, 2000a).

Interestingly, not only do roundabouts make good sense from a safety perspective, they can also save the community money. Electricity and maintenance savings compared with a conventional lighted intersection are estimated by IIHS at up to $5,000 per year, plus savings in costs associated with congestion and traffic control (IIHS, 2000a). Fuel savings, less noise, and reduced air emissions are also positive results.

Many steps can be taken to get people out of their cars in the first place. The historic city of Ghent, Belgium, shows how pedestrians, bicyclists, and public transit can be given priority and accommodated in the context of a very compact urban form. Here, a number of changes have been made in recent years through a comprehensive reconfiguring of mobility options for the city center. Trams and electric buses operate throughout the center, while autos are restricted from entering during certain hours of the day. Signage guides drivers to one of several underground, public parking garages located at the edge of the center, providing a real-time count of the number of spaces available in each. Extensive improvements have been made for bicycles, including extensive bike lanes, numerous bike parking areas, and signage permitting bicyclists to move with greater flexibility (e.g., allowing them to ride in the opposite direction on one-way car streets). Intersections have been reconfigured to provide space for bicycles to move to the front of cars. These areas are painted red, with bicycle symbols, as are bicycle travel lanes on either side of roads (and again, in some cases, with bicycles moving in the opposite direction to cars). These improvements have clearly made a difference. The city center of Ghent is a delightful pedestrian space, easy to get to, and the number of both pedestrians and bicyclists enjoying the city on a typical day is encouraging.

Many communities in the United States and Europe have sought to discourage car driving and car traffic through pricing policies. Road pricing or congestion pricing holds that roads are a scarce economic commodity and their use ought to go to those willing and able to pay for them. Although there may well be some equity concerns here, making car driving more expensive, signaling economically that cars inflict serious social and environmental harm on our communities, makes considerable sense.

There are many good practical examples of these kinds of congestion pricing systems. One of the boldest recent examples is Mayor Ken Livingstone's new road pricing scheme for London. Beginning in February 2003, drivers entering central London were required to pay a congestion charge of £5 (about US $8). Policed through a network of 260 cameras that check license plates to ensure that payment of the charge has been made (which is possible through the Internet, at gas stations, or by phone), the goals of the system are to generate revenue for transit and to reduce car traffic in the center of the city. The area over which the charge applies is about 8 square miles. In its first year of operation the charge reduced congestion by about 30 percent (Transport for London, 2004). The success of London's program had lead to proposals to extend the idea to other cities throughout the United Kingdom. And in May, 2004, Mayor Livingstone made the provocative proposal of doubling the congestion charge for SUVs—not a bad idea for these space-hogging vehicles that do special harm to environment and place.

European cities and countries have for many years been using a variety of economic pricing tools to discourage auto dependence. Generally higher road taxes, higher parking charges, and of course much higher gasoline taxes are the norm. The latter have been particularly important both in generating revenue for public transit investments and in discouraging car ownership and use, although both of these are on the rise throughout Europe. Increasing gas taxes remains an elusive and politically tricky step in the United States, but one that would do much to help strengthen place and support patterns of community sustainability.

Reform of traffic laws at the state level is also needed. This is brought home in my own hometown of Charlottesville, Virginia, by how difficult it often is to cross streets even at well-marked crosswalks. On Rugby Road, a main movement corridor near the University of Virginia, you can wait for some time on the sidewalk before a benevolent motorist takes notice and stops to allow you to cross. Indeed, Virginia law does not require motorists to stop for pedestrians waiting to cross; pedestrians have the right-of-way, requiring motorists to stop, *only when they are actually in the crosswalk*. This creates the perverse and unsafe situation that to gain the right-of-way, pedestrians must first place themselves in harm's way. Strange, but true.

There are signs that some state laws are changing. In 2003, Oregon adopted a much more stringent pedestrian safety law, a result of active lobbying by the relatively new national pedestrian advocacy group American Walks. The new law requires that drivers come to a complete stop for pedestrians, even at intersections where there are no crosswalks. The driver must remain stopped until the pedestrian has cleared not only the driver's traffic lane but also the adjacent lanes. Unfortunately, though, for the provisions of the law to apply, the pedestrian must first step into the intersection (Dietz, 2003). Further strengthening these pedestrian laws, and further acknowledging pedestrian rights, would be an essential step in creating the conditions of walkable, livable communities.

Greater transit ridership—getting more people out of cars and into trains, trams, and buses—would do much to address many of the current traffic problems. On a per-passenger-mile basis, public transit consumes much less energy, produces much less carbon, dramatically reduces emission of conventional air pollutants (only 5 percent as much emission of CO, again per passenger mile traveled) and would help reduce our insane dependence on foreign oil (Breen, 2002).

Figure 4.11 | Hasselt, Belgium, decided to provide free public transit to its citizens and to convert an inner ring road into a "green boulevard." The city saw a nearly 900 percent increase in public transit ridership.

The city of Hasselt, Belgium, is an excellent example of a city that has done many things to encourage walking and bicycling. Most notable are pedestrianizing much of its city center and reconfiguring its inner ring road into a "green boulevard." Roadway space has been dramatically reduced for cars, and in its place a new bicycle way and a rather wide pedestrian promenade, flanked by a row of trees on each side. This green boulevard is 2.5 kilometers (about one mile and a half) long and contains more than 400 trees. Cars travel on two lanes going one way, and buses are given their own lane. Buses are, in places, moving contra-flow, so they do not have to travel completely around the ring. As well, spaces for cars to enter have been removed, new public plazas created, and the entire center designated a 30 kilometer per hour (a little less than 20 mph) restricted zone.

Although not a large city, about 70,000 in population, perhaps the boldest innovation in Hasselt has been to make riding the buses free. Through an agreement between the city and the regional bus company, De Lijn, whereby the city covers what would have been generated from the farebox, all city buses (i.e., those operating within the city) are free. Regional buses are also free for Hasselt residents for trips beginning and ending in the city zone (with an identification card). This move, in combination with a substantial increase in the coverage and frequency of bus service, has seen a dramatic increase in bus ridership, rising an astounding 870 percent.

Hasselt's mobility innovations appear to be working well. The green boulevard has recaptured space from cars, and people do seem to be using it. At points the spaces may actually be a bit too large, and the two lanes of cars, often speeding, do not encourage quiet strolls, but these community improvements, along with numerous other curtailments on car access and movement, do much to improve the walkability of this city and indeed its overall quality of life. Interestingly, Hasselt's approach was defended for economic reasons. Expanding bus service and increasing pedestrian space and bicycle routes were seen as less costly alternatives to building more roads. And, with the mayor at the time deciding to forgo the building of a third ring road, the economic results have been positive: business in the city has gone up, municipal revenues have risen, and taxes for residents have actually gone down.

Hasselt is not alone, of course, among Belgium or European cities in its efforts to increase space for pedestrians and bicyclists. Opportunities to enhance mobility through bicycling are especially promising as a viable alternative to driving. Compact cities certainly help make bicycling a real possibility for residents; conversely, though, investments in bicycle infrastructure will help to bring about the compactness we desire. Even though our best examples are European, every American city can be fundamentally bicycle-friendly. A combination of providing safe spaces for bicyclers (bike lanes, paths, trails, and separate protected spaces and lighting at intersections), and secure facilities for parking and leaving bicycles at home, work and major destinations will accomplish much. In some cities, like Toronto, Canada, programs exist for teaching prospective riders about how to comfortably commute to work by bike. And, of course, the education of motorists about bicycles and sensitizing them to their presence (something that perhaps comes about more easily in European cities) is also important (see Beatley, 2000).

Providing places for secure bicycle parking ought to be given as much importance as we usually give to auto parking. Many European cities have made special strides here. In Freiburg, Germany, for instance, a major multistory bicycle parking facility has been built by the city adjacent to it main train station (and an important bicycle- and pedestrian-only bridge). Here, several levels of *valet* bicycle parking are available, along with car-sharing cars, a travel agency office, an office of the Deutsche Bahn (the German national train system), and a café. The building has a green rooftop and powered partially by photovoltaic panels. It is a fantastic and special addition to that community and very well-used.

In the United States, cities like Chicago are following the lead and are making a variety of impressive and necessary investments in their bicycle infrastructure. In that city, some 125 miles of new bikeways have been installed and there are now some 9,400 bike rakes. Most impressive has been the opening (summer, 2004) of its new Millennium Park bicycle depot—a facility similar to Freiburg's where bicycles can be parked, and where a variety of other bicycle services, such as showers and lockers, repair and rentals, and even internet service, can be found. It's also where several car-sharing cars can be found (operated by I-GO carsharing). And, also like the Freiburg facility, some of the power needed for the station is generated from PVs. Even before the opening of this facility the city had been providing free valet bike parking for major events in Grant Park, such as the Blues Fest and Taste of Chicago. Cities like Chicago demonstrate convincingly that it is possible to foster a bicycle culture and that bicycles, given the infrastructure investments and leadership, can provide viable alternatives to cars.

Designing-In Connections to Other Communities

Our dismal inability in the United States to provide sensible alternative transportation options for traveling from city to city is another major aspect of the problem of place building, and adds to the difficulty in creating compact communities. In thinking about the possibilities of living a car-free existence, most Americans have a difficult time imagining how this is possible, when thinking about the full spectrum of mobility possibilities that they have (or don't have, as the case may be). Even where people find themselves living in compact, walkable urban neighborhoods with good local transit, they may see a strong need to have a car (and to use it) when visiting their aging parents in a nearby city or when traveling to see a show or visit a museum in a city in a nearby state.

In this case, European commitments to rail, and especially to high-speed rail, represent an excellent model to emulate. For many years, an increasingly integrated network of high-speed rail lines and systems has been under development, especially in northern and northwestern Europe. A number of fantastic high-speed options exist for European travelers—the Thalys, the Eurostar, the TGV in France, and the ICE in Germany, among others. An article in *Business Week* reports on the "dramatic expansion" of this high-speed rail network. It is projected (by the Community of European Railways) that over the next eight years the number of kilometers of high-speed rail track will double (an additional 3,300 km). Major new high-speed rail ties are also being built in Spain and Italy. As well, early high-speed technology will gradually be replaced by trains that move even faster, on average 350 kilometers per hour (217 mph) as opposed to today's 300 kph trains. And the amenities and comfort offered riders on these trains continue to expand.

In Spain, major new investments in its high-speed train system are set to pay tremendous dividends in improved convenience and quality of life. There, its new AVE high-speed routes will dramatically cut travel times between that country's major provincial cities. Travel time from Madrid to Barcelona will be reduced from 7 hours to about $2^1/_2$ hours when the system is fully completed. The benefits to a compact city like Barcelona are tremendous and its progressive mayor Joan Clos has been using the high-speed rail improvements to strongly argue for extending and expanding the city's transit system. There will now be even less need for a car in Barcelona.

The European experience does show convincingly that high-speed rail can shift substantial movement away from plane travel and, especially important in the American context, *from cars. Business Week Online* (2002) reports on one such experience:

> Before the high-speed Thalys train connecting Paris with Brussels was launched in the mid 1990s, 61% of travel between the two cities was by car and only 24% by train. Now, the Thalys has 50% of the market and cars only 43%, according to the International Union of Railways. That's not surprising, considering that driving from Paris to Brussels takes at least three hours. And taking into account highway tolls and Europe's $4 per-gallon gasoline prices, it costs

Figure 4.12 | Germany's ICE high-speed trains provide excellent connections between cities there. Europe is poised to extend and expand dramatically its high-speed rail network.

about $50 each way to drive—not that much less than a $63 one-way Thalys fare.

And it turns out that almost 60 percent of airline trips are 500 miles or less (Bernstein, 2002). Clearly, many intercity trips in the United States, especially in highly populated corridors and states, would be faster, more convenient, and more pleasurable by train than by air.

Admittedly, these great European transit systems come with substantial government subsidies and an apparently greater (intrinsic?) willingness to financially underwrite high-speed rail, at least compared with the United States. Yet, given the high degree of recent subsidy to support ailing U.S. airlines, and the traditionally very high subsidy afforded cars and highways, directing more financial resources toward rail, high-speed in particular, is very justifiable.

Americans might be convinced if they were to experience firsthand the pleasures and ease of traveling on a high-speed train. Many American tourists have done so, and they usually came away convinced. Several years ago, when leading a group of American planning students on a tour of sustainable European cities, I insisted that at least part of the trip be made on ICE trains, the German high-speed system. I think the trains had an impact on the students, who were able to watch the kilometers per hour on interior speedometers, located and highly visible on the ends of the cars. I suspect that getting Americans on these trains for even a short trip might have similar, positive results, and perhaps play effectively into their approach at home to new gadgets and technology.

Good planning and design is also an important part of the story. In the Dutch city of Arnhem, a new multiuse, multifunctional train station is now under construction, and will provide a new and important intersection point between high-speed rail and other transport modes. Not only will the station be located near the city's center, and provide access to all aspects of transport (local transit terminal, regional trains, bike rental, storage, repair), it is designed to include extensive housing and office uses.

Investments in intercity rail, especially high-speed rail, serve to further strengthen local transit as well, as European research shows (see van den Berg and Pol, 1998) and the experience of cities like Barcelona demonstrate. The advantage of traveling quickly from one city to another is quickly lost if the passenger is forced to spend the last leg of the journey on a very slow bus or train. And, strategies for integrating and melding together the different modes of mobility make it easy, indeed effortless, to move from one to the other. For example, I can travel from Brussels to Frankfurt on the ICE high-speed train and move to the S-bahn, or regional rail, to get to my final destination. No car is needed in this scenario, and I have the time and ability to focus on the place and the people I'm seeing.

Conclusions

There is considerable consensus today that unchecked sprawl is a major culprit in diminishing and destroying genuine place. Low-density, excessively car-dependent development, with its accompanying onslaught of chain stores, fast-food restaurants, and big box commercial, is deserving of much attention in any place-building strategy. Sprawl is, moreover, not sustainable for many other reasons: it is highly energy-consumptive, polluting, land- and habitat-destructive. The remedies explored in this chapter are many, though not necessarily easy ones to implement: more compact, urban development, organized around good transit and the potential for walking and bicycling; strategies that build upon and tie into existing community land use patterns and fabrics; and architecture and design solutions that value diversity, creativity, and that are place sensitive. Connections and connectedness are major themes. Good places and places that people will love and be committed to provide spatial connections of many kinds—walkable street connections between neighborhoods and neighbors, between homes and schools and shops, and easy and sustainable connections between cities (i.e., by high-speed rail).

Notes

1. Not all is perfect in Vancouver. Some people have been critical of the similar architectural look of many tall towers, especially in Concord Pacific Place. Partly, this seems a result of the fact that several of the buildings were designed by one architect, Jim Chan. But, the speed and short time frame in which so much construction is happening is as much a culprit.

2. Conservationists and environmental groups in Maryland are, however, concerned about the land protection and conservation side of the program and are less convinced about the governor's commitments here. See Dresser, 2003.

3. Several so-called green Wal-Marts have already been built, including the first and best known in Lawrence, Kansas. For a description of this building, see Beatley and Manning, 1997.

Nature and Place: The Role of Natural Environments in Strengthening Commitments to Place

There is little doubt that we need natural systems to survive, physically and biologically, and we need them for our emotional, psychological, and spiritual health. The ecology and natural elements of our communities are essential place assets. They provide us with innumerable services and benefits and do much to make communities attractive and livable. There is ever-increasing appreciation that these green features—the *green infrastructure*—are as important to the life and economy of a place as is the more conventional infrastructure (roads, sewer lines, etc.). The natural functions and ecosystem services are of many kinds; for example, trees and vegetation preserved on an urban or suburban lot can do much to reduce stormwater runoff, air pollution, and the energy consumption needed for mechanical cooling and air-conditioning. The results of a number of studies done by the tree advocacy group American Forests show convincingly that trees and forests provide tremendous benefits and ought to be acknowledged explicitly. In an ecosystem analysis of the Washington, D.C. Metro region, for instance, American Forests (2002) calculated that area forests provide almost $5 billion per year in stormwater conventional retention benefits (based on what it would cost to build retention structures) and about $50 million per year in air quality benefits (particulate reduction). Although these ecological services are not generally accounted for in our present economic framework, individual homeowners and landowners ought to give them some amount of credit.

Greenness, or the presence of nature in all its possible forms, is one essential place-fixing element, and we have much quantitative and anecdotal evidence of the power it exerts on our place sensibilities. This greenness can of course take many forms and be expressed in many ways. It is important to remember that these are qualities and conditions of place over which we have considerable control, and which help in moving us closer to sustainable living.

Maintaining large blocks of natural land in close proximity to urban residents, and seeking creative ways to educate and connect residents with the biodiversity and landscapes that surround them and support them is an important goal. A number of U.S. cities have been able to do this effectively. Greenbelts exist in many of our cities; for example, Boulder, Colorado, has set aside some 40,000 acres of land within a close walk of many homes, Portland has preserved more than 8,000 acres of fish and wildlife habitat as part of a regional green spaces plan. In Boise, Idaho, preservation of surrounding foothills and open space is a major place-enhancing strategy; in 2001, Boise residents approved a special foothills levy to raise $10 million and purchase and protect these important surrounding lands. In Albuquerque, the cottonwood forests along Rio Grande, known as the Bosque, are an important open space resource and the focus of restoration efforts.

At the landscape level, we can and must find ways to reconnect citizens to the important ecosystems and landscapes that support them and nourish them biologically and emotionally. Creative initiatives that aim to both educate the public about the richness and history of landscape and build commitment to these places are numerous.

In Hannover, Germany, the 80-kilometer-long (about 50 miles) Green Ring (*Der Grüne Ring*) has been created to encircle the city, providing a continuous hiking and biking route, and exposing residents to a variety of landscape types, from hilly Börde to the valleys of the Leineaue River. Coordinated by the regional government, the Greater Hannover Association (KGH), each of the individual municipalities in the region has designed its own distinctive trail marker for this network of connected farm roads and trails, all painted

Figure 5.1 | The Hannover Green Ring is an 80-kilometer-long walking and biking trail that encircles the city. (Map compliments of Region Hannover.)

a consistent shade of blue. Green Ring maps and landscape guidebooks have been published and are widely distributed, further enhancing the educational role. The Hannover strategy illustrates well that we must provide easy physical access to these rich landscapes and work hard to ensure that even those living in dense urban environments have the opportunity to learn about and connect with these environments.

In the United States, a marvelous emerging example of building appreciation of landscape can be seen in an initiative called Chicago Wilderness, a collaborative effort of more than 160 different environmental and community organizations. With substantial funding from the U.S. Fish and Wildlife Service and the U.S. Forest Service, the initiative has undertaken a variety of impressive efforts to document the richness of the biodiversity in the Chicago region, to educate the public about it, and to work to restore and protect it. The name Chicago Wilderness also refers to these lands and landscapes—some 200,000 acres representing the considerable remaining remnants of tallgrass prairies, oak woodlands, swamps, dunes, and other habitats and species that existed before European settlement of the region (Chicago Wilderness, 2000).

The variety of educational and biodiversity awareness-enhancing initiatives of Chicago Wilderness is truly impressive, recognizing the importance of building a public constituency. The group has recently published an exemplary *Atlas of Biodiversity* that documents the richness of nature in the region. Beginning its discussion of the region's geology 26,000 years ago, the atlas describes in vivid detail the habitat and living communities in the region and past efforts to protect them. A number of other educational tools are being successfully employed, including the monthly magazine *Chicago Wilderness,* educational videotapes, and model school curricula. Chicago Wilderness has also produced a Biodiversity Recovery Plan, which lays out in considerable detail a vision of future protection, management, and restoration needs, and has been adopted by the Northeast Illinois Planning Commission.

Spring of 2004 saw the release of an impressive extension of the thinking of Chicago Wilderness—the *Chicago Green Infrastructure Vision,* a strategic region-wide map depicting places where wetlands, prairies, parks and green spaces could be restored, extended, expanded. Its essence is a powerful visual expression of the region's Urban Biodiversity Plan, and if followed would protect and restore nearly 2 million acres of land. The map actually derives of a series of workshops in which local experts came together to collectively put on a map the lands they felt to be most biologically valuable and the places where strategic protective steps could be taken. Spearheaded by Chicago Wilderness and the staff of the Northeast Illinois Planning Commission, the process began with a series of key ecological overlays—watershed boundaries, wetlands, streams, woodland cover, among others. The vision map is seen as just that—not a site-specific template for land acquisition or restoration. It is already being used to guide regional transportation decisions, and is, like Chicago Wilderness itself, already shifting the perspective of the city and region as a place of nature, and as an interconnected, coherent whole.

The vision will undoubtedly serve as a guide to more specific land planning and conservation actions through the urban region.

Interestingly, the City of Chicago has done as much as any local jurisdiction to value this biodiversity heritage, notably under its Nature Chicago program. An active participant in Chicago Wilderness, the city has developed and is implementing a variety of impressive urban greening and urban ecology initiatives. It has recently signed an urban conservation treaty (only the second in the country) designed to better protect the estimated 7 million migratory birds that travel through the city each year. Under this treaty, the city has agreed to do a number of things, including utilizing bird-friendly landscaping in city parks, mapping bird migration routes, educating residents about what they can do to promote bird habitat in their own backyards, and, most dramatic, instituting a plan to turn off downtown building lights during key migration periods—certainly one of the most vivid demonstrations of commitment to place. All of these activities have the potential to further educate and instill public understanding of and appreciation for the unique natural heritage of Chicago. Such steps are essential to building local support, to nurturing a new appreciation for the natural settings of place, and really laying the foundation for deeper, richer meanings and experiences that can come from understanding *local* nature and natural systems.

Communities Like Forests: Rethinking Cities and the Built Environment

With the publication of such books as Janine Benyus's *Biomimicry,* (1998) and the work and writings of Paul Hawken, Bill McDonough, Amory Lovins, and many others, there is new interest in applying the many lessons of nature to buildings, commerce, and other aspects of society. Little of this thinking has actually been applied to the functioning of cities, towns, and regions, but I believe there is great promise in those areas. The metaphor of a city or community functioning as a forest does is a powerful one. Communities should be fundamentally natural—a rich habitat for biodiversity, embedded in ecosystems and watersheds that function in natural ways (e.g., minimizing impervious surfaces, preserving or restoring free-flowing creeks and riparian areas), and have important ecological features and qualities that provide ecological services (e.g., trees and urban forests providing shade, capturing particulate matter, controlling stormwater runoff, etc.).

Every building and project constructed in the "community as forest" acts to further respect and advance these natural and organic qualities. Parking lots and other conventional elements of the built environment can be designed in fundamentally different ways to replicate natural systems. There is now considerable positive experience with biofiltration design—essentially rethinking parking structures as "rain gardens" to act as a natural water treatment and recycling device. This is quite a different way of viewing parking lots. As the Europeans have learned, every aspect of the built environment can be profoundly greened—gardens, shrubs, and ground covers can be planted on rooftops; walls can be greened; sterile, gray, hard surfaces can be taken up, or "desealed," with trees and other types of vegetation and community gardens installed in their stead.

Urban rooftops represent a particularly promising way of injecting nature into our cities. Common in Europe, this idea is beginning to take hold in the United States. Especially the extensive green roof, or eco-roof, where a carpet of sedum or grass or bushy plants covers an entire rooftop, providing insulation, sequestering carbon, providing bird and invertebrate habitat, retaining stormwater, and generally improving the feel and quality of urban life (e.g., Peck and Kuhn, undated; Beatley, 2000). Some dramatic U.S. examples now exist, such as the one in Chicago. Under the leadership of Mayor Richard Daley, Chicago's City Hall has been retrofitted with a dramatic green rooftop—about 20,000 square feet, containing some 20,000 plants.

Already the roof is viewed locally as a great success—energy savings for the city have already been significant, and owners of buildings with views of the roof have been rumored to be contemplating raising their rents. The marketplace clearly rewards such urban greening ideas. The city hall roof's ability to attract and nurture wildlife in the center of downtown continues to grow each year. A monitoring effort by local volunteers is finding remarkable (and growing) diversity of species living or visiting the roof—birds, spiders, grasshoppers and other insects, and even native bees (Mallett, 2004). The educational value of the city hall retrofit, and its impact in showing others that it is possible and desirable has been tremendous. There are now an estimated 70 green roofs completed or in progress within the City of Chicago.

Figure 5.2 | Chicago's City Hall has been retrofitted to include a beautiful green roof, which has resulted in significant energy savings.

Bringing Nature Back into Cities and into Our Lives

Reconnecting urban residents to nature and the natural processes upon which they rely is a special challenge for planners, but one with tremendous potential place-enhancing benefits. Much of our current human condition involves a physical disconnect from natural processes, much the result of what ecological architect Sim van der Ryn calls our "flush and forget technology." Restoring nature to urban environments, and making natural processes transparent and visible, will demand both small and large actions.

Every city will have opportunities to reestablish connections to its preexisting natural conditions and to those elements of its natural heritage that may have been overlooked or covered over. A city need not have a spectacular environmental backdrop like Denver or Honolulu or Cape Town to do this. Communities in less visually spectacular places, such as central Ohio, are also blessed with tremendous opportunities. In a recent Ohio State University (OSU) city planning class that I co-instructed, a number of these opportunities for the Columbus plan were explored. A careful look at the history of city development and growth in Columbus demonstrates just how much natural beauty and complex hydrology once existed there. The students unearthed the oldest known map of the city, dating to 1824, which shows clearly a network of streams and creeks draining into the Scioto and Olentangy Rivers. This "natural paradise," as the students describe it, consisted of a site of dense forests, springs, ponds, wetlands, streams, and rivers. For the most part, this natural system has been covered over and ignored, the grid street pattern overlaid onto this natural system with little sensitivity.

The OSU city planning students have proposed some bold actions, including starting a program of daylighting streams, beginning with the Iuka Ravine, a culverted stream. This proposal, as the students rightly point out, would be a "revolutionary project for Columbus," symbolizing its "commitment to restoring its natural hydrology" (Ecocity Columbus, 2001).

Daylighting streams that were channelized and paved over during development is a bold stroke indeed, and some cities have accomplished it. Zurich, Switzerland, for instance, has been implementing a program to bring back to the surface covered streams and creeks, eventually 40 kilometers (about 25 miles) of stream length will be uncovered in that city (Beatley, 2000). In the United States, Seattle is leading the way in stream restoration and repair of its natural hydrologic systems, for the most part out of necessity. In the late 1990s, the city received a lightning bolt thanks to the federal Endangered Species Act. Two species of salmon were placed on the federal list of endangered species—the result of massive human alteration of the natural watersheds of western Washington State—mandating considerable new protective and restorative responsibilities on local officials. Since the mandate, Seattle has been exploring creative opportunities to retrofit and redesign the urban landscape to make it "salmon friendly." Indeed, the city aspires to be a salmon-friendly city, though it's just beginning to understand what this will require.

The Seattle Public Utility (SPU) has played a key role in pushing such investigations. In the spring of 2000, SPU sponsored a four-day "Salmon Friendly Seattle" design charrette. Bringing together notable designers and environmental scientists, five teams were given the charge of analyzing five different sites in the city and coming up with design solutions to restore the natural hydrology of these sites and their ability to support salmon. The solutions from the charrette were imaginative and inspiring—for example, a high school was redesigned to reduce paved surfaces with increased native plantings; and a residential block was redesigned to capture and treat stormwater via an underground cistern. Other initiatives of SPU include sponsoring an educational display methodology on "salmon-friendly gardening," and an urban creek celebration (Amaya, 2000).

Part of the task will be rethinking every aspect of our built environments to find ways to inject nature. In Seattle, the even broader, more expansive concept of *green streets* is gaining momentum. The idea is to convert conventional streets into green flowing mixes of trees, community gardens, rainwater sculptures along the sides of urban buildings, and a water runnel collecting rooftop runoff winding its way down the street.

Urban and suburban streets can be greened in ways that allow them to function more like ecological systems, which also contributes to more pedestrian-desirable spaces. The Street Edge Alternatives (SEA) program, a pilot project initiated by the Seattle Public Utility, is a creative effort to address the problem of excessive stormwater runoff from urbanized areas, as well as its water quality and habitat-destroying impacts. The project has produced a prototype of a different kind of street in northwest Seattle—a retrofit on 2nd Avenue designed to better contain and manage rainwater, specifically to control on-site runoff from a two-year, 24-hour event, such that peak is no greater than predevelopment conditions (SPU, 2001). The residential road has been redesigned to incorporate rainwater swales, trees, and native vegetation.

Part of Seattle's Urban Creeks Legacy program, the 2nd Avenue site was selected in part because of expressed interest and support by residents (six different blocks submitted petitions to have their streets retrofitted). Blocks were encouraged to submit petitions, and at least 60 percent of the residents on the street had to support the retrofit.

In addition to the swales and stormwater retention, a more organic, significantly auto-calmed street has been created. The road has been narrowed (to 14 feet wide) and turned into a curvilinear green street, with a sidewalk on one side and 11 percent impervious street surface (SPU, 2001). More than 100 trees and some 1,100 shrubs have been planted along the street, adding significant new green along with the contoured swales. To address concerns about fire and emergency vehicle access, there are no curbs and only a 2-foot-wide grass shoulder provided on each side. The street has advantages in addition to stormwater management, including a lower cost and

Figure 5.3 | Seattle's Street Edge Alternative (SEA) initiative is converting conventional suburban streets into pedestrian-friendly linear rain gardens. (Photo compliments of Seattle Public Utilities.)

reduced long-term maintenance when compared with conventionally engineered stormwater collection systems.

The design of this more ecologically functioning street sends many messages. It shows that we need not pave as much as we do to achieve the same public function—that is, moving traffic. Multidimensional design in the ecologically designed city is essential. Arnesen, Chollak, and Dewald make these points about the 2nd Avenue street and note that this project is many things:

> A sidewalk design that not only serves but attracts pedestrians, together with a street design that reduces vehicle speeds, provides a setting that is safer for those who live on the block and for those who simply pass through. The project sets a new standard for neighborhood involvement and collaboration, which builds community. The idea that the enhanced street serves the higher purpose of protecting natural ecosystems is one that benefits the public welfare directly and indirectly.

The Growing Vine Street initiative, also in Seattle, is a neighborhood and grassroots effort to green Vine Street. The community has been involved every

Figure 5.4 | Buster Simpson's *Beckoning Cistern* captures and stores rainwater from rooftops and will eventually be part of an innovative green street in the Belltown neighborhood of Seattle.

step along the way. Indeed, as much as it is a design for greening a street, it is also an exercise in democracy and in community building. Founder and architect Carolyn Geise sees the mission as one not only of greening the city but of strategically using the street as a way to overcome ethnic and income differ-

Figure 5.5 | A drawing of what Vine Street, in Seattle, will eventually look like. The Growing Vine Street initiative envisions a major street retooling: more space for pedestrians, a community garden, trees, and a stormwater collection "runnel" system alongside the street. (Rendering by Carlson Architects, Seattle; Design team included Greg Waddell of Carlson Architects, Buster Simpson, Peggy Gaynor, and SvR Designs.)

ences, and as a kind of community and neighborhood "glue." It brings people together in support and pursuit of common goals.

What Geise and the neighborhood have envisioned, and what a design team has given expression to, is a profoundly different point of view of a street. As figure 5.5 renders wells, the street is less a thing for cars, and more a place for walking and socializing, for trees and growing food, where water from rooftops is collected and sent along in "runnels" or meandering waterways, *cleansing* (and celebrating) this water on its way to the Puget Sounds. A street, then, becomes a living thing, an organic vein in the green city.

The most dramatic feature of the elements of Vine Street so far completed is Buster Simpson's *Beckoning Cistern*—a blue corrugated tank, with a striking hand reaching up to the façade of the 81 Vine Street building, the index finger of the hand collecting rooftop runoff from a long tube extended from near the top of the building. On the street level, the water collected in the cistern will be sent trickling through the runnels and a series of stepped basins. Simpson's bold design, described in some of the promotional material as "a poetic utility sculpture," was dedicated in a major neighborhood event in March 2003.

Although the green vision of Vine Street extends its entire length, only a few selected pieces of the street, such as Simpson's sculpture, have been completed or are under way. This is partly explained by the paucity of community resources, but probably speaks more significantly to the difficulties of rethinking such conventional infrastructure. This does not trouble advocates like Geise—she sees it as an organic transformation, an ongoing work in progress. In her mind, the street will never be finished, meaning it will always be in some process of emerging and reinventing itself, of being what residents of the neighborhood feel it should be.

The Growing Vine Street initiative shows how an unusual small project can help move dialogue and discussion along in a community. Geise and her collaborators used the street greening proposals as a way of sponsoring community events; the need to raise neighborhood support and money for her vision was part of the reason, but it also served as a broader vehicle to allow neighbors to better understand and get to know each other. Geise has been pleasantly surprised that these street greening ideas have developed so much credibility in such a relatively short time. It is not unusual today to hear positive references to Vine Street from those on the city council, for instance, and there is the view that similar approaches can and should be taken in other parts of the city.

Other forms of urban infrastructure can be reconceived of in a green and organic way. In London, a *green bridge* has recently been unveiled, connecting two sections of parkland in the Tower Hamlets borough, and capping five lanes of gray roadways with a green forest of mature trees and grass. Designed by Piers Gough of CZWG Architects, and funded through the Millennium Commission (which also funded the Millennium Dome), the goal of the bridge is "to give the impression of the park floating over the road" (Powell, 1999). This "green carpet" has already injected a highly visible new element of nature into the neighborhood, made the presence of the existing Mile End Park more prominent, and helped to breathe new economic life into the area. Interestingly, the bridge design has also created rentable space below it, enough for a restaurant and several shops. The rent charged to these establishments is now underwriting the management of the Mile End Park.

Figure 5.6 | The Green Bridge, in the Tower Hamlets borough of London, is a pedestrian- and bicycle-only bridge. With mature trees and vegetation, it provides an impressive "green carpet" that seemingly "floats" over several lanes of vehicle traffic.

From ecological rooftops to urban forests and wildlands, to efforts at converting wasted land around buildings into wildlife habitat, there are tremendous opportunities to restore a connection to nature in urban environments and to build constituencies of people who will love and care about these places as a result.

Reestablishing native vegetation and replacing turfgrass and conventional monocultural urban landscaping, wherever feasible, can be another bold action. A side-yard, a corporate entrance, or a window opening can be an opportunity to reestablish a connection with native habitats and vegetation. The Metropolitan Water District (MWD), in Los Angeles, for instance, has recently funded a series of projects to reestablish native vegetation in public spaces. Under its City Makeover Program, the MWD has given grants to eleven cities in the area. The education and place-enhancing benefits of this project are clear and not lost on program supporter and actress Rene Russo: "We lost our landscape heritage so long ago, we wouldn't know a native plant if we tripped over one. This program goes a long way toward helping us rediscover our sense of place" (Metropolitan Water District, 2003, p. 1).

Green Urban Neighborhoods

Designing new urban neighborhoods and regenerated areas with wildlife and nature in mind is another important place-strengthening move. The Greenwich Millennium Village, the new ecological district in London (a portion of a larger Millennium Village regeneration effort), demonstrates the possibilities. A first phase of development puts fairly dense and compact ecological housing in close proximity to an impressive park. The park, a restored wetland and marsh system, provides unusual access via boardwalks and walkover structures to this area of abundant bird habitat. A series of bird observation blinds and a carefully planned spatial configuration make visual enjoyment and access for residents (and visitors) easy, and equally unintrusive for the wildlife. And the new residents of the village appear already to be fully enjoying these natural connections. Residents of upper-floor flats can be seen, binoculars in hand, watching birds, and at one time, monitoring the progress of a pair of nearby nesting swans.

The Greenwich Peninsula Ecology Park offers an especially impressive aspect of the neighborhood, and an unusual green amenity. A network of wooden walkover structures allows residents to get close to nature and adds significantly to the pedestrian elements of the neighborhood. By restoring this preindustrial marsh, the park provides new ecological infrastructure to the area and opportunities for nature strolls and bird-watching. Managed by the Trust for Urban Ecology, several different habitats have been restored on the site, in addition to the marsh and two lakes. These include a beach, alder and willow woodlands, and a wildflower meadow. A series of bird blinds and observation points are included along the walkways, and the main nature center itself provides expansive windows for observing and watching. Four special habitat features are also included: a bat tower, a kingfisher tunnel (a riverbank hole where the birds like to nest), tern rafts, and standing deadwood (Greenwich Ecology Park, undated).

The Viikki ecological district in Helsinki, Finland, further demonstrates the possibility of new design with connections to nature kept in the fore.

Figure 5.7 | The Greenwich Peninsula Ecology Park, a key element in the brownfield redevelopment project Greenwich Millennium Village, in London.

Figure 5.8 | The new Viikki ecological neighborhood in Helsinki includes community gardens and food production as a central design feature.

Here, these natural connections are at both a neighborhood housing scale and the broader master plan level for this district of Helsinki. The housing design provides for a series of green fingers or wedges that are reserved for community gardens and rainwater collection. A large adjacent nature area is easily reached through two pedestrian and bicycle bridges, opening up terrific opportunities for nature exploration and wonder for neighborhood children. A relocated stream has been designed to collect and treat stormwater and to meander naturally, restoring habitat and ecosystem functions. A walkover structure and the two architecturally significant bridges also provide important connections to the stream. Compact housing, then, is provided at the same time as extensive preservation and tremendous neighborhood nature amenities and access for residents.

Kronsberg, the new ecological district in Hannover, Germany, is another excellent example of a relatively dense, compact neighborhood organized to minimize traffic and cars and to incorporate natural features. The first phase of about 3,000 units (the area will eventually contain about 6,000 units and a population of about 15,000) is designed to reduce impervious cover throughout and to retain stormwater on-site. Blocks of housing are organized around extensive green courtyards, where community gardens, children's play areas, and water features are found. Green, grassy stormwater collection swales are located next to sidewalks and highly calmed roadways, themselves draining into two spectacular stormwater collection boulevards. These are grand vegetated green fingers that collect and treat stormwater, with photovoltaic-powered pumps that recycle whatever does not percolate back into the ground. A series of check dams along the way provide important pedestrian walkovers, connecting the blocks of housing on either side. A beautiful walkway bends along and through each of these large stormwater collection streets, and the flowers and vegetation produce a real green amenity for the district.

Green retrofits of existing older neighborhoods are also possible and can profoundly adjust the perception of these neighborhoods and strengthen commitments to them. Malmö, Sweden, is completing an ambitious urban greening project aimed at retrofitting and redeveloping the older central-city district of Augustenborg, built in the early 1950s. With a population of about 3,000, this neighborhood has endured many indignities over the years. Flooding in the district and a combined sewer overflow problem has plagued the area in recent years. And, once considered the epitome of modern, high-quality housing, the district has become an area of relatively high turnover and impermanence.

The neighborhood's green retrofit consists of several key measures. Most impressive are the efforts to reduce the historic problems of flooding and urban stormwater management. An impressive new on-site water collection system has been designed, converting land surfaces in the neighborhood into a network of ponds and wetlands, drainage swales, and drainage channels. One significant side effect of this effort has been to reintroduce water back into the neighborhood, becoming a new amenity for residents. The new strategy also involves a major green roof program, and new green roofs have been placed on the buildings of industrial complexes, on a neighborhood school, and on the rooftops of neighborhood waste collection centers.

Other elements of Augustenborg's green effort includes establishment of a car-sharing program, utilizing electric vehicles, and, to provide greater mobility especially for elderly residents, a new (small) electric trolley. The green trolley is a visible sign of change, and has already made life easier there for many residents, especially the elderly, in getting around and accessing doctors' offices, pharmacies, and other services beyond an easy walk.

The program for ecological rebuilding in Augustenborg has taken an admirable grassroots emphasis. This has included community workshops, evening meetings, and community committees formed to study specific topics. Groups of community residents have gone on "study tours" to other Swedish cities, and residents of the community with special ideas and interests have been tapped for special roles in the rebuilding process. One resident, an amateur hydrological engineer, has been especially involved in designing the new stormwater elements of the district. Formation of community businesses has also been a key element; for example, a new local company, Street Tram Sweden, now manufactures the green electric mini-buses that serve the district.

There are many ways to reconnect to nature, many ways to re-earth our communities, and many levels at which this can happen. Streets, neighborhoods, and even tall buildings can be places of nature, such as the Commerzbank in Frankfurt, Germany. There are nine sky gardens in the Com-

Figure 5.9 | The Kronsberg ecological district in Hannover, Germany, features an innovative on-site stormwater collection and treatment system. The major stormwater collection boulevards (as shown here) collect stormwater from side streets and provide a delightful walking trail and lush greenspace for the community.

Figure 5.10 | One of the nine lush sky gardens in the Commerzbank building in Frankfurt, Germany.

merzbank, each garden four-stories high. Each garden contains full-sized trees and lots of vegetation. The garden structure and layout is the same in each, but the trees and plants vary depending on the direction the garden faces. (A tenth garden is completely open to the outside and not accessible to occupants of the building.) There are three planting schemes, each repeated three times: east-facing gardens contain Asian plants, south-facing contain Mediterranean plants, and west-facing contain North American plans. These gardens are well frequented, used for lunching, breaks, and informal meetings. Their four-story height means that many offices have windows looking out over the gardens, providing tremendous visual benefit in addition to their positive functions in moderating temperature and improving air quality. The gardens have been described as the "green lungs" of the building.

The Rhythms of Nature in Cities and Everywhere We Live

One of the primary goals of ecological place-building or community-building should be to find ways to make urban life rich with the experiences of nature.

Cities, towns, and communities should seek every opportunity to facilitate a closeness with nature, to allow the rhythms and dynamic flux of nature to find a presence in our communities every day. This can occur in many different ways—through community forests that shift in color with seasons, through farmers' markets and urban agriculture that actively connect us to the cycles of the growing season, or perhaps through urban wildlife programs and initiatives that educate about and provide experimental opportunities to understand the ecological rhythm of local biodiversity.

Designing water into our communities is one special opportunity in this regard, I believe. Water is an essential element in human life, and a natural element that bestows tremendous appeal on cities. People want to be where water is; they enjoy seeing it, jumping through and frolicking in it, hearing it, feeling its coolness. There is also something very primordial about it; children, without the inhibitions of adults, can't resist the urge to touch or play in water, often sans clothing.

Few individuals have built as impressive and creative a body of work dealing with and celebrating water in cities as Herbert Dreiseitl, a German artist and designer. Incorporating waterways and water flows in city-center plazas, courtyards, and buildings has become his forté with spectacular results (see Dreiseitl, Grau, and Ludwig, 2001). Town squares in the German villages of Gummersbach and Hattersheim have been transformed through and by new and creative interventions of water. The steps of Hattersheim's town hall now have a flow form, with water pulsating down, meandering through the town hall plaza, through a town park, purifying and aerating the water along the way, ending in a retention pond and wetland. Water has become a new presence in this center, a creative way of linking the town hall and a nearby park, and a "way of taking people to the water" (p. 18).

Called the Klein Trinkwasser, the Hattersheim waterway is strikingly unusual. Water cascades down a series of curved stone surfaces, sculpted from the stone steps of the town hall. It gurgles and pulses as it makes its way down in waves. Animated and active, it is water you might expect to find in a waterfall. The sounds are impressive and gently resonate throughout this pedestrian core. Once reaching the floor of the town center, the water disappears underground, then resurfaces, zigzagging and winding its way through an area of cafés with outdoor tables arranged beside and around the water.

Figures 5.11 and 5.12 | This waterfall and stream begins at the steps of the Hattersheim (Germany) town hall. It provides tremendous beauty and vitality to this town center, and is an almost irresistible feature for children.

The brick-and-stone channels contain relatively large rocks and an occasional distinctive utility cover, and three large trees provide shade along the course of this urban stream.

This water element brings the feel, sight, and sound of water to the center of Hattersheim and then, by extending to a nearby park, serves in a very visceral way to connect the gray and the green. It becomes a more natural stream as it moves into the adjacent city park, eventually ending in a large pond. The allure of this feature to children is especially undeniable. On a recent visit during a hot July day, a group of about fifteen elementary school children could be found frolicking in the waterfall steps. The design makes this easy. Traveling down thirteen steps, the watercourse fans out into a series of four larger basins. Children can walk and slide up and down the steps, but the basins, in a kind of heart shape, provide flat places to stand and sit with feet and legs in the water. Another fascination for children is watching objects float down the waterway from the top to the bottom. Later that same day, a young boy and girl were having limitless fun by going to the steps and dropping tree limbs, leaves, and Styrofoam pieces, watching them float down, collecting them at the bottom, and then starting the process over again.

There is something incredibly enjoyable about seeing and experiencing water in such places, in dense cities, where we know intellectually that water is being whisked about, delivered to taps and hydrants and kitchens, but through invisible networks. One thing lost in this modern and artificial delivery system is an experience of the base physical qualities of moving water—the pulses, the tumbling, the gurgling exhilaration of water. The connection with the natural physical world is immediate and therapeutic.

The marvelous water and green courtyard in the Nicolas-Cusanus-Haus, a home for the elderly in Stuttgart, Germany, is another positive model. The interior courtyard, a Herbert Dreiseitl design, is a rich, vegetated area, full of plants, light, and water. Water is a central element, cascading down through a series of stone channels, the sound soothing and therapeutic. Dreiseitl (2001) describes the difference such sounds can make to the comfort and feel of a building:

> It is often first noticed on a different level of perception, because sometimes it can only be heard and not seen. But the residents are particularly fond of these sounds.
>
> The constant splashing and glugging creates a comfortable, indeed luxurious acoustic background, masking distant scraps of conversation and keeping people's own intimate conversations private. (pp. 133–134)

Such water systems as urban design also have the strange ability to push us out of our self-obsessions, to bring us down to the moment and to the people and human events occurring around us. Watching and awareness are key qualities that beautiful, sustainable places induce in us. We are forced to step over to the side to avoid that channel or that step that is watery, not solid. Occasionally, we end up with a wet shoe, reminded that the natural is all around, and ever to be experienced with full senses.

These urban circumstances force on us a kind of intensity of focus that we often lack in daily life. In another of Dreisetl's designs, the water elements of Potsdamer Platz in Berlin, visitors are confronted with a narrow set of steps through water. There are no railings here, and Dreiseitl (2001) notes that here, in such settings, people are "responsible for their feet and not their insurance companies" (Dreiseitl 2001, p. 133). As Dreisetl tells us, water provides many benefits. Among them, he says, is "atmosphere"; it helps in strengthening the uniqueness of a place, its individuality, the sense of being home.

Seeking beauty through waterscapes and water design is a marvelous response to our present, unsustainable relationships to water. These unsustainable aspects take many forms, including water shortages and overconsumption, flooding and disruptions of natural hydrological systems, and contamination of water from urban runoff and nonpoint-source pollutants. The possibility of hope and renewal and new connections to water are evident in these urban waterscapes.

Reestablishing and Sustaining Connections with Land and Landscapes

There are many actions that can be taken to strengthen community bonds through connections to urban land resources. Often, they present special opportunities to achieve other important social goals, such as providing employment for the unemployed and a sense of hope about the future.

Grassroots urban gardening initiatives around the country illustrate well this potential. One of the better known organizations with this mission is the San Francisco League of Urban Gardeners (affectionately referred to as SLUG). Among its many efforts has been to promote urban gardening in and around low-income neighborhoods in that city. The best functioning example is the St. Mary's Urban Youth Farm, started in 1995, on a former dump site adjacent to the Alemary public housing project. Here a functioning urban farm has emerged, complete with row crops, fruit trees, and raised flower beds. The farm employs teenage garden interns who work for a small wage and learn about horticulture, landscape management, and business.

The farm also represents a microcosm of sustainable living. Recycled materials from the site, such as waste concrete, were used to build retaining walls and walkways, and compost and mulch produced on the farm is now sold as a product. Restoration of the ecology of the site, including a nearby wetland and stream, are also part of the agenda. Food from the farm satisfies many important needs, including providing a direct source of nourishment for residents of the Alemary complex and for local soup kitchens. Much of the food is processed and marketed under the organic label "Urban Herbals" and sold in local stores.

A working farm is also a key ecological design element of the new EVA-Lanxmeer neighborhood in Culemborg, Netherlands. This adjacent farm will eventually provide organic produce for Lanxmeer residents, and will also provide the opportunity for residents to work on the farm. It provides an important open-space amenity, accessible to walking and bicycling. More broadly, the farm will provide local, ecologically produced food for the town of Culemborg. Existing orchards have also been integrated into the neighborhood and will be managed and harvested as well.

Another inspirational model of local leadership in promoting sustainable local food production is Intervale, in Burlington, Vermont. A 700-acre agricultural floodplain, partially within the city limits, it is now home to twelve organic farms, providing some 500,000 pounds of food to Burlington area residents (see www.intervale.org). About half of the farms operate as CSAs, or Community Supported Agriculture. Based on an idea originating in Japan, local residents buy shares in these farms, entitling them to a basket of vegetables (and often flowers) each week during the growing seasons. CSAs overcome the typical anonymity of the food production/consumption process, establish direct personal connections between farms and local residents, and help to keep income and money local. The number of CSA farms nationally continues to grow each year, and currently number more than 1,000.

One of the special initiatives at the Intervale is a Farm Venture Program, a kind of farming incubator effort that assists, educates, and nurtures new small farmers, recognizing the need to help proactively in the creation and successful running of new local farms and farmers. Other unique programs include a food security initiative that provides opportunities for youth in the city to spend time learning about farming and seeks to make healthy food grown at Intervale available to residents of more disadvantaged neighborhoods in the city; a native tree nursery; and a municipal compost facility (that generates and sells 10,000 pounds of finished compost each year). Also on the drawing board is a Community Food Enterprise Center, which would provide shared greenhouse, food processing, and storage space; a community kitchen; and a venue for a variety of education and research activities.

Figure 5.13 | A working farm is a key element of the new ecological community EVA-Lanxmeer, in Culemborg, Netherlands.

Urban food production in Chicago has recently received some deserved attention, with positive stories in the *New York Times* and the *Chicago Tribune* (Abdur-Rahman, 2003; Davey, 2003). Food is grown on vacant city-owned land and a nonprofit organization called the Resource Center, started by urban farmer and recycler Ken Dunn, employs local residents and generates a fair amount of cash from pedaling their wares to local gourmet restaurants.

It is remarkable what can be produced on such small snippets of land. Ken Dunn and his partner, Kristine Greiber, with the help of their 3-year old (highly enthusiastic) son Soren, and a handful of young employees, produce food on five small parcels. The most visible site is on the north end, across from Cabrini–Green, a notorious public housing project. Only 3/4 of an acre, this site produces about $20,000 worth of income from the sales to local restaurants. The vegetables are sold to local residents from an on-site farm store, but fetch even higher prices by local restaurants. The farm produces thirty different varieties of heirloom tomatoes. The restaurants are often upscale, such as the Ritz-Carlton Dining room, and chefs covet the freshness and taste of the locally produced food, and are willing in turn to pay more for it. The land is intensively farmed, and Dunn estimates the annual production of tomatoes at about 5,000 pounds. The taste and freshness of these tomatoes is legendary with local restaurants. The secret, Dunn believes, is growing the plants in nearly 100% compost. The compost comes from their own composting facility that takes among other things, the organic wastes from several restaurants. A nearby stable brings their manure, also, relieving them of a major disposal headache.

The land is rented from the city for a dollar, and free water is also provided from a nearby city hydrant. The whole operation is designed to be movable, and given short-term nature of the leases, the understanding from the beginning is that the land will eventually be developed. The fence has actually been used elsewhere before, and will be transported later to a new site, and even the 18 inches of compost will be scooped-up and transported when the time comes. Dunn and partner Greiber view what they are doing in Cabrini Green as a model, as an experiment, as a prototype that shows the possibilities of small-scale sustainable urban agriculture. Dunn's future vision for Chicago is one where urban farms would sprout up throughout the city, or some of the estimated 9,000 acres of vacant land in the city, some 40,000 parcels. Ken's future vision to see these movable farms as a generator of local jobs, as community focal points, as places where it makes sense for the city to provide a variety of social services (including soup kitchens and community food dispersal points).

The benefits of this urban farm are many and not always obvious. Its location means there is a steady stream of people, many from the nearby public housing, and a nearby elderly complex, and the farm is a green resource for them, a place where they can purchase healthier food at an onsite farm stand. Many passersby stop to chat or ask questions. It is a green oasis that helps anchor the community, provide a pleasant view from the windows of public housing units. The farm provides training and apprenticeship to young urban farmers. Dunn estimates that if the model were used through out the city it would generate some 20,000 jobs. School groups make visits to the farm, and during the summer it is the site of organized dinners. Ken Dunn and his group clean up the sites, add value to the neighborhood, and inspire hope in a green urban future.

Local food production, reconnecting food consumers to the land, and landscape that produce the food they eat, can also help address basic food security and equity concerns. A new sustainable food initiative in the Austin community on the west side of Chicago, for instance, offers some promise. Part of the Kellogg Foundation's food security initiative, Chicago State University students are engaged in a comprehensive study of food availability, quality, and price in this predominantly African-American community. Eventually, the hope (or vision) is that a community cooperative grocery will be formed, and that low-income black farmers in rural areas south of the city will be able to directly sell their produce here (Peterson, 2003). Organically and locally produced, and providing a fair price to these farmers, the outcome provides less expensive, healthier food to this poor community, and at the same time reduces the carbon and energy footprint of the food. There are a multitude of creative variations on this theme, but such strategies simultaneously strengthen the economy of surrounding rural areas (and the value of rural land for these sustaining functions), improve urban neighborhoods, and connect these places to each other in some direct and visceral ways.

Every new housing development and new urban (or suburban) neighborhood should design-in the opportunity to grow food. Viikki, in Helsinki, rep-

Figure 5.14 | This city farm in Chicago produces vegetables for nearby restaurants, sells food to the nearby Cabrini Green housing project, and is a compelling model for regenerating economy, community, and environment.

resents a fantastic example of integrating gardens and food production into this new mixed-use neighborhood. The result of a design competition, the winning master plan by Petri Laaksonen envisioned a series of green fingers or wedges between major blocks of housing, the spaces available for garden allotments. Stormwater is collected on-site and retained in underground cisterns, with hand-operated water pumps making this water available at key points near the gardens. The allotments are preciously guarded and shepherded by residents. As one resident working in her garden on a spring afternoon explained, she was extremely happy to see her plot from her upstairs flat. The plots are well used and a key synthesizing feature of this unique neighborhood. The Viikki plan also includes a larger area of garden allotments available to residents of the area, including a gardening information center to help would-be gardeners. The ability to grow food was important enough to Helsinki officials that it was explicitly incorporated into the minimum eco-design criteria that projects have to satisfy.

Growing food on-site or within the neighborhood is one important community-building step, but there are also many ways to forge real and sustainable relationships between local and regional farmers and urban residents who increasingly care where their food comes from and how it is produced. The Good Food Box, an initial of the Toronto nonprofit Food-Share, is one possible model for how to do this. Started in 1994, it is essentially a service that assembles boxes of fresh vegetables and fruits and delivers them to 200 neighborhood drop-off points in that city. Lower-income neighborhoods are targeted, and the boxes are sold at a discounted price. The program has been very successful; it distributed some 4,000 boxes every month in 2003, and has been able to connect local producers with local residents in need of affordable, healthy, fresh food. Emphasis is given to buying from Ontario farms, and more than half the food comes from these local producers. (FoodShare, undated; Scharf, undated). Relationships with a number of local farms have been established and nourished. With the neighborhood drop-off points and distribution of food boxes undertaken by volunteers, it's also a good example of social capital building.

Of course, other creative ways of more effectively connecting consumers with local farmers abound. Making it as easy as possible to support local producers means looking for commercial endeavors that bridge the inevitable gulf between the process and the places where food is produced and where it is commonly prepared and eaten. And unfortunately, the separation between consumers and producers is maintained through inertia and routine. Many of us just can't imagine any other way to collect our sustenance then the trip to the large grocery store.

David van Seters represents some of this new entrepreneurial spirit of place making. In 1998, not long after receiving his MBA, van Seters started a company called Small Potatoes Urban Delivery (SPUD) in the greater Vancouver region of British Columbia. SPUD customers place their orders for more than a thousand grocery items by e-mail, with the produce and grocery goods delivered to their doorsteps. The best part is that most of the goods are sourced from local producers, a primary goal of this environmentally minded business. SPUD now has some 5,000 customers, makes 2,700 weekly deliveries with its fleet of natural gas–fueled delivery trucks. Delivered produce comes from more than fifty local growers (Bhatty, 2004).

Restaurants can also play an important role here. The Frontera Grill in Chicago, and its owner, Rick Bayless, not only buys from and strongly supports Ken Dunn's urban farm, they see an obligation to support small, local, ecological farms more generally. They have developed long-term relationships with a number of growers in the region, and have even recently formed the Frontera Farmer Foundation to provide small grants to "small, sustainable midwestern farms serving the Chicago area." (See www .fronterakitchens.com). The menu at Frontera is scrumptious and authentic Mexican, and Rick Bayless even hosts a PBS shows "Mexico One Plate At A Time." But at the end of the menu, below the Crema de Quelites and Taquitos de Pollo, is a commendable statement to its customers: "Our goal is to serve you seasonal sustainably raised vegetables, meat and poultry; fish from sustainable fisheries. We support local artisanal farmers." (www .fronterakitchens.com).

There is considerable support for organic, locally grown food, in every sense (buying it, eating it, ordering it in restaurants), and in turn for taking responsibility for the secondary effects of our individual food-purchasing decisions. In a recent telephone survey of 372 residents of Madison, Wisconsin, for instance, 73 percent of the respondents expressed concern about "the presence of chemical and nutrient residues from food production and processing in Madison-area wells, streams, and lakes" (Stevens and Raja, 2001, p. 9). About 70 percent expressed concerns about the solid waste produced from food packaging, and 50 percent indicated concerns about soil erosion and consumption of oil associated with the food production system.

Respondents in the Madison survey furthermore expressed support for farmers' markets and locally produced food. Although residents of this progressive university city may be more aware of food issues than average Americans, such a survey does reflect, I believe, tremendous support for rethinking our contemporary food production and delivery system, as well as a growing market for a new system. (Other surveys provide similar evidence; see, for example, New Economics Foundation, 2003.) For most Americans, the challenge is likely to be in seeing easy ways to give meaning and expression to these values. What easy alternative is there for a Virginian buying a California-grown tomato, or a Washington-grown apple, at the local chain grocery?

Buying a share in a CSA is one option; frequently, the local farmers' market is another. Farmers' markets, while increasingly appreciated by urban residents (there are now more than 3,000 farmers markets throughout the United States), face tremendous challenges in cities today. One of the most significant is in finding spaces for them. It is not uncommon for such markets to experience considerable impermanence and instability, as more lucrative businesses outbid them and displace them from established sites. As markets are forced to move from site to site within a city, residents are understandably frustrated at knowing where they are and how to find them.

This "instability" is precisely what is threatening farmers' markets in Pittsburgh, for example. New commercial development, including a Kmart, and road construction projects are taking priority. In the words of one frustrated farmer, "There's got to be someplace they can put us. We've been pushed and shoved around pretty good" (as quoted in Gaynor, 2001). Some blame the mayor for not making the markets a priority, and for giving priority to larger projects like a new downtown stadium.

Finding permanent sites is a challenge, to be sure, but an essential condition for farmers' markets. Comparing the status and importance given to community markets in cities like Pittsburgh with their centrality in most

European cities is striking. In my temporary home of Leiden, the market occurred in central, regular locations on days known to everyone. The market itself comprised both sides of a major canal in the center of the city, in the historic core, accessible to many residents by walking or bicycling.

Farmers' markets provide many benefits to both community sustainability and community strengthening. They help support local production of food, reducing substantially the problem of unsustainably produced food being transported hundreds of miles, consuming considerable energy, and sending the economic food dollars outside the community. That farmers who sell at farmers' markets rely on this income to a large degree is evident. A recent survey of farmers at Pittsburgh markets found that such markets supplied some 75 percent of their income (survey by Pittsburgh Citiparks, cited in Gaynor, 2001).

Supporting regional farmers' markets with larger, more permanent locations, closer perhaps to Leiden's model, is an option for American cities as well. Developing a coordinated plan or strategy and giving markets permanent space must be part of the answer. In Pittsburgh, under the leadership of Sustainable Pittsburgh, a Farmers' Market Alliance has been created to advocate and push for these interests and to coordinate information and planning activity.

Figure 5.15 | Farmers' markets help to connect local producers and local consumers, and have grown in popularity and number.

Larger permanent public markets (often enclosed) are an important strategy as well. These spaces, like Washington D.C.'s Eastern Market, become important community and neighborhood hubs, offering a large array of foods and goods, and have the advantage of stability and (relative) permanence in terms of locations. Indoor space is desirable in harsh climates, making these markets a year-round resource for communities. The Portland Public Market, in Portland, Maine, is one of the most successful. Opened in 1998, it provides a permanent space for some thirty vendors selling locally grown foods and goods. The Westside Market in Cleveland's Ohio City neighborhood dates to 1912, and is itself housed in a lovely and recently renovated "neo-classical/Byzantine style" structure. Markets like these also serve as public spaces, and places for community and public events and activities and meetings of various sorts. The Westside Market was not long ago the site of rally and protest against the Iraq war, by the Cleveland Nonviolence Network. Kansas City's permanent City market, north of its downtown, contains a farmers' market, restaurants, and a music venue for the city. The Portland Market in Maine contains a demonstration kitchen, and offers cooking classes. The building itself is a positive addition to place. Its large timber-framed structure built by "Maine timber craftsmen" includes a large granite fireplace (from Deer Isle granite).

The Bounty of Local Landscapes: Producing and Consuming Locally

More generally, the concept of a sustainable place argues that what can be produced and consumed locally is preferable to systems of excessive importing of goods and services, with the concomitant exporting or externalizing of the environmental and other costs associated with this consumption. This does much to build understandings of and commitments to place. From a sustainability perspective, there are important reasons to support such regimes. When production and consumption are brought closer together, there is greater accountability for environmental impacts, and a greater sense of connection and bond between consumer and producer, and the common landscapes that support them both.

Fostering sustainable local production, and developing markets for these sustainably generated goods is not always an easy task, but it does have great potential for strengthening a unique sense of place. In southwest Virginia and northeast Tennessee, for example, the nonprofit organization Appalachian Sustainable Development (ASD) has been working hard to nurture markets for local lumber and wood, harvested from small woodlot owners, using sustainable techniques including pulling logs out with teams of horses. ASD has developed a set of strict environmental standards and their own Sustainable Woods label for marketing the wood. A solar-and-wood-waste-powered drying kiln, in combination with a portable sawmill, has the potential to produce some 240,000 board feet of lumber (see www.appsusdev.org; Still, 2003). The ASD sustainable forests and wood initiative holds the potential to connect producers who are striving to be better long-term stewards of local forest resources, and protecting these important natural qualities of place, with consumers willing to keep their dollars closer to home. A local school and library are two examples of recent use of ASD-certified timber, with beautiful results. ASD Executive director Anthony Flaccavento has embarked on a broader effort to market the timber regionally, in towns and urban centers such as Charlottesville, Virginia, and Asheville, North Carolina. Stronger places benefit on several levels.

Figure 5.16 | Anthony Flaccavento, executive director of Appalachian Sustainable Development, stands in front of its solar drying kiln. ASD's sustainable forestry program works to support low-impact, sustainable forest management in southwest Virginia and northeast Tennessee.

Production and consumption can be brought even closer together. Many spaces in cities represent excellent opportunities for planting fruit trees and edible landscapes, opportunities for both sustainable living and the further development of local economy. In Asheville, North Carolina, the nonprofit *City Seeds* has planted what may be the first "edible park." With one acre of land provided by the city, an array of edible-fruit-bearing shrubs and trees were planted, including apple, peach, pecan, mulberry, currant, and fig, as well as herbs of various sorts. An outgrowth of the Bountiful City Project, other sites for edible parks within the city have been identified.

The Asheville park illustrates the possibility of consciously viewing cities and urban areas not just in terms of generating demand for fruits and vegetables, but as places where food items can be grown and with a view that cities are fertile, if unconventional, bountiful fields. Spaces in and around buildings could be used to grow berries and other fruit, urban forests can be the source of many kinds of nuts and fruits.

And these harvestable goods can be the sources of considerable economy in urban neighborhoods. Collecting can provide many of the goods sold in community markets and can be used as a way for community groups to raise money. Those who focus on urban agriculture and forestry have a name for these goods—urban nontimber forest products (NTFP). As a category, NTFP include a variety of edible and economically valuable materials, including mushrooms, maple syrup, berries, cones, and medicinal plants, among many others. NTFPs often provide important supplemental food and income for communities, and represent a method of forest use that generally conserves the resource and is both born from and strengthens a sense of connection to environment and place. As a recent fact sheet about NTFP notes, these activities help strengthen our awareness of the seasons and cycles of nature:

> A meal that includes wild onions . . . fiddleheads . . . or dandelion greens . . . is
> a harbinger of spring. A mushroom hunt on a damp autumn day confirms the
> end of summer and provides a rewarding excuse for the pleasure of a day in the
> woods. Many gatherers speak of the personal importance of maintaining their
> connection to the natural world and its cycles through their harvesting activi-
> ties. (Emery, 2001, pp. 2–3)

A 2000 study of NTFPs by a Baltimore group called Community Resources found a remarkable number of collecting, growing, and economic uses in that city. They found over 103 products generated from 78 different species, and that there had been considerable economic benefits (as high as $100 per year per tree for mature fruit trees) (Community Resources, 2000). Several categories of use were identified, including edible, medicinal, horticultural or nursery, and uses as craft items and decorative products (www.communityresources.org).

Jahnige (2002) observes that in urban neighborhoods where these growing and collecting opportunities exist, not only are viable economic options and alternatives expanded where they are needed most, but the acts of collecting and growing can build bonds between and among neighbors and help strengthen place.

> Many people collect urban NTFPs to give as gifts and share their harvest bounty with neighbors or friends. Sharing and gift giving is an important form of social reciprocity and an example of how urban NTFP collection can help build connections between people in urban communities.

Urban forests, community forests, offer tremendous potential in creating more sustainable places, and in binding us to specific places. Positive and compelling examples exist of cities and communities owning and managing community forests, variously as a source of timber and income, and for the recreational and ecological benefits they provide. The community forest in Arcata, California, is one of the most interesting, in that it is managed to yield a sustainable yearly harvest level, with the resulting wood sold as certified sustainably managed.

The city of Arcata actually owns two forests, both managed sustainably: the Arcata Community Forest is about 600 acres, and the Jacoby Creek Forest is 525 acres. An initiative passed by the citizens of Arcata in 1979 called for a management plan based on principles of ecological forestry. The harvested wood is sent only to local mills, and the logging occurs only through local logging contractors. A substantial amount of income is generated for the city from the harvest, which goes into managing the forests and funding stream and habitat restoration.

Arcata's forests provide important environmental and ecological services, and the Arcata Community Forest provides an incredible recreational resource for residents. Included are 11 miles of spectacular trails close to the city and within easy access of many. This forest is part of the enjoyment of living in Arcata, a part of what makes Arcata a distinctive place, and a critical aspect of moving in the direction of more sustainable forms of production and consumption.

In London, the borough of Croydon has become perhaps the first *entire* community to become certified (by the Forest Stewardship Council) as a sustainable forest. Here, the city literally *is* the forest. Not only does Croydon have its own blocks of forestland, which are used locally for lumber, but its street tree trimmings and cuttings are used for fuel in local combined heat and power plants.

In both Arcata and Croydon these forested landscapes provide important ecological and watershed services and are important in place building, by creating enjoyable green urban living environments. At the same time, they

Figure 5.17 | The Arcata Community Forest in Arcata, California. This forest is owned by the city of Arcata and sustainably harvested.

express the hope and potential of sustainable consumption and productive patterns—where local and regional landscapes, sustainably managed, not only provide local goods and services, but build clear and direct connections with the land while also building local economy.

New housing projects and neighborhoods in our communities can as well be designed and planned in ways that utilize local resources, minimize the drawdown of resources and ecological systems from outside one's region, and creatively recycle waste as a productive good. It is now common, for instance, to stipulate that building materials come only from within a certain distance or radius of a building location. In the case of London's Beddington Zero-Energy Development (BedZED) (discussed in greater detail in Chapter 11), most of the building materials come from within a 300-mile radius—bricks from a local company, wood from Croydon's forests, and so on. These projects and initiatives show convincingly that it is possible to build and live more lightly on the planet, strengthen connections between people, and build community, and in the process strengthen our commitments to actual places.

Conclusions

Humans need nature, and as the examples in this chapter demonstrate, there are many, many ways to integrate and design-in nature and the natural environment in all the building and city planning that we do. From green rooftops to urban forests to green streets, a major challenge in creating places that work and places that matter is to find creative ways to green them and to make them full of nature. Green neighborhoods and green cities will both instill greater love of and commitment to these places and address a host of ecological challenges and problems faced today, from climate change to biodiversity conservation to energy self-sufficiency, among many others. Cities and urban places have historically been viewed as antithetical to and the opposite of "nature," and this is one obstacle of perception and attitude that must be overcome in future place making. The greener and more full of nature are our neighborhoods and communities and cities, the healthier will be our local population and our planet. To modify Henry David Thoreau somewhat, "In *urban* wildness is the preservation of the world."

Pedestrian Places

Places that provide abundant opportunities to walk, to spend time socializing with others, and to simply *be* in public spaces and in the collective realm are likely to be places to which our ties are greater and our emotional bonds more significant. But current attitudes and community policies in the United States make it hard to actually live a walking life. Adults spend close to 90 percent of their time indoors (Klepeis et al., 2001). In a sample of more than 9,000 individuals, total time spent indoors was 86.9 percent. An additional 5.5 percent of time was spent in vehicles, and thus only 7.6 percent of time outside. This is not a good beginning in imagining a walking culture and society.

Not only is this unhealthy but it will also not do much to create community or strengthen place. Snowstorms like the one that paralyzed much of the East Coast in February 2003 tell us many things about how our communities function (or don't) and provide us glimpses of how they might work. The roadways are inevitably cleared first, while sidewalks are left uncleared or, rather, have snow heaped on them from the street plowing. Real snow days are a glorious throwback to former times when cars were less important. What you see on these days provides some hope for the rebuilding of community. Neighbors wave at each other as they shovel driveways; children sled; there is friendliness and sense of common predicament that binds, at least for a fleeting time. And we seem to have more time, of course, as many shops and businesses are closed and many roads are still treacherous or impassable. It serves to neutralize, at least for a short time, the isolating, separating effect of cars. These experiences further reinforce, of course, the need for compact land use and connected streets, but more fundamentally they provide an unusual insight into the possibility of a pedestrian, community-centered life. Perhaps we need more snow days, but perhaps we ought to look for ways to create these conditions and opportunities and feelings every day.

Too many of the choices about the trips we make and the ways we shop, get to work, and get our kids to school involve the car. We no longer walk to our jobs, often because they are far away, because we need to run errands during the day, or because we need to drop off or pick up our children from school or band practice or a soccer game on the way. According to the 2000 Census, a dismal 2.7 percent of home-to-work trips are by foot, and even fewer (.04 percent) are by bicycle. Children, of course, are in turn walking less, and a walk or a bicycle ride to school seems a rarity. Although just thirty years ago about two-thirds of school-age kids in the United States walked or rode their bikes to school, today fewer than 20 percent do so. The causes are predictable but not irreversible. It is perhaps not hard to understand—the car is typically always waiting for us in the driveway or garage; we worry about the dangers our kids might face in walking to school; and in communities where car traffic has really taken over, it may be virtually impossible to physically get to where we want or need to go by any means other than the car.

It is ironic perhaps that many of the cities that Americans most want to visit and spend time in—for example, Paris, New York, and Copenhagen—are cities with abundant public spaces and where walking is the main tourist activity. And Americans walk a lot when they visit such places, but don't seem to make the connection that these same qualities are possible in their hometowns and cities as well.

The Compelling Nature of the Pedestrian Realm

The social functions of public spaces—streets, plazas, courtyards—are especially important to us all. William Whyte (1980) tells of this dynamic in terms of "triangulation," or "that process by which some external stimulus provides a linkage between people and prompts strangers to talk to each other as if they were not" (p. 94). This can take the form of an object or piece of public art or a performer such as a street musician. Whyte elaborates eloquently on the value of these spontaneous exchanges:

> Street characters make the city more amicable. Mr. Magoo, who volunteers as a traffic director in midtown New York, will always draw a crowd, and his performance will draw its members together. The person standing next to you is likely to tell you all about his history, or ask you who in the world he is. The witch, a raunchy woman who jeers at the dignified and spits at little children, is quite deplorable. Strangers exchange shocked glances. But they smile, too, as if they were on her side. (p. 94)

I think we all have similar stories and similar experiences. I remember a few years back the ubiquitous presence of a street character in the Adams Morgan neighborhood in Washington, D.C. Known to all as the "compliment man," his modus operandi was to shower every passerby with effusive (and loud) compliments. The experience was a bonding one, at least momentarily, for those within earshot.

The Barcelona Rambla (or Las Ramblas), the main pedestrian street in that city, epitomizes the concept of streets as public stage. Over the course of

Figure 6.1 | Street musicians on Las Ramblas in Barcelona, Spain.

a day or two, a visitor is likely to see as many as thirty different street acts, mimes, dancers, and musicians, ranging from the common or mainstream to the unusual. Typical musicians include classical guitarists, harpsichord players, and even solo vocalists. The scene also includes dancers; flamenco dancers and even break dancing are common sights. The quality of these performances varies, but some of the musicians are astoundingly talented. Among the more unusual might be the woman lying under a boulder waiting to be (for a few Euro-cents) rescued, or the pilot sitting in a home-made, human-powered airplane, waiting, again for a few Euro-cents, to begin his fanciful flight.

There are many lessons to be learned from these best pedestrian cities of the world. In Venice, Italy, it is a rich mixture of *campi,* or the small public squares that dot the old city, and a maze of pedestrian routes leading to and from these squares, taking one along canals and across bridges. Many of the smaller pedestrian routes have little more than space enough for one person to walk comfortably in one direction. The *campi* and *calli* (streets) are well marked and contain a diverse and interesting mix of uses and activities. Restaurants and cafés, stores, vegetable stands, art stores, and galleries are all together, side by side. Buildings, for the most part, are four or five stories tall, and seem an appropriate scale; taller structures, one feels, would overwhelm the public spaces of the *campi.*

But Venice itself has been going through many changes and facing many challenges. Maintaining a vibrant, viable resident population is but one challenge. About five years ago, local planning laws were changed to allow residential structures to be converted to small hotels—a questionable move, some believe. Long-term residents bemoan the expansion of these small hotels, and the general proliferation of tourist-oriented businesses. (There are many, many shops that sell Venetian masks, for instance.)

Venice's high water, or *aqua alta,* which happens with increasing frequency, also presents special challenges for pedestrians and for the movement of goods. One overriding impression when water in the streets is knee-high in some places is that it does not stop the movement or the pedestrian life of the city. Residents, and the many individuals involved in movement of goods, from furniture to luggage to store deliveries, find creative ways to cope. Partly, it means finding alternative routes. Elevated scaffolding in some

Figure 6.2 | Campo San Luca, one of the smallest but most active and delightful of the small squares in Venice, Italy.

places, and a supply of high boots that await those who need them, are other adaptations. Ground-level cafés, restaurants, and stores are prepared: most have portable flood doors that are quickly put into place; pumps work to expel water, hotels put down paper covers to protect carpeted stairs, and doors are taken off hinges and placed above the water line.

The *aqua alta* is an occasion for celebrating cooperation, though, and in some ways, for building community. Those with boots commonly give "piggyback" rides to strangers, and strangers routinely exchange information about alternative routes to avoid high water. During one recent event, two teenage students without boots found themselves unable to walk more than a few feet in any direction; frantic on their cell phones, they were eventually given rides to safety on the backs of kind strangers.

Beyond Auto Worries

Few cities provide as much experiential evidence of the power and potential of a walking life as Venice, and as much relief from the worries about cars and car traffic felt especially by parents of small children.

Venice has relatively few gardens and parks, but the complete absence of cars makes it safe for children to play anywhere, even in the middle of the street. The entire city serves as their playground, and, as children grow, they can safely walk to each other's homes, even from a very young age. Younger children walk to school, and older children sometimes take the ferry.

In Venice, there is an incredible positive feeling of space, literal and mental, created by neutralizing the auto—that is, designing-out the auto. People walk because they must, but also because they enjoy it. Even on these very narrow streets, 4 or 5 feet wide, an incredible number of people are able to pass by. The daily life schedule incorporates time for strolling. The evening hours from 5:00 to 7:00 are universally considered the strolling period—the hours before dinner, when kids kick the soccer ball around the *campi*, couples window-shop, and families enjoy time together outside. When travel to farther destinations is required, most people use the water-based public transit—an excellent system of water-buses, or *vaporetti*.

Further contributing to this rich pedestrian life is a general feeling of security and safety on the streets. Even fairly late into the evening, there is little fear of being mugged, accosted, or otherwise harmed. The incidence of street crimes is very low. One of the clear reasons for feeling secure is the presence of many different shops and businesses, all with a clear view of streets and, indeed, often with open doors and windows. One is never very far from a corner café or trattoria or market.

Here Jane Jacobs's ideas, articulated so profoundly in her classic 1961 *Death and Life of Great American Cities,* remain as important as ever. A vital street life—pedestrian sidewalks, sufficient urban densities, short blocks, mixed uses, diverse housing, and efforts to reduce and moderate car traffic—all combine to create vibrant, safe neighborhoods, and neighborhoods with a rich social life and network of social relations. Her vision of an inherently walkable city endures today. Jacobs's own Greenwich Village, and other neighborhoods in New York City, are certainly positive models of pedestrian districts, as are parts of Boston, San Francisco, and New Orleans, to name only a few. Increasingly, it seems there are impressive and creative initiatives in North American cities to promote walking. Several U.S. cities, including Portland, Oregon and Oakland, California, have prepared Pedestrian Master Plans, putting pedestrians and walking on a more equal footing with cars, and putting forth both a comprehensive vision of a walking city and a tangible set of projects and actions, including investments that expand pedestrian infrastructure, that can be taken to reach this vision.

The City of Toronto has done much to elevate pedestrian concerns in local government decision making and planning. In 2002, Toronto took the bold step of adopting a "pedestrian charter," which, among other things, "upholds the right of pedestrians of all ages and abilities to safe, convenient, direct and comfortable walking conditions" (City of Toronto, 2002, p. 1). While not a legal document, its intent is to promote awareness, to encourage walking, and to elevate attention to pedestrianism in the city's urban design and planning (City of Toronto, undated).

And so I am drawn back to Venice for inspiration. For me, one of the more compelling spaces is the Campo Santa Margherita. One of the larger *campi* in Venice, it bubbles with activity and energy even in winter. Configured as a rectangle that narrows and curves on one end, forming a point, it can, like most *campi,* be entered from different directions. As you enter the square, your senses are fully engaged, you see the variation in the buildings, the different architectural details and color façades. There is a fish market and a small vegetable stand. Cafés and restaurants surround the square with tables, and awnings to cover them in winter, extending into the *campo,* though not at all taking space away from pedestrians. There is a feeling of spaciousness to this *campo.* The spaces feel right, and the relationship between buildings (which are no more than four stories tall), spaces, and people feels natural. The surrounding development could be denser, but the design qualities of these spaces are superb. One can sit at one end of the *campo* with clear views of virtually the entire space.

Many cities and towns in Spain offer similarly impressive street qualities—function, beauty, and activity. In Gavà, in Barcelona province, for instance, the downtown is organized around an impressive linear walking street, or *rambla.* Las Ramblas of Gavà actually consist of three different named *ramblas*: beginning with Rambla de Lluch, extending to Rambla de Vayreda and Rambla de Casas. The street begins at one end of the city's bustling train station, with other pedestrian streets branching off from it. It balances well in a way similar to the *ramblas* in Barcelona, the pedestrian and car realms. With a pedestrian corridor in the center of the space, about 20

Figure 6.3 | A diversity of small shops and a high degree of pedestrian activities characterize Venetian *campi* like this one, Campo Santa Maria Formosa.

feet wide, car traffic is permitted by way of a single lane along the side of the street (one lane in each direction, plus a row of on-street parking). Traffic is permitted to cross the pedestrian street at six different points, though again at very low speeds.

The street is alive and full of pedestrians much of the day and into the night, and for the most part because of the key reasons already mentioned: there are extensive shops with considerable diversity, the positive synergy with an active train station, and fairly dense housing (six- to seven-story apartment buildings) along the street and above the shops and businesses all along the corridor. The highest-density apartments are to be found on the corners of intersecting streets. As there is considerable variation in building height throughout the block, with many buildings in the three- or four-story range, there is no particular feeling of claustrophobia or crowdedness.

There is a considerable diversity of activities and commercial establishments along the Rambla Gavà. More than eighty stores and shops, ranging from banks to stores selling everything from electronics to clothing, furniture, cameras, real estate, and jewelry. Evidence that this is a neighborhood shopping area—that is, an area for people living nearby—can be seen through the presence of extensive bars and restaurants, dry cleaners, a bakery, and a dentist. Small grocers, though not on the *rambla* itself, are to be found on nearby side streets. The stores and commercial life of the Rambla Gavà seem to be thriving—the construction of a new suburban-style mall, with a multiplex theatre and very large grocery store, has been a serious threat. So far, the Gavà downtown appears to be holding its own, likely for many of the basic reasons these spaces work—their attractiveness, their function, and the fact that they are places people want to be and hang out.

There are also many things about Gavà's *rambla* that work very well. A busy train station at one end, feeding pedestrians into the center, certainly helps. The *ramblas* of Gavà, though not very wide—perhaps 100 feet—work very well. Two rows of trees define the edge of the pedestrian spaces, along with a short row of bushes. Extensive rows of benches along the way provide ample seating.

At the other end is a well-designed and well-used multifunctional park. It contains an open field (for soccer playing), a public stage and space for music and public events, a municipal museum and café, and an extensive children's play area. The playground runs along much of the edge of the Rambla Gavà, and can be seen from it, though it is accessible only from specific gates. The play area functions well and is flanked by benches that allow casual play with relaxed supervision and parental socializing. On the opposite side is a police station, with police vehicles parked out front, giving an added sense of security to the space.

The spaces of Gavà also show how new plazas can creatively emerge from the intersection of pedestrian streets. This happens with the Plaza de Josep Tarradellas, which is formed from the triangular spaces to the west of the *rambla*. Benches, trees (eight fairly large trees in this small space, forming the perimeter), and a spectacular example of public art in the center provide a beautiful space for respite and conversation. A walkway on the north edge of this space allows those passing through to skirt along the side. The edge itself is a wall about 1 foot high and 1 foot wide, which provides additional seating for the plaza.

Measuring Important Space Qualities

The places and spaces we are attracted to, that we want to visit, stroll along, and hang out in, have important and special qualities. They are interesting, they feel comfortable and safe, and they are functional in the sense that there are things to do, reasons to be there, distances and spaces that are not overly daunting to travel to or through.

Many of these qualities are not immediately obvious, but can be discerned in some of our most treasured pedestrian destinations. In a recent field study undertaken in Venice, I took some approximate counts of the diversity of uses and activities around and within a short distance of *campi*. Several different types of *campi* were chosen, including one that is a more commercial-center *campi,* and several smaller, neighborhood *campi*. More specifically, counts were made in a (roughly) 100-meter (about 330 feet) radius of the *campi,* measured from the edge of these *campi*. The conclusions suggest a remarkable diversity of uses and commercial establishments within this small circle. In the case of Campo San Luca, a more commercial-center *campo*, the district around the *campo* is quite bustling. Directly on the *campo* itself is a good mix of activities: two banks (three ATMs), a corner store, a clothing store, a cosmetics store, a fast-food restaurant, a bookstore, and three cafés. By my count, within this approximate 100-meter radius are another 103 shops, reflecting a substantial diversity of services and goods. This amazing diversity is important for several reasons. In the same way that diversity of architecture is stimulating, so also is the variation in the shops and restaurants and services available in a community. There is a resulting visual and social texture that is place strengthening. Such a small-scale commercial scene ensures that more money and resources are recirculated locally, and allows for greater local control of the products and services offered. Moreover, these small shops carry with them shop owners and shopkeepers, a kind of living infrastructure—people who typically care about their neighborhoods, have the time for casual conversation, and provide "eyes on the street," in Jane Jacobs's words (Jacobs, 1961).

In Campo Santa Maria Formosa, the shop and store count is even higher than in Campo San Luca. A larger campo in physical size, it feels more em-

Figure 6.4 | The Campo Santa Maria Formosa, Venice, Italy, is a popular gathering spot for teenagers.

bedded in a neighborhood, and less central, and less likely visited by those outside the very immediate area. Like Campo San Luca, lots of stores front directly on the *campo*—a hotel, a clothing store, a restaurant, a pharmacy, two banks, a music store, even a mortuary. The interior of the square is also active space for commerce, with an outdoor vegetable stand, a news kiosk, a clothing stand, and a flower vendor. Here the number and diversity of stores within 100 meters is even greater—111 stores, by my count, with an equivalent level of specialization.

When recording and counting different kinds of stores, it is often hard to categorize and to lump them together. One store might be a bakery, but with other market goods; another might be a small chocolate store, but with some pastries and bakery fare. One news shop might sell toys; another, tobacco products. This diversity is remarkable for the preponderance of small and very small stores. Average square footage is low, and storefronts are relatively short—in most cases, 8 to 12 feet in width, usually including a shop window. Some store widths are even narrower—I measured some less than 6 feet.

For the most part these are not chain stores, but are clearly local and locally owned stores. Venice is unique in comparison with many other historic European cities in the few number of large chain establishments—the one large store is a Benetton, which itself is a four-story urban store that fits nicely into its location near San Marco. There are several McDonald's, but they are very small and relatively inconspicuous.

One clear conclusion from this analysis of *campi,* and an explanation for why they seem to work, is the importance of having reasons for people to visit them and be in them in the first place. For most *campi* there are multiple reasons—visiting the stores, restaurants, and cafés; stopping at a cash machine or running an errand; and, very important, moving across a *campo*—essentially using it as a street—in traveling from one point to another in the city. These public spaces are not only destinations and places to be (to sit, play, talk), but they are vibrant avenues and movement corridors that add further to their life and energy. And, these *campi* support a relatively large residential population—Campo San Luca is formed by mostly five-story buildings, and thus, in virtually every case, extensive homes and apartments are above, behind, and around the shops and cafés.

The movement or flow of people through a *campo* must certainly have much to do with its energy and its functionality. In the case of Campo San Luca, there are seven different points of entrance, and so pedestrians from many routes and different directions are guided to, and often crisscross, the square. Even during the night or early morning a steady flow of pedestrians can be seen.

The attributes of the *campi* themselves make them delightful places to be, or to pass through. Campo San Luca, for instance, has interesting façades with clocks, sculptures embedded in the exterior walls, and building detailing worthy of stopping and looking. Typical *campi* have a cistern (that historically collected rooftop water, though today these systems are no longer in use) and water fountains near the center, and many have statues and other physical aspects that further enhance the spaces. The larger spaces, such as Campo San Stefano, are used for public functions and events, and for holiday festivities, such as the annual Christmas market.

The size, layout, and use patterns of *campi* further contribute to feelings of intimacy and safety. The combination of foot traffic, the relatively small

Figure 6.5 | The Campiello Dei Sequelini, Venice, Italy.

size (it's not really possible for someone to hide), and the large number of apartments looking directly over the *campo* create perceptions of safety (and the reality is that they are indeed rather safe!). A count of windows directly looking onto *campi* yields a surprisingly high number, giving further credence to their importance in generating feelings of safety and intimacy. At Campo Santa Maria Formosa, for example, I counted an amazing 466 windows looking directly onto the square. Even the windows that are shuttered or at vacant apartments contribute to the overall feeling of community. Another measure of the activity levels of *campi,* and comings and goings, is the high number of doors or entrances fronting on them. Like the windows, these entrances help explain, I believe, feelings of safety and security.

Public spaces in Barcelona also work extremely well—they are places where people want to be, where strolling is a way of life, where many activities of daily life are centered. Spaces like La Rambla, perhaps the best walking street in the world, exemplify pedestrian designs that work well. Extending about 1.5 kilometers (less than one mile) from Plaça de Catalunya to the city's famous statue of Columbus, it is the center of life for this city. It has all the essential qualities of good pedestrian spaces—reasons to be there, in the form of

Figure 6.6 | Las Ramblas, the main pedestrian street in Barcelona, is full of life and activity well into the evening.

restaurants, cafés, museums, and impressive architecture all around. The space itself is attractive and functional—two long rows of large trees; lots of green and shade in the summer months. There are chairs and places to sit, lots of things to do, and many people to see.

Barcelona's *Rambla,* while itself a linear street, also exemplifies a high degree of connectivity with the spaces and neighborhoods around it. Two lanes of highly calmed traffic (one-way) move on each side of the pedestrian street, but numerous pedestrian crossings make lateral moves off the La Rambla rather easy. One civic space leads to another. Adjoining spaces include the impressive Plaça Reial, which has more than thirty palm trees and a fantastic fountain that attracts people to its edge and presents great opportunities for sitting and watching. The square is flanked by street-level restaurants and cafés with outside seating looking over the goings-on in the square, with six- or seven-story flats above.

The linear pedestrian route has, for all practical purposes, been extended, with the completion of the Rambla de Mar, which provides access to a new entertainment area created on the water. This spectacular wooden bridge provides a new and already very popular pedestrian route to Mare Màgnum, a shopping area, cinemas, and the city's aquarium. One can walk nearly an

Figure 6.7 | The pedestrian street Morsstraat, in Leiden, the Netherlands. A short street, it contains a remarkable diversity of uses and activities, and many different building façades.

additional kilometer to the venues on the water, again with lots to see and experience along the way, and not much of a sense of having walked very far at all. For residents of Barcelona, and visitors as well, the amount of walking done in the center is indeed impressive. It is a street that pulls you along, to paraphrase Tony Hiss, that results in pedestrians walking much farther than they probably realize. La Rambla itself is about a kilometer long, and it would not be uncommon for Barceloneans to walk the length of it several times in an evening or on a weekend day.

There are many things, of course, that we can do to make such public spaces more inviting. Many practical issues, such as providing abundant places to sit and adequate bathrooms, are not to be underestimated. Especially for families with children, restroom access is an essential part of what makes spaces attractive or unattractive. Partly, I think, this is a planning regulatory issue. Many of the stores and restaurants along the busiest streets and plazas restrict access to their restrooms to patrons only, even though they benefit undeniably from proximity to these public spaces. Although it may not be fair to demand public restrooms, per se, shops, restaurants, and offices should be expected to be welcoming, especially to families and children.

Places to sit, rest, and watch are critical. A new pedestrian street created in Turku, Finland, shows the potential role of benches. Here, even though cars have been prohibited, the look of a travel center has been preserved through borders and bricking patterns. The result is that faster-moving traffic—bikes and fast-walking pedestrians—tend to stay in the middle, while slower traffic moves over to the wide sidewalks on either side. Benches facing the center also help to define this interior "roadway," and sitting in the sun on these benches, watching the brisk foot and bike traffic move by, is a popular pastime.

In Pori, Finland, a significant move toward enhancing the pedestrian environment can be seen in two prominent ways: the city's effort at pedestrianizing much of its center, and its creation of a 4-kilometer-long (2.5 miles) public promenade. The promenade partly includes the main pedestrian street, but it does much more. It crosses the Kokemäenjoki River and connects with a major park and swimming area. To the north, the promenade passes under a railway line and major highway, connecting with the city's main hospital. The promenade routes and pedestrian areas in the city are heavily used. A bicycle and walking culture has emerged (bicycles are allowed to ride on the

Figure 6.8 | The Promenade in Pori, Finland.

pedestrian streets), aided by the city's growth and development policies that promote development of closer-in areas.

In the city of Herne, in the formerly industrial Ruhr Valley in northwestern Germany, its Hauptbahnstrasse has been converted into a lovely and very interesting pedestrian street. Two lines of young trees have been planted, about seventy in all, and many interesting things along the way keep the attention, especially of children. Items of interest include a stone globe floating and spinning (at least, seemingly) on upward shooting water, and a silver flying saucer that beckons for kids to climb up the ladder and to take off.

The design of the North End, the main pedestrian street in the London borough of Croydon, utilizes trees, street furniture, and street drainpipes to give it form and to divide up the spaces of this outdoor room. Pedestrians make decisions about how to move through these spaces almost like drivers on a highway—those wanting to move along faster choose the narrow faster-moving pedestrian corridor, hugging close to shop fronts. Those lingering or sitting move to the interior spaces, again with useful demarcations by tree lines and drain lines. Bike traffic is permitted on this street, with abundant bike parking provided in clustered blocks along with benches.

Undoubtedly an important element in the success and activity levels at Croydon's North End Street is the abundantly good access provided this area through public transit. Tramlink, a regional tram service, runs along one edge of the pedestrian street. The frequency of service is high, and the passing trams are a reassuring sight when walking or sitting along the pedestrian area. There are many reasons to be on the North End, especially shopping—the Whitgift Shopping Centre's main entrance is on the street, for instance. The presence of trees in the Croydon pedestrian area is a major part of its attraction; mostly planted in a single row, there are about thirty trees on this walking street.

The main walking street in Kaunas, Lithuania, is really two connected streets, Vilnius Street in the old center and Laisves Aleja. Connected through a pedestrian underpass, together these streets make up a nearly 3-kilometer-long (almost 2 miles) pedestrian street, with the old city hall as one terminus, and a large church as the other. The most impressive part of this street is certainly the Laisves Aleja portion. Quite an old street, it consists of two rows of densely planted trees, with a pedestrian promenade in the center. Benches are placed all along the way on both the inside and outside of the

Figure 6.9 | The main pedestrian-only street in Kaunas, Lithuania. This pedestrian corridor extends nearly 3 kilometers in length and contains more than 500 trees.

main promenade. In 1972, the city pedestrianized the remaining sides of the street that had allowed for car traffic—one lane in each direction, on either side. The result today is an impressively wide pedestrian area. Most remarkable perhaps are the trees—by my count, more than 500 linden trees on the main pedestrian street, but also scores of additional trees on side streets branching off from the main promenade.

The level of activity along this street is quite high—it is clearly the main place to go, to hang out, to be seen in Kaunas. People are lingering and people are moving quickly, using the street as a key movement corridor in the city. Reasons for the high levels of use are many. A great many destinations and activities are located along the street—for example, a zoological museum, the new city hall, a major concert hall, and several schools (including what is considered by some to be the best school in the city). Located here as well are many restaurants, shops, and pubs, many with outside seating. There are, I think, some other good reasons that suggest why this space works well. There are many places to sit and relax. The perception of an abundant number of seating opportunities is something I had to demonstrate to myself by counting them. There are, by a quick count, some 130 benches on the main street, in addition to other available seating in the area (around fountains, on ledges of walls, and seating on side streets). The main street, moreover, does not stand alone; on each side are active streets, with flats and other important points of interest. These points of interest are many, to be sure. That such a street is a *public* street is undeniable, and there are many ways in which it attracts visitors. Major public buildings and functions are situated along it, and statues and monuments to important people and events appear throughout.

Walking areas can be incorporated within new development areas in other creative ways. The Millennium Peninsula in London, a former industrial zone that has been regenerated in some exemplary ways, shows this. Here, an overall master plan (by London-based architect Richard Rogers) has sought to minimize car traffic, and major investments by English Partnerships, the British Regeneration Agency, in a network of bikeways and trails makes spending time out of one's car both practical and enjoyable. The new Greenwich Millennium Village, with site plan and building designs by Swedish-based architect Ralph Erskine, is the centerpiece of this newly regenerated area (along, of course, with the visually notable Millennium Dome). It has many green features, but important from a pedestrian perspective is its proximity to the Thames trail (a bike and walking trail along the Thames River), its central park and green area, and the Millennium Ecology Park. Together, there are tremendous opportunities for nature walking and bicycling, for the most part, protected from cars and car traffic.

Steady bicycle and walking traffic can be seen on the Thames trail. Some traffic comes from outside the peninsula, and there are places where one can park, but most foot or bicycle traffic seems generated from within the district. Strolling families and bird-watchers with binoculars can be seen; a small group of teenagers sitting along the river is engaged in intense and animated conversation. The residents of the new compact dense housing here benefit immensely from the use of this trail and from the direct and visually impressive access to the river. Quality of living here has been greatly enhanced, and affection for this unique place has been strengthened.

The streets and public spaces of Leiden, my home in the Netherlands for many months, also provide many important lessons for creating walkable places. Here, emphasis has been placed on restricting car access, expanding the pedestrian realm, and gradually connecting pedestrian streets (e.g., through new canal bridges). My last home in Leiden was on Morsstraat, a street that, in itself, is an important lesson in place building. This relatively short street, about 200 meters long (660 feet), exemplifies what makes pedestrian streets attractive. Here organic, historic growth has yielded a remarkable level of building and façade diversity, for instance, and a tremendous mixing of uses and activities (we conveniently lived above a travel agent!). Uses on this short yet remarkable street included pubs and restaurants, a laundromat, several art galleries, a hobby store, a pet groomer, an ecological store, and a bicycle repair shop, among others. By my count there were a remarkable fifty-six different building façades on this street. It was enjoyable to walk along it, and I noticed something different every time. It is an absolute pleasure and a joy to live in a truly walkable city.

Opportunities to Build a Walking Culture in North America

Appreciating and connecting to the physical and hydrological conditions of a city can also provide opportunities to strengthen a walking culture. A number of cities in Europe and North America have developed promenades or trails systems along their rivers and waterfronts. Prominent North American examples include Milwaukee, Chattanooga, and Vancouver, among others. The city of Milwaukee, Wisconsin, in 1993 took the successful step of creating the new Riverwalk to connect downtown to its river. Riverwalk has spurred tremendous private investment, strengthened that city's downtown, and raised property values there. Richard Killingsworth and Jean Lamming of the University of North Carolina Active Living by Design Center (2002) describe the success of the project:

> The Riverwalk introduced healthy new walking options for downtown workers. It also does a better job connecting downtown's restaurants, apartments, stores, and offices. New river views inspired building owners and developers to transform empty buildings into condominiums with dining on the first floor, making the riverside a destination. Rowers travel the river, attracted by the audience of walkers and diners who cheer them on. The Riverwalk connects

downtown to nature: trout, steelhead, and salmon have added the fishing crowd to the downtown mix. (p. 16)

Chattanooga, Tennessee, has similarly rediscovered its riverfront and created a successful new Riverwalk. The vision is of a connected greenways system that will extend 22 miles, with 7 miles already completed. Other elements of these connected waterfront spaces include Coolidge Park, with its restored, hand-carved carousel; the Walnut Street bridge (purported to be the longest pedestrian-only bridge in the world); fishing piers; and outdoor stages and performance spaces (where events like the city's Riverbend music festival are convened). As Councilman David Crockett says, "The Riverwalk has done more to bring people together than anything else" (quoted in Porter, 2000).

In Vancouver, British Columbia, a pedestrian, bicycle, and in-line skating trail follows the water's edge, providing a popular and prized recreational amenity in that city. It began in the early 1900s as an erosion control wall, circling Stanley Park, Vancouver's impressive 1,000-acre green oasis. The seawall has been wisely extended and now comprises about 12 miles, beginning at the downtown waterfront on the north, then circling around Stanley Park, and on to False Creek and Granville Island to the south. The seawall has become an important amenity in that city's new Concord Place development, with strategic public art installations inserted long the way, and providing important pedestrian connections between sections of this project. At almost any hour of the day, one finds strollers and joggers and in-line skaters enjoying these special spaces along the waterfront edge of this vibrant city.

Certainly, what is important about the experiences of Vancouver and Chattanooga, and which could be applied to other cities, is the emphasis given to the special environmental qualities of these places, and the focus on pedestrian investments and opportunities. Chattanooga's Riverwalk, it is often said, is about celebrating and rediscovering and reconnecting with the Tennessee River. Providence, Rhode Island, has undertaken a major effort to reconnect to its riverfront, in this case the three rivers running through the city. Reconfiguring the rivers has created greater public access and more waterfront public spaces. Citizens and visitors in Providence are now enjoying its riverfronts—strolling, jogging, and picnicking and eating—and spending time at the city's Waterfront Place Park.

Many efforts at creating European-style pedestrian malls have been seen in U.S. cities, especially in the 1970s, but many of these efforts failed. The pedestrianized main street in my own home city of Charlottesville, Virginia, has been a success and offers some important lessons in creating successful pedestrian spaces. This exemplary space was created in 1974, implementing a plan for the mall prepared by noted landscape architect Lawrence Halprin.

One of the most distinctive features of Charlottesville's pedestrian mall, and a major element in its success, are its large shade trees. About sixty trees, mostly willow oaks, extend the length of the mall and create a verdant green canopy that keeps the space remarkably cool during the summer months. And the trees are an attraction in themselves for many visitors. The Charlottesville pedestrian mall conveys the feeling of walking in a forest as much as being in the center of a city.

William Lucy (2002), a planning professor at the University of Virginia who has spent much time studying the mall, discusses the importance of these trees:

> The number and height of these trees is important in three respects. They create an atmosphere of natural beauty in a dense built environment that is aesthetically pleasing, partly because this combination of trees and buildings is unusual. They contribute to a congenial microclimate with low pollution and pleasant bird sounds. They also serve an eminently practical shade and cooling function. (pp. 25–26)

Other important lessons from the Charlottesville mall include the importance of maintaining city government offices downtown; the need to expand the amount of housing on or near the mall, and thus the number of people there; and the importance of a design vision that emphasizes historic preservation and adaptive reuse. Another key lesson is that these spaces will not necessarily be immediately successful but require a longer-term timeframe and commitment and a certain amount of patience. Today, there are few downtown pedestrian spaces anywhere in the United States that are as delightful and functional as Charlottesville's mall.

There are many other places, many other ways in which Americans might be enticed to walk, and to return to the walking habits that we had only a decade or two earlier. Developing habits and interest in walking early in life

Figure 6.10 | The pedestrian mall in Charlottesville, Virginia.

is critical. As noted earlier in this chapter, not long ago most children walked or rode their bicycles to school, and there is much potential to restore these healthier patterns of mobility. Tremendous opportunities exist to return children to a walking life, and in particular to create the conditions for them to at least walk safely to their schools. There are now a number of successful "safe routes to school" initiatives under way and new interest in them around the country. One common element of these initiatives is the idea of "walking school buses"—a very creative idea that seeks to promote walking to school but is sensitive to the safety and security concerns parents have today. The idea is essentially that one or two parent volunteers collect children in a neighborhood each morning and walk with them to school. Sometimes one child carries a flag or a sign in the shape of a bus. The "bus" follows a fixed route, collecting children along the way.

Walking school bus programs can be found in many places around the world—the United States, the United Kingdom, and Australia. There are many advantages, of course, of getting children outside and walking, including the obvious one of getting some physical exercise. Less obvious benefits include developing a better understanding of one's neighborhood and community as well as socializing with other children and parents.

Chicago has an active walking school bus program. Although more students in Chicago than in most major cities already walk to school, the results of the walking school bus program have nonetheless been impressive. Of some 422,000 children in Chicago public schools, an estimated 90 percent walk to school. This compares with a dismal national average of less than 10 percent. Much of this is made possible by the city's land use pattern, but much is attributed to the neighborhood-based initiatives (www.cityof chicago.org). In Chicago, the program is viewed also as a way to address neighborhood crime, and indeed the city's police department is a major partner.

A major benefit of the walking programs is the potential to reduce traffic congestion at pick up and drop off times. Indeed, the congestion itself is seen by parents as a reason not to encourage their children to walk to school. Walking school bus initiatives in British Columbia are reported to have reduced school congestion by 25 to 60 percent (Casey, 2000). One more indirect benefit, though completely understandable, is that students who walk to school may be more alert and ready to learn when they arrive there. Ninety percent of teacher respondents in a survey of primary school teachers in the United Kingdom indicated that they believed students were more alert when they walked to school (www.walkingbus.com/school_news.htm).

Getting people to walk, and to spend more time in public spaces, will likely require more than just changing the design and configuration of the physical environment, though this will do much to help, of course. Sedentary lifestyles are also a function of mind-set and behavioral patterns that may be hard to overcome. Most people in the United States are couch potatoes, and it will take more than simply the *opportunity* to walk to budge us from our polyester and leather lairs. We need to relearn the tenets of a walking life, and just as it takes collective encouragement to stop smoking (or drinking, or littering), so also will it take a proactive push to move us back to a healthier pedestrian existence. How this might be done is seen in initiatives like Wheeling Walk, a media and advertising campaign in Wheeling, West Virginia, that is the brainchild of Bill Reger, a faculty member in the Department of Community Medicine at West Virginia University. Reger sees the logical need for media messages that might (help to) overcome the vast advertising supporting unhealthy lives and living (e.g., McDonald's annual advertising budget is more than $1 billion).

During 2001–2002, residents of Wheeling were exposed to a variety of media messages encouraging thirty minutes of walking each day—in all, 683 television ads during prime-time viewing, 1,164 ads on local cable television, almost 2,000 ads on local radio, 14 full-page ads in community newspapers, as well as press conferences, a speaker's bureau, and other efforts to get the message out to the community (Reger-Nash et al., undated). In follow-up research, the campaign appears to have had an impact on behavior, with an estimated 14 percent net increase in walking. With postcampaign place interviews suggesting that a very high percentage of Wheeling citizens had seen the ads, we might actually have expected higher results; it probably shows the difficulty of overcoming lifestyle patterns and personal interaction.

Conclusions

Building a pedestrian culture responds at once to a number of place ills—for example, our car-dependent ways are unhealthy in many respects and especially in locking-in our sedentary lives and lifestyles; we have gone to war, some believe, in defense of the oil that we need to sustain these auto-centric lives; we are increasingly isolated from each other and from the civic realm. Pedestrian places, moreover, are experienced and lived at a slower pace and through a deeper experiential mode. I'm not sure we can truly love places that we only drive by at high speeds. Genuine places, good places, and, certainly, sustainable places are pedestrian places. And our sense of social connectedness—our contacts and bonds with each other—requires pedestrian spaces. Building true community, building social connections and commitments, simply cannot happen in automobiles. Streets, plazas, and *campi* are where we have conversations and political debates, where we exchange recipes and shopping tips, where we learn about the health of friends and neighbors, and where we establish personal and meaningful relationships.

There are many creative ways to design and redesign our cities to allow and encourage walking, and we now understand many of the prerequisites necessary to get people out of their cars and onto plazas, *campi,* trails, streets, and greenways. At the most basic level, as former Bogotá mayor Enrique Peñalosa eloquently reminds us, walking is about being human and about doing what is natural and necessary to express our humanness: "God made us walking animals; pedestrians. As a fish needs to swim, a bird to fly, a deer to run, we need to walk, not in order to survive, but to be happy" (Peñalosa, 2001).

Place Building through Art and Celebration

Art can contribute immensely to the creation of real places. A sustainable, enriching place is one where, at every turn, we are challenged visually and spiritually. Art and the creation of art have become important strategies for place making in several respects. Just as every work of art has its own uniqueness, a city full of unique art becomes a unique place, different in some important respects from all others. Art in many ways makes us feel alive, deepens and expands our perceptions of the world, and helps us to see value and importance in people and buildings we may have otherwise overlooked. In a sense, public art lays the groundwork and opens us up for loving and caring about the neighborhoods and communities in which we live. Art also is ideally a participatory activity, and art in cities is often about infusing and disseminating individual and group creativity, in this way building a real sense of ownership and commitment.

We should find art everywhere, and in every place, from streets to building façades, to the rolling stock of buses, trash trucks, and other vehicles that pass through our communities. It is a premise of this chapter that art is an essential ingredient in our cities, and then, importantly, that many things can be done to support and extend these artistic dimensions of place. Art is itself often celebratory, and celebrations and collective events that encourage us to come together to appreciate and enjoy each other and the special qualities of place, reflect our creative and artistic impulses. Celebrations of place, then, represent a second major category of place-strengthening activities (highly related to and interactive with art) addressed in this chapter.

Nurturing and Supporting Local Artists

There are many creative ways to bring art to the city, and to passionately and artistically celebrate place, and many of them involve rethinking or reconceptualizing where and what art actually is. In a number of cities, artists have literally saved the day by inhabiting buildings and neighborhoods that others had abandoned or had given up, thereby revitalizing many areas. This happened in SoHo in New York City, in the 1960s and 1970s, where abandoned warehouses and industrial buildings were taken over as artist's studios and living quarters. In Europe, the salvation and preservation of the Temple Bar district in Dublin, Ireland, is another wonderful example. Much of this historic urban district in Dublin was scheduled to be razed for a new transit center when artists moved in to take advantage of the low rents and short-term leases, eventually establishing the neighborhood as a cultural and arts center, and propelling the impressive regeneration of this mixed-use pedestrian district. There are many more examples that show convincingly how in very real ways artists and artistic communities represent a tremendous place-building resource.

A number of U.S. cities have developed programs to fund and support local arts and artists. Chicago and Seattle have exemplary efforts under way to build art-enriched places. The Seattle Arts Commission, for instance, is a major facilitating force in that city, providing extensive grants and assistance to support the arts. The impressive range of programs and initiatives there include production of online art and culture walking tour maps for many neighborhoods in the city, and an arts education link, which provides an online resource for teachers to incorporate art into their classrooms. Most recent has been work to develop an Arts Resources Network, a mostly Web-based service that provides extensive information about arts events, galleries and arts organizations, grants and training, and public art, among many other topics that might be of interest to local artists and the general public (see www.artsresourcenetwork.org). One of the most interesting new initiatives of the Seattle Arts Commission is its ARTS UP program, or Artist Residences Transforming Seattle's Urban Places. Under this initiative, artists are teamed up with community groups to help them in creating neighborhood arts projects that explore issues of special concern to the community.

There are many ways to promote art and the development of a rich arts community. Some cities pursue the creation of arts or artists overlay districts, providing a special set of regulatory zoning standards in places where art and artist activities and communities might be promoted. The Lowell, Massachusetts, artists overlay district, recently profiled in a report by the National Trust for Historic Preservation, is a good example of this strategy. Under the overlay, Lowell artists are permitted to use second-floor spaces for both living and working—they can have both a studio and a business, as well as their home, in the same unit. The ordinance has already had the effect of stimulating rehabilitation of several buildings with this purpose in mind (National Trust for Historic Preservation, 2002).

The South Downtown (SODO) Business District in Seattle is home to an interesting effort to promote and stimulate art along a 2-mile corridor. Called the SODO Urban Art Corridor, this community focal area, just south of the Kingdome, is an area of warehouses and low-rise industrial use. It has been a marginal area in many respects, a place of graffiti and trash and a hangout for at-risk youth. A nonprofit organization called ArtWorks has been created in an attempt to change the area and to use public art as a way to guide, inspire, and uplift youth in the community. With some funding from the city, along with private donations (such as paint from stores such as Sears), and with many volunteers, ArtWorks works with youth to create spectacular murals along this stretch of 5th Avenue South. Beginning with a summer program, ArtWorks now operates year-round and has teaching and gallery space (rent-free space). More than fifty murals now grace the walls and façades of buildings along this corridor. Many can be found on the city's Web site (www.ci.seattle.wa.us/community/sodo/sodo.htm).

The initiative shows what can be done through personal commitment, creative energy, and a little bit of community seed money. ArtWorks and the Urban Arts Corridor were the brainchildren of Mike Peringer, who was recently given the Jefferson Award, a distinguished public service award in Washington

State, for his outstanding community work. A recent story in the *Seattle Post-Intelligencer* pays tribute to Peringer and reports on the power of these murals: "They not only instill pride in the young artists, but also command respect from taggers. They bring the community together, Peringer said, recalling one mural worked on by an unlikely alliance of elementary school children, gang members and senior citizens" (Virong, 2003).

Many U.S. cities have adopted the policy that a certain percentage of the cost of public projects must be spent on public art, and this has been a real boost. In Seattle, 1 percent of the public project budget (including the infrastructure projects of Seattle Public Utilities) must be spent on public art. Chicago adopted its Percent-for-Art Ordinance in 1978, and requires that at least half the allocation be made to local artists. Public art in Vancouver, British Columbia, is flourishing. Under that city's urban design guidelines, developers seeking zoning changes are required to make a specific contribution to public art. At a rate of about Can$1 per buildable foot, this public art requirement has funded numerous, impressive installations (see City of Vancouver, 1994).

The Power of Artful Place

Encouraging early experience with the arts is another essential element of a child-friendly city. The arts have tremendous potential to expand and uplift and shape positive perceptions of the world at an early age. Exposure to and involvement in the arts is also important in the early development of cognitive and intellectual skills. The 1999 study *Champions of Change: The Impacts of the Arts on Learning* summarizes much of this compelling research to date. Among its findings are that participation in arts programs helps develop critical thinking, helps strengthen academic performance overall, and helps especially to lift children from disadvantaged neighborhoods and backgrounds. The benefits for kids of involvement in the arts extend to other seemingly unrelated subjects, as well, such as mathematics (Arts Education Partnership, 1999). And, as the report makes clear, arts programs help to build interpersonal connections among kids, between adults and kids, and between kids and schools and other community institutions.

Champions of Change, really a compilation of studies, provides strong evidence and justification for getting kids involved in the arts early and working to sustain this involvement into adulthood. Such involvement, the study concludes, allows "unparalleled opportunities for learning, enabling young people to reach for and attain higher levels of achievement" (Arts Education Partnership, 1999, p. xii). The potential impacts in changing learning environments, in shaping the future lives of students, and in facilitating new community commitments and optimism is great.

Many cities have risen to this challenge of actively involving children. The Seattle Arts Commission, for example, has developed some exemplary new initiatives, including spring break and after-school arts training programs (e.g., Arts Corps). Chicago has an impressive grants program to support the arts. City Arts, administered by the Chicago Department of Cultural Affairs, awards about $1 million each year to support about 240 arts organizations. Grant sizes range from $1,200 to $8,500 (www.ci.chi.il.us).

Since it began in Chicago in 1991, *Gallery 37* has provided some 25,000 jobs to student artists and 2,500 jobs for professional artists (Gallery 37, undated). The program was founded by Maggie Daley (wife of Mayor Richard M. Daley) and Louis Weisberg, the city's Commissioner of Cultural Affairs, and its funding comes from a variety of mostly private sources. Many of Gallery 37's programs are accomplished through partnerships with other galleries, theaters, and organizations in the art community, some fifty each year (Gallery 37, 2002).

Chicago's Gallery 37 has one of the earliest and best-known job training programs for young artists, and has been emulated by other American cities. Under the program, young artists (ages 10–21) are provided a financial stipend and given apprentice positions with established artists, who serve as teachers and mentors. To date, some 20,000 young people have participated in the program, which has led to the creation of a great deal of art around the city.

Gallery 37 also operates a program called "connections" for students 10 to 14 years old. Described as a preemployment arts program, it is aimed at students with physical or cognitive disabilities. A key goal is to use art as a way of building self-esteem and confidence in these children, and reports are that the

Figure 7.1 | Gallery 37 in Chicago provides a variety of arts education and hands-on artist training. Here, a ceramics class displays the impressive results.

program is successful in doing so. The Neighborhoods Program, which employs students during the summer to work on arts projects in their own communities, is one of the most interesting aspects of Gallery 37. These projects, in about fifteen neighborhoods, leave a lasting legacy and have the potential to enhance significantly and positively the aesthetics of the places people live.

The space available for Gallery 37 programs is truly impressive—some 65,000 square feet downtown, on four levels, contains studios and classrooms, film and media production equipment, soundproof music studios, a dark lab, a culinary kitchen/classroom, a dance studio, and a fairly large gallery space, as well as a street-level shop selling the artwork. There is also a small theater and stage that is available for community theater productions. The Storefront Theater, as it's called, puts on about fifteen productions each year. The building and space are provided rent-free by the city.

The students are not just talking about or learning about art in some abstract sense, but they are producing art, and the city of Chicago itself is reaping much of the benefit. Students at Vaughn High School, for example, are making a mosaic mural that will soon be installed on the main outside wall of the school. A colorful mural adorns a Chicago Transit Authority (CTA) bridge, not far from the Gallery 37 building. Sponsored by the Mexican Fine Arts Center Museum, the CTA mural is titled *Rites of Passage*. Students' murals are also appearing on the highly prominent sides of old warehouses visible to drivers on the Kennedy Expressway. The LaSalle Building has become known as the "mural building," and some 300,000 people see the murals each day (Lobiskey, 2001). Murals are cycled on and off the space, and LaSalle Bank sponsors Gallery 37 apprentices to design and paint them. (To see the current murals, go to http://mural.lasallebank.com/home.html.) And Gallery 37's production goes beyond paintings and murals: each year a CD is produced of the work of the Gallery's apprentice musicians, and literary work is also published.

Watching and talking to students in some of the Gallery 37 classes, I noted a sense of community building through this process; and the classes that I have seen represent a great ethnic, cultural, and gender diversity, suggesting the very positive role the arts can play in overcoming the things that divide us. As the Gallery 37 literature claims, "the arts provide a common ground that leads to camaraderie and mutual respect" (2002, p. 3).

Figure 7.2 | The *Rites of Passage* mural, painted on a prominent Chicago Transit Authority bridge in that city's downtown.

Figure 7.3 | In Chicago, even the city's fleet of municipal trash trucks is seen as an opportunity for artistic expression. This is "rolling art" in the truest possible sense.

Infrastructure as Art

Some cities are recognizing the inherent connections between art and aesthetics, and the many functional aspects of the built environment that make a city work. All could be designed with art in mind, with artistic elements incorporated into them; indeed, in some cases, buildings can be viewed entirely as works of artistic expression.

Systematically integrating art and artistic views is a challenge, but there are some good models of how this might be done. Seattle Public Utilities, the agency responsible for that city's water, sewage, and solid waste, has undertaken an "artist in residence" program, and noted artists Buster Simpson and Lorna Jordan have come up with a number of creative ideas for thinking about how art and public utilities can be blended together. For her part, Jordan has worked on developing a long-term vision called "Watershed Illuminations," which would connect utility and art over a long period of time (see Arcade Journal, 2002).

Buster Simpson's work exemplifies these possibilities for fusion as well. His *Beckoning Cistern* in Seattle's Belltown neighborhood shows how art—

in this case, a beautiful metal hand reaching to a building's rooftop, guiding its bounty of stormwater to a cistern, and eventually to a streetside runnel or waterway—can be both infrastructure and ecological restoration. (See Figure 5.5 for a photograph of this interesting installation.)

Artist Michael Singer has had significant success in changing our views about what a city's utilities and infrastructure might look like and how they might function. One of the most acclaimed examples is the solid waste management facility in Phoenix, Arizona. Designed along with fellow artist Lennea Glatt, and in collaboration with the engineering company Black and Veatch, the building serves as a combination sorting and waste transfer and recycling facility; it accommodates some 500 trucks daily, arriving with some 3,500 tons of waste. This facility does its job, to be sure, but does much more. It includes a visitors center and has a designed-in amphitheater where visitors can view the waste sorting and recycling process. It is at once a facility for servicing and sustaining the city, an expression of the civic realm, and an embodiment of artistic expression.

The Phoenix building is, as well, an ethical statement (the building demonstrates the recycling and reuse of some of the city's waste stream), an educational opportunity (a facility that teaches the community about the waste and material processes upon which we all depend), and a new addition to the civic landscape (a place where people meet).

Instead of hiding away the gritty process of waste disposal, this building brings it front and center. The Phoenix community appears to have welcomed this new kind of civic venture; some 10,000 school children visit the facility each year. In a way it is as much a public school as a waste facility—it teaches, informs, and conveys lessons about personal and collective responsibilities.

Traditional infrastructure such as bridges can also be designed and reconceptualized as works of place-based, community art. An excellent example can be seen in Tucson, Arizona—a pedestrian bridge in the shape and form of a rattlesnake. Designed by Simon Donovan, a Tucson artist gaining considerable local acclaim, the Diamondback Bridge is a fantastic merging of the functional—a foot and bicycle bridge—with the beautiful. It is, moreover, the beauty *of the place*—the form, color, and subject—that is at once striking and unusual (one does not always see a large snake bridge crossing a highway) but at home, something that clearly belongs here and could have found its way from of the nearby desert. Designing a bridge as a sculpture is part of what this special project involves; seeing the structure and form of the bridge in the anatomy of a snake is also what this is about. As artist Donovan says, "The architecture of a bridge, the skeleton of a snake, with the ribs and spine, were perfect for creating this pedestrian bridge" (Regan, 2003). The bridge has met with almost universal affection by local residents. Spanning 300 feet across busy Broadway Boulevard, the bridge rewards a pedestrian or bicyclist with the sound of a rattle passing through the snake's tail. The bridge cost $2.3 million to build, funded through local government's 1 percent for art program. The *Tucson Weekly* recently called the snake bridge "the coolest thing to slither across this town in years" (*Tucson Weekly,* 2002, p.1). It has also won three engineering awards.

Transit stations represent similar venues for artistic expression, and a number of cities worldwide have seized this opportunity. The New York Metropolitan Transportation Authority's (MTA) Arts for Transit is one im-

Figure 7.4 | The Diamondback Bridge in Tucson, Arizona. Designed by artist Simon Donovan, it exemplifies place-sensitive public art, merged with the functional. (Photo compliments of Tucson Pima Arts Council.)

portant example. To date, some 185 different public arts projects have been sponsored at transit stations since the program was started in 1985. In a creative partnership between MTA and the Museum of Natural History, the 81st Street Station, which includes a direct entrance to the museum, has been transformed into stories of the evolution of various life-forms. On the walls and floors of the station, artwork portrays a story of the earth's natural history for those passing through (see www.amnh.org).

One can cite many more impressive examples of art that brighten and enliven subterranean subway spaces, where it might be a surprise and unexpected delight to travelers. José Ortega's mural *Una Raza, Un Mundo, Universo* (One Race, One World, One Universe), installed in seven panels below Third Avenue/149th Street, is described on a City University of New York (CUNY) arts Web site:

> Just below the bustling streets of what is affectionately known as "The Hub" lie seven mosaic murals making a connection between the natural world and the human world. Circular forms emerge to unify the murals and sustain a universal dialogue between the sun, the earth, and the human face. José Ortega also captures the diversity of the neighborhood above, allowing scenes of daily life to meld seamlessly with the abstract and symbolic. Pre-Columbian and African influences infuse the imagery with timelessness in direct contrast to the surroundings. The result is a brightly colored celebration of harmonious relationships, diversity, and the enduring human spirit. (http://bronxart.lehman.cuny.edu/pa/ortega.htm).

The murals and other arts elements are typically funded and commissioned at the time of transit station renovations. Artists compete for the chance to create their art here, and typically a panel that includes representation from the local community selects the winners (Delatiner, 2001). Thus, an installation often tells a story about or relates in important ways to the surrounding neighborhood. The result is progress at making individual stations distinctive and unique in identity and feel.

Many communities have initiatives aimed at displaying literature and poems on the sides of buildings. Leiden, in the Netherlands, is a marvelous case in point. Here, at seemingly every turn of a corner, lies another poetic nugget on the side of a building or a vacant wall. Offered in a number of different languages, they are not always readable (to me, at least) but are a great and beautiful addition to the urban landscape.

Other cities have treated their rolling stock—their buses, trams, and trains—as opportunities for literature, also. Many communities have imitated "Poetry in Transit" programs, which display poetry on the spaces in and around buses and other transit vehicles. Typically, the poems are by local authors, exploring local themes. They stay up for a couple of months at most, then are replaced with new creations. Funding is provided from many different sources, including the transit agencies themselves, local businesses, and local associations of book publishers.

Art on Streets and Sidewalks

A number of cities have had positive success with promoting what might be called pop art, temporarily installed on public streets—an idea that origi-

Figure 7.5 | One of the Washington, D.C., "party animals." The 200 brightly colored elephants and donkeys graced the streets of that city during 2002. (Photo compliments of the D.C. Commission on the Arts.)

nated in Zurich. In 1998, the City Association of Zurich sponsored local artist Walter Knapp's plan for placing what would eventually be more than 800 ceramic cows on the streets of that city. Some 400 artists were commissioned to paint and creatively adorn them, and the cows were later sold for charity. A number of American cities have followed suit. In 1999, Chicago sponsored "Cows on Parade," in which some 300 cows of widely diverse artistic treatments were installed throughout the city.

Many benefits are often cited as coming from the "cows on parade" style of art initiatives. Typically, at the end of the exhibit period, most of the art objects are sold or auctioned off, with the proceeds going to local charities. The art is also credited with increases in tourism and the ensuing local economic benefits. In Chicago, the tourism benefits from Cows on Parade have been estimated at some $200 million. Cows on Parade has led to other arts promotion around the city—Suite Home Chicago (fiberglass furniture as art), and city critters at Lincoln Park Zoo, among others.

Cows on Parade has become an international event and experience, with New York, London, and Sydney, Australia, among the many other cities sponsoring such events. Some other cities, however, have built on to the basic idea and chosen a different animal or theme. These include the "Big Pig Gig" in Cincinnati, Ohio; "Peanuts on Parade" in St. Paul, Minnesota, with colorful Snoopys gracing the streets; and New Orlean's "Festival of Fins," with artistic fish the center of attention. Erie, Pennsylvania, similarly sponsored "Go Fish"; Toronto had its "Moose in the City"; and Rochester, New York, its "Ewe Review."

The version of this whimsical public art trend in Washington, D.C., was "Party Animals"—200 artfully decorated donkeys and elephants, building on the palpable partisanship that pervades that city (an equal 100 for each, of course). Seven hundred artists submitted applications for the chance to embellish one of the animals, each receiving a $1,000 grant and $200 for supplies. As with the similar programs in other cities, the "animals" met with generally positive praise. At the end of the public display period, the animals were sold, through both an online and a live auction, raising more than $1 million for the D.C. Arts Commission—in addition to the $400,000 contributed by corporate sponsors and local governments to fund the program.

A follow-on public arts project in 2004 has placed 150 very colorful plastic pandas on Washington Streets. Called PandaMania, it builds on the special affection of this city for pandas, dating back to donation by the Chinese government in the 1970s of Ling Ling and Hsing Hsing. Giant Pandas are an important adopted species for Washington and a symbol of détente. The designs are clever and appealing and irresistible climbing objects for kids: there's Bearra Cotta Warrior Panda, a Patriot Panda, an E Pluribus Panda, a Panda Melon (one of the more colorful), and a Panda of the Opera, among others (See http://www.pandamaniadc.org/ for a full gallery of the completed pandas).

Initiatives such as the Party Animals and PandaMania provide the opportunity to turn a city into a collective treasure hunt. One admirer of the Party Animals reports in the *Washington Post* her delight in seeking out, via bicycle, all the "animals" in the various locations around the city. It took her three months to do it, with the help of a map published in the paper, but the experience clearly had the perhaps unintended effect of educating her about D.C. "Along the way, I saw parts of the District that were new to me, some that were familiar, all helping me revisit my native roots" (Hodskins, 2003, p. C10).

In addition to adding new color and generating interest in cities, public art of this kind can also generate controversy, sometimes in ways not expected. In the case of the Party Animals, perhaps reflecting the special pathologies of Washington, D.C., objections were heard from independent and third-party organizations and voters that they ought to be given an equal chance to participate. As Scott McLarty of the D.C. Statehood Green Party is quoted as saying, "What if the commission had chosen just the elephant? . . . The Democrats would have gone on the warpath" (Cass, 2002). Placement of the colorful animals became an issue as well, with some concern that an elephant or donkey too close to a facility or establishment might signify a particular political endorsement.

PETA (People for the Ethical Treatment of Animals) sought to use the animals to make some points about cruelty to animals. When denied by the Arts Commission the right to depict a "weeping, shackled elephant," PETA took the commission to court claiming a violation of free speech rights and won. Public art even of the more whimsical sort, does seem to have the ability to stimulate discussion and controversy, to stir people's emotions on many levels, and in this way must be considered a good thing.

And the focus of this form of public art can also certainly take its cue from the native flora and fauna of a community. The recent Prairie Dog Art Project, organized by public station KGNU in Boulder, Colorado, is an example. Here, more than sixty-five prairie dogs made of polyethylene resin have been creatively and courageously adorned in an artistic and public celebration of this native citizen (see www.kgnue.org/prairiedogs/index.html). In Florida's Tampa Bay area, sea turtles have become the object of attention in a similar public art display, with efforts to educate the public along the way about the dire plight of these fellow place citizens.

Art and beauty can be expressed by and mixed with the more utilitarian elements of streets and urban infrastructure. In a number of cities, efforts have been made to preserve historic and distinctive elements of traditional street infrastructure, including manhole covers, tree grates, and street lamps. Manhole covers, for instance, have been the focus on new artistic expression in several American and European cities. In New York City, artist Michele Brody has received funding from the Lower Manhattan Cultural Council to design ten new sets of manhole covers, a project called Recovering the Cityscape. Her resulting designs incorporate specific architectural and historical details of buildings that have been demolished. The new manhole covers have been placed at the approximate location of these lost buildings, and in this way are a combination of public art and historic plaques. The designs are interesting and richly detailed—for example, one design incorporates the distinctive architecture of the Jefferson Market Prison on Greenwich Avenue. (To see the other designs, see www .recoveringthecityscape.org.)

In Vancouver, the public has been encouraged to submit unique designs for new and replacement manhole covers in that city. Under a public arts initiative called Art Underfoot, the city will select two designs—one for sewer covers and one for stormwater covers—with the intention of also visually demonstrating the city's commitment to addressing its serious combined-sewer and stormwater overflow problem. The winners of the design competition will also receive a cash award of Can$2,000 (see www.city.vancouver.bc .ca/commsvcs/oca/publicart).

Using Art to Enhance the Presence of History and Heritage in Communities

Finding creative ways to highlight the history of a community, and to incorporate it into the built environment, becomes an important challenge. This can happen in potentially a number of ways including, as it does in many communities, through murals, sculptures, and outdoor art. Perhaps the most famous creative use of murals can be found in the small Canadian town of Chemainus, located on Vancouver Island in British Columbia. A mill town facing hard times, Chemainus decided it would attempt to promote tourism and celebrate its history by commissioning murals on the walls of its buildings. Inspired by the religious frescoes one of the town fathers saw on the walls of Romanian monasteries, and with a revitalization grant from the British Columbian government, the town embarked on this unique strategy. Twenty years later, the town boasts thirty-four large murals depicting its history and attracts 400,000 visitors each year.

Chemainus demonstrates well how with determination and vision a new strength of place can be brought about. Its 3,500 residents were facing hard economic times with the decline of the logging economy and the closing of the town's mill (which reopened several years later). Known now as the "mural capital of North America" (and the world!), the town began this creative strategy in the early 1980s. A Festival of Murals Association has been formed:

> More than a quarter of a million dollars has been invested in the mural project by private, corporate, federal, provincial and municipal investors. As a direct result, Chemainus has attracted in excess of one hundred new businesses, 350–450,000 visitors a year and a $3.5 million dinner theater. From the dependence on a single industry, it has broadened its economic base to offer a range of service and tourist related activities. (Chemainus Festival of Murals, 1993, p. 7)

The idea found its inspiration deep in a history book about the Chemainus valley written by local author W. H. (Harry) Olsen, *Water Over the Wheel—The Story of the Chemainus Valley and Its People.* It chronicled the history and key historical events, dating to the earliest Native American beginnings.

The murals depict these events and periods in breathtaking detail. One mural shows the British gunboat *Forward,* one of four Royal Navy vessels sent to search for suspects in a local murder spree in 1863. Others depict a steam donkey at work pulling felled trees; railroad scenes; the arrival of a British sloop to Chemainus harbor; and logging with oxen (the main technique of logging in the late 1800s).

Sculpture and wood carvings have also been added to the town in recent years. The economic activity generated from the murals has been considerable, with a variety of secondary businesses popping up, from galleries and studios, to bed-and-breakfasts, to cafés and bakeries.

Other communities have now emulated the creative example set by Chemainus. Several communities in Southern California have commissioned murals, including the town of Santa Paula, whose murals depict different historical periods in its history (Ritsch, 1998). In the Chicago suburb of Naperville an initiative called the Century Walk (operated by the nonprofit Century Walk Corporation) was inspired by the Chemainus example but extends the idea in some interesting ways. The Naperville walk consists of a series of murals, tile and glass mosaics, and statues depicting that town's history, located on the walls of businesses and in front of important public buildings. With funding from the Illinois Arts Commission, there are now fourteen stops on this historical walk.

Other North American cities have similarly used murals and art to tell the history of a place. Chicago has commissioned artist Ellen Lanyon to create a series of ceramic murals on the Riverwalk that tell the story of the Chicago River and waterfront, from early exploration up to modern times. Called *Riverwalk Gateway,* Lanyon's installation consists of a series of 6-feet-high decorative and narrative panels (Chicago Dept. of Cultural Affairs, undated):

> The narratives, which are told through a combination of scenes, vignettes, and objects, begin in 1673 with the explorations of Marquette and Jolliet, followed by a mural with scenes from 1782 of Jean Baptiste DuSable and 1803 when Fort Dearborn was built. Paintings record the development of Chicago's bridges and commemorate landmark events and important sites along the river and the lake, concluding in 2000 with the recreational use of the Chicago River.

Public art can in significant ways build upon and strengthen our understanding and appreciation of the unique cultural heritage of places. The artwork of First Nations and indigenous peoples can deepen connections with place, educate about local history and culture, and inject beauty into daily life. In the fall of 2003, Vancouver saw the unveiling of a 14-foot bronze sculpture by master Haida carver Jim Hart. Provided in response to the city's public art requirement, it now graces the entrance to an apartment building. The piece, entitled *The Three Watchmen*, draws on traditional Haida totems. "Traditionally, Watchmen figures looked out for danger emanating from both the supernatural and the everyday world, and were often incorporated by the Haida on the tall cedar totem poles in front of their houses in villages throughout Haida Gwaii—Queen Charlotte Islands" (Kennedy, 2003). The sculpture was unveiled in a ceremony that included a traditional Haida prayer and dance. A remarkable piece of public art, it makes the heritage and culture of First Nation peoples alive and visible. Spiritual art, art with deep

Figure 7.6 | Haida sculpture, *The Three Watchmen*, by master carver Jim Hart. (Photo by Barbara Cole, compliments of the City of Vancouver public arts program.)

local meaning, graces a common local landscape, in this case, and does not require a visit to a local museum or art gallery.

Street Celebrations, Parades, and Other Active Community Art

Art in cities can, of course, take a more active form, expressed through street celebrations, processionals and parades, and art-based community activism. Celebrations of place help to foster commitment, as well. These can take many forms, but all aim to educate, appreciate, and highlight the unique dimensions and special qualities of our communities.

Local arts can be promoted and supported, and local economy enhanced, through a variety of arts events. A number of North American and European cities have, over a long period of time, had successful experiences with arts festivals—events that bring in substantial income, change perceptions of place, and enhance the lives and life experiences of the residents of these cities enormously. Many cities around the world have had impressive experiences with annual or semi-annual arts and ideas festivals. This is yet another way to both support and stimulate local artists and musicians as well as bring into the community the music, art, and ideas of the world.

In the United Kingdom, a history of arts festivals goes back to the postwar period, where such events were seen as a way of lifting spirits and morale in war-dispirited places. The Edinburgh Arts Festival, now billed as the largest in the world, is perhaps the granddaddy. It grows larger each year, with a staggering number of events, artists, venues, and attendance levels during August that actually cause the city's population to double. This event, which has spawned many others, generates some £150 million (about US$100 million) in revenue for Edinburgh and has certainly done much to create a positive arts image for the city.

Despite its successes, Edinburgh offers a cautionary story. It is often criticized for being elitist, for failing to reach local audiences sufficiently (rising ticket prices raise affordability concerns), and for not enough nurturing or showcasing of Scottish and local talent (e.g., see Fox, 2002; Thorncroft, 2002). These issues can be addressed, however, with greater efforts to sponsor local artists financially, to provide free concerts and events, and to ensure that venues are selected so that all, or as many citizens and neighborhoods as possible, have access to these artistic and musical opportunities.

A number of other creative arts festivals can be found in the United Kingdom, offering similar positive stories. Glasgow, Bath, and Belfast all have long-running and successful arts festivals. Some cities have sponsored street-based festivals, like Brighton's Hat Fair, where musicians and performers are supported by hat collections (Thorncraft, 2002).

In the United States, large arts and idea festivals occur in many cities, such as Spoleto in Charleston, South Carolina. The annual festival in New Haven, Connecticut, is relatively new but has already been immensely successful; in 2004, it lasted 16 days with hundreds of events—music, dance, opera, theater, art, literature, and ideas. Almost a million people attended, representing many different nationalities. The events were geographically scattered over the New Haven area. The variety of performances and media are striking. There are stilt performers and outdoor films; the Warsaw Village Band plays on the same bill as the Slammin' Nor'easter hiphop band. Other interesting events include bicycle tours, food tours (sampling the fares of local restaurants), and fieldtrips to neighborhood projects and University venues (e.g. Yale's Robotics lab this year). In this sense, there is much about the Festival that involves learning about the creativity and innovation at-home and the artistic and creative work present all around one. For the kids there was the so-called Wiggle Wall, an "ongoing multimedia collage where they can paint pictures and weave fanciful patterns onto an awesome visual display" (New Haven International Arts and Ideas Fesival, http://www.artidea.org/).

Clearly some of the more interesting and stimulating pieces are the "ideas" events. In 2004, these included a conversation with Harvard biologist E.O. Wilson on his "thoughts on the natural world and the future of life on Earth," a discussion by physicist S. James Gates on superstring theory, and a review of research on the human genome, among many others. Uniquely, the festival also included a "day of debates" where notable experts debated each other of some of the most divisive and controversial issues of our time: biotech research, no child left behind, immigration reform, and gay marriage. The Festival in New Haven is as much about creative and stimulating ideas as about more the traditional artistic pursuits and happiness.

Celebrations can take many forms and provide special opportunities to connect with the special places and environments in which we live. The focus of these might be a river, a mountain range, a watershed, and the means of celebration may be unique and unusual. In New York City, efforts to celebrate the Bronx River there, result in an annual flotilla of boats and residents who pass along a large golden ball, not unlike the way in which the Olympic torch is passed. The ball, 3 feet in size, is floated from 219th Street to Starlight Park. The South Bronx River, long a neglected and polluted waterway, has been the center of much community activism in recent years, from canoe trips to grassroots cleanup efforts. This activism is culminating in a $60 million restoration plan, envisioning a riverfront greenway and network of connected parks.

The Bronx River initiative shows dramatically how citizen groups can restore a sense of connection to the natural environment (many Bronx residents did not even know there was a river there) and, in the process, to strengthen the quality of life and commitment to staying in the community. At a recent conference promoting sustainable development ideas in the city, Bronx

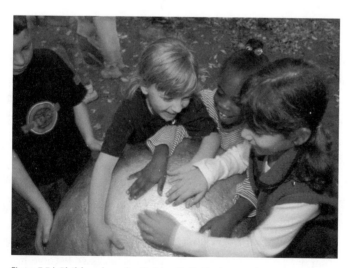

Figure 7.7 | Children hug the Golden Ball. Each year the Bronx River Alliance holds an event to celebrate that river, pushing and floating along a distinctive golden ball from venue to venue like an olympic torch. (Photo compliments of the Bronx River Alliance).

activists talked of the prevailing view in the past that the best, most desirable option, if you could manage it, was to escape this environment. Building a sense of place there, improving and respecting the environment, means that over time residents will want to stay.

In the case of the Bronx River it is perhaps not surprising that residents had little sense of connection to this physical resource. Until recently it was physically impossible even to reach the river because it was surrounded by fences and industrial uses that blocked any visual or physical connectedness. Providing physical access to these special places, illustrated as well in the cases of the Ontario Waterfront Trail and the Hannover Green Ring, are essential requisites.

Community events can help bring people and neighborhoods closer together, help develop lasting community relationships, and build commitments to place. We need more community events that rally people together, that call upon them to demonstrate (physically) their bonds to one another and to the community as a whole. In Portland, Oregon, a community organization called The City Repair Project, has been sponsoring and organizing such events. One of the more notable is the semi-annual "Hands Around Portland." Described as an "enormous human circle," it is literally an event where people in that city hold hands, along an agreed-upon route, at a designated date and time. This "remarkable gesture of interconnectedness" has linked as many as fifteen Portland neighborhoods (www.cityrepair.org). Such events, while fleeting and periodic, can evoke in us all a kind of feeling of the significance and importance of "others" in our lives—other neighborhoods, other families, other organizations and groups—whose interests and fate, in place, are inextricably bound together.

Few cities have nurtured these active impressions to the extent of Vancouver. A nonprofit charity, the Public Dreams Society, has been promoting and facilitating activities in that city since 1985. With financial support from the City of Vancouver (and others) and a strong base of volunteer labor, this organization has been instrumental in staging what have become important community events, in putting on workshops and in building grassroots capacity to organize and pull off these events.

Two important annual events in Vancouver are the Luminaries Lantern Processional and the Parade of Lost Souls. Both mark seasonal transitions;

Figure 7.8 | Luminaries Lantern Processional, a production of the Public Dreams Society in Vancouver, British Columbia. (Photo compliments of Public Dreams; Photographer: Tim Matheson.)

for example, the latter occurs near Halloween, marking the seasonal shift to the Northwest's dark winters. Other events include a First Night Vancouver, the Vancouver International Children's Festival, and community circuses (where there are no live animals—only participants dressed as animals!).

For several years Public Dreams has also been running a Spectacular Young Artists and Performers Project, with the aim of training and involving youth in the community. Workshops are held on such subjects as torch building and handling, lantern making, and giant puppet building. These young artists then become actively involved in putting on events like First Night Vancouver, the city's New Year's Eve celebration.

The community-strengthening, place-building benefits of these Public Dreams events are often emphasized in their descriptions. The notion of developing a "shared culture" is often mentioned, and the value of creating "safer neighborhoods by bringing together people whose lives do not otherwise intersect, and by reinforcing community pride and optimism" (www.sfu.ca/cscd/gateway/sharing/chap7bx1.htm).

The explicit charge of the Public Dreams Society is "to revive and redefine community arts and the role of the artist in the community. Our mission statement is to produce theatrical events and participatory community events, integrating artists, performers, and the public; and to integrate theatre performance with ritual, myth, celebration and community activism" (www.publicdreams.org).

The Parade of Lost Souls is an especially valuable addition to the texture and life of a northern city like Vancouver. Held each year on the last Saturday before Halloween, it has become an extremely popular community event. It is at once a celebration of those deceased, a remembrance of family and friends who are still important in our lives, a connection to the past, and a recognition of the seasonal transitions. Celebrating and marking the seasons through community celebration like this happens too infrequently in cities. One participant and volunteer has written eloquently about this spectacle (Miles, 1999):

> The Parade of Lost Souls is about the dissolution of the boundaries of time and the reinforcement of the bonds of community. On one level . . . it is about joining life and death together in a cycle without end or beginning. Cross-culturally, this is a festival about the passing of the old and the resurgence of the new. The boundaries dissolve for one night, the two meld into one.
>
> By remembering its dead, the community retains a sense of itself, a connection to its living history, and internal bonds are strengthened. As a piece of theatre, the parade breaks down the barriers between performers and audience, between producers and receivers. Everyone is in costume, and the leitmotif of the Parade incorporates all the players into the show.

There is no doubt, then, that public events can serve to break down barriers between people, nurture a sense of connection and connectedness between people, and help to strengthen commitments to place. In Vancouver, organizations like the Public Dreams Society and events like the Parade of Lost Souls are part and parcel, for many, of why this city is such a special place in which to live. These kinds of active and participatory arts help to overcome, moreover, a prevailing sense of the passive nature of art—that it is about perceiving something (typically created by someone else), that it is something one stares at in a museum or gallery. As a city is a vibrant, active, dynamic place, so also should be the artistic experience. There is no better way to develop an inclusive vision of art than to invite citizens to become part of the art itself.

In Providence, Rhode Island, the spectacular and highly unusual WaterFire—the burning of 100 floating torches on that city's rivers, accompanied by music and other performances and events—draws many to its center. The event began in 1994, the brainchild of sculptor and photographer Barnaby Evans. The 100 floating fire braziers are lit by volunteers on boats (some 150) and stoked with wood from 8:00 P.M. to 1:00 A.M. on event nights. A musical score, also prepared by Evans, accompanies the flames. (See Diffily, 1998, for a good history.) Avant-garde performances, public dances, and side events are also now commonly a part of the events, typically around ten in a season, which are held from April to November.

WaterFire Providence, a nonprofit arts group, describes the event as "a powerful work of art and a moving symbol of Providence's renaissance" (www.waterfire.com):

> WaterFire's sparkling bonfires, the fragrant scent of aromatic wood smoke, the flickering firelight on the arched bridges, the silhouettes of the firetenders passing by the flames, the torch-lit vessels traveling down the river, and the enchanting music from across the world all engage the senses and emotions of those who stroll the paths and bridges of Waterplace Park. WaterFire has captured the imagination of many thousands of people, bringing life to downtown, and continues to revitalize Rhode Island's capital city."

That events like WaterFire bring us together and give us reasons to be in public spaces in cities is undeniable. As Barnaby Evans, the creator, observes, "When you boil things down, its about making our lives special. I think there's a transformation that happens at WaterFire that's very life-affirming and also very poignant" (as quoted in Ziner, 2002). The event is becoming a tradition, now that it is approaching a decade's existence (see also Van Siclen, 2002, 2003).

Forming a nonprofit arts group to carry the event forward was an important step, and the cost of WaterFire is covered through a combination of corporate sponsorship, private donations, and funding from the city. The event has been so popular that Evans has been asked to help create similar installations in other cities. Despite their popularity, however, these events that make cities and towns special are often on a tenuous financial footing. A precipitous decline in corporate sponsorship, a result of the economic times, threatens WaterFire's continuation (Van Siclen, 2003).

Conclusions

Humans need art in a profound and deep way, and these impulses and expressions of creativity and meaning can and must manifest throughout the places in which we live. Cities must be reconceived as grand artistic palettes, where art in many, many forms can find application. Building façades, transit bridges, sidewalks, and plazas provide opportunities for injecting thoughtful messages and exhilarating images, for incorporating art that entertains, uplifts, and challenges us to think of our world in new ways. And each city will express its artistic impulses in different and unique ways, leading in turn to unique place qualities and experiences. Art, then, plays an essential role in building place and place commitments, and in enhancing quality of life. It shifts our focus from material consumption to spiritual growth and interpersonal connections, and lays important foundations for creating sustainable communities.

Learning by Design: Communities That Teach

Education about place must be a centerpiece of any long-term vision of sustainable places, and a key prerequisite for rebuilding commitments to place and community. If we have little understanding of the communities and ecosystems in which we live, we will perceive little visceral or personal connection to them, tend not to care about them, and have little sense of what actions, behaviors, or policies will be necessary to nurture and steward over them. Education about place—about our neighborhoods, communities, regions—should be seen as an essential element in growing an intelligent and caring and responsible citizenry.

Few Americans actually know very much about the places in which they live. Long-term commitment to place will require place-based educational initiatives at a number of levels and in a number of creative ways. This chapter provides several ideas about how we may begin to tackle the challenge of place-based education. A key point is that education and learning about place can (and must) happen in many ways, some outside of the usual spheres of education. Particularly for those of us beyond school age, the main vehicles for place learning will necessarily be outside the formal classroom. I argue that there are many (profound) ways in which our design and planning decisions represent opportunities to teach. Each building constructed or renovated, each new infrastructure project undertaken, every instance of civic design, represents an important place-teaching moment that should be seized. Even the act of buying a new home represents a chance to impart new understandings of the nature, uniqueness, and special qualities of place, as well as opportunities to give effect to new place ethics and sensibilities.

For most North Americans, the modern home, whether a single-family suburban residence or a multistory urban apartment building, has been fundamentally "de-physicalized," or disconnected from the landscapes and ecosystems that support it. The average homeowner couldn't accurately tell you the name or physical dimensions of the watershed in which the house is located (or, indeed, even that their home is in a watershed), where the water and energy comes from, where the wastes are treated and disposed of, and so on. Food comes from the grocery store and energy from the power grid (or even more basically, from the light switch). Nurturing commitment to place, then, demands a reconceptualizing of home—indeed, a fundamental re-physicalizing of where (and how) people live. Correspondingly, there is a need to redefine home as a venue for a variety of important ethical choices, and home ownership or household management as important extensions of citizenship.

We must search for strategic points in which to intervene, to educate and instill a different deeper understanding of place. One such point is indeed during the research for a new home. For most Americans, such research is guided by a few basic things: price, housing style and size, and desired location. Yet, few homebuyers (or renters) are ever challenged to view their choice of a new home as an ethical choice, and especially in terms of its potential long-term impact on the environment. The possibilities here are substantial, and a number of creative ideas exist for involving a different, or at least broader, set of considerations in the process of selecting a new home. Once a home is selected, additional opportunities for education and the building of a place ethic emerge, as new residents move into their new homes and may be especially receptive to knowledge and insights about their new home settings at that time.

Building sufficient local capacity to educate residents, new and old alike, about environment and place, ought to be a high priority. At Kronsberg, the new ecological district in Hannover, Germany, a serious effort was made to put in place an institutional structure to educate new residents of this community about its ecological features and more generally about how the residents might live more sustainably. A unique organization was formed— KUKA (Kronsberg-Umwelt-Kommunikations Agentur) or the Kronsberg Ecological Education Agency. KUKA, with an office on-site, has played an indispensable educational role, including offering workshops and training, answering questions and inquiries of residents, and organizing environmental campaigns and initiatives in the district. KUKA also works with the local schools on environmental education, provides advice and guidance to local architects and builders, and gives guided tours. Impressively, KUKA gives to each new resident of the neighborhood an information binder (published in several different languages), a kind of "ecological owner's manual" that explains the environmental features of the district, its landscape, where and how one recycles, how to reduce energy and resource consumption, and the like.

KUKA is unusual even in environment-conscious Germany. It was created by the City of Hannover, with substantial funding from the Deutsche Bundesstiftung Umwelt (German federal environmental foundation), and is intended to eventually disband or sunset. Undoubtedly, finding ways in which to fund such a mechanism would be an issue in other places, and whether such an educational function was seen as necessary would be a major point of discussion. One suspects, though, that such an approach would pay many dividends in both the long and short terms (e.g., energy savings) and could serve as a compelling justification for staff and administrative costs. Place- and environment-educated residents will translate, I believe, into more economically efficient and socially resilient places, and providing such an educational push at the time new residents are moving into a new area makes considerable sense.

Landowners and homeowners alike need to be encouraged—indeed, challenged—to think beyond their own narrow self-interests. They should be expected to take the broader impacts and implications of their decisions into account. Chicago Wilderness's Good Neighbor and Parks project, for instance, seeks to enlist those with properties adjacent to parks, forest preserves, and other natural areas to begin to take the health and condition of these adjacent lands into account. There are many helpful things that can be done, such as making habitat improvements or nurturing natural vegetation that can, in a sense, help to extend the natural area functionally. Equally important are the many potentially damaging practices, such as the heavy usage of pesticides and lawn fertilizers that can harm adjacent lands, that landowners and homeowners might be asked to curtail.

One of the more interesting new models for educating homeowners, one with protected broad future implications, comes out of the United Kingdom. The British building society Norwich and Peterborough (N&P), in partnership with Future Forests, began offering customers a carbon-neutral mortgage in 2000. What makes the mortgage carbon neutral? For each participating home, 40 trees are planted to compensate for their expected carbon emissions (about 26 percent of the carbon emitted in the United Kingdom comes from the housing sector). Eight trees are planted each year for five years. Homeowners have the option of continuing the forest planting after this five-year period, again through Future Forests. New homeowners are not typically thinking about such things when shopping for mortgages. Price and interest rates are, at least in the American context, the usual driving considerations.

N&P reports that some 7,600 trees have already been planted (as of July 2003). All the trees have been planted in two U.K. forests—one in Lin-

Figure 8.1 | Representatives of the building society Norwich and Peterborough, in the United Kingdom, planting a tree and showing how a carbon-neutral mortgage might work. (Photo compliments of Norwich and Peterborough.)

colnshire and another in East Anglia. The carbon offset, though, could happen anywhere, and could be done locally or in a developing nation where the effects of global warming may be even more severe and the need and benefits of tree planting yet greater. For proprietary reasons, the building society declined to give me precise numbers about how many people had taken them up on this new kind of mortgage, but the idea does seem to be growing in popularity.

Such initiatives have the potential not only to educate about the environmental and place-destructive impacts of our lifestyles (heating and cooling one's home generates carbon emissions), but also to admonish an ethic of taking responsibility for these impacts. They also provide tangible tools and actions for assuming responsibility.

North American examples of educating residents and enhancing new home building sensibilities also exist. One promising example can be seen in Spring Island, South Carolina, a development designed around ecological and land conservation principles. Education of new residents about the island's rich biodiversity and natural environment has been a key goal, reflected in the building of a nature center and hiring of a resident ecologist. Most interesting has been the practice of giving each new resident as they move into the project a binder describing the nature on the island—a kind of biodiversity owner's guide. We might expect that new homeowners be given information at least equivalent to what they received about how the washing machine works or how the heating system ought to be maintained. And, in the process, it might be possible to instill in new residents not only a greater appreciation for the richness of place, but a civic responsibility to work, in both small and large ways, to protect and nurture it. Similar to the education provided by KUKA, such efforts educate but also exhort and challenge residents to be stewards of their larger *home*—the city, landscape, planet in which their individual dwelling unit lies.

From Real Estate to Living Places

The task of educating about place can be assumed by many different individuals and groups in a community. It just makes good sense to involve, for instance, real estate agents in any deeper, place-building initiative. Given the face-to-face personal relationships they forge with new residents and prospective buyers, and the sheer amount of time spent in home searches, the opportunity for awareness building about place and environment is great indeed. As one Washington State agent was recently quoted as saying: "You know, we realtors are educators too. . . . We spend from 16 to 50 hours with each client. We explain how things work, where people can go for information, and how they can get involved in the community" (quoted in Puget Sound Action Team, 2003, p. 5). One important way to pass along information is through an educational packet, which realtors are including with the other information typically given to clients.

In Jefferson County, Washington, an interesting initiative seeks to creatively inject such information into the process of buying and selling homes. The "Welcome to the Watershed Project" trains and enlists real estate agents in this environmental education mission. Training has been provided on watershed issues to agents through the State's Cooperative Extension Service, and with funding from Puget Sound's Public Involvement and Education (PIE) program.

In Rochester, New York, the creative "Homeroom: City Living Resource Center" conducts classes (among other things) for realtors on how to market historic structures successfully. This initiative recognizes that many homebuyers will be hesitant about buying a home in an urban neighborhood, and may need special help in appreciating the history and unique qualities and living opportunities in such places (see National Trust for Historic Preservation, 2000).

Instilling a fuller awareness of landscape and place in homeowners (and renters) could take even more fundamental forms. Ecological deeds, which describe the habitat types, ecological functions, and biodiversity of a parcel of land, might be required to accompany the more typical metes-and-bounds legal description of land and property found in a typical property deed. Local property tax systems could be adjusted to reflect these natural connections and in turn encourage more responsible management. A typical land deed describes a property in a limited legalistic way. Perhaps we must explore the notion of an ecological deed that would explicitly attempt to list some of the natural conditions and qualities of the site, and perhaps the ecological assets and infrastructure present: the trees, the biodiversity, and the habitat qualities of the site. Would such deeds make a difference in our outlook on property? It is hard to say, but it might begin to set in motion a broader, deeper view of land and place, and a recognition that the home one owns is tied to and interconnected with a larger ecosystem.

The greater the protection of ecological functions and services maintained on a parcel of land—whether protecting mature trees, existing wetlands, groundwater regeneration sites, or the like—the lower the property taxes should be. An immense accounting headache, to be sure, but such a system would increase awareness of place—native landscapes, vegetation, ecosystems—as well as provide economic incentives for protecting these qualities. In some western U.S. cities, largely to conserve limited water, citizens are given financial rebates for replacing their conventional turfgrass with desert landscaping. In Las Vegas, for instance, the local water authority will offer homeowners as much as $400—no small inducement. Such programs, while creating positive economic incentives for good practice, are also educational and alert homeowners to the preciousness of water.

Finding creative ways to educate the public and homeowners about the environment will help build connections to local watersheds and nature. In some communities, learning about the location of preurbanization streams, creeks, and watersheds becomes the basis for community walks. Stenciling storm drains is one technique done in many communities. Toronto took the interesting approach of mapping where streams and creeks *used* to be. Working with schools, local students painted roadways where the surface streams have been buried. Called "Paint the River" day, the project resulted in the installation of plaques commemorating the former location of the stream before development occurred.

In Toronto, the nonprofit community group North Toronto Green Community has been sponsoring Lost River walks since 1995. Residents participate in guided walks, in which they learn about the hidden hydrology of their neighborhoods. The goal of these walks is to "help people appreciate their intimate connections to the water systems that form an essential part of their lives" (www.lostrivers.ca). The walks sometimes draw several hundred people, but typically have 15 to 60. Nearly 5,000 people have participated in these walks since they began. As a flavor for what is covered, here is how the walk schedule reads for a May walk in the Ashbridge Bay neighborhood of North Toronto:

On this walk we will discover at least 11 lost creeks in four distinct subwatersheds that once flowed into Ashbridge's Bay. Highlights include a secluded, century-old Jewish cemetery that once overlooked one of the creeks, as well as various reminders of the brick-making enterprises that once flourished along the creek's course. Finally, we will be rewarded with a live creek, still flowing in a forested ravine. (www.lostrivers.ca)

One way to strengthen community resolve in support of place is to encourage and facilitate individual or family commitments. Such declarations of commitment to place can take many forms, but need essentially to be visible to others. In this way they serve as a vehicle for neighborhood and community education. Again in Toronto, the group North Toronto Green Community has led the way, starting a Chemical Free Zone Residential Pesticide Use Awareness Program. Over 700 residents have participated thus far, by buying and putting up "Chemical Free Zone" signs on their lawns. Through this relatively simple program, homeowners are able to declare their ecological homeowner values in a very effective way, and to educate others about the importance of these type of homeowner decisions.

Figure 8.2 | A Lost River walk in Toronto, Canada. These walks are organized by North Toronto Green Community. (Photo by Peter J. Hare.)

Prospective residents of the new ecological neighborhood EVA-Lanxmeer, in Culemborg, Netherlands, are asked to acknowledge and accept the special ecological goals and philosophy of this neighborhood. They are required to read and sign a contract that states the special qualities and conditions of EVA-Lanxmeer, specifically that the project seeks to minimize the presence of automobiles, that residents realize that there may be some things that cannot be put down their drains (e.g., because they may damage the graywater reed-beds), and that the landscape plan will impose some limits, as well (e.g., no walls, only natural hedges, and use of native vegetation). There ought to be as much emphasis on what is required (of the homeowner or new resident) to take care of the local watershed as on how to clean and care for interior surfaces, perhaps, or the maintenance schedule for the garage door opener.

New developments such as Civano, on the edge of growing Tucson, Arizona, have placed special emphasis on native landscaping, which impressively reduces water consumption, adds beauty to the community, and acknowledges the desert ecosystem into which it has been placed. One finds cactus, mesquite, and palo verde trees in the yards of these homes, not turfgrass. And the layout of Civano facilitates direct exposure to the abundant native flora and fauna. A series of wedges of desert ecosystem and open

Figure 8.3 | Civano, in Tucson, is a new development that emphasizes native vegetation and connections to the surrounding desert ecosystem.

space—brown wedges, if you will—with low-impact walking paths extend through residential areas, with a number of homes with backyards and spaces adjoining these natural areas. Some 30 percent of the land area of this project is to be set aside for these kinds of natural lands.

The residents of Civano are helped along in the use of native plants by a relatively large on-site nursery. The Civano Nursery and Garden Center has already salvaged some 2,400 plants and 500 mature trees from the development site, reportedly some 65 percent of the sizable trees (www.terrain.org) have been replanted. The nursery also conducts workshops and training about native landscaping and, perhaps most importantly, works directly with homeowners in designing a unique plan for planting and landscaping one's home.

The use of native vegetation helps in conserving water, a precious resource in the Southwest. Native, drought-tolerant plants are uniquely adapted and suited to local climatic conditions. Starting with landscaping that requires much less water in the first place, Civano also incorporates rainwater harvesting from rooftops and the reuse of water. Each home in Civano is fitted with water lines delivering potable water and less-clean recycled water. Civano uses close to 65 percent less water than a conventional development in the Tucson area. In this case, using local flora both strengthens connections to environment and sense of place, and conserves a scarce and important local resource.

One of the community's key design tenets is about "creating a sense of place that fosters community and connects people to one another and their natural environments" (www.terrain.org). The architecture has also been designed with the idea of connecting residents to place. Use of adobe and other materials and building styles native to this region provides a right "fit" to the place. The adobe structures, however, are not meant to replicate or fool, and are clearly contemporary. The visible presence of solar panels, for instance, makes it clear that these are not new homes trying to be old homes. A mix of the modern and the traditional Southwest might best describe the style.

In Prairie Crossing, a conservation development in Grayslake, Illinois, the position of a full-time environmental coordinator exists. Among other duties, the coordinator educates and works with residents in thinking about how their homes, and the spaces around their individual home are managed.

Covenants running with the properties, which require, for instance, use of native plants and mandate organic and slow-release fertilizers only (and applied no more than twice a year), further strengthen understanding of homeowner environmental obligations (Lehner et al., 1999).

One way to build active community involvement with land management while strengthening local ecological knowledge is through initiatives that train and enlist citizens to do research, monitoring, and stewardship activities. Under the many activities of Chicago Wilderness, for example, the development of an army of "citizen scientists" is one of the most promising. Here, citizens are enlisted to learn about plants, birds, and frogs through workshops and training, and then to actively manage monitoring programs for the local species.

Local grassroots organizations can certainly do much to promote awareness of local ecology and ecological connectedness. Along the Anacostia River, a watershed that includes some of the poorest neighborhoods in Washington, D.C., reconnecting with and recommitting to this river offers hope of community renewal and a richer quality of life for its residents. The Anacostia Watershed Society (AWS), formed in 1989, is working hard in many ways to improve water quality and other environmental conditions and make this

Figure 8.4 | EVA-Lanxmeer, a development in Culemborg, Netherlands, seeks to instill in a variety of ways new ecological sensibilities in its residents.

impressive river and watershed meaningful to residents, a source of civic engagement and pride. Its goals are to "develop an enlightened community of citizen stakeholders who are aware of the connection to the natural world and who work to promote the healing of the Anacostia River and its watershed communities." Among the important activities raising citizen awareness of the river have been river cleanups throughout the year, weekly river tours, storm drain stenciling, a water quality monitoring program, tree planting and wetland restoration events, paddling clinics, and an annual paddlesport regatta. The accomplishments have been considerable, including the participation of more than 30,000 volunteers, the planting of some 11,400 trees, and the pulling out of some 7,500 tires from the watershed. The organization has worked extensively with local schools to promote watershed education there, and has involved the students in cleanup and restoration work as well. Some 6,700 students have gone on canoe trips of the river. Through the Watershed Explorers and River Habitat programs, local students learn in class about the ecology of the river, and through river tours and hands-on activities build new understandings of their watershed homes.

Often the task is about researching local and neighborhood ecology and making this knowledge accessible to community residents. One of the more creative recent examples can be seen in the work of the nonprofit group Fairfax Trails and Streams, a group promoting stream restoration and trail building in this heavily populated northern Virginia county. Through the tireless work of one of its members, Steve Dryden, a beautiful, historical and ecological map of the little-appreciated stream Pimmit Run now exists. Dryden, over a five-year period, pieced together an elaborate history of this stream, both its ecology (what was there and what remains) and the historical events that occurred along its banks. He learned of duels that took place, and the amazing story of how in 1814 our nation's most important documents—the Declaration of Independence and the Constitution—were whisked out of the capital and hidden from the invading British in a gristmill along the stream. The resulting product of Dryden's great research is a map depicting the stream and its history, produced with the help of watercolorist Ann Chenoweth Sader (Kunkle, 2002). With a grant from the local historical society, a number of these maps have been published and are now available at a local wild birds store and a community center.

Although examples like the Pimmit Run map, which fuse historical and ecological knowledge, and collect and present it in ways that educate and motivate, are to be commended, their impact may in the end be rather modest, of course. But, when this kind of historical, landscape, and ecological research becomes standard practice that homeowner associations or neighborhood groups commonly undertake, the potential for impact is great.

(Re)connecting Students to Place: New Educational Missions for Schools

Place-based learning must be incorporated in serious ways, especially into primary and secondary education. History of cities, towns, and regions—environmental and human settlement history—should be given at least as much importance as traditional American history courses. Learning about the ecology and natural heritage of a place also suggests redefinition of the role of a school and the essential "equipment" needed for this educational mission. In addition to the typical ingredients of books, computers, sports equipment, and the like, we might imagine schools that represent direct connections to place. Perhaps a functioning native forest, wetland, or other local ecosystem or biotope ought to be considered essential equipment for place-based education.

One example of this is the "Little Prairie by the School" initiative, a collaboration between the Naperville, Illinois–based Conservation Foundation and Lucent Industries. Under the program, small grants are given to schools to design and plant their own small prairies on-site (and to pay for maintenance for five years). The stated goal is to "develop an awareness and appreciation of native prairies in local schoolchildren, parents, school staff, and communities through long-term programs that stimulate a holistic understanding of prairies" (Little Prairie Proposal Guidelines, undated). School prairie restoration workshops are held, and educational materials about prairies are provided. Initiatives similar to this one can be replicated everywhere, and schools can be redefined to include a fundamental place- and environment-educational mission.

Municipally owned properties may form the basis of nature or ecological schools—places where schoolchildren visit; where environmental education programs are held; and where, through recreation and visitation, residents of a community learn about the geology, natural history, and flora and fauna of a region. Such a lovely place exists in the municipality of Nacka, Sweden, adjacent to Stockholm. The Nacka Nature School, once a seventeenth-century manor estate, is now owned by the municipality and serves as a nature preserve of considerable size (700 hectares) and as an education center. Several of the buildings on the estate have been converted to environmental classrooms and exhibition sites. In one main building, students can see a small functioning "living machine"—a collection of plants and aquatic organisms that take up and naturally treat effluent—as well as other sustainability technologies. Moreover, in addition to the opportunities to learn in the classroom, the spectacular water and forests on the property make for a fantastic mix of outdoor laboratory and learning opportunity (Nacka Kommun, 2001).

Many schools and school buildings are now being designed to incorporate green and ecological features, features that are evident and visible to students and become as important to the learning environment as the usual book, blackboard, and classroom. One example is the Roy Lee Walker Elementary

Figure 8.5 | Roy Lee Walker Elementary School, a sustainable school in McKinney, Texas. (Photo compliments of SHW Architects and Planners.)

School, located near Dallas, Texas, and designed by the SHW Group. It has been winning awards for its ecological design elements and has been recently described by the National Institute of Building Sciences as the "most comprehensive sustainable school in the United States" (National Institute of Building Science, undated). This school for about 600 students has many elements of green thinking in its design and construction: use of nontoxic paints, use of local products and materials, landscaping with native vegetation, recyclable carpets, and daylighting throughout. Its rainwater collection system, which provides water to the landscaping and the school's pond; the solar panels on the rooftop; an eco-garden; two large sundials; and a 30-foot windmill are all highly visible, making nature and sustainability a key aspect of the experience of being in school.

Schools must also be enjoyable, physically nurturing, and inspirational places for students (and others) to spend time. Designing every new school so that ample sunlight bounces through the halls and classrooms is a basic and essential requirement. Durant Middle School in Wake County, North Carolina, is one outstanding example. Designed by the Raleigh architectural firm Innovative Design, every classroom is filled with daylight: "Rooftop monitors aligned on an east-west axis bring daylight down through mitigating baffles and into classrooms. Sensors adjust artificial lighting to compensate for cloudy days" (McQuillen, 1998, p. 46).

Designing schools to take advantage of daylight also substantially reduces energy consumption in these buildings. Nicklas and Bailey, at the architecture firm Innovative Design, conclude from monitoring studies that annual energy consumption at daylit schools is between 22 and 64 percent less than conventionally lit schools. The potential long-term cost savings are impressive, to say the least: "In North Carolina, a 125,000-square-foot middle school that incorporates a well-integrated day lighting scheme is likely to save $40,000 per year over what is typically constructed. And, if energy costs go up by 5% per year, the savings on just this one school, over the next ten years, would exceed $500,000." (Nicklas and Bailey, 1996a, p. 7). The Durant Middle School building is saving about $77,000 per year in reduced energy consumption, with a payback period of less than two years. The economics of daylighting in a school like Durant Middle School, then, are rather convincing. While the extra daylighting feature added some $230,000 to the cost of the building, lower energy demand reduced the mechanical electrical system cost by $115,000. As the architects note, the final cost of daylighting is less than 1 percent of the total cost of the structure. And the payback time is extremely short.

Designing schools to be green, energy-efficient, and uplifting learning environments is a good place-building strategy and accomplishes many things at once. Studies indicate that daylit schools will help tremendously the primary mission of schools. Students will be more attentive and happier, learn more effectively, and miss fewer days from schools. Daylit schools have been shown to result in higher student grades (Smith, 2002). A study of three daylit schools in Johnston County, North Carolina—two middle schools and an elementary school—found that students attending these schools outperformed students at nondaylit schools by 5 to 14 percent (Nicklas and Bailey, 1996b, p. 10). And the longer students attend these daylit schools, the greater the difference in performance becomes. Students are also more likely to want to come to school in the morning. Of the 100 schools in Wake County, North Carolina, the Durant School has been at the top in terms of attendance rates (number one in 1996).

The definitive study remains a two-year analysis conducted by the Alberta (Canada) Education Ministry, which compared student attendance and performance of those attending schools with natural, full-spectrum lighting and those with conventional lighting. Students exposed to natural light were found to be healthier (attended more days of school each year), had more positive moods, grew taller, and even had significantly less tooth decay (as reported in Nicklas and Bailey, 1996a).

It is sad that in designing and funding school construction we often appear to overlook those features so essential to the health and well-being of students and the effective learning and human growth that we increasingly expect from our schools. Just as it is essential to design schools to provide natural light, it is equally important to incorporate trees, nature, and green wherever possible. There is growing evidence of the psychological and physiological effects of exposure to nature in the built environment, and again, as with daylight, there is simply no excuse not to design children's play and school environments with these qualities foremost in mind.

Schools would be an obvious place to ensure exposure to nature, and there are now considerable numbers of schools having gone through some form of greening or ecological retrofit, as a way of improving the environment of these places and also as an opportunity to educate students about the planet. Los Angeles, in many ways the poster child of sprawl and the antithesis of a city full of nature, is another emerging site of inspiration for urban ecology and city greening initiatives, many of them focused on schools. The grassroots advocacy group TreePeople, in particular, and its founder, Andy Lipkis, have put forth some exemplary concepts for restoring natural hydrological functions of the city and region. Spurred by plans by the Los Angeles Public School District to resurface schoolyards (to the tune of an incredible $200 million), Lipkis and his group saw an immense opportunity to redirect these investments in a more natural direction:

> We were able to show that by reducing much of the asphalt surface and planting thousands of trees, we could reduce some of the runoff which leads to periodic flooding and pollution of local rivers and beaches. We were able to prove that the district could save between 12–18 percent annually in air-conditioning costs, because the trees help to cool the buildings in the Southern California heat (as quoted in Amaya, 2000).

An outgrowth of Lipkis's advocacy is the Cool Schools Tree Planting and Energy Efficiency Program, sponsored by the Los Angeles Department of Water and Power (LADWP). Under this program, thousands of trees have been planted on school campuses throughout the city. The program involves the students at these schools directly by educating them about the trees and tree care, and students are actually helping to plant them. Thousands of students will have been involved, as wells as volunteers from the community, and at-risk youth are hired.

The green retrofit of Broadus Elementary School in the Los Angeles area, a collaborative effort between several groups, including the LADWP and TreePeople, shows how schools and schoolyards can be positively transformed. Here, perennial flooding problems due to a highly paved-over environment have been addressed by pulling out about one-third of the site's asphalt surfaces, installing grass and bioswales, and planting some 170 trees in its place. The green retrofit actively involved parents, students, and teachers and accomplished several goals at once: alleviating the flooding problem, reducing the energy consumption of the school, and creating a greener, more inviting school. This new landscaping was also seen as an opportunity to teach. A curriculum addressing area watershed issues was developed, and the design itself encourages students to appreciate and understand the hydrology of the neighborhood. "The landscaping was designed to model a watershed and provides a living textbook for Broadus students" (TreePeople, 2002, p. 1).

Schools can also be places where children learn about and participate in growing food, in healthy and sustainable ways, of course. An early effort to integrate schoolyard food production into the school operation can be seen in the Willard Greening Project, an effort to supply two elementary schools in Berkeley, California, with fresh greens actually grown on the grounds of the Willard Elementary School. The on-ground production involved tearing up considerable paving and asphalt and installing raised beds. The program produces 15–30 pounds of fresh lettuce each week, which stocks the school cafeteria's salad bar. Any remaining produce goes to a homeless shelter and a local farmers' market. Students are also directly involved in the production, with some 124 sixth-graders working each week, and being instructed on

Figure 8.6 | Berkeley Edible Schoolyard Program. (Photo compliments of Edible Schoolyards, Berkeley, California.)

"the cycle of life (decomposition), nutrition, ecological systems, plant biology, and hands-on gardening" (Huang, 1999).

Support for school gardens in Berkeley and elsewhere has been helped immensely by a champion—Alice Waters, famous San Francisco chef and restaurateur (founder of the well-known restaurant Chez Panisse). For Waters, this mission began in the early 1970s when she began to notice the depressingly gray look of the Martin Luther King, Jr., Middle School, in Berkeley, which she would pass on her drive to work. When called by the school's principal to see if she might help (in response to a print interview in which she mentioned the school's neglected condition), her notion of the Edible Schoolyard emerged, and this particular school has emerged as a model. Students here, as Waters believes all students should be, are challenged to become personally involved in growing the food they eat, and to connect in a visceral way to the natural cycles and earth upon which we all depend. And the teaching is also about slowing down, learning to appreciate food and sustenance and community and people.

Martin Luther King, Jr., Middle School is quite a different place because of the Edible Schoolyard program. In 1997, an acre of asphalt was ripped up and converted to garden space. A kitchen was created out of a 40-year-old bungalow adjacent to the school. These spaces have been integrated into the life of the school, with sixth- and seventh-graders frequently visiting the garden during the week, and being taught about food and cooking in the kitchen. Students themselves are, moreover, directly growing, cooking, and eating food, alongside their teachers. The nonprofit program now has a full-time staff of six, including a kitchen teacher. (See www.edibleschoolyard.org for much more information.)

The obstacles to such programs are not insignificant, however. In the Willard Greening Project, for instance, supplying school-grown lettuce ran into a variety of objections from the school district's Food Services department, including concerns about cost, difficulty of preparation, and concerns that schoolchildren are not particularly interested in eating fruits and vegetables. Interestingly, the cost issue often looms important because food services operations are typically structured in ways that require them to operate at a profit. As one recent observer notes, sadly, they tend to be "budget driven, not menu driven or nutrition driven programs" (Huang, 1999). In the case of the Willard Greening project, it was possible to overcome many of the obstacles simply by clarifying the issues and working cooperatively with the Food Services department.

Students can be creatively challenged to imagine more sustainable community futures and the creation of more satisfying and fulfilling places. A recent project undertaken by the students at Emery High School, in Emeryville, California, provides an inspired example. Some thirty juniors and seniors there produced a "solar mural," depicting what their town might look like if radically powered by the sun. A kind of cross between a sculpture and a map, the work was guided by artist Therese Lahaie and took six months to complete. Sun shines on the mural and solar cells power whirligigs and lights (thus the kinetic dimensions of the sculpture!). It now hangs in city hall as a piece of community art that educates as well about the possibilities of solar power.

The Emeryville project, officially known as the Solar Art Workshop, was sponsored under that city's youth arts program, where community artists, in exchange for a stipend, spend time teaching in the schools. Artist Therese Lahaie met with her solar mural students weekly, and in addition to planning and designing and building the mural, she used these meetings to teach about

Figure 8.7 | Emery High School Solar Mural. (Photo by Paul Herzoff; compliments of Therese Lahaie.)

solar energy and to conduct experiments that demonstrate scientific principles and the potential for solar power. The project impressively combines creative design and art with education about the environment, in an activity and process that is fun for students. A recent article summarizes the benefits and accomplishments of this project (found at www.thereselahaie.com, 2003):

> The solar mural project helped the students to imagine a sustainable way of relating to their world, and to share this understanding with others through art.
>
> As students' understanding of solar power grew, Lahaie discussed the importance of solar power in response to pollution and the depletion of fossil fuels. Lahaie asked students to imagine a city powered by solar energy, rather than gas and oil. Through drawing and painting, the students reflected their urban surroundings, and these drawings were the basis for the design of the solar cell–driven whirligigs.

In Almere, a new town east of Amsterdam, and a city with many sustainability qualities, a unique effort has been aimed at involving local schools in educating about and promoting wind energy. Here, a creative approach has been taken to engage students in the planning of a nearby wind farm. Specifically, a color designer was commissioned to identify three alternative color schemes for painting the Almere turbines. A contest was held among grade-school children (all students in grades 6–7) to choose which paint scheme to apply. Students were asked not only to choose which color but to put forth a convincing argument for that selection. In the end, thirty-six classes participated, learning much about wind power in the process, and developing a sense of ownership about the park. The color scheme chosen, and by far the most popular among the students, was "fire" (red, orange, and yellow).

City Vision is yet another example of engaging youth in community affairs and building confidence and competence in community participation. Created by the National Building Museum in Washington, D.C., in 1993, the program is largely staffed by volunteer architecture and design professionals. City Vision involves students from five D.C. middle schools in thinking and crafting real-world design and planning solutions to neighborhood and city problems. During this three-month-long program, students visit, observe, and seek to understand their neighborhoods, develop basic technical and interpersonal skills, and working in teams, prepare a specific proposal for addressing a community problem (see www.nbm.org). They present these proposals to a panel of professionals, public officials, and representatives from the community. Past projects have included how to promote reuse of vacant lots and abandoned buildings, how to address graffiti problems, and concerns about littering and vandalism (Langholtz, undated).

Landscapes That Teach

Every community will have opportunities to create places that teach about landscape and bioregion and city ecology. Albuquerque, New Mexico, for instance, has been engaged in developing a master plan, recently completed, for a 2,700-acre nature reserve and educational center called La Semilla ("the seed"). Adjacent to the large Mesa del Sol master-planned community, which is itself designed with environmental sustainability in mind, La Semilla will become a recreational and educational resource for the city's residents. La Semilla will incorporate several elements, including a renewable resource research park (the northern one-third of the site, to promote and research such ideas as solar wind and biomass energy) and an environmental education campus (including a visitor's center, museum, library, and classrooms), and will "emphasize methodologies and techniques that can reduce our reliance on water and other resources that will preserve biological diversity and ecosystem health" (La Semilla Master Plan, 2002, p. 7). The (working) McCormick Ranch comprises the southern portion of the site. The Environmental Education Campus will house a native plant garden and arboretum, a native tree and agricultural orchard, a wildlife rehabilitation center, and an urban ecology field research program (which, among other things, will be monitoring the environmental effects of the nearby Mesa del Sol development). The McCormick Ranch is envisioned as a place where residents can see and learn firsthand about ranching and farming practices in New Mexico, as well as provide opportunities for research and demonstration for more sustainable forms of these practices (La Semilla Master Plan, 2002).

Landscape and ecological teaching opportunities can be inserted in some very imaginative and unconventional ways. In Tampa, Florida, a creative design for a restorative parking lot at the Florida Aquarium illustrates how urban landscapes can educate. A joint initiative of the Southwest Florida Water Management District and the Florida Aquarium, the parking lot has been designed to funnel and treat stormwater runoff so that at the end of the process the water entering the Tampa Bay (and actually the Gulf of Mexico) is remarkably clean. The treatment process involves several steps. Runoff from the parking spaces is guided first into a series of vegetated swales between parking rows, then into forested wetlands (or "strands") where pollutants are absorbed by the trees and vegetation, and finally into a wet detention pond. Space for the 4-foot swales came from creatively shortening each parking space by 2 feet (the fronts of the cars now hang over these grassy areas).

Education is a key element of this project. Visitors to the Florida Aquarium are handed a brochure that describes the parking lot and its stormwater management and other unique environmental features. Displays have also been installed in several places in the parking lot. Some 600,000 people visit the aquarium each year, and potentially a large proportion of them learn about watersheds, threats to water quality, and application of natural systems thinking to the common spaces and places—including parking lots— where we spend time. The Florida Aquarium has also been developing an environmental curriculum for ninth-graders and has been using the parking lot as a site for field trips.

A unique park adjacent to a wastewater treatment plant, in Renton, Washington (near Seattle) further illustrates creative landscape education. The 8 acres of the Waterworks Gardens is organized as a series of habitats and functional elements. What the designer, Lorna Jordan, calls "rooms" move from the top of a hill and wind down to wetlands at the bottom. These five garden rooms tell visitors the story of the water cycle. This path is both a winding trail and a functional treatment train, with much of the area in a series of sensitively nestled ponds, collecting and treating stormwater until reaching the final wetlands stage. Always looming in the background is the large conventional wastewater treatment plant, reminding visitors that this is not your typical park.

Funded through Metro King Country's 1-percent-for-art program, the Renton park is educational at the same time that it creates a high-quality walking environment. The trail meanders in and out of the collecting ponds and wetlands, and connects to other trails. An article in *Landscape NW* describes succinctly the function of these different rooms:

> Stormwater flows under a grate below "The Knoll," a paved overlook dominated by a basalt column "colonnade." "The Funnel" consists of a series of terraced leaf-shaped ponds connected by the path, or stem. At the bottom of a hill, stormwater cascades into "The Grotto," which is shaped as a seed pod. Undulating shotcrete walls covered with a richly patterned mosaic provide a place for repose. "The passage" provides a calming experience as the path passes by a row of Lombardy poplars and three circular ponds that symbolize the fruit of the plant. In "The Release," cleansed water flows from the last stormwater treatment pond to the ribbonlike islands and channels of a wetland and then to Springbrook Creek. (Enlow, 1998)

Even on a weekday morning there is considerable use of this small but extremely interesting space. Walkers, birdwatchers, and joggers are all present. It is a remarkable combination of art, technology, and nature in a single place

Figure 8.8 | The Waterworks Gardens in Renton, Washington, which educates about stormwater runoff and the nature of water cycles, is a creative use of an area adjacent to a wastewater treatment plant.

and facility that actively teaches, albeit in subtle ways. The only limitation of this fantastic project may be that it suffers as part of our typical attitude toward sewage treatment plants—we want to keep them away from us. The site feels remote from where people live or spend time in Renton, off the beaten path (despite a steady and annoying flow of car traffic on adjoining Oakdale Avenue).

Infrastructures That Teach

Santa Monica's Urban Runoff Recycling Facility (SMURRF) demonstrates the integration of art and infrastructure and the creative designing-in of public education. This innovative new facility collects and treats up to 500,000 gallons per day of urban runoff, during the dry season, providing tremendous pollution reduction benefits. Draining an area of 4,200 acres, fed by one major storm drain line, this polluted urban runoff would otherwise end up directly in Santa Monica Bay. But SMURRF has another benefit, one equally as important as its ability to reduce pollution: it recycles treated water back to the city for landscaping and dual-plumbed buildings (toilet-flushing).

The facility was designed from the beginning (by engineering firm CH2M Hill) to maximize its public education potential. It has been dubbed the "first full-scale, dry weather runoff facility in the United States" (Antich, Gobas, and Salgaonkar, 2003). A short distance from popular Santa Monica Pier, the treatment equipment and machines have been arrayed sequentially so visitors can see and better understand the stages of the treatment process. A partnership between Santa Monica and the City of Los Angeles, the facility opened in spring 2001. An education plaza further adds to the learning:

> The design team met the city's mandate, laying out the equipment in a fashion that would be logical to visitors, emphasizing each piece of equipment with a prominent base, dramatic lighting, or colorful tile work. The water, as it moves through the facility, is daylighted in five places so visitors can see the results of the purification process. From overlooks at two points, visitors can see the array of equipment. Educational material about the working of the facility, the local urban watershed, and the citizen's role in preventing pollution are presented as well. (Antich, Gobas, and Salgaonkar, 2003)

An artist was an important member of the design team for SMURRF, leading to some significant aesthetic elements. This was also seen as an important dimension to fitting this facility into the community:

> The genuine concern for aesthetic issues signaled a sense of respect for the local citizenry. By investing this potentially mundane facility with carefully considered architecture, landscapes, and art, a unique contribution was made to the quality of life in Santa Monica. (Antich, Gobas, and Salgaonkar, 2003)

At the Cambridge, Massachusetts, water treatment plant, several public art installations were developed to inject beauty into this functional facility, and to educate about water supply and watersheds. Artist Michele Turre has created a scale map of Cambridge's watershed and reservoir system, mounted on a second-floor wall of the plant. Even more dramatic is the installation by artists Mags Harries and Lajos Héder, called *Drawn Water*, which is located in the lobby of the plant and consists of a 2,500-square-foot terrazzo map of

Figure 8.9 | The SMURRF—the Santa Monica Urban Runoff Recycling Facility—incorporates education about urban stormwater runoff and the need to conserve precious water directly into a facility intended to treat and recycle it. (Photo compliments of City of Santa Monica.)

the city's water distribution system. Also included is a "transparent water column," indicating the location of the city's main reservoir on the map, and connected to an outside water fountain at the plant. The artists also designed thirteen distinct bronze manhole covers, placed in each of the city's neighborhoods, "to encourage a treasure hunt in the neighborhoods" (www.ci .cambridge.ma.us). Both projects were funded by the Cambridge Arts Council, which provides the following detailed description of *Drawn Water*:

> *Drawn Water* combines real drinking water, symbolic elements, and a 2,500 sq. foot map that focuses attention on the importance of water in our lives. The underground pipes that bring the water throughout the city are marked on the map, along with water fountains, swimming pools, and ponds. Actual water pipes form functional seats and suggest the sizes of pipes in the map. A transparent water column is placed on the map at the site of the city's holding reservoir, Payson Park. The art continues outside the building. A shallow depression on both sides of a path reveals a 42-inch pipe, reminding us of the connection between the treatment facility and Fresh Pond, the city's reservoir. A circular opening in the fence around the pond focuses views of the water intake.

Buildings That Teach

A single building or structure, in its design and functioning, can do much to teach about place and about ways of living sustainably and respectfully in that place. For many of us, the true extent of our consumptive lifestyles—the amount of energy we consume, water and gas we use up, waste we generate—is difficult to gauge or fathom on a daily (or even momentary) basis. In today's American buildings, we in the United States seem to go out of our way to hide the meters and dials that show how much we are using of these things. Many schools, for instance, now incorporate energy meters in prominent locations that show real-time consumption of power as well as production of solar, wind, and other renewable energy sources. The Solar Tower, a high-rise office building in Freiburg, Germany, has a street-level panel showing photovoltaic production and output from its visually dramatic vertical array. It is hard to walk by this structure, and certainly hard to walk through the lobby, without actively scanning the solar display.

Even the more typical and mundane urban buildings and cityscapes can be designed to better reflect (and teach about) green values and to function according to ecological principles. The opening of the new Sainsbury's ecological grocery store, as part of the new Millennium Peninsula regeneration project in London, is a dramatic case in point. The energy features of this grocery store, which opened in 1999, are special and many. The goal was to reduce energy consumption 40 percent compared with a more typical supermarket (Sainsbury's, undated). These features include a natural ventilation system, which pulls fresh air in from ground-level ventilation ducts, a floor heating system that uses waste energy from a combined heat and power system, insulation from the building's earth bank design, thermal mass from concrete walls, and cooling in summer from deep ground wells. Other important environmental features of the store include the planting of 4,000 native trees and shrubs, on-site rainwater collection and treatment through a reed-bed system (and re-use in store toilets), use of Forest Stewardship Council (FSC) certified

Figure 8.10 | Freiburg Solar Tower, Freiburg, Germany.

wood, use of recycled material (entrance flooring made from recycled tires), and a program for reducing packaging waste.

Two of the most visually distinctive features of the grocery store are the pair of wind turbines (and photovoltaic array) at the front of the store, and the daylighting on the inside of the building. The daylit roof is a key feature of the structure, but perhaps one that shoppers may fail to appreciate adequately. The curved roof (the building looks a little like a spaceship) employs a sawtooth design, with north-facing windows sending a tremendous amount of natural light into the interior of the structure. Interior artificial lighting is minimal and is adjusted automatically through light sensors. Each window has a movable louver that closes at night to reflect light back into the building and to retain the building's heat. Light-colored floors further serve to reflect light back.

Other unique features of the Sainsbury's store, and that tell you that you're somewhere different, have to do with the transportation possibilities: there is extensive bicycle parking, a bus-only going right by the entrance, and even an electric car recharging station. Moreover, the space in front of the structure has become a public plaza, with outside seating for a café—a

Figure 8.11 | The Sainsbury's ecological grocery store, London.

Starbuck's, unfortunately, but nevertheless an improvement over the spaces found outside most American-style grocery-chain buildings.

Perhaps the most intriguing—and certainly the most visually distinct—element of the Sainbury's green grocery store is its two wind turbines. Prominently operating on 12-meter-high towers placed on ground near the entrance to the store, these turbines produce 2.5 kilowatts of power (together with the photovoltaic panels) and have a rotor length of 3 meters. These turbines pivot into the wind and can rotate 360 degrees. They are convincingly benign in an urban setting: these turbines essentially make no noise, not even the sounds of air movement of larger turbines.

Interesting indeed is to watch the steady flow of shoppers entering and exiting with grocery carts directly under and next to the turbines. Perhaps the windmills have become transparent for most shoppers going about their mundane tasks of grocery shopping. But I have to imagine that for some, at least, this picture still looks a bit unusual (in a good way) and that it may provoke a question or two or induce a speculation about the promise and beauty and special qualities of wind turbines. I certainly hope it does.

In the so-called Green Zone in Umeå, Sweden, is another interesting example of teaching by design. The project was the idea and passion of Per Carstedt, the owner of a Ford dealership. Looking for a larger new site for his business, he saw it as the perfect opportunity to give expression to his ecological ideals. This new green commercial complex would contain not only the car dealership, but other elements familiar to suburban American communities—a gas station (Statoil) and a McDonald's.

The green rooftops on the buildings (especially the McDonald's) are perhaps the most visually dramatic elements, but others certainly catch the eye as one enters this unusual Ford dealership. Specially designed, mirrored light boxes bring daylight into the showroom and the other workspaces of the building, and reduce the need for artificial lighting. Ventilation air is drawn through the building through a series of small fans—silver flicks in the sun, turning, pulling air through an underground pipe that cools the incoming air as well.

The air is cleaned and humidified through a series of plant boxes distributed throughout the building. The plant boxes are an odd sight in this Ford showroom. A commercial system, Levander R filters, meaning "living filters," each of these boxes is equipped with an overhead spray nozzle that gives the plants a one-minute shower twice an hour. As a result, the box both cleanses the air (particles wash off and are captured in the soil) and cools and humidifies the environment. The plants in these boxes are bushy and flowering and obviously doing quite well.

The dealership's construction and materials are not only intended to create a healthy work environment, they are assembled in ways that allow them to be easily reused. All building elements are either bolted or screwed, and a dry building method was employed. Utilizing prefabricated sections that permit quick assembly, and not painting concrete (allowing it to fully dry), are some of the other strategies employed.

The emphasis on circular material flows can be seen in a number of aspects of the design. Wastewater is to eventually end up on farm fields, or be processed in a new way resulting in pellets to be used as fertilizer or burned in power plants. Stormwater runoff from the development is minimized by way of the greenroofs and permeable paving. Gray water from the carwash in the complex was to be treated through a circular system, utilizing a pond and wetland system, but this process was stopped because the buildup of iron clogged the distribution pipes. (There is a high concentration of iron in the soil.) The complex's wastewater system also follows a circular path.

Figure 8.12 | A day-lit car dealership in the Green Zone, in Umeå, Sweden.

The unique environmental philosophy of this complex is also evident in the Statoil gas station, where customers are given a greater selection of environmentally labeled goods (like foods certified under the national KRAV organic label). Bio-diesel and ethanol fuels are available. Groundwater is protected under the station through the installation of a protective rubber mat.

The garage of the car dealership is itself sparkling clean—more like a semiconductor plant than the messy place where brakes are repaired and oil replaced. A series of hoses suck away the old fluids, another tube delivers the new. A new kind of "environmental plug" makes this possible, without any physical contact with the oil. Vegetable oil is used in the car lifts.

The green dimensions extend beyond the visibly obvious; all three of the companies have been certified under the environmental management system, ISO 14,001, which assures that the companies are making serious efforts to reduce the environmental impacts of their operations. (For a more detailed explanation of ISO 14,001, see www.ISO14000.com.) All employees go through extensive environmental training. Important energy elements of the Green Zone include electric power from a windmill (not on-site, but owned in part by Carstedt), a ground-source heat pump, and a solar warming system on the south side of the dealership's building that heats intake air. One especially creative element involves the recycling of heat. A heat recapture system collects waste heat from the grill in the McDonald's and the refrigerators in the Statoil station. The energy savings of these features is impressive—an estimated 60 percent less energy is consumed when compared with a conventional array of commercial buildings (Green Zone, undated).

One of the more interesting dimensions of the Ford dealership in the Green Zone is the set of workplace reforms that have been put into place. Unlike a typical dealership and garage, there are no receptionists and no shop chiefs. Customers deal directly with a mechanic and typically develop a relationship with that person over some period of time. There is a decided deemphasis on hierarchy and an importance given to personal responsibility. The combination of these reforms to the way work is done, and the building's ecological features, make the dealership an unusually pleasurable place in which to work (and visit).

At the college level, few buildings teach by design as effectively as the Lewis Environmental Center at Oberlin, in Ohio. The brainchild of Professor David

Orr, and designed by William McDonough and Partners, this building is more than classrooms and office space—it is a physical manifestation of how to design and build sustainably, and a building that "teaches" its students, faculty and visitors much. Use of green and recyclable materials throughout, on-site stormwater collection and treatment that are made a visible part of the site, and treatment of all bathroom wastewater in the building's living machine (again, highly visible), are some of the key features. Although some people have been critical of the building's performance in its first few years of existence, there are teaching and learning opportunities even where systems may not always work perfectly. As an example, when the wastewater delivered to the living machine were not sufficient to sustain the plant life there, a creative incentive was offered to students to utilize the bathrooms in the Lewis Center—25 cents per visit. A humorous movement to some, and perhaps a technical issue of how to size living machines appropriately, it was also the chance to extend understanding about this unique structure and how natural techniques might be used to treat our municipal wastewater.

Figure 8.13 | The Lewis Environmental Center at Oberlin College treats all the wastewater from its bathrooms onsite through a living machine. Housed in an attached greenhouse, the living machine becomes a visible part of the structure and an opportunity to teach and learn about more sustainable forms of waste management.

Conclusions

Despite the expressed and probably sincere commitment to teaching about the environment heard for many years, our collective knowledge about our communities and planet is actually rather sparse. What is known—perhaps something about tropical rain forest destruction or global fisheries depletion—is also rather abstract. Building sustainable places and nurturing commitments to particular places will require new commitments to education—education that extends to new and creative ways. The obvious opportunities for teaching about place are our community schools, and we must seize these opportunities and recognize the potential for every school to be a *center* of knowledge about place and environment. Integrating local habitats and restoration projects onto school grounds themselves is promising, and broadening our notion of what is needed to be a good school is essential (e.g., perhaps a functioning wetland or a community garden ought to be seen as being just as essential as the jungle gym or basketball hoops). We should view the school building itself and the organization and operation of that school as an opportunity to teach about energy, water, and sustainable and responsible living. But we must think even more boldly and look for other, perhaps less conventional, opportunities to teach. Private home ownership, new housing projects, and the design and construction of public buildings and facilities, all represent important teaching moments. Green building labels, watershed and place maps, and public art are all potential means for teaching, and we should use every creative tool at our disposal. The more we know, and the more we are expected to know about our "home," the more we will tend to care.

Strengthening Place through Sharing Institutions

Looking for creative ways to share our spaces, resources, and, in fundamental ways, our lives has the potential to bolster our interpersonal relationships and commitments to community, place, and a more efficient use of our natural resources. Sharing is an impulse and value we possess, I would argue, in equal measure to the selfishness and hoarding and individualistic consumption that receive much negative press.

How exactly might we go about institutionalizing sharing at the local level, and what might be some of the creative local approaches and structures and sharing institutions that might be put into place? Good ideas and examples of ways to make sharing easier, more natural, and a standard part of our communities abound. This chapter explores some of these sharing possibilities, and the potential for creating and strengthening community through them.

Shared Housing and Living Spaces

Perhaps the most obvious opportunity for sharing is that of sharing spaces— providing many and varied public spaces in which people can come together. Many of the design issues surrounding traditional public space—squares, plazas, streets—were addressed in Chapter 6. There are also many relatively new ideas for designing and organizing urban living, notable for the prominence given these extrapersonal collective realms. These include co-housing, eco-villages, and conservation communities that, among other things, provide physical designs that emphasize the public realm.

The physical structure and organization of co-housing makes sense on many levels, and facilities sharing in many ways. An idea with its origins in Denmark and Northern Europe, it entails clustered housing, sited around a plaza or pedestrian area, with a common house and other common facilities (McCamant and Durrett, 1994). These are marvelous communal spaces that provide children, among others, a highly desirable level of independence. Shared nightly meals in the common house further strengthen community. Minimizing the presence of the automobile and creating quiet, pleasant, pedestrian spaces facilitates interaction and informal conversations. Residents know and care about each other.

Figure 9.1 | Hilversum Commons, in the Dutch city of Hilversum, is the first example in that country of *centraal wonen*, or central living. A compact community clustered around pedestrian spaces, families share meals and many other things, from tools to garden plots.

Co-housing projects can and should be embedded within cities and urbanized areas. Dutch co-housing, which is called *centraal wonen,* or central living, is often situated in more urbanized, higher-density locations. The first Dutch *centraal wonen—Hilversumse Meent,* or Hilversum Commons, in the city of Hilversum—illustrates how the concept can be creatively woven into the form and street pattern of a city. Completed in the late 1970s, the homes are oriented around one long pedestrian street, with several side streets. These streets connect with surrounding neighborhoods and are occasionally used as walking routes by adjacent residents.

Sharing is a key underlying philosophy in Hilversum Commons, and sharing spaces is an obvious central design element. The beautiful pedestrian spaces are the heart of this community, suitable for common gathering, as play areas for children, and as spaces for outdoor meals and informal conversations. These pedestrian spaces, away from the noise and danger of cars, are marvelous environments in which to nurture a sense of connection and relationship between residents. Hilversum Commons incorporates a number

Figure 9.2 | The pedestrian streets within Hilversum Commons provide safe and sociable spaces for children to play and adults to interact, with lots of trees and greenery, as well.

of other shared facilities, including a meeting room, a tool and hobby shop, a sauna, a café/bar, a community garden, and guest rooms.

In the Hilversum example, community and sharing are nurtured at several levels. The community is organized into ten different family clusters. Each cluster of five dwelling units/families shares one common kitchen area, and uses this space in different ways. They may decide to eat meals together each evening, or less frequently; there are no hard-and-fast rules about this. Beyond the cluster community, the broader set of fifty families shares many things at this neighborhood level, as well.

Indeed, co-housing, eco-villages, and other community designs that provide shared spaces offer tremendous potential for reducing the material consumption needs of an average household. Co-housing residents commonly share a variety of things, minimizing the need to individually own such things as lawn mowers and grass-cutting equipment, outdoor grills, tools of various kinds—even automobiles. Australian researcher Graham Meltzer has conducted some interesting research of American co-housing, specifically visiting eighteen communities and surveying the residents about resources consumption. Meltzer found, for instance, "a 25 percent reduction in the number of freezers, washing machines and dryers and a 75 percent reduction in lawn-mowers from what they had used in their previous housing" (Gardner, 1999, p. 17; see Meltzer, 1999).

Although sharing is a key idea, it does not mean that residents sacrifice privacy or their private lives; indeed, reaching a comfortable balance between the public and private realms is an important goal in co-housing. Each of the units generally has its own private kitchen and private space.

Clare Cooper Marcus, of UC-Berkeley, reports on the social functioning of Hilversum Commons through the eyes of two residents, Rod and Moniek, who report a "strong sense of community" in the neighborhood, "fostered both by events and by shared amenities." There are annual social events which attract many people, such as a summer flea market, a New Year's party, a bicycle rally. In terms of shared physical spaces, Rob and Moniek felt the most important were the pedestrian street, the café/bar, and the gardens. But most of all, it is cluster-eating that provides the social focus for Rob and Moniek and their family (Marcus 2000, p. 148).

My own periodic visits to co-housing projects in Denmark and the United States and elsewhere confirm the importance of both organized and informal events. Celebrating the birthdays of residents and organizing parties and celebrations in the common house are frequent occurrences and certainly help to further strengthen bonds between residents.

Eco-villages, in the United States and around the world, combine the ideas of co-housing with notions of ecological building and living, and include many of the same opportunities for sharing and resources. The new EcoVillage in Loudoun County, Virginia, outside Washington, D.C., offers some insights into this type of development. In addition to ecological homes and buildings (e.g., use of recycled materials, energy-efficient designs) and impressive site restoration and sustainable use (e.g., extensive tree planting, stream restoration, setting aside large amounts of open space), common space and common features are present. A common house will include community washers and dryers, and also guest rooms, in turn freeing up space in the individual homes. There are undoubtedly many other ways that sharing can happen and where sharing is facilitated and made easier as a result of co-housing and eco-village configuration.

Although the homes in American co-housing and eco-village projects are not small by most standards, they do represent the potential for smaller, less space-intensive housing. The inclusion of guest units in the common house at Loudoun EcoVillage, for example, means, in creator/developer Grady O'Rear's eyes, that each home need not worry about designing-in a guest room.

EVA-Lanxmeer, a new ecological neighborhood being developed in the Dutch town of Culemborg, illustrates further the ideas of space sharing. Here, about 230 homes, many designed as home-work units, will eventually be built. The neighborhood includes a number of ecological and green features, including very low energy designs (each individual unit must be designed to use no more than 40 gigajoules per year), south-facing units, solar hot water heating and photovoltaics on rooftops, treatment and recycling of gray water from the homes, a farm that will produce organic food for the neighborhood, edible landscaping, and efforts to minimize hard surfaces throughout, among other features. Plans include treatment of wastewater

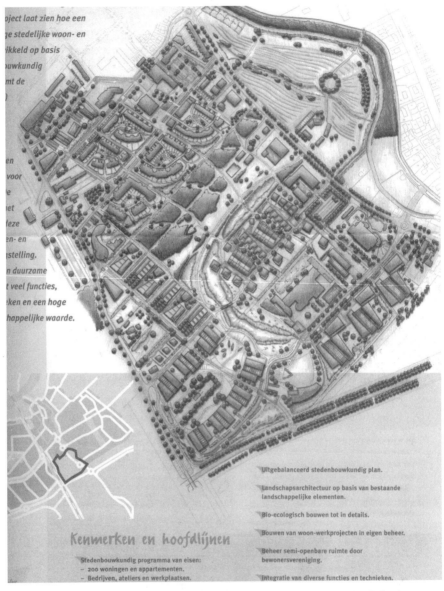

Partial visible text within the image:

oject laat zien hoe een
je stedelijke woon- en
ikkeld op basis
uwkundig
mt de

en
voor
e
iet
leze
en- en
stelling.
n duurzame
t veel functies,
ken en een hoge
happelijke waarde.

Kenmerken en hoofdlijnen

Stedenbouwkundig programma van eisen:
– 200 woningen en appartementen.
– Bedrijven, ateliers en werkplaatsen.

Uitgebalanceerd stedenbouwkundig plan.

Landschapsarchitectuur op basis van bestaande
landschappelijke elementen.

Bio-ecologisch bouwen tot in details.

Bouwen van woon-werkprojecten in eigen beheer.

Beheer semi-openbare ruimte door
bewonersvereniging.

Integratie van diverse functies en technieken.

Figure 9.3 | Master plan for the new ecological community EVA-Lanxmeer, in Culemborg, Netherlands. (Image compliments of Stichting EVA; masterplan design by Joachim Elbe of *Econnis* and Hyco Verhaagen of *Copijn Utrecht*).

through a living machine, extraction of biogas from waste to be used for power generation, and the installation of small wind turbines on rooftops in the neighborhoods.

A car-free living environment is a main feature of EVA-Lanxmeer, with cars restricted to several sites on the edge of the neighborhood; and while access to homes by car is possible (e.g., for dropoff or pickup), physical barriers prevent driving through. These small roadways, along with footpaths, mean that pedestrians and bicyclists dominate. The neighborhood has unusually close access to the city's main train station, just a few meters away from the entrance to the project.

And, the homes in neighborhoods, mostly attached, are tightly clustered around green interior courtyards. Each home has a small garden behind it, the private space, which then transitions into a common green courtyard—not a formal garden, but a rich, green, lush area with paths and typically a common table or two, chairs, and child-play structures. How to use and configure these common spaces is a joint project among the neighbors. These delightfully lush green commons are places for afternoon play, for community

Figure 9.4 | Many of the homes in EVA-Lanxmeer are sited around beautiful common green areas, embedded in a highly pedestrian-friendly environment. A working farm and orchard are also within a short walk.

dinners and events, and for casual socializing. The spaces are not large or hidden, and can be viewed easily from the houses. The residents of these clusters seem to know each other particularly well and have an extensive friendship network.

Conservation communities in the U.S. provide similar benefits. Tryon Farm, near Michigan City, Indiana, conceived by Chicago architect Ed Noonan and wife, Eve, has taken an existing Indiana farm, preserved the farm landscape, yet added to it a cluster development. Specifically, eight clustered "settlements" are envisioned, each with eight to twenty homes. Two of these clusters have been built: a farm cluster, adjacent to the original farm buildings, and a forest settlement. Although the homes are clustered close together, they achieve a fine balance between desires for privacy and the need for social interaction.

The design of Tryon Farms is very creative. The first of the eight community clusters, the Farmstead, is a tight cluster, with shared pedestrian and car parking space. While some peripheral parking is available, most resi-

Figure 9.5 | At Tryon Farm, a conservation community near Michigan City, Indiana, homes are sited in tight settlement clusters, with large amounts of green space and nature left untouched.

dents have a garage along one of the two central parking courtyards. Access to the homes, sited close together, is by way of narrow paths, emanating from several central areas. Creatively, these garages have housing on top. On one side, a structure designed in the shape of a barn has three loft units above the garages. Residents meet and greet each other coming and going in this central area, parking their cars, visiting the central mailboxes, or relaxing in the garden areas adjacent to the older buildings that comprise the original farm.

Conservation of the open land is a major objective, of course, and about 120 of the 170 acres of the farm have been protected in pasture and forest. A dairy farm has been converted to a community center. Creating opportunities for casual and spontaneous interaction with neighbors is certainly a key goal, and the relatively tight clusters certainly are a contrast to the conventional suburban designs. As architect/developer Noonan observes (quoted in Schneider, 2001, p. 513):

Modern subdivisions aim everything at the big spaces inside—fancy kitchens, bigger bathrooms—and the private backyard. The sequence of arriving at a

Figure 9.6 | In many European cities it has become a trend to design-in space for car-sharing cars. Here, a resident of Vauban, in Freiburg, Germany, makes a stop at his home before returning a car-sharing car.

modern subdivision home is to drive into the garage and walk directly into the house. There is very little chance of connecting with your neighbor.

While the Farmstead was the first of the settlements at Tryon Farms to be completed, the Woods settlement was the second. Future settlements will include Meadow, Village, Dune, and Pasture (Buck, 1999). In the end, Tryon may accommodate about 150 homes on this former farm.

The new district Vauban, in Freiburg, Germany, is another excellent example of compact, pedestrian development. Eventually to house about 5,000 people, it is built on the site of a former army barracks. Vauban has especially received much attention internationally for its efforts at promoting car-free living. Now residents are asked whether or not they intend to own a car, and if so, are confronted with a charge of about US$14,000 for the cost of a garage parking space. In this way, the cost of housing and car spaces are disentangled, and a strong economic incentive is created for new residents to find alternative ways of getting around and living instead of depending on cars. About half of the residents have so far chosen to be car-free.

The physical layout and pedestrian-friendly configuration of Vauban is impressive in a number of ways. A relatively compact and dense pattern of housing—primarily attached and multifamily housing—and limited roadways allow residents to use cars to drop off needed items and temporarily access their homes. A set of U-shaped access roads limit the extent to which traffic penetrates into the interior living spaces and keep traffic speed down. Cars are relegated to several perimeter parking garages, where car-sharing cars are also available for short-term uses (more on this below). The area receives excellent bus service and will eventually be served by the city's trams.

The life of this community happens in the interior pedestrian spaces where cars are not allowed. Rocks, trees, rope swings, and play equipment are all found in these spaces, creating excellent places for children to play and adults to socialize. An extensive set of walkways and paths connect the different housing areas. Vauban represents an unusually sensitive balancing of the need for some auto access and mobility with the safety and pleasure of car-free living and play environments.

Making physical room and space for civic and social life of a community is indeed an important planning and design principle. Less common today, integrating parks, plazas, public squares into new development, and organizing events and creating reasons for people to come together in these spaces is essential. New urbanist projects, described earlier and in more detail in Chapter 4, do, to their credit often integrate such spaces. One of the most impressive recent examples is a project called Port Warwick, in Newport News, Virginia. This mixed-use neighborhood located on a former Eveready Battery industrial site, is already breathing new life into this midtown section of this tidewater city. At the heart of the community is Styron Square, a beautiful London-style town square, where already people—neighbors and city residents alike—are coming together to listen to jazz every Wednesday evening during the summer months. At the center of the square is a beautiful open pavilion with a spectacular spire on the top. On the perimeter of the square are sycamore trees, walkways, and many wooden benches. Close by are some 350 new homes, within a brief walk, and restaurants and shops, as well as an office and a seniors housing project. There is much talk of future parades, art fairs, wine festivals and the many other public and social events that might happen in this space and that would further infuse a sense of commitment to and affection for this new community. In addition to the large central square, there are four smaller squares interspersed among the residences. More intimate in size, they are nicely nestled among the homes. Although the project is a bit sterile and new today, the developer, Bobby Freeman, imagines that it will be transformed by the residents over time to meet their own needs and ideas. And in this project there are many other design features that help to create a unique feeling, including the installation of public art—visually dramatic sculptures in prominent locations—an architectural style utilizing unusual brick patterns and colors. The centrality and status this square will have are important to the possible emergence of a real sense of place and community. It is certainly harder to grow these qualities in new communities like this, but designs like Port Warwick will help.

Every neighborhood, of course, has opportunities to create places and spaces where people can come together and socialize. These shared spaces can take many different forms, from community gardens, to sidewalk areas where width allows chairs, to a vacant corner lot where tradition and space may permit neighborhood gatherings. The small Washington-based initiative *Community Greens* is devoted to facilitating and advocating for small parks and greenspaces within residential blocks, and argues that community-binding spaces and secret gardens can often be formed from the backyards and other underutilized spaces that already usually exist. (See Drayton, 2000; Inerfeld and Blom, undated.) More creatively utilizing suburban backyard spaces, and creating connected walkways and common areas for picnicking and child play from these private spaces is also possible. I've often thought that we need new ideas for inserting meeting and socializing spaces in the layout and design of even suburban housing, perhaps an occasional indented area of common space, every so often along a sidewalk, where neighbors might sit, converse, interact. These spaces could be the important social glue for building a sharing society and community.

Many spaces in and around neighborhoods can be used of course for food production and edible landscaping. Sharing the vegetables, berries, fruits generated from these community gardens and orchards is itself a potentially important dimension to sharing and helps to build bonds between people. In my own neighborhood, good spirit is generated by the presence of a pair of apple trees. The owners, reflecting a sense of the collective nature of these

Figure 9.7 | Port Warwick, a new housing project in Newport News, Virginia, and built on a brownfield site, has incorporated a series of neighborhood parks within easy walking distance.

trees, displayed a sign in front of them that said simply: "Good cooking apples. Please pick as many as you want!"

Public spaces can be reconceived in radical ways to offer opportunities to come together. A neighborhood park is not just a place to walk the dog, but perhaps to join with others in a variety of other fate-sharing, community-building activities. One of my favorite examples is Dufferin Grove Park, in Toronto. Here, thanks to the creative ideas of community activist Jutta Mason, an underutilized park has been transformed into the center of energy and activity for the community. One of the special and unique aspects of the park is the installation of two public baking ovens, available for those who want to bake bread or pizza. An unusual feature for any public park, the ovens have had valuable secondary impacts. As Jutta Mason notes: "An oven attracts festivals and community events. This only makes sense. People want to share food on special occasions" (Friends of Dufferin Grove Park web site www.dufferinpark.ca/home/dufferinpark.html). The park also boasts a farmers' market, a skating rink, and a variety of music and cultural events from storytelling to jazz concerts.

Figure 9.8 | Residents of Prairie Crossing, in Grayslake, Illinois, participate personally in the restoration of the prairie habitats around and near their homes.

At Prairie Crossing, a community in Northern Illinois, residents are invited to participate directly in the ecological management and restoration of the landscape. This includes extensive opportunities to volunteer for prairie and wetland restoration work throughout the development, and at nearby Liberty Prairie Preserve. Residents are especially encouraged to join together in restoring the natural habitats around and in close proximity to their homes. Periodically burning-off invasive species and accumulated biomass is a necessary step for native prairie species to return and flourish, and many residents have gone through training to learn how to do this safely (affectionately referred to as "burn school"). On one recent visit, I found two residents burning the grass near their homes—one directing the flame, the other close behind with a shovel to ensure the burns didn't get out of hand. These two individuals were enthusiastic and clearly proud of what they were doing, and show the possibilities of the comradery and community-building that can result from shared management of public spaces (and in their case private spaces managed to achieve a community goal).

Shared Mobility

Sharing community mobility may be one of the most practical means of giving expression to this community value. Public transit, for example, in all its specific forms is an important alternative to private auto mobility. It makes sense for communities in many ways: it uses much less energy, generates much less pollution, takes up much less of our precious community space, and represents a tangible expression of commitment to others and the broader community. Many have written about the variety of creative transit programs and initiatives around the world (e.g., see Newman and Kenworthy, 1999; Beatley, 2000; Cervero, 1999). Several exemplary public transit efforts were described in Chapter 4, including the unique approaches taken by the Belgian cities of Ghent and Hasselt. These cases demonstrate convincingly the place-enhancing effects of good transit—effectively getting residents and visitors out of cars, and walking around, meeting and enjoying each other and their historic, charming cities. It is clear, then, that trams, street cars, subways, buses, and all manner of public transit are essential to creating sustainable places and to helping overcome our tendency toward excessive private consumption.

Several special cases of shared mobility, however, warrant particular attention and examination here: car-sharing and bicycle-sharing. Car-sharing, as a practice, began in Switzerland and has emerged as a popular and growing mobility option in many European cities. The basic idea is that of a network of neighborhood-based cars, accessible to members of a car-sharing club or organization, to be used for short trips and short periods of time. Typically, subscribers must pay a membership fee and a monthly fee, and then pay for the use of the cars on a kilometer and time basis. The number of car-sharing companies and organizations, and the number of subscribers, has grown steadily in Europe over the last decade. It is estimated that more than 100,000 subscribers now exist, with car-sharing services available in some 500 cities.

The economic and ecological advantages of car-sharing are significant. As most private cars remain parked for most of the day, car-sharing represents a more efficient use of collective resources—many fewer cars are needed to pro-

Figure 9.9 | Car-sharing is growing in popularity in the United States. Shown here are cars available from Zipcar, a Boston-based company that has been gradually extending coverage to cities nationwide.

vide mobility. Car-sharing may discourage car use overall, and does appear to strengthen local public transit use. From an economic and affordability perspective, car-sharing also makes good sense. Ownership and full responsibility for a private automobile is an expensive proposition; car-sharing helps create at least the possibility of living in a community without owning a private auto (or having to own a second automobile), and with a significant savings in personal resources. With use of smart card technology, using neighborhood-based car-sharing cars offers considerable convenience, as well.

Car-sharing is actually making significant inroads now in the United States, with programs in operation in a number of cities. Two private U.S. car-sharing companies, Boston-based Zipcar and Seattle-based Flexcar have been expanding aggressively, proving the considerable market for and appeal of the idea in this country. In the Washington, D.C., region, Flexcar cars are now available at a number of Metro stations, joining, as has been common in European cities, the benefits of car-sharing and public transit.

There are many ways in which local governments can support car-sharing initiatives and the move toward similar types of mobility service. The cities of Boston and Cambridge, Massachusetts, and Portland, Oregon, for instance, have set aside parking spaces in public garages and other places for car-sharing cars. Spaces are either provided free or at a discounted rental rate. Seattle, Washington, and Edinburgh, Scotland, have provided substantial financial subsidies for start-up of car-sharing companies or clubs.

Development regulations and planning requirements can be modified to reflect the contributions made by car-sharing. Local governments should be prepared to relax the parking standards for new developments where car-sharing services are available and incorporated into the project. The Beddington Zero Energy Development (BedZED) in the London borough of Sutton, for example, was given relief from normal parking requirements—indeed, it allowed only 50 percent of the usual number—in large part in response to plans to establish car-sharing on-site and the argument that fewer spaces would thus be needed. Increasingly, car-sharing is an option in new housing development designs. Residents of Vauban, in Freiburg, Germany, are given the option to purchase a "special mobility package" that provides membership in a car-sharing company, and also a one-year local transit pass, as well as a 50 percent reduction on train tickets (Enoch, 2002).

In the large new ecological district Hammarby Sjöstad in Stockholm, the oil company Statoil was permitted to construct a new gas station on the condition that the resulting service station would provide rental cars. So, the station now has four or five on-site cars that, although not rented for less than a day, will add substantially to the mobility flexibility of residents. There are many different ways in which collective mobility options such as this can increasingly be seen as a necessary and essential form of public infrastructure. Following the Stockholm example, perhaps service stations can be reconceived as important points of sharing—at least those located in places (not the ring road or beltway) reachable by walking or public transit.

Public Bike Programs

Sharing bicycles is another creative way to reduce environmental impacts, strengthen community, and enhance appreciation of place. Few public bike programs have been as successful and as large-scale as Copenhagen's City Bikes. The Copenhagen public bike program was the brainchild of Ole Wessung and Morten Sadolin and intended to address the problem of bicycle theft—much of which in that city had been attributed to one-time users (e.g., someone looking for a ride home). In the first five years of the program, bicycle theft has declined by 30 percent. Today, 2,500 of these bikes are available to residents and visitors. The bikes are sturdy, with adjustable seats, and are designed so that their components cannot be taken apart without specialized tools. The bikes are free, but with a 20 kroner coin deposit (a little over US$3). A clip system is employed, similar to that used for grocery carts. Put the coin in, release the clip, and the rider is on her way; bring the bike back, insert the clip, and the coin is returned. Moreover, the advertising on the wheels and frames pays for cost of the bikes. (Companies purchase the bikes, put on the advertising, then donate them to the program.) Maintenance of the bikes occurs by hiring underemployed people in the city.

Helsinki, Finland, started its own city bike program, similar to Copenhagen's, in 2000. Smaller in scale, it has about 300 bikes in circulation at about 25 dispersal points in the city. The bikes are a colorful lime green, also with distinctive advertising. The deposit is a EUR 2 coin (a little less than US$2). Watching one prominent location in front of the city's main

Figure 9.10 | The City Bikes Program in Helsinki, Finland, provides public bikes in the central city for a EUR 2 coin. The bikes are very popular and heavily used.

train station, on a Sunday afternoon in spring, I saw the bikes coming and going and in wide use. One frustration may be not being able to find a bike, but checking back in a few minutes often yields results. Another frustration is disrepair. These bikes get hard use and, though sturdy, often show the wear. On the day I watched, a couple checked out a bike lacking a seat; transportation is provided even without this seemingly essential element of bicycle anatomy.

Private companies can also help by promoting bike sharing. The ecologically oriented hotel chain Scandic offers bikes for rent at their hotels, facilitating a more sustainable mode of travel for guests. At the Scandic in Umeå, Sweden, for instance, you can rent a bike for 30 kroner for a half day, or 50 kroner (about US$6.50) for the entire day.

An essential element of these programs is providing a generally bicycle-friendly environment. In the Helsinki city center, the level of bicycle use is impressive. Bikeways, well-marked and separated from road traffic, are found throughout much of the city, allowing one to ride quickly and safely through the center, balancing pedestrian and bicycle space nicely.

Theft of public bikes does remain a concern, of course, in many American cities, giving rise to what DeMaio (2003) calls a "third generation" of public bikes—"smart bikes." Systems where a smart card or other magnetic strip identity card is used to check out or rent a bicycle allow much better tracking of the bicycles. DeMaio notes the existence, as of fall 2003, of smart bike programs in ten cities, almost all in Europe.

One interesting "smarter" public bike program, not included in DeMaio's survey, is the City Bike initiative in Sandnes, Norway. In this small city of about 56,000, both a Copenhagen-style coin-deposit system and a more controlled subscriber system have been used. Sandnes has found the latter to work well and continues with this subscriber approach. Specifically, the city uses a special locking device with an electronic key that subscribers obtain by requesting and paying a small annual fee (100 kroner, or about US$14). This electronic locking system allows a user to borrow a bike from a public station, and then if she needs to lock the bike along the way, only her key will open it (until she is done and the bike returned). In this way, the city knows

Figure 9.11 | Scandic Hotels, a Scandinavian hotel chain with a strong environmental ethic, makes bikes available to its guests for rental.

Figure 9.12 | Die Bahn (DB), the German national rail company, has started a smart bikes program, making bikes available in cities like Frankfurt shown above.

who has checked out the bike, and there is greater sense of personal ownership involved. The program is operated by the City Bike Foundation, which is funded through advertising boards in the city center, given by the city under a twenty-year agreement.

The smart bike system in use in Rennes, France, is even more high-tech. Here, the bike system, run by the firm Clear Channel Adshel, utilizes a smart card. Inserting the card into one of the twenty-five stations frees a bike from its docking station, and also identifies who is borrowing a bike. The use of these bikes is also free, paid for through advertising. Similar Adshel Smart-Bike® systems are now in use in Singapore, Oslo, Norway, and soon to come to London, England, and Annapolis, Maryland, the first city in the United States where the technology is to be applied.

Die Bahn (DB), the German rail company, has been providing some interesting lessons in thinking more systematically about these kinds of mobility services. The company has recently added both car-sharing and bike rental services for its train customers. Through partnering with existing car-sharing companies in many German cities, car-sharing cars are now available at many train stations. In Frankfurt, DB has partnered with the "book'n'drive" car-sharing system, for instance. It is encouraging when traditional transportation companies recognize that what they ought to be doing is providing mobility more generally, not necessarily promoting a single method or mode. Combinations like car-sharing and trains recognize that the travel needs are best served through a package of options and alternatives.

Die Bahn is also currently implementing an ambitious smart bike program, known as "Call a Bike." At the Frankfurt central station, for instance, a DB customer can find some twenty-five sturdy white bikes for rent. Customers call a central reservation number and are given an electronic number code that can be used to unlock the bikes. Each bike is equipped with an electronic locking device and a built-in computer keypad. The cost to use the bike is 6 (euro) cents per minute (a little over 7 US cents). The bikes are high quality and although containing no advertising, they carry the DB logo and a distinctive curved carriage rack on the rear.

The DB system appears to work well and is relatively easy and convenient. Smaller numbers of bikes are distributed around Frankfurt city center, available at more than sixty points. Because the bikes have an independent electronic locking system, there is no need for any kind of elaborate stand or depot. The bikes are simply left standing on their kickstands, and if the locking pad is flashing a green light, they are ready to be taken out and used by a new customer. The DB operates Call-a-Bike in Munich and Berlin, as well.

A number of American communities have experimented with public bikes, though none to the level of sophistication found in European cities. A community bikes initiative has been under way even in my own small city of Charlottesville, Virginia. The Yellow Bike Program has been sponsored by the Charlottesville Area Bicycle Alliance (CHABA)—and it has been an admittedly low-tech endeavor: donated used bikes are being repaired and painted yellow by volunteers, and placed at a number of specially installed bike racks around town for those who wish to use them. The Charlottesville effort was not especially successful and shows the challenges of operating such a program in a U.S. city: most of the bikes put out disappeared. The Charlottesville yellow bike program, despite its difficulties, remains alive, although evolving into a different kind of program. Many additional bikes are being readied, and a decision has been made to convert the system to a library or check-out system.

Other American public bikes programs have similarly evolved into some form of "library bikes" system, in which a user borrows a bike from one or more check-out sites. In Arcata, California, a library bikes program gives residents there the ability to borrow bikes, with a $20 deposit, for up to six months (and with the ability to renew). Bikes are available from four locations in the community (as well as the new repair facility): a co-op grocery store, a coffee shop, a frozen yogurt store, and a city recycling center. The program is run by volunteers and essentially takes donated bikes (and bicycle parts) and converts them into working bicycles. The organizers in Arcata emphasize that in addition to providing a healthy, sustainable mode of transportation, they're also diverting materials from the city's waste stream:

> Library Bikes are created from bicycles that were likely sitting in someone's garage or backyard broken down or unused. Many of these bikes would eventually end up in the landfill. This is where the real power of the bike program lies. Humans generate incredible amounts of waste in nearly all aspects of modern life. The bike program is fundamentally a vehicle for resurrecting otherwise difficult to restore bicycles, eliminating bicycles from the solid waste stream, and conserving mineral resources that would otherwise be spent creating new bicycles or cars. ("Arcata Community Library Bike Project," at www .culturechange.org).

Such projects not only have the potential to create greater opportunities to share things, but they are themselves created and brought about through grassroots participation and volunteer work. The tangible rewards of connection to others and the broader community of such initiatives are often underappreciated and underestimated. One of my recent students, Sarah Rowe, has been an active volunteer, and attests to these less quantifiable benefits. In her words (Rowe, 2001, p. 8):

> I have painted fifteen bikes, inflated more than eight tires, changed tubes and solicited sign companies. The work has been truly enjoyable. I have met new friends and learned how to repair my own vintage ten-speed.

Sharing regimes might be thought to bump directly up against issues of trust and honesty. If we put bikes out for public use, will they be stolen or vandalized? This has certainly been the experience in some cities, such as Portland, Oregon, where early experiments with public bikes occurred, and in my own city of Charlottesville. Civic and environmentally responsible behavior is not automatic, but requires nurturing, guidance, and mentoring. Successful sharing requires a similar process of learning. Whether borrowing a tool or a bicycle or participating in car-sharing, time and effort will be necessary to build an understanding of the collective etiquette and "rules of integrity" expected of everyone. We should expect the best from all Americans, but education and learning must be a part of these initiatives.

Sharing and Reusing a Community's Material Assets

The potential for community reuse was made abundantly clear to me recently on a visit to our community recycling center. Disposing of, for the most part, papers and cardboard boxes, I brought with me an old microwave oven that I had hoped the center would be willing to take and help to find a new home.

Figure 9.13 | The Loading Dock, in Baltimore, Maryland, promotes recycling of a variety of building and construction materials, including the plumbing fixtures shown here.

The microwave was an old model to be sure, but potentially had a few years of life left. In this beehive of activity, in the time it took me to snatch the oven from the car and carry it to the recycling office, a very enthusiastic young man approached: "Do you mind if I take your microwave?" Of course, I was delighted an enthusiastic new home had been found, demonstrating to me on a very personal level that many of the things we discard, for whatever reason, have value to others. Finding local initiatives and regimes for facilitating exchanges, such as the one I had, becomes an increasingly important role for local government, I believe.

Creating regimes for reusing goods and materials in the community can be given a higher importance than is typically the case. Support for neighborhood-based networks of material reuse is one idea. Models such as the Loading Dock in Baltimore, Maryland, or the Harmony Warehouse in Charleston, South Carolina, or Urban Ore in Berkeley, California, suggest that much can be done to redirect waste streams to productive reuse.

The Loading Dock is a creative nonprofit warehouse, which collects and sells excess and recycled building material for use by low-income and affordable-housing groups. A 20,000-square-foot warehouse displays an exotic array of building materials, available to members at bargain prices. Described as a cross between Home Depot and the Salvation Army (Ruban, 2002), it both responds to the need for affordable building materials, and reduces the waste stream entering local landfills. The old wood floors from a local high school, the toilet fixtures from a demolished building, the unused paint from a construction site—all make their way into the hands of individuals and organizations who can put them to productive use. Waste is no longer waste, but again a productive input to something else, in this case with an important social goal, namely, the building and rebuilding of affordable neighborhoods and housing.

In Charleston, South Carolina, the Harmony Warehouse collects slightly damaged or previously used building materials and makes them available to low-income families and organizations building or renovating affordable housing. Often, materials are donated by larger home improvement and building supply stores, such as Lowe's, and then sold by the warehouse for a fraction of their retail cost. An initiative of the Harmony Project, the warehouse serves to reuse and recycle materials that would otherwise end up in the landfill, and at the same time helps to build community and social capital in Charleston. As a recent story in the *Charleston Business Journal* notes:

> Rather than throwing away or continuing to store leftover materials, Buck Lumber donates an average of 10 high quality doors and 8 high quality windows a week to the Warehouse, along with lumber and roofing shingles. Each week Lowe's also donates some 50 gallons of incorrectly tinted but otherwise usable paints. (Beach, 1998)

There are many other successful examples of building economy and community through reuse of materials. A for-profit company, Urban Ore, in Berkeley, California, is a leading case in point. Founded by Daniel Knapp in 1980, the company operates a building materials exchange and a general store, where one can find almost any kind of reused good or product. The economic value generated by rediverting this community waste flow is impressive, directly employing twenty-five people and producing $1.5 million in retail sales. And, these waste recycling efforts have spawned more than 200 other local businesses, some located in the city's resource recovery park.

Urban Ore provides an inspiring practical example of how local economy can be strengthened through creative waste recycling, how opportunities for doing the right thing concerning our waste can strengthen community and place. The efforts of Urban Ore have also managed to avert the planned construction of an unwelcome waste incinerator in Berkeley (see California Integrated Waste Management Board, 2003).

Some cities and counties are now aspiring to the goals of becoming zero-waste communities—that is, developing and implementing aggressive recycling and reuse programs so that nothing, or virtually nothing, ends up in the municipal landfill. As these examples show, community-sharing institutions like the Loading Dock and Urban One can do much to advance sustainability. Del Norte County, California, is one of the first places in the United States to have set the goal of becoming zero-waste. Such a relatively simple idea appears to work well and is perhaps an important first step in the direction of dematerializing our homes and neighborhoods.

There are indeed many creative ways of collectively sharing our material goods and what has become perceived as the essential "stuff" of modern living. We sometimes forget the historic importance of sharing institutions like

Figure 9.14 | Residents of Takoma Park, Maryland, often check out tools (posthole diggers and ladders, in this case) from the city's tool library.

libraries, which provide important cultural, educational, and entertainment benefits that are difficult to secure individually. In this era of vast Internet resources and megabookstores like Barnes and Noble, and Borders, the value and use of public libraries has perhaps diminished. But libraries are quite different in their civic intent, in their functioning as centers of civic life, and a visit to a public library, which is more likely to stock books and material of less commercial value, is a special and different public act than a visit to a commercial chain bookstore. Strengthening our commitment to institutions of community sharing such as public libraries helps to strengthen our sense of and commitment to place.

There are interesting and valuable ways, moreover, to extend the concept of public libraries that help reduce our ecological footprints and make our communities more sustainable. A number of communities for instance, have instituted some form of "tool library," a facility (often separate from book libraries) where residents can check out infrequently used, but perhaps immediately necessary, tools and equipment. The tool library created by the city of

Takoma Park, Maryland, is one of the oldest. Operated out of a trailer be-hind city hall, it contains just about any tool one might need. Chain saws and rototillers, perhaps for obvious reasons, are about the only items not to be found there. The tools are available for borrowing by residents only and a de-posit check and photo-identification are the only things needed.

The Takoma Park tool library is run by a colorful Vietnam veteran, who belligerently follows up on unreturned tools and adds to the flavor of the whole operation. The value of this service can be easier grasped by watching the steady flow of tools coming and going. On one recent day, a father and son picked up posthole diggers and several ladders—items they badly needed at the time, but if purchased individually, would be infrequently used. Such a rel-atively simple idea appears to work well and is perhaps an important begin-ning step in the direction of dematerializing our homes and neighborhoods.

There are undoubtedly many different ways to organize such institutions. The city of Columbus, Ohio, for instance, has a *mobile* tool library, which brings the borrowing to different neighborhoods on a regular schedule. And, other items extending beyond tools might also be loaned, say, outdoor furniture or barbeque equipment or sports equipment, as many colleges and universities do.

Conclusions

The general trend in our communities today is in the direction of strengthen-ing the private realm, the realm of the individual. The signs are everywhere, from increased auto driving (often in a single-occupancy vehicle), to the growing popularity of gated communities, to time spent on-line and isolated from others. Places, real places, need people who need each other, and who interact with and care about others. There is, then, the strong need for com-munity institutions that emphasize the public. There are many opportunities to strengthen place and place commitments through sharing institutions. This institutionalized sharing strengthens human bonds and connections to the broader community; it can also substantially reduce natural resource con-sumption, and is thus a key element in creating a more sustainable place. There are potentially many good ideas and institutions for doing this, and only a few—car-sharing, bike-sharing, tool libraries, communities that emphasize sharing spaces and resources—have been discussed here. Much sharing can, of course, arise informally, as well, but a major contention here is that cities, towns, and communities have an interest in facilitating sharing and helping these sharing patterns emerge and flourish. However we do it, sharing can build community and strengthen the bonds and commitments to place.

Multigenerational Communities: Places That Sustain and Cherish Children, Families, and the Elderly

The careless community landscapes that we have created in the United States, which are described at length in earlier chapters, are particularly harsh on the most vulnerable populations in our community—the very young and the very old. The challenges of being a young person or an older person today are daunting, to say the least. The problems facing children today include rising obesity rates (the results of poor diet and/or sedentary lifestyle), diminishing personal independence, dangerous play environments, and an alarming disconnect from many societal and community structures. Television, computer games, and the Internet discourage creative play, physical exercise, community engagement, and true place learning. Unsafe streets, stultifying schools, and a landscape of fast-food franchises and shopping malls, accessible only by car, collectively yield emotionally and ecologically impoverished places— not the sort of places that reflect, as David Orr observes, a society that loves its children. Young families are challenged, moreover, in numerous ways in raising healthy children; challenged by unsupportive landscapes and built environments and by the social and economic pressures that make life taxing (expensive and limited housing options, the press of work, pervasive materialistic values and media messages).

Equally serious are the ways in which elderly Americans are marginalized.

As with children, the elderly often lack mobility and independence, are too sedentary, and are equally disconnected from community. They often have poor access to medical care, limited networks of family and friends, and special physical and emotional challenges in the later years of their lives. New efforts at designing and planning communities that are multigenerational in nature are badly needed.

The age-truncated and overly narrow age-focus of our community design and planning is a serious dimension of our contemporary crisis of place for several reasons. A genuine place, a place that feels real and authentic to us, is a place, as I have argued earlier, that is diverse, and this must necessarily include age diversity. Achieving the socially vibrant, caring communities that we want is simply not possible in the absence of young and old. The young are the embodiment of our optimism and commitment to the future; the older members of our society hold the perspective and judgment and knowledge to understand where we have been and where we are heading. The older members of our communities are, in a sense, the living history of a place, and creating environments where they are able to impart their knowledge to younger residents (and receive the energy and enthusiasm and optimism of the young in turn) is an essential aspect of good place building. It is also simply a matter of fairness, and I have always believed that the sanity and humanness of a society should ultimately be judged by how it treats its oldest and youngest members.

There are many things that can and should be done in community planning to turn the current situation around. Giving special consideration to needs of children and the elderly is only logical. Designing communities that nurture the young is a strategy for creating the next generation of smart, caring people who will be the eventual stewards of community and environment. Equally true, the elderly have spent a lifetime learning the lessons and wisdom of life, and to waste this by warehousing or marginalizing them is remarkably shortsighted from a societal point of view.

Urban Form That Allows Independence and Mobility

At the most basic level of planning and design, communities need to permit and facilitate independence and independent mobility for all their residents.

Car-dependence for both the young and the old means reliance on others, constrained personal freedom, and low quality of life. American teenagers see life beginning at age fifteen years and nine months (or whenever one qualifies for a learner's permit to drive); their European counterparts, on the other hand, grow up having tremendous personal mobility, thanks to investments in pedestrian, bicycle, and public transit infrastructure. In the Netherlands, with an inexpensive piece of equipment—the bicycle, which is the most used form of transportation—kids can travel independently to most places, including the store, the park, the city center, and the soccer field. This mobility, in turn, reduces the stresses on parents and opens up space in the daily family schedule that would be consumed in shuttling around in the car in most American communities.

Changing the physical environment of our communities may, of course, be only part of the battle in an era when there are increasing temptations to be sedentary. Using computers, playing computer games, and, of course, viewing television are important competing pulls. It has been estimated that the average teen watches between twenty-one and twenty-eight hours of TV per week, and actually spends more time in front of the screen than in the classroom. Teenagers in the United States perhaps have special pressures from the limited ability to get around or even out of the house when they would like to.

The costs of this kind of youth inactivity, and accepting the kind of community and urban landscapes that encourage such sedentary lifestyles, are extremely high. The Centers for Disease Control and Prevention are now calling the rising rates of child obesity an epidemic, and as youth depression, the percentage of young people on antidepressant drugs, and the youth suicide rates are all on the rise, healthy, sustainable, real places are needed even more than ever before. Our communities are ignoring the special needs of youth. We are letting the youngest members of our society down.

While some data on personal travel choices is available from the National Personal Transportation Survey (NPTS), Weston (2002) makes the observation that many of the response categories relate to adults, and that teens will tend to emphasize other kinds of travel behavior and purposes. One important travel behavior is "cruising"—not going to a particular place, but just going out to see and be seen. These are socially significant kinds of mobility, and we ought to take them into account in designing places.

Figure 10.1 | The elderly and children are the most negatively impacted by heavy dependence on automobiles, and the most in need of vibrant, public spaces like these in Venice, Italy, where it is common to see the generations together.

Mobility for the elderly is equally problematic. Driving for many elderly people becomes especially difficult, raising important planning concerns similar to those raised for the very young. Car-dependent landscapes are equally inhibiting for the elderly, and looking for strategies that permit them—as with the pre-driving-age young—to lead independent, high-quality lives becomes critical.

Ironically, in the responses to this problem to date, much of the emphasis has been on keeping older Americans in their cars—for example, driving and skill-building classes, such as organized by the American Association of Retired Persons (AARP) 55 Alive Driver Safety Program—or testing older drivers to make sure they're taken off the street when found to be dangerous. Or, more recently, there have been efforts to identify ways that technology or car design can facilitate safe driving by the elderly (see Phelps Deily, 2002). Although these initiatives are undoubtedly justified given the realities of our excessively car-dependent society, more proactive forms of elder-friendly and multigenerational place building are needed.

Providing older Americans with reliable, elder-friendly public transit is one essential element, as equally important as it is to the mobility of the young. This means transit with frequent service, going to places where elders need to go (shopping, senior centers, health care and medical centers), and designed in ways that make it physically easy to use (e.g., low-carriage trams). Traditional transit must be supplemented by other mobility options. The Netherlands, for instance, has a system of subsidizing taxicabs, which allows elders and disabled citizens to travel for essentially the price of a bus ticket. To qualify, these residents must register for the service and can at that point take advantage of the taxi service as frequently as they want. If the taxi takes more than thirty minutes to arrive, the trip is free. This is a tremendous life-enhancing benefit and service to those who need it.

Designing community environments where walking is easy and enjoyable, and where daily destinations such as a local grocery are nearby, is important. An abundance of elder-friendly third places—parks, cafés, and libraries—is also important. Mixed-use, walkable neighborhoods are an especially valuable resource in keeping elders active and healthy and engaged in their neighborhoods and communities.

Part of the answer is in anticipating the challenges of mobility in the later years. Joseph Coughlin, of MIT's Age Lab talks of the need for "lifelong mobility," advance thinking about where seniors will live, and strategies for mobility when and if driving is no longer possible (see MIT Age Lab http://www.web.mit.edu/agelab/).

These concerns should be major considerations when siting and designing new eldercare facilities or apartment complexes. Permitting such facilities to be plopped down in a sea of cars, roads, and parking lots, disconnected from any real community, should be forbidden. The Dutch have taken an interesting approach in creating a certification and labeling system that evaluates new and proposed housing for the elderly against certain criteria, including such things as lighting, elder-friendly doorway widths, and bathroom and kitchen design. If the housing meets the criteria, the complex or building is permitted to display the *Senioren* label and logo, and to use it in advertising. Such labels help those looking for housing to judge which buildings, projects, or locations might be the most elder-friendly. Although most of the criteria

Figure 10.2 | Pelgromhof, a senior housing project in the Dutch city of Zevenaar, incorporates many green features and is within a short walk of the town center.

have to do with structural and building design issues, the criteria also explicitly consider the location of the facility. To receive the Senioren certification, the building must be within a specified short distance from shops and a town center, and have easy access to public transit. This label has since been merged with a broader housing quality certification system, but remains an important idea and tool.

One elderly housing project to receive the Senioren label is the impressive Pelgromhof in the eastern Dutch city of Zevenaar. This project includes a number of elder-friendly features, including an "open architecture" that gives residents direct involvement in designing the desired layout of their flats, radiant floor heating that reduces particulates in indoor air, and use of natural paints. The project contains a mix of units for independent living, a "sheltered nucleus" of units for those who need greater care, and extensive social and recreational facilities (theater, restaurant, etc.) (Canada Mortgage and Housing Corporation, undated).

The most striking features about Pelgromhoff, however, are its green aspects, a priority of architect Frans van der Werf. The entire rooftop, some 7500 square meters, is green. Covered with sedum, the rich colors of the roof's vegetation—pink, green, brown—change over time, and are visible throughout the interior courtyard spaces of the building and from the apartments. Actually the green roof is multi-layered, the large roof draining onto smaller lower level roofs, including one above the complex's dining area, and in turn sending water to the green courtyard below (see Janssen and Keultjes, 2000). At the center of the project, on ground level, is a lush vegetated wetland, complete with footpaths and bridges bringing nature into the very core of this elder complex. An effort was also made to preserve the existing trees on the site (and to relocate some). Green vegetation is seemingly everywhere one looks, and contributes much to the quality of life for those living in this unusual project.

There are other compelling examples of creative housing for older residents that integrate abundant green interiors and look for ways to establish physical connections to the earth, water, and environment. Herbert Dreiseitl's work on

Figure 10.3 | The pedestrianized city center of Umeå, Sweden, is a delightful car-free space in which old and young, indeed all generations and age groups, can come together.

the project Arkadien-Aspen, for instance, an elder housing project in Germany, is impressive for the environmental qualities it provides its residents. Interior spaces bask in sunlight and are lush with green plants, as well as the sights and sounds (therapeutic and relaxing) of a small waterfall.

Access to Parks and Nature

Direct physical access to nature and natural areas, for both the young and the old, is another design and planning necessity. Many of us remember that having direct access to nature was an important element of our childhood. My own experience of growing up on the west end of the northern Virginia city of Alexandria bears this out. Many hours were spent exploring surrounding woodlots, climbing trees, building tree forts, playing in and around creeks, and rearranging the stones and forest litter in these natural urban areas. The element of freedom was phenomenal, at least by today's standards. My friends and I would walk considerable distances, setting our own agendas for the day, following whatever spur-of-the-moment impulse might have struck us. Some of those forested and natural spaces around Alexandria are now gone, but for the most part the city still retains a highly walkable environment.

Access to "urban wilderness" must be considered a key design principle in city planning, and an essential strategy for raising smart, engaged children who grow up to be adults who care about environment and the communities in which they live (see Nabhan and Trimble, 1995; Kahn and Kellert, 2002).

More intentionally planned parks and play areas should also be designed to facilitate creative, nature-oriented play. Important is recognizing that children need places that are interesting and diverse, and environments that allow "exploration and experimentation" and encourage them to set their own agendas. Frost and Jacobs (1995) are critical of the kinds of play opportunities available today: "Today's children simply do not have the same freedom to choose where and what to play that their parents and grandparents had when growing up. Many contemporary children rarely or never experience the wonders of the farm, the wilderness or even a creative challenging playground" (p. 20).

The American attitude about play areas is evident when contrasted with the spaces incorporated into the built environment in compact European cities such as Leiden. Families with toddlers, especially, need safe outdoor spaces, where the kids, prone to darting and dashing away, not always forward in a straight line, can be contained. Areas to explore and play, and slides and climbing equipment, embedded in an urban, walkable environment are key.

The Lombardy Park in the Fan district of Richmond, Virginia, is a good example of such a park. Surrounded on all sides by housing—townhomes and four-story apartments—the park has lots of "eyes" on it. Slow-moving car traffic can weave along the adjoining streets. The park, not a large one, is surrounded by a brick wall with large metal gates; the wall is high enough to effectively contain those darting kids, but low enough to maintain strong visual connections with the surrounding neighborhood and sidewalks.

The delightful interior spaces of Lombardy Park work exceedingly well. The play equipment is in the center of a large sand-bottomed area, with attractive metal benches allowing parents to relax while watching their kids play. Sandbox toys are strewn about for everyone to use. Several large mature trees shade the area and make for an outstanding space to spend time in, for both toddler and parent.

Older residents need nature and natural surroundings as much as children and everybody else. The restorative, therapeutic values of plants and greenspaces can and should be used to create more uplifting and enlivened living environments that can add substantially to the quality of life in one's latter years. Encouragingly, there are now many good examples of elder facilities, such as Pelgromhoff, incorporating natural elements.

Bringing Young and Old Together

Finding ways to bring the young and the old together in communities is a challenge, especially in an age where extended families are not very common. In more traditional communities, in the past, extended families were quite common; and grandparents, who often lived in the home, played important roles in caring for the young.

Older people have, of course, much wisdom, history, and care to offer; things that children and young people need desperately. In turn, interaction with children provides energy, optimism, and excitement that benefit older citizens. There is a natural and essential symbiosis here that works to everyone's advantage, and helps to strengthen communities and the bonds between generations.

Separation and isolation of different age groups is more common today, but there are ways to overcome this age-isolation. Finding creative ways to integrate and combine care for the young and old is one possibility. A number of intergenerational or multigenerational centers exist where, for at least a portion of the day, the young and old interact.

The McClure Multigenerational Center in Burlington, Vermont, is one of the best examples of this. Since 1999, the Champlain Senior Center and the Burlington's Children Space, a nonprofit child-care provider, have been under one roof. A variety of services are provided for the elderly here, including daily meals (some 10,000 served per year), exercise and dance classes, and other wellness services. The child-care facility is an especially important resource for low-income working parents, and has extended hours (7:30 A.M. to 11:30 P.M.). The facility serves the broader community as well, providing a much needed meeting space for neighborhood organizations.

Figure 10.4 | At the McClure Multigenerational Center in Burlington, Vermont, the young and old come together for mutual benefit. (Photo compliments of McClure Multigenerational Center.)

Interaction between the young and old occurs at the McClure Center in both programmed and spontaneous ways. Every day, the seniors read books to the children. This program, called Book Buddies, promotes literacy in the young while engaging the elderly in activities and interaction across generations. Other activities here have included a multigenerational summer barbeque, art classes, a drum ensemble, and a dance group—all opportunities for intergenerational bonding.

One unexpected benefit of this multigenerational facility has been the development of relationships between the parents of children and the seniors. In the words of Syndi Zook, director of the Senior Center, "the parents of the children are captivated by the elders. In many cases parents have practically taken the seniors into their families. Many parents invite them to dinner and bring them gifts at the holidays. It's been a real plus for the community" (as quoted in Fieldworks, 2000). Combining these facilities under one roof has also had other interesting advantages, such as allowing more efficient fundraising to occur and reducing operating costs.

Designing new housing to provide similar opportunities for interaction between generations ought to be a goal, as well. One recent example in Fairfax County, Virginia, can be seen in the brand-new Gum Springs Glen, an affordable seniors apartment complex. Also located there, in the lower level of one of the buildings, is a new Head Start program, providing opportunities for senior residents of this complex to become volunteers, if they wish. The presence of the Head Start program, and the prospect of interaction with youngsters, has been prominently cited in the marketing of the project (Fairfax County, undated). In an article about the new project in the neighborhood newsletter, the president of the Gum Springs Civic Center Association talks of the virtues of bringing these generations together: "[The seniors] will be able to provide the young children a sense of history about where they live while the children will put a 'spring in their step' and a look into the future" (Hunt, 2003).

Schools as Community Centers and Intergenerational Centers

There is no reason why schools cannot be fundamentally reconceptualized to be the very *centers* of our neighborhoods and communities, multi-use places where generations come together, not simply large single-use facilities in use only a portion of the day. Progress on these new ideas about schools is being made, and a number of cities and school districts around the country are experimenting with these types of new ideas (e.g., Elliott, 2002; Paquette, 2002). Often faced with substantial expenditure for new school construction and renovation, this construction is increasingly viewed as an opportunity to do something differently.

A nonprofit organization called New Schools, Better Neighborhoods, for instance, is helping the Los Angeles Unified School District to rethink the direction of a massive school building program. The new schools, or "smart schools," would be, at the core, multiuse community centers, open to the larger public, providing service and community needs:

> Smarter schools should be inviting places rather than foreboding institutions. These locations should encourage community use and their shared public spaces should be accessible—day and night, all year round—to the community. Schools should be places where creative configurations of space expand their use to encompass early learning and adult education; where learning occurs "after hours," at night and on weekends; where school-to-school partnerships, links with businesses and collaboration with higher education are encouraged and supported. They should enable learners of all ages and serve as centers for lifelong learning.
>
> All these examples point to ways that schools can better serve as the center of their communities, either by playing a more integral role as a community activity center or by extending the learning environment further out into the community to take better advantage of a wider range of community resources. Schools that are more integrated with their communities in these ways can strengthen a community's sense of identity, coherence and consensus. Like a new version of the old town square, they can serve as a community hub, a center for civic infrastructure, a place where students and others can learn to participate and support the common good. (www.nsbn.org; "What If" report)

The vision of multifunctional, neighborhood and community-strengthening schools expressed above is a compelling one, and there are already ten joint-use schools under development in the Los Angeles Unified School District. The district is developing these schools with partners, an important element in funding and operating the series of facilities serving the broader public. In the case of the new (still to be constructed) Conoga Park School, the partner is the nonprofit organization New Economics for Women (Gao, 2002).

Some multiuse schools of this sort already exist around the country. One example is the Cesar Chavez Elementary School in San Diego, California. Here, a number of typical school functions are doing double service to the broader community. The school health center serves as a community clinic, its library as a community media center, its playfields as community recreation areas. The Millennium Primary School in the Greenwich Millennium Village in London, England, is another excellent example—at once an elementary school, a day care, and a community health center.

The trend over the years has actually been toward larger schools, often located on more peripheral locations, along a major road, that virtually pro-

Figure 10.5 | The Millennium Primary School in Greenwich, London, is a good example of a multifunctional community school. In addition to serving as an elementary school, it contains a day care and a community health center.

hibit much walking. The shift toward large schools appears to be driven by a number of factors, but most insidious are state school facility guidelines that indicate minimum parcel sizes necessary for different types of schools. Behind these standards appear the goals of reducing costs by achieving certain economies of scale. As Salvesen and Hervey (2003) note, however, the direct savings, though considerable, are not overwhelmingly large (in the lower 20 percent per student cost range, over smaller schools) and don't take into account the more indirect costs of, for example, having to transport students longer distances by bus. The health costs and the costs of time spent traveling are critical and need to be considered.

Moreover, as Salvesen and Hervey suggest, there are many creative community approaches for implementing neighborhood schools that reduce their costs. These include joint-use agreements that allow sharing of, for instance, athletic fields or parking areas, and providing flexibility in the code standards applied to renovation of older schools (smart codes).

Smaller schools also appear more effective as learning environments. Drop-out rates are lower and academic achievement higher (Lawrence, 2002). Reducing the time students spend on buses en route to far away schools (often very large ones), and making walking or bicycle travel to school a real possibility, are other important objectives. Citizens of Dayton, Ohio, recently (fall 2002) passed Issue 4, a ten-year school bond measure that hopes to reinstate the concept of nearby walkable neighborhood schools. Under this plan, nearly all the city's school-age population will be within 1-1/2 miles of an elementary school (Elliott, 2002). The middle school will also be scrapped in favor of students staying in one elementary school until high school age. As the superintendent of the city's school system, Percy Mack, says: "It makes sense. When children don't move from school to school, students and their parents can develop stronger relationships with their school" (as quoted in Elliott, 2002).

Key to making this return to a vision of neighborhood schools was resolution of a thirty-year desegregation case, which until recently has forced busing. Many other U.S. cities will certainly have a similar need to consider the impacts on racial and economic diversity, and this is a real and important concern that must be carefully taken into account.

Chicago has also endorsed the concept of schools as community centers and is moving forward with 20 such schools, with the goal of 100 over the next five years (Grossman, 2002). In Chicago, the idea is to create schools that serve as "anchors" for the community, in the words of the Chicago Public School Chief Executive Officer Arne Duncan (Chicago Public Schools, 2002). A Chicago Public Schools press release further describes the initiative:

> Each community school involves a partnership between the city and a nonprofit organization that contributes half the funding and takes the lead in developing the programs offered at the school. These schools are viewed as "full service" schools and are typically open well into the evening providing a variety of educational and community service, including academic and extracurricular programs such as tutoring for students, adult education/GED preparation, sewing, technology training, health services, homework support and childcare. (Chicago Public Schools, 2002, p. 1)

A community school coordinator is hired for each school, and direct involvement by the parents and the neighborhoods in which the schools are located are essential elements. Already, results in Chicago show the value of this idea: student attendance and truancy rates for these schools have improved, test scores have risen, and students tend to stay enrolled in the schools (i.e., reduced student mobility rates). The transition to a community school appears then to help solidify commitments to place and community, while addressing a host of practical needs and issues in the community (Coalition for Community Schools, 2002).

Jane's Place at the Nettelhorst School in the East Lakeview neighborhood of Chicago is an example of how community schools work in practice. A collaboration between the Jane Addams Hull House Association, and Chicago Public Schools, Jane's Place operates essentially as a "community center" within the school, offering a host of free and fee-based child and adult programs. For younger kids there are story hours, fairytale ballet, Spanish classes, and open gym time. For older kids there are music classes and book clubs, and photography. Evening classes for adults include computer literacy, yoga and dance, cooking classes, and book clubs, among others. Many of the classes are offered on weekends. The school is quickly becoming a venue for classes and activities that might otherwise not happen there, making new opportunities available to students, and injecting new resources and amenities that help make them comparable to private schools. The local athletic club is installing a pool, for instance, and the local yacht club sailing school is offering sailing lessons there (Jackson, 2003).

Communities for a Lifetime

Enhancing mobility options for the young and old, finding opportunities to bring generations together, and rethinking schools, are all potentially important steps in building multigenerational places. But probably what is needed are broader, more comprehensive community analyses and strategies. Perhaps as much as anything is the need to nurture a new philosophy or attitude about how we design, plan, grow our communities—one that looks at the whole, at how these many pieces might fit together to create an elder/youth-friendly community, a multigenerational community, or as the State of Florida has been touting "Communities for a Lifetime."

Few other states have done as much as Florida in trying to encourage cities and localities to take the steps necessary to be more accommodating to younger and older residents, the latter especially. Few states, of course, have such a number and proportion of older residents: the 2000 Census shows that 17.6 percent are over the age of sixty-five years (Canedy, 2002).

The most impressive statewide initiative, started in 2000 under the leadership of then Secretary of Elder Affairs Gema Hernandez, is the Elder-Ready communities program. Now called Communities for a Lifetime, the initiative encourages communities to undertake an extensive assessment of how elder-friendly they are, and to identify steps that can be taken to improve living conditions for older Floridians. The change in the name of the state program reflects not just a change in secretaries but a shift in philosophy. Communities for a Lifetime extends the generational coverage; it is intended to be more inclusive and recognizes that communities must be "friendly" and "ready" for all age groups. As Peg Cummings, the coordinator of the Communities for Lifetime program for the city of Dunedin, notes, "An elder-ready community is a family-ready community."

Once analysis is completed (a comprehensive review of such things as access to transit, walkability, safety for elder residents, community resources available to address special needs), a city or county may then be "certified" as a "Community for a Lifetime," a designation that can be proudly touted. Once a locality is certified, the state will help in promoting it. Currently, there are more than forty localities participating in the program, on their way to this certification.

Typical elder-friendly community improvements include wider sidewalks, longer crossing lights at intersections, larger and easier to read street signage, and installation of emergency call boxes. Expanding services at local senior centers is also common, as well as support for elder-friendly businesses, and home delivery and medical services.

St. Augustine, Florida, the oldest American city, has been an early participant in the Communities for a Lifetime program. Spearheaded by Cathy Brown, the charismatic executive director of the St. John's Council on Aging, there are a number of interesting strategies under way here to better integrate elders into the community. The area has two very active senior centers. I visited one—the Coastal Community Center—and was impressed by its creative design and programs. On the day of my visit, the lunch crowd was treated to a dance performance from a group of students from St. Augustine High School. Some 500 meals are served at the center each day, and the staff proudly tell me that unlike many (perhaps most) senior centers, the food is freshly prepared right there in the senior center kitchen. The day's menu was turkey, broccoli, and sweet potatoes. Groups of friends were sitting together, conversing, laughing, exchanging friendly glances and smiles up and down the tables. Other activities were under way, including an exercise class in one room, and computer instruction in another. Additional amenities include a library, a billiards table, an office for legal advice, and rooms for various classes offered there. The Coastal Community Center—a former health department building—is also embedded in a fairly walkable environment, not far from the center of the old city of St. Augustine (though many elderly visitors come by car or by way of the center's bus).

Meals for a Meals-on-Wheels program are also prepared in the Coastal Community Center kitchen. A portion of the kitchen is organized as a kind of

Figure 10.6 | The Coastal Community Center, a senior center in St. Augustine, Florida, provides many important services and functions for older residents, including meals, computer training, and social and entertainment events.

assembly line, where plates are prepared, sealed and placed in coolers. The meals are delivered by volunteers, many of whom are elderly. As director Brown notes, the philosophy behind the meals delivery program is not simply the delivery of food, but social contact. For many housebound recipients of the meals, the delivery may represent the only contact with another person all day.

Another elder-ready step undertaken by the St. John's Council on Aging is the establishment of its bus company and system. Called the Sunshine Bus Company, it provides the only public transit for elders (or anyone) outside of the urban area of Jacksonville. As director Brown observes, not only does it serve as a lifeline and a critical means to get people around, some ride it just to get out and about. The fare is a reasonable $1.

Perhaps most impressive about the St. John's Council on Aging is the underlying philosophy that guides it, and that its director, Cathy Brown, articulates consistently. First, the elderly in our communities are, in Brown's words, to be venerated, respected, valued, cherished for their wisdom and life experiences. The elderly ought to play a central role in the life of the community, and not be marginalized as they typically are in the United States. Second, caregivers and those who work for the agency are to be valued and appreciated. In-home caregivers are to be paid equally with those working similarly in other settings. It is recognized that unhappy and disgruntled workers will pass these ill feelings along to those they care for.

The city of Dunedin, Florida, one of the communities farthest along in the program (and a community where 40 percent of the population is over sixty-five), began participating in the Communities for a Lifetime program in 2000, following a stop by then-Secretary of Elder Affairs Hernandez on her "awakening tour" of the state. Support and interest from Dunedin's mayor, Tom Anderson, was strong, and the town began the first step—preparing the report card, a diagnostic process intended to identify the aspects of the community that could be improved and made more elder-ready. The resulting report document, completed in early 2001, is comprehensive and thorough.

Through a partnership process, several different groups in the community carried out various steps of the analysis for the report card. For example, a group of pediatric nurses from the nearby community hospital visited and evaluated some forty-two restaurants in the city. They looked at the extent to which restaurants were elder-friendly—everything from walking hazards and physical access to dietary issues, to the font size of the menus. Perhaps most important, at the end of each assessment, the nurses would meet with and discuss their findings with the restaurant owner. Often these owners were quite interested in making the suggested changes (of course, in part out of self-interest). Other steps in the analysis include mapping access to transit, areas served with a stop within one-quarter mile, extent of sidewalks, and the location and distribution of parks and recreational facilities as compared to where older residents lived in Dunedin. Those areas in the city with the highest concentration of residents fifty-five years and older are also mapped. Overlaid on this map are existing pharmacies and grocery stores—critical services for the elderly.

Dunedin has especially worked hard to make its downtown pedestrian-friendly for a number of years, beginning in the late 1980s with the creation of a community redevelopment district, which captures tax base increases and directs them to improvements in the downtown. This tax-increment

Figure 10.7 | Dunedin, Florida, is one of the first communities seeking to become an elder-ready community (now officially called "Communities for a Lifetime").

financing mechanism now supplies more than $200,000 in yearly revenue for improvements and maintenance.

The city has recently prepared an action plan, a number of which have already been taken: changes in intersection crosswalk signals (adding an extra 15 seconds for crossing; at one intersection it is possible to stop traffic in both directions); an expansion of the homestead exemption for elderly (property tax reduction); satellite post offices, including a small post office downtown (in a boxcar); auto-pay systems for paying utility bills; a new adult day care facility that will open soon; and a new senior center.

A number of future changes are being actively pursued, including working with and encouraging businesses to provide home delivery, gradually replacing street signage with larger letters, and working with the Pinellas Transit Agency to provide more bus shelters and call boxes.

The pedestrian- and bicycle-friendly atmosphere of the city is further strengthened by the Pinellas Trail, a 47-mile-long trail that runs the length of Pinellas County, and intersects Main Street at about its midpoint. One sees quite a few older bicyclists on the Pinellas Trail. Dunedin is in the heart of the trail and a logical stop and center of activity for riders.

Dunedin's Main Street and downtown have indeed been impressively pedestrianized. Wide sidewalks, trees in the streets, extended curbs, and strategically placed vegetated medians all effectively slow traffic. There is a healthy abundance of shops and businesses to overcome feelings of a dead downtown, as well as numerous pocket parks with benches and seating. Distinctive brick cross-paths and slightly elevated brick surfaces at intersections slow auto traffic.

For the most part, the stores and restaurants on Main Street have done well, and the economic benefits of the pedestrian improvements have paid off. Clearly, there are multiple reasons for undertaking these kinds of community improvements, and this is a key lesson from Dunedin. Not only are the environments created better for older Americans, but they are also better for the local economy. Elder-friendly streets and shopping areas are also child- and family-friendly, a factor that families with small children find attractive.

The city also does an excellent job bringing people to the town, by organizing an impressive array of events during the year. These range from arts and crafts festivals, to wine tasting events, to a Mardi Gras celebration. Many elderly residents are transported downtown for these events by bus.

Infill housing has also been part of the strategy for Dunedin's downtown redevelopment. An interesting approach can be seen in the Grant Street townhouses. Here, an effort was made to encourage shops and businesses one street over from Main Street. Residential structures have been designed to include a small extension, with a street-oriented entrance, for a home business or to be rented to a small merchant. Only partially successful so far, they represent an interesting example of flexible zoning and planning and encouragement and support for fine-grain mixing of uses, and a pedestrian multigenerational environment.

Much of the land use here would indeed seem to work from a multigenerational perspective. Not only are shops and coffee places available on this pedestrian route, but a major hospital is close by. Residents of one of the nearby retirement homes, for instance, are within a brief walk of many destinations. The same is true for elderly residents living in single-family homes in adjoining residential neighborhoods.

If you are a resident at the Park Place retirement home on London Avenue, it is an easy walk to shop at, say, Cindy Lou's antiques or Allen's Florists, or to take a bite to eat at Café Alfresco or the Chili Shop, or the old Boxcar (which also houses the post office), among other places. There are also several churches along Main Street.

The lessons here are at least perhaps twofold: (1) It is important to create pedestrian centers like Dunedin's everywhere, so that *wherever* one lives, the physical landscape is accommodating and accessible and interesting. Along with the pedestrian improvements, there is need to find ways to locate new elder-care or elder living projects so as to take best advantage of such marvelous walking environments, to provide exposure to a stimulating mix of activities and uses, and to provide opportunities for interaction with others (including children and families).

Conclusions

Today's communities are designed around, and function well for, those in their middle years—especially those who are old enough to drive (when life begins for many kids, at least in American society) but not too old that driving becomes difficult or dangerous. While auto-dependence for the young and the old in our society is the most obvious problem of our age-truncated community design, there is a host of other ways in which the youngest and oldest members of our communities are not considered. A sustainable and just place can be judged by its treatment of the young and the old, and on many fronts and in many ways we fail on this essential measure. Multigenerational place is the goal, and it brings into play an array of design and planning issues and needs—good transit, walkable environments, schools that better serve all age groups, and proactive community policies that provide care and safety and security and richness of experience to the young and the old alike, in ways that convey that they are loved and valued as our most essential community assets.

Energy and Sustainable Place Making

Few aspects of our lives and lifestyles have as much planetary impact as our energy use and, at the same time, as much potential to strengthen place and to build sustainable communities. We Americans consume a tremendous amount of energy to heat our homes, fuel our cars, and power the industries and offices in which we work. The negative impacts of this consumption are often devastatingly destructive of place. Our demand for coal has ravaged much of the highlands of West Virginia and eastern Kentucky, for instance, and the burning of coal and oil has had similar deleterious effects. Moreover, our monthly expenditures on energy could be a significant source of community wealth if directed to support local businesses and economic activity, and if used to help build rather than undermine community and ecology.

The production of energy can occur in many locally specific ways that build upon the special character and circumstances of a community and region and serve to reinforce place. An important part of the mission of building a place-based or place-strengthening economy is to find primary ways to generate jobs, income, and economic activities from local resources. Locally generated electricity, produced from locally produced biomass, is a growing possibility and one that is widely used in Scandinavia and Germany, for instance.

The extent of serious discussion about alternative energy options in the United States has been depressingly limited, and the interest in local or place-based energy solutions and renewable energy has generally been rather meager. Producing energy in the fastest, cheapest way has been the goal, with little effort made to see energy needs and the sustainable and place-sensitive ideas for addressing them as *local* concerns and opportunities. There is a largely disingenuous mantra of "hydrogen" at the federal government level that has distracted us from the immediate possibilities of moving significantly toward a self-sufficient, zero-emission, local-based energy future. But, we need not wait for some magical technological breakthrough—we don't need one. Each community, each place, each neighborhood and home, can be reimagined with renewable, ecologically sound energy in mind. This makes sense from the perspective of concern for our planet and its precious ecosystems, and also from the good that comes from building distinctive, resilient places.

Chicago, Renewable Energy City

Cities ought to aspire to be energy-neutral, to produce the basic energy they need in renewable, nonpolluting ways. This can serve to strengthen and enhance sense of place and can help build economy. Few large cities in this world have taken as many steps toward building a renewable-based energy strategy as has Chicago, Illinois.

In the summer of 2001, the City of Chicago signed a groundbreaking agreement with ComEd to purchase green power, or electricity produced from renewable sources—20 percent of its total municipal demand—the full amount to be provided by 2005 (10 percent in the first year). Strongly supported by Mayor Daly, this move is viewed as a way of building a renewable energy economy, as well as simply doing the right thing. Fully implemented, the purchase will reduce annual CO_2 emissions by nearly 250,000 tons (Office of the Mayor, 2001). As part of the agreement, ComEd will contribute (forgo) the profits it would have made from the sale (above the regular electricity rate) into a Special Reinvestment Fund, which will be used to further support local renewable energy projects.

Leading by example is a hallmark of the Chicago approach. The city is taking direct actions to reduce energy in a number of other ways. It has com-

Figure 11.1 | Chicago has taken a number of steps to promote and advance renewable energy, including installing photovoltaics on the rooftops of its public buildings. Shown here is the rooftop of the Midwest Center for Green Technology.

mitted to retrofitting 15 million square feet of public building space to be energy efficient. It has also sponsored a design competition—Green Homes for Chicago—to spur energy-efficient design and construction in the city.

Chicago leads the way with the notion of "brightfields"—turning brownfield sites into places where renewable energy is generated. The first completed brightfield is a 17-acre, former rock-crushing site that has now become the Midwest Center for Green Technology. The city cleared some 600,000 cubic yards of construction debris from the site, most of which was recycled. The old building on-site was renovated and redesigned to incorporate a number of green features, including extensive roof-mounted photovoltaics, a green roof, a rainwater collection/cistern system, a geothermal heat pump system, bicycle parking, and shower facilities. At least half the materials for the building were produced within 300 miles of the site. The first occupants of the building are Spire Solar Chicago, a solar panel manufacturer, and GreenCorps, the city's green job-training program.

Chicago's move in the direction of renewable energy is exemplary in many ways, and represents a model for other cities. It is part of an overall new vision of the city as a green city, and part of a broader set of actions taken in pursuit of this vision. A willingness to invest public monies upfront to underwrite the development of a local renewable energy industry, and to throw the city's purchasing power behind these goals, is impressive. The city has committed $2 million to purchase solar products from Spire, in combination with ComEd's investment of $6 million. Already, a number of public buildings contain photovoltiac panels, including most of the city's major museums, community centers, and public schools (e.g., the Peggy Notebaert Nature Museum, the DuSable Museum of African American History).

Chicago's most ambitious energy plan invokes restoration of the Calumet region, in the south of the city, a former center of heavy industrial activity. The city is envisioning this major cleanup and restoration project as another power-generating opportunity—building a solar power plant on the site, as well as harvesting the biogas from its landfill. A new environmental center is also planned.

Lessons from Aero Island

The historic and progressive island of Aero (Ærø), in Denmark, stands out as an inspirational case study. This beautiful island, south of Jutland, offers a model for moving in the direction of a place-strengthening energy strategy. Ninety square kilometers (about 35 square miles) in size, and with a population of about 7,400, its agricultural and small-town land use offers a contrast to Chicago, to be sure, but a powerful one nonetheless. Through a deliberately inclusive grassroots process, the island has developed an impressive vision of an ecological island—one where locally produced, renewable energy is the cornerstone. The official goal is to provide 80–100 percent of the island's energy needs from renewable sources by the year 2006. The island has already reached an impressive 40 percent.

As a small, largely rural island, it is perhaps an unlikely epicenter for energy innovation. Yet, Aeroe's lessons are many. On the road to completely renewable energy sources, the island has pioneered some new ways of building energy-independent communities. Aeroe has become most famous for its creative combining of solar energy technology and district heating. It has three solar district heating plants, with a fourth likely in the future. The Aeroskobing (Ærøskøbing) district heating plant, the island's oldest, is an interesting mix of solar and biomass power. The 4,900 square meters of solar panels on the south-facing roofline send hot water into the system. The remaining heating needs, especially during winter months of the year when solar production is low, are satisfied through the burning of wood pellets and straw, both renewable resources. The straw comes in bales, produced on local farms; whereas the wood pellets, compressed from wood waste from Danish furniture and lumber-processing plants, are shipped in. Ash, a by-product at the end of the burning, goes back to area farmers to be applied to the land. The architecture of this plant is compact, distinctive, and, many (including me) would say, beautiful.

The solar heating plant serving the town of Marstal is perhaps the most famous on the island, and one of the very largest of its kind in the world. It consists of rows of south-facing panels, some 9,000 square meters in all. These solar panels currently provide about 15 percent of the hot water needs

Figure 11.2 | Aeroe Island, Denmark, has three district heating systems that utilize solar and biomass energy. The plant shown here serves the town of Aeroskobing.

Figure 11.3 | The power plant for the town of Marstal, on Aeroe Island, heats hot water through 9,000 square meters of solar panels, shown here. A herd of sheep meander through the panels and keep the grass short.

for Marstal over the course of the year. During the several months of the summer, the solar panels typically provide all, or at least the lion's share, of the hot water for the town. Plans are already in the works to add an additional 10,000 square meters of panels, which (the locals proudly proclaim) would once again put it ahead of Swedish rivals, making it the largest such plant in the world, allowing the town to increase the percentage of heating and domestic hot water provided by this innovative facility.

Another organic element of the Marstal plant is the (somewhat startling) herd of sheep that lives in and around the rows of solar panels. They perform the important job of keeping the grass short—something that would otherwise need to be done through more conventional (and likely energy consumptive) means.

The most recent of Aeroe's three plants, completed in 2002, serves about 130 homes in St. Rise and in many ways demonstrates best the great potential of this place-based technology. Here, about 50 percent of the hot water is from the solar panels, with the remaining heat provided from wood pellets.

The environmental footprint of the building and panels is modest, and the boiler for the pellets is small and unalarming. In addition, the boiler only needs to run for the three summer months of the year because enough heat from the solar panels can be stored in its storage tank to carry the operation through the fall without the need to burn pellets. Consequently, most of the year there are no emissions at all from the plant's small smokestack, and labor costs are small to none, except during the three months the burner is operating.

The technology of solar heating panels has improved greatly over the years. Temperatures in the panels can easily reach 200 degrees Celsius (though they are never allowed to reach this temperature). The panels, consisting of a mix of water and glyco (a substance that prevents freezing in the winter), receive solar rays that are captured and bounced around, much like in a greenhouse, heating the metal plates through which the liquid is pumped. Variable-speed pumping allows better circulation of the liquid and reduces the electric consumption of the pumps. The actual speed of the pumps is regulated by the solar production coming from several photovoltaic panels.

Aeroe's plans for, and vision of, the future are bold indeed. Part of the vision is to continue to grow the local economy around renewable energy. Already, for instance, a local resident has started a solar panel production facility, which has served as the source of panels for the new St. Rise plant. The island continues to move ahead with the installation of new windmills that will further extend its energy self-sufficiency and bring it closer to its ambitious goal.

Aeroe residents believe that a key lesson is that smaller is often better. The strategy has been one of making concerted progress through a number of relatively small, decentralized energy investments—not a single solar heating plant, but three, and perhaps eventually four. Other power sources and energy strategies will be necessary, including further development of new technologies, including a proposed biogas facility that would capture energy from farm and livestock waste, as well as from town wastewater. Other important lessons include the need to build support from the ground up, and to involve many local players in a partnership, something Aero has worked hard to do.

Not all is perfect even in Aeroe, of course. Worries related to the solar heating plants include a concern about the price and availability of wood pellets, disposal of the pesticide residue from the straw burning (it presently goes to the landfill), and how to ensure that the water returning to the plant is actually not too hot. The most serious challenge to Aeroe's renewable energy vision has been opposition to six proposed windmills, which together would have satisfied all of the island's electricity needs. Considerable and vocal opposition to the windmill plan developed, with concerns expressed both about the size of the windmills (2-MW units) and their original planned placement near a historic fort. A new proposed site avoids the fort, but the issue of size remains contentious. Opponents of the project argue that smaller windmills would better fit the island's scenic landscape. But, proponents counter that, at least in Denmark, smaller windmills are not yet being manufactured, and that, in any event, the visual effects would not be much different. A recent compromise means that the island is moving ahead with three of the windmills, which together would satisfy 50 percent of the island's electricity needs. Not a bad beginning.

London's Zero-Energy Neighborhoods

Crafting new places to live—indeed, entire new neighborhoods that use little energy, or ideally produce more than they need, and are carbon-neutral (or produce no net increase in carbon emissions)—is one of our most significant place-making challenges.

The Beddington Zero-Energy project, or BedZED, in the London suburb of Hackbridge, is one of the most inspiring examples to date. This project is a redevelopment of 1.65 hectares of brownfields, the borough's former wastewater treatment works. Included are 82 units of housing, alongside 14 work units, and office space, a village square, and adjacent spaces provided for a soccer field. The housing is mixed, with about a third standard owner-occupied, a third joint ownership, and another third social rental housing.

The borough of Sutton, long known for its environmental leadership, agreed to sell the land to the Peabody Trust for 10 percent less than fair market value, reflecting the monetary value of the environmental benefits—the CO_2 reduction, in particular—that would be provided.

Energy is the most important ecological design feature. It begins with south-facing housing units, with intentionally cooler north-facing work-spaces. Exterior walls are rather thick, with a 300-millimeter-thick layer of insulation between brick and block. The high thermal mass conserves energy, as the buildings cool down and heat up more slowly. Each housing unit has a south-facing, double-glazed conservatory. In addition to a sedum roof, some 777 square meters of photovoltaics have also been installed, or what has been calculated as sufficient to power forty electric vehicles.

Efforts to make the community energy- and carbon-neutral extend be-yond the buildings, with a special effort to give residents easy alternatives to driving cars. Parking areas for bicycles are provided, a car-sharing organiza-tion has been formed (now with thirty members and two cars), and available parking has been cut in half compared with what would normally be pro-vided (indeed, required) with a development of this size. The car-sharing club is now a legal commitment; the result of negotiating with the borough to per-

Figure 11.4 | BedZED, the Beddington Zero-Energy Development, is designed so that living spaces are south-facing and require very little energy. Natural ventilation, ther-mal mass, and photovoltaics are also utilized.

Figure 11.5 | Building materials for BedZED come from within a 300-mile radius of the site, and include lumber sustainably harvested from the Borough of Croydon.

mit the fewer parking spaces eventually allowed. Each resident must pay an annual fee (though fairly small) for their parking space.

Some of the other impressive green elements of BedZED have to do with the sources of building materials and energy fuels. The neighborhood's heating and electric needs will, for the most part, be taken care of by the new combined heat and power plant. This plant, which will produce 130 kilowatts of electricity and about twice that amount of heat, will burn wood waste from local "tree surgeries." About 1,000 metric tons of tree waste each year will become fuel for the project's combined heat and power plant (CHP). In addition, wood siding comes from the nearby Croydon borough's forest. And, uniquely, this borough—Croydon—is itself considered a sustainable forest; the trees and forests throughout the city have been certified by the Forest Stewardship Council as sustainably managed. Bricks for the exterior walls are manufactured just 20 miles away. Overall, more than half of the building materials used in the project have been derived within a 35-mile radius of the site (BioRegional, undated). A number of building materials have been recycled, including structured steel reclaimed from demolition sites. Concrete pavers in the village square lie atop a bed of recycled crushed glass.

Perhaps the most unique and distinctive feature of the design is the ventilation system. Especially important in tight energy-efficient homes like these (about 60 percent of the interior heat in the winter is estimated to come from body heat and cooking), fresh air is circulated through an innovative system of "wind cowls" that scoop air and direct it into the buildings. The cowls, painted in bright colors of red, green, and yellow, each have a wind rudder that ensures they're always pivoting into the wind; air is scooped through large funnels, and incoming and outgoing air is passed through a heat exchanger. Desai and Riddlestone (2002) describe the function in more detail:

> The wind cowls, which have become a distinctive feature of BedZED and a sometimes controversial local landmark, point into the wind and air is forced down into the rooms. Stale air is drawn out from the kitchen, bathrooms and toilets (removing odors and excess moisture) via the rear of the wind cowls, where negative pressure is created by the windflow. This negative pressure is accentuated by the curved roofline which has been refined in a wind tunnel, generating lift in the same way as an aeroplane wing, which helps to draw air up out of the homes. A heat exchanger extracts any warmth or coolth from the outgoing air, maintaining the internal temperature of the homes.

All the windows and doors are operable, and as conservatories heat up in the summer, residents are expected to make these temperature adjustments themselves. The energy techniques are decidedly low-tech, and that is one of the lessons from BedZED. In the words of one BedZED project architect, the buildings are essentially "well-insulated sunny coves."

The model unit of a three-bedroom flat is stylish and most impressively full of light. Skylights and conservatories result in full light throughout the flats, and little need for artificial lighting during the day. The BedZED units demonstrate pretty convincingly that low-impact sustainable living need not be painful or sacrificial. The quality of living in these units is high, and the amenities numerous.

Among the special amenities in this compact urban development are the "sky gardens." Almost all the housing units have gardens, with many physically detached from the units and accessible only through an elevated walkway. This is a feature the residents appear to like a great deal and allows for "maintaining greenspace and bioproductive land in a high density development" (Desai and Riddlestone, 2002, p. 93). Being able to look out the living room windows and see their garden gives them an extra feeling of spaciousness. A 30-centimeter layer of soil exists in each garden, which allows vegetables and plants to be grown, and also serves as building insulation.

Wastewater from the units is collected and treated in a living machine—a device that breaks down and takes up wastes through green plants and aquatic organisms in a completely natural and chemical-free process, with the resulting clean water collected in underground cisterns and used again for toilet flushing. Rainwater is also collected from rooftops and added to this cistern storage. Along with permeable paving and the sedum rooftops, the project sends no runoff into the municipal storm drains.

The energy and environmental results are already impressive. The housing units are so well insulated (and ventilated) that they require very little heating, and the power demands of this small community are low, to be sure. What power is needed is provided through a sustainable, circular means. Desai and Riddlestone (2002), of BioRegional, estimate that the new residents of BedZED, if they do nothing more than occupy the units, will have already

Figure 11.6 | The brightly painted wind cowls of the BedZED, which scoop in air and provide natural ventilation, also add a colorful, distinctive look to the neighborhood.

reduced their ecological footprint to about 4 hectares, from the 6-hectare average for the United Kingdom. Further green lifestyle choices (e.g., using the car-share club) could, they believe, reduce the footprint further, to about 2 hectares or around the global average or "global fair share target" (what each person on the planet is entitled to emit—a function of what the planet can sustain, divided by total global population).

Educating and working with the residents of BedZED is also viewed as important. Considerable work went into producing an attractive, accessible residents guide, explaining the special energy and other features of the buildings. BioRegional is also undertaking a green lifestyle initiative to help make it as easy as possible to live in more environmentally friendly ways.

Strengthening Place to Solve Energy Problems

Building a place-based energy system means taking full advantage of local climate and landscape conditions. A creative example of a climate-sensitive energy opportunity can be seen in the storage and use of snow for cooling in climates with cold and snowy conditions. Sundsvall, Sweden, a famously progressive city, has been utilizing snow storage for cooling since the year 2000, when its hospital cooling system began to operate. Here, seasonal snow storage provides all the summer cooling needs of the city's 190,000-square-meter structure. Some 40,000 metric tons of snow, most collected from streets and sidewalks, is stored with a layer of wood chips to provide insulation. The cooling services are provided by the slowly melting cool water, which is sent to the hospital, and recirculated back to the cold storage site. It is estimated that the payback period for this project is a modest three years, with a project life of around forty years (Skogsberg and Nordell, 2001).

The Sundsvall project illustrates a climate-sensitive energy production strategy, taking advantage of the essentially free services of place, in this case melting snow. Other place opportunities will emerge. In agricultural areas, utilizing farm waste produced locally is another idea with great potential. Power plants fueled by methane from poultry and livestock wastes have become common in Germany, the Netherlands, and Denmark. New plants are also coming on-line in the United Kingdom. One such new plant in Holsworthy, Devon, takes the poultry wastes from a cooperative of about thirty farms. It should handle up to 150,000 metric tons of slurry per year, producing more than 14 million kWh/year in electricity and heat for the region. The best part is the locally based nature of the production—utilizing waste material from an 8–16-kilometer radius of the plant, and turning a polluting waste problem into an energy opportunity (Renewable Energy World, 2001; BBC news, 2002).

Burlington, Vermont, provides an excellent example of sustainably generated, locally produced energy. The McNeil Generating Station, built and operated by the Burlington Electric Department (50 percent owned by them), is powered from wood-harvest residue and lower-quality trees harvested from private lands in the area (70 percent), in addition to sawdust, chips, and bark purchased from local sawmills. The plant produces 50 megawatts of energy at peak, about enough for the entire city of Burlington. Wood ash, a by-product of the wood-burning process, is recycled in the form of soil conditioners (mixed with limestone) and used in building roads. Pollution control devices monitor particulates to a much greater degree than required by state or federal law (emissions are one one-hundredth of that permitted by federal law).

The Burlington wood-based plant has many advantages from a sustainability point of view—it uses a renewable resource, diverts a substantial amount of waste from landfills, and helps strengthen the local economy. As a U.S. Department of Environment case analysis states:

> Using wood as a fuel for electricity generation puts money back into the Vermont economy while improving the condition of its forests and providing jobs for Vermonters. Forty people are employed at the McNeil Generating Station, including a maintenance crew, equipment operators, fuel handlers, foresters and administrative and engineering support personnel. In addition, it takes approximately 76 tons of wood per hour to run McNeil at full load. Using this in-state fuel resource adds to Vermont's economy. Fuels other than wood have to be imported from other states because wood is Vermont's only indigenous fuel. (www.eere.energy.gov/biomass)

A proposal to use the residual waste energy from the Burlington plant to provide district heating to the city is now being explored. Of course, using wood waste, agricultural wastes, and biogas extracted from wastewater and to generate electricity and heat are common strategies in many European cities (Beatley, 2000). In the Swedish city of Växja, local waste is also used to power transit vehicles; in Upsalla, some forty municipal buses are powered by biogas from organic household and kitchen waste.

One of the most impressive new European examples of place-based energy production can be seen in Malmö, Sweden's redevelopment of its Western Harbor. This former industrial port area is being redeveloped as part of a large building exhibition, and has taken sustainability as its key design theme. The project, Västra Hamnen (also known as the "city of tomorrow"), will eventually contain 1,000 dwelling units in its first phase, and represents a car-free district close to the city's historic center. A highly pedestrianized district, the street layout is decidedly not a grid, but arranged so that buildings are pushed askance, so that the pedestrian is never quite sure what might be around the next corner.

The district's environmental features are many, and reflect a strong desire to minimize its ecological footprint and to incorporate nature through the design. It contains an impressive array of energy features. One of the goals of the project was that it be powered 100 percent from local renewable energy sources. This goal has been accomplished largely through the construction of a 2-megawatt wind turbine. Smaller amounts of energy are also produced from rooftop photovoltaics, and heat is provided in part through vertical south-facing solar heating panels. The latter provide a rather dramatic visual addition to the side of the one main building of flats, which also has a ground-level ecological restaurant. As well, energy is extracted from groundwater via a heat pump.

The Kronsberg ecological district in Hannover, Germany, another positive example, represents an amazing laboratory and demonstration of how many local and place-centered energy ideas can be combined in a single urban district. Beginning with very low-energy housing designs, the neighborhood is heated through two combined heat and power (CHP) plants and a district heating grid. Creatively, one of the CHP plants, providing heating for about 600 dwelling units, is actually located in the basement of a building of flats. Designed to dampen noise and vibrations, the residents of this building scarcely know the plant is located there (the two stack pipes at the rear of the

Figure 11.7 | The new ecological re-development of Western Harbor, Malmö, Sweden. Called Västra Hamnen, 100 percent of its energy is produced locally through renew-able technologies, like these façade mounted solor hot water heating panels that feed hot water into a district heating system.

building are the only visible signs). Use of CHP plants is a much more effi-cient way to produce heat and electricity, and has become standard in new developments in northern Europe.

Kronsberg demonstrates a number of solar technologies, including one of the largest centralized solar hot water heating systems in a residential develop-ment. Rooftop solar collectors on a large section of multifamily flats send heated water to a large 2,700-cubic-meter storage tank, which is partially un-derground. The aboveground section of the tank serves as a popular children's play "mound" (with ladders and slides leading to and from the top). This sys-tem covers about 40 percent of the hot water needs of these 100 or so flats.

The energy needs of this district are minimized in other important ways, as well. Perhaps most important is the new tramline serving the neighbor-hood with three stops and very frequent service to the center of Hannover. No resident of Kronsberg is more than 600 meters (about one-third of a mile) from a tram station. A nearby grocery and an area of shops provide destina-

Figure 11.8 | Energy production at Kronsberg, in Hannover, Germany, happens on-site. Here, a 1.8-megawatt wind turbine sits just a few hundred meters from homes.

tions that are easy to walk to, and extensive bike paths and facilities make movement by bicycle very easy, as well. The first phase of the development also includes a primary school and three day-care facilities.

Other exemplary new projects with bold energy ambitions can be cited. EVA-Lanxmeer, in Culemborg, in the Netherlands, will eventually contain 230 homes, as well as green office buildings and studios. The neighborhood aspires to be carbon-neutral and to rely on locally produced renewable energy. The homes and buildings throughout are designed to use a small amount of energy in the first place, and must incorporate photovoltaic panels and solar hot water heating units.

Creatively reducing energy consumption in cities can happen in both big and little ways. Small actions such as replacing conventional incandescent bulb lighting with compact fluorescent lights can have a remarkable cumulative reduction in energy needs. A creative illustration of this is seen in the results of the Philips Lighting initiative to "relamp" an entire block of buildings in Berkeley, California. A joint initiative along with the Lawrence Berkeley National Laboratory, an energy audit was first conducted of the buildings on Telegraph Avenue (between Channing and Durant Streets), and then, with products donated by Philips, energy efficient lighting was installed. The calculated savings in energy and dollars is impressive. Pre-retrofit consumption for the block is reduced from about 147,800 kWh/year to 85,142 kWh/year, or about a 60 percent reduction (Lawrence Berkeley National Laboratory and Philips Lighting Company, undated). Total savings to building owners is estimated at about $8,772, and about equal reduction in the cost of electricity. Simple initiatives like this can further reduce the carbon emissions and ecological footprints of urban areas, and at the same time strengthen the economic bottom line for shops and businesses there.

In Search of Windy Cities

Wind energy has found important applications within urban areas, and represents a potentially important part of the energy mix to move cities toward energy self-sufficiency. Windmill parks erected near cities have fast become new, positive elements of place. One of the most dramatic cases is the Middlegrunden wind farm, just offshore from Copenhagen, Denmark. Extensive analysis of site alternatives was conducted, with special concern about visual impacts. In the end, the twenty 2-megawatt turbines, providing enough power for an estimated 32,000 Danish homes, were sited along the old harbor fortifications.

Wind power has been integrated into some prominent new examples of ecological development. The ecological district, Kronsberg, in Hannover, Germany, already mentioned includes three wind turbines, one of which is 1.8 megawatts, all within just a few hundred meters of homes. There is virtually no sound or vibration from these turbines, until one gets right underneath them and hears a surprisingly pleasant "whoosh." These turbines provide much more than the power needed by residents of this new neighborhood.

The windy coastal city of Pori, Finland, has made a major commitment to wind energy. An excellent place for wind power, Pori has already installed eight 1-megawatt turbines and two 2-megawatt turbines. Plans are under way to build as many as thirty turbines offshore, and the city has just been given approval by the national government to begin a study of different potential sites. A visitor's center has been constructed very close to the meri-Pori wind farm and hosts school visits each day. The center answers questions and provides wind energy information, and has itself become a major tourist stop.

Integrating wind turbines into building design is another promising direction. Indeed, there is a long history of utilizing microturbine technologies in this way. One of the most visually dramatic examples was the design for the Dutch Pavilion at the 2000 Hannover World's Fair. The structure, with the overall theme of creating space, was unusual in many respects, but capped on its roof were six small turbines especially designed by the engineering firm Lagerwey for use in urban environments.

Figure 11.9 | Wind turbines in Pori, Finland, have been sited to minimize their visual impacts.

Strengthening Urban Form through Low-Energy Building

Renewable energy and energy efficiency can also be nicely linked to other place-strengthening land use strategies. Historic buildings might be adaptively reused with substantial energy upgrades, for instance. Infill housing that helps to bring new life to struggling neighborhoods could also be designed and built to use small amounts of energy, further strengthening local economy and ecology. And where renewables are designed-in, they will perhaps add a distinctive look and feel to this housing. The promise of infill development that dramatically reduces energy consumption and incorporates renewable energy technology is shown by new development in the historic downtown Tucson, Arizona, neighborhood of Armory Park. Built on a parcel of vacant land, the victim of urban renewal, the Armory Park del Sol is an urban solar village where, as its literature boasts, "historic meets high-tech." Developed by John Wesley Miller, a local builder who has spent much of his life advocating solar energy, the project is an excellent example of sensitive neighborhood redevelopment. The first decision made was to utilize an open street plan—connecting with and integrating into the surrounding neighborhood; no gates or walls, which has become a standard building practice in Tucson. Instead, nice sidewalks and interior walkways add a neighborhood continuity to the project. All of the ninety homes include solar energy elements. Most have solar hot water heaters and photovoltaic units, and utilize concrete-filled block walls with excellent thermal mass qualities.

One of the most interesting aspects of this project are the incentive arrangements made with the local power company that further entice potential buyers. Specifically, Tucson Electric Power (TEP) operates a Guarantee Home program, which provides an assurance to homebuyers that their monthly energy bills will not exceed a certain maximum, usually for a three-year period. This maximum is typically expressed in cents or dollars per day and, in Armory Park, prominently displayed on signs in the front of model homes. Builders participating in this program receive a number of incentives, including training, advertising, and the ability to offer the guarantee as a powerful enticement to potential buyers. TEP staff review building plans, make suggestions for improving the energy efficiency of the homes, and conduct inspections of the homes along the way during construction. For TEP, reducing peak demand in this way makes much sense; for the builder, it helps to sell homes. And to the buyer, the promise of lower operating cost (and the ability to receive TEP's lowest electric rates) is very attractive. In the end, perhaps most impressive about this program is the way it gives visibility and prominence to home energy consumption (and the possibilities of reducing it!).

Monitoring of the homes has only just begun, but early anecdotal evidence suggests Miller's homes are living up to their expected small energy footprint. Miller relates a recent story of one owner complaining that his total energy bill that month was $27, actually below, Miller says, what should be anticipated.

The homes in Armory Park are extremely well insulated—the solid masonry construction provides a good thermal mass for the homes. It utilizes low-emissity windows (that reflect long-wave heat back into living spaces and provide greater insulation), fluorescent lights, and energy-star certified appliances are found throughout.

Figure 11.10 | The homes at Armory Park del Sol, in Tucson, Arizona, demonstrate that energy efficiency and solar technologies can be integrated into new, infill housing projects like this one.

Armory Park del Sol also has one of the four zero-energy homes sponsored by the National Renewable Energy Laboratory. The home is designed
to produce at least as much energy as it will use over the course of a year.
Among other things, the home's roof hosts a much larger array of photovoltaics, though in every other sense it blends in. The home sold quickly, and
the owners speak of the beauty and quality of the home as well as its zero-
energy feature. Miller called TEP to check the first monthly bill for the home,
and the clerk was shocked to see that the house had instead racked up a
credit. The surprised employee said this must not be right and that she had to
go talk to her supervisor! Miller has worked hard to blend in and hide many
of the solar and energy features of the project, responding to the expressed
concerns of the neighborhood. Solar water heating units are low profile on
the roofs, a black color that blends into the background roof color. Photovoltaics have been placed on garage roofs in the back of the homes, away
from streets and mostly beyond neighborhood view. Miller talks of learning
over time how to perfect the integration—replacing shiny metal on solar
heating units that draw attention to them.

Bold Buildings for a Low-Energy Future

In very urban environments a sense of place is often a function of the skyline
and the architecture and configuration of larger, taller buildings. Increasingly,
the aesthetics and design work involved in these taller buildings permit dramatic reductions in the energy needed, at the same time providing distinctive
new visual texture to cities. Here, again, energy and architectural design can
be fused to strengthen place.

Skyscrapers will in many cities be an important part of the sustainability
answer, and have the potential to achieve much higher levels of energy
efficiency. The Commerzbank, in Frankfurt, Germany, completed in 1997
and until recently the tallest building in Europe, represents perhaps the best
of the new generation of green skyscrapers. Designed by Norman Foster and
Partners, the forty-eight-story building is designed around a triangular form,
with a long center atrium, and a series of nine sky gardens that wind their
way up and around the uniquely shaped building. These enclosed gardens are
important in providing natural ventilation, in moderating temperatures, and

in generally enhancing the working conditions in the building. The design incorporates a number of energy features, including a double-skin façade providing an important thermal buffer, with built-in sun-shading screens, operable windows in offices, a tremendous amount of daylight (all offices have large windows, many with pretty spectacular views of the River Main and the city skyline), and a ceiling cooling system utilizing chilled water. The amount of daylight throughout the building is one of its most noticeable features; this abundance of natural light results from the large interior atrium, the gardens, and the glass partition walls throughout. Motion sensors and light sensors moderate and adjust the artificial lighting that is needed.

Together these design features make for a very energy efficient building compared with conventional skyscrapers. Commerzbank staff estimate that the building uses almost 40 percent less energy than a conventional structure of its size would. And employees are reported to be very happy with the work environment of the building and its innovative green features.

And, the size and density, along with the downtown location of structures like the Commerzbank suggest even greater energy savings. While the Commerzbank did include parking, most travel to and from the building is via public transit. The Kaiserplatz metro station is nearby, and the Frankfurt Main Train Station is just a few minutes walk away.

The new Swiss Reinsurance building, under construction in London, demonstrates as well the ecological and energy-conserving potential of new, large, office building designs. This forty-one-story structure, affectionately labeled the "erotic gherkin," takes on the shape of a cigar, tapering at the top and bottom. The winding and tapering shape maximizes the amount of daylight brought into the building, and a double layer of building skin acts as a thermal buffer, further reducing its energy consumption. The tapered bottom also allows more room for public space.

Parametric modeling and wind tunnel testing have been used to design optimal wind flow around this structure, and to minimize downdrafts experienced at street level. Because the wind moving around the structure will "caress rather than buffet" the structure, the building can actually be lighter (and thus fewer materials and less energy to build it; Glancey, 2001). The design directs airflow into and through the building through a series of window vents. Six-story-high sky gardens spiral around the building, treating the air

Figure 11.11 | The new Swiss Reinsurance building in central London is an innovative design that minimizes energy consumption. It also represents a spectacular new aesthetic statement modifying in a positive way (I believe) the London skyline.

as it moves through the building and providing important trees and green-spaces for occupants and visitors.

Large ecologically designed, energy-efficient buildings are increasingly common now in U.S. cities, as well. In New York City, the Conde Nast Building at 4 Times Square blends in and extends the unusual feel of that neighborhood, at the same time incorporating a number of interesting green features that substantially reduce its environmental impacts. Its green elements include recycling chutes on every floor, substantial use of recycled materials in construction, low-flow water fixtures, heating and cooling through gas-fired absorption chillers, energy efficient windows and extensive use of day-lighting, a system for managing and recycling construction waste, and delivery of a much higher amount of fresh air than required by building codes. Thin film photovoltaics are incorporated on the south and east façades (of the top nine floors) and a 280-kilowatt fuel cell provides all the building's electric needs during the evening (allowing the structure to be off the grid). Designed by Fox and Fowle Architects, this forty-eight-story building was completed in 2000, and has quickly set a green standard that other buildings in the city have sought to meet.

Its most distinctive feature is perhaps the ground-level plasma screen, consistent with the look of Times Square, with the photovoltaics generating the power needed for it. While not mandatory, tenants are given a set of environmental guidelines, and are encouraged to utilize and decorate the interior spaces in ways that reduce energy consumption and environmental impacts (e.g., using light-colored paints and surfaces to reduce need for artificial lighting).

It remains unclear to me why we have not done more to harvest the free bounty of sun in our building designs. In some European countries, notably Germany, strict building laws mandate designing for daylighting, for instance, and sets maximum distances that workspaces are permitted to be from windows. But increasingly in Europe and elsewhere the project examples are moving much beyond what the law or energy codes mandate. Several notable recent buildings seek to utilize the sun through the tried-and-true principles of greenhouse design. The Mont-Cenis Academy in Herne, Germany, is one of the most unusual recent demonstrations of the potential. Inspired by the Crystal Palace, built for the London World's Fair in 1851, Mont-Cenis consists of a large wooden outer structure, encapsulating a series of interior buildings. Structures within the envelope include a state training facility and seminar rooms, a hotel, a canteen, a library and a district town hall. This "microclimate envelope" provides the opportunity for comfortable temperatures (and very sunny conditions) year-round, shifting (as the architects predicted) to a Mediterranean climate. This interesting sheltering approach means that interior structures need not be constructed as tightly and that generally the energy needs of occupants and activities are greatly reduced. Windows on the top and sides of the structure are opened automatically to adjust temperature when needed.

The glass structure has 10,000 square meters of photovoltaic panels on its roof, making it the largest solar building in the world, with a maximum potential production of 1 megawatt. The photovoltaics are arranged on the glass roof in interesting cloud patterns (through the aid of computer modeling), providing shading within the envelope and extremely pleasant light. And the building also relies heavily on local materials. For example, the large pine timbers that hold up the outer structure come from sources less than 100 kilometers away from the building's site (about 60 miles), and the photovoltaic panels for the roof and façade come from a local assembly plant.

The structure of a greenhouse offers a great opportunity to reduce energy consumption, infuse green features, and create high-quality working and living conditions. One of the most impressive examples of an office structure utilizing a greenhouse design is the Alterra Building, in Wageningen, the

Figure 11.12 | The Mont-Cenis Academy building in Herne, Germany, contains 10,000 square meters of photovoltaics on its rooftop, configured to simulate the look (from the inside) of clouds.

Netherlands. Designed by German architect Stefan Benisch, two connected greenhouses form the core of the building, with offices, seminar rooms, and a library opening onto these delightfully lush greenhouse interiors. The building uses a standard commercial greenhouse roof, which can be opened and closed depending on the season and time of day. Within these greenhouses are three levels of offices, accessible both from interior hallways and through a series of metal stairs and walkover structures. Uniquely, every office has both a hallway door and a door directly opening onto the garden. Even in winter, doors and windows are opened to the greenhouse.

The greenhouse design has many advantages from the perspective of energy conservation. It allows, obviously, for the capturing of tremendous daylight. There is a bright open feeling to the work environment and little need for much artificial lighting. Air circulates and passes through the structure, moving from a cool underground chamber laterally through the building and through automatically opening side glass panels. A major element of the building's ability to cool in summer is the tremendous level of evapotranspiration occurring from the interior plants and the flowing water moving through the interior ponds and water features. The building employs a clever water cycle. Stormwater runoff from the roof is sent to a pond system behind the building (really more like a lake). From this pond, water is pumped into the interior, filtered, and then used for toilet flushing.

Perhaps most fascinating is to watch how the building automatically adjusts and moderates its mechanical elements to fit changing climate and weather conditions. As the building heats up in the morning, the glass roof and side glass panels gradually open up. Watching this occur one July morning, I heard a slow buzzing of motors as the roof's shading system unfolded. In a few minutes the interior gardens took on an entirely different look, more like a hidden palm oasis with tree shading and an immediate feeling of coolness.

Although no measures of productivity are available, surveys of workers in the building suggest that this environment is highly appreciated. Users of the building have also pointed out two unexpected problems. One is the higher than expected hallway noise, a result of the combined acoustic qualities of wood floors and cement ceilings. The second discovery is that users feel the building is often too cold in the early hours of winter mornings. The build-

Figure 11.13 | The Alterra Building in Wageningen, the Netherlands, is structured as two connected greenhouses, providing substantial energy savings and lush greenery and water in the interior spaces.

ing's radiator system provides low heat, and the effects of computers and body heat are not yet felt in these initial early morning hours. These are minor issues, to be sure, and there is no sense of them being problems that need in some way to be "solved." Indeed, the latter issue especially is one that conforms to the underlying philosophy of the building—that, as under natural conditions, sometimes it is hotter or colder and that users must adjust accordingly (put on a sweater in the morning, perhaps?).

Especially important will be connecting energy-efficient and low-energy designs with affordable housing. Indeed, they must go hand in hand. Colorado Court, a new low-income project in Santa Monica, California, provides an inspiring example of what is possible, and demonstrates that city's commitment to sustainability and renewable energy. This five-story single-residency occupancy (SRO) structure is designed to be 100 percent energy-neutral. A natural gas–fueled combined heat and power system provides the base electricity needs for the building as well as hot water for the residents.

Façade-integrated photovoltaics send power to the grid, producing much of the electricity needed. Impressively, even though the units are rather small—375 square feet—they feel spacious as a result of a decision to include 10-foot-high ceilings.

Other environmental elements of the Colorado Court building include design to take advantage of prevailing winds and natural ventilation, sunshades on the south side, energy-efficient lighting and appliances, and a rainwater collection system that retains water on-site, storing it below the structure and allowing its percolation into the ground. Among other things, this building demonstrates that every new major structure or building can and should be designed to be energy-neutral, producing at least as much energy as it needs.

Conclusions

Energy represents a significant opportunity for every city and every community to strengthen its place qualities. Becoming energy self-sufficient and energy- and carbon-neutral are no longer pipedreams but, as the examples in this chapter show, clearly within the realm of the feasible and the possible. Local renewable energy production can be a significant boost to the local economy, can greatly reduce the negative global effects of local lifestyles, and can at the same time serve as the basis for strengthening unique and distinctive place qualities. Indeed every place and bioregion will have its own special energy solutions, resources, and assets that can be harvested and employed in sustainable place building. Phoenix has abundant sunlight; cities in the Baltic region rely on the constant temperature of seawater; cities in the upper Midwest of the United States have the great potential for harvesting wind. A renewable and place-based strategy for energy need not mean quality of life is reduced. Quite to the contrary. This is certainly evident at the individual building level, as the energy-efficient (yet) high ceilings of the Colorado Court building and the sun-drenched units of the BedZED project show convincingly. And it is true at the neighborhood, city, and regional levels also, as the examples of Chicago and Hannover show. Locally-produced renewable energy, and a strong economy and high quality of life clearly go hand-in-hand.

The New Politics of Place

It is a common plea for a new form of politics that is less divisive, less conflicting, less ineffective. I, too, have hope for a new politics and believe that concepts of place and sustainability have the power to unite and bring communities together. I am optimistic that local politics can change in some significant ways, and in this chapter I explore some of what will be needed. But there is no silver bullet. We need a number of changes. And the responsibility for creating a new politics of place falls on the shoulders of many—citizens, local interest groups, elected officials.

Effective place building is clearly about democracy and participation. Those places to which we will feel most committed are also the places to which we feel we have some degree of ownership. Giving citizens many robust ways to participate in their communities, and giving them effective opportunities to have their voices heard, will help nurture these place commitments. A place-based politics, then, is very much about building the capacity for grassroots governance and participation. Local institutions for strengthening social capital—those important networks of social relations and shared values—are critical to bringing about many, if not most, of the place-strengthening initiatives discussed in this book. Indeed, sustainable places can be judged by the strength of these social institutions and their ability to adapt and respond to changing place-based needs. Building and sustaining rich social capital is a major goal.

Many strategies for building social capital are possible. Local Agenda 21 initiatives in Europe and elsewhere show what can be accomplished by giving citizens a voice and a structure in which to participate and providing some (often relatively modest) financial underwriting of these community efforts. Local Agenda 21 efforts typically involve the grassroots participation of neighborhoods and citizens in shaping a local environmental agenda. Meetings and community forums, the formation of a sustainability steering committee and more focused task groups (e.g., addressing energy, transport, greenspaces), and ultimately the preparation of local sustainability action plans are common steps in the process. Local grants and technical support for a variety of neighborhood and community projects, from mural painting to tree planting, will help to grow and support grassroots groups. Many communities, moreover, have planning and governance structures that provide some level of official recognition and input to neighborhood organizations.

At the same time that meaningful participation in governance is good, a new place-based politics strives to overcome the understandable "Not-in-My-Backyard" tendencies, or "NIMBYs," that frequently characterize local politics. Long-term commitment to sustainable places will require a politics in which people and organizations work together to create a positive future, not simply to oppose specific projects or decisions they deem threatening. A proactive anticipatory community politics is desirable and indeed possible. Many of the place-strengthening projects and designs and initiatives described in the preceding chapters, whether the unique Phoenix waste recycling center or the Diamondback Bridge in Tucson or the examples of industrial site reuse, are about shifting NIMBYs to YIMBYs ("Yes, In My Backyard"). A politics that encourages and facilitates neighbors to come together to redefine and reconceive of a bridge as a forest (e.g., the London green bridge) or a street as a stream and garden (the Growing Vine Street initiative in Seattle) is a more positive place-strengthening form, to be sure.

The framework of sustainable places offers special potential as an effective community umbrella under which groups with often disparate concerns can work together. Recent efforts around the United States and Europe suggest that much can be accomplished in this way. Green building organizations in

Figure 12.1 | A group of volunteers in Seattle, Washington, stencil storm drains as a way to educate citizens about watershed protection. (Photo compliments of Puget Sound Action Team).

several U.S. cities have served this umbrella and convening function, including the Atlanta Sustainability Roundtable, the Cleveland Green Building Coalition, and the Pittsburgh Green Building Alliance. Providing a community forum, and reasons and opportunities for groups to come together to develop and work toward a common agenda can do much to advance the cause of local sustainability and place building.

Participation and engagement at the local level by citizens—whether through a neighborhood association or a service group, by campaigning for a local candidate or writing a letter to the local newspaper, or by volunteering—is a central element in place-strengthening and place-building politics. Such acts and patterns have many positive effects on place building; they are not only educational but provide tangible acts of commitment that, in turn, lay the foundation for future actions. They help build bonds of commitment and loyalty, and they infuse "local knowledge" that will likely lead to better decisions and policy outcomes that better reflect the uniqueness of individual places.

A Politics of Inclusion; a Politics from the Bottom Up

One of the key impressions when looking around the United States today is how many small community and environmental organizations there are despite trends toward apathy and declining social capital, and how, through their stories, you realize what can be accomplished with few resources. Sustainability often becomes a powerful framework or unifying vision for these groups.

Organizations such as Eco-City in Cleveland, Ohio, with a tiny staff and its impassioned founder and director David Beach, have over a number of years transformed the debate in that city from typical infrastructure and economic development discussions to envisioning a new kind of inspired city, a green and sustainable city, that builds onto its industrial past, and indeed views this past as a catalyst for its transformative green future. Eco-City Cleveland seeks to educate about and advocate green and sustainable ideas and issues and in doing so has changed the agenda there. This small group has undertaken many creative projects that promote good planning and awareness of ecological city ideas—for example, conducting visual preference surveys for northeast Ohio, preparing and distributing a beautiful bioregional map poster, publishing an extremely informative and attractive newsletter journal, and awarding each year "Bioregional Heroes." One of the most impressive projects in this regard is the Urban Eco-Village, an ecological redevelopment district—a close-in neighborhood, adjacent to a transit station, that is already being transformed into a new model for urban living, with green housing, restored greenspaces, community gardens, and a renewed sense of its value.

In many of the innovative place-building examples discussed in earlier chapters it has often been community-based and nonprofit organizations that have been responsible for getting things done. Building and strengthening places will be benefited immensely by the existence of a variety of forward-looking, nongovernmental organizations. Impressive and unique projects like BedZED, the zero-energy neighborhood in London, would not be possible, to be sure, without the strong support and leadership from nongovernmental organizations. The Peabody Trust, London's innovative housing association, must be given considerable credit for thinking outside the box, and recognizing the critical importance of linking sustainable and green housing with its goal of providing affordable housing. Its annual report states this philosophy: "Sustainability lies at the core of everything we do. Short-term solutions may provide temporary relief, but effective long-term strategies are essential for future growth and prosperity" (Peabody Trust, 2002, p. 2). BedZED benefited as well, of course, from an enlightened municipal government in the form of Sutton borough. This London borough has a long tradition of supporting and advancing environmental issues, and it played a key role in providing land to the Peabody Trust at a below-market price. The borough has also shown leadership in other ways, for instance, entering into an agreement with the Trust that BedZED would reduce its consumption of fossil fuels by half and, consequently, be afforded some creative relief from the borough's parking standards.

New Collaborations and Coalitions

The new politics of place is about joining forces, about finding common ground and common agendas on which often substantively disparate groups can collaborate. Such collaborations require both structures or organizational space (and literal space as well) to come together, and changing attitudes on the part of organizations and agencies about their turf and mission.

Chicago Wilderness shows what is possible through coalition building. This organization, described in more detail in Chapter 5, is a coalition that now includes more than 160 different organizations, all rallying behind the vision of a protected, restored, healthy regional ecosystem. Some 9,000 volunteers are actively involved in its many programs and initiatives. With only six full-time employees, Chicago Wilderness depends heavily on the contributed time, resources, and goodwill of partner organizations and their staff. Much of the work happens through a series of four different topical teams. For example, the Sustainability team is in charge of looking at relationships between the region's natural heritage and its built environment; part of its task, in the words of one of its co-chairs, is to identify new strate-

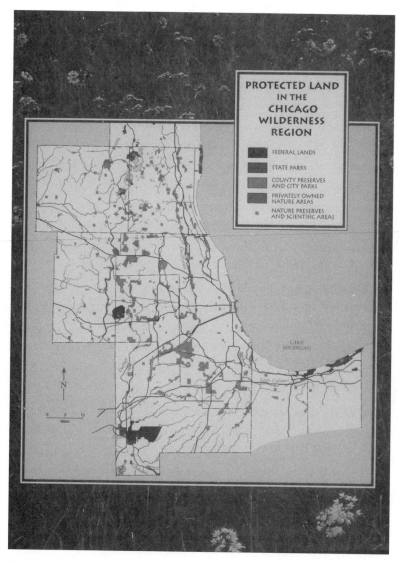

Figure 12.2 | The map prepared by Chicago Wilderness shows some 100,000 acres of already protected land in that region. (Map compliments of Chicago Wilderness. Map produced by Richard Vaupel and Leonard Walther of the Cartography Lab, Northern Illinois University, Dekalb, Ill.)

gies that "can be cooked up and tried." This collaboration is one that stimulates much forward-looking thinking.

The Bay Area Alliance for Sustainable Communities, in the San Francisco Bay Area, is another case in point. Describing itself as a "multi-stake-holder coalition," the group has brought together a diverse number of organizations, many not always on the same side of issues. Its members include environmental organizations such as the Sierra Club, civic and governmental organizations, and the business sector (including, for example, the Homebuilders Association of Northern California!). This Bay Area Alliance has over a number of months prepared an impressive regional sustainability compact, which each of these local groups and governments have been asked to sign (Table 12.1). Such efforts can both build political support around community sustainability and advance discussion and debate about what is needed to create sustainable and unique places and regions.

A positive European example of local governments and businesses working together on a sustainability agenda is Norway's interesting Eco-Lighthouse program. Created by the municipality of Kristiansand in 1996, through funding from the Norwegian Ministry of the Environment, the program seeks to

---

TABLE 12.1 | Ten Commitments to Action: Compact for a Sustainable Bay Area

The Ten Commitments to Action, which forms the centerpiece of the compact, contains the following 10 strategic commitments:
1. Enable a diversified, sustainable, and competitive economy to continue to prosper and provide jobs in order to achieve a high quality of life for all Bay Area residents.
2. Provide housing affordable to all income levels within the Bay Area to match population increases and job generation.
3. Target transportation investment to achieve a world-class comprehensive, integrated, and balanced multimodal system that supports efficient land use and decreases dependence on single-occupancy vehicle trips.
4. Preserve and restore the region's natural assets, including San Francisco Bay, farmland, open space, and other habitats.
5. Improve resource and energy efficiency; reduce pollution and waste.
6. Focus investment to preserve and revitalize neighborhoods.
7. Provide all residents with the opportunity for quality education and lifelong learning to help them meet their highest aspirations.
8. Promote healthy and safe communities.
9. Support state and local government fiscal reforms.
10. Stimulate civic engagement.

SOURCE: Bay Area Alliance for Sustainable Communities, www.bayalliance.org

encourage local businesses of many different kinds to examine their environmental impacts and to develop programs for becoming less resource consumptive and more sustainable. In Kristiansand, one company in each of several sectors (including a hotel, an ice cream factory, a housepainter, and a wood product manufacturer) was asked to participate. For each company, the municipality pays for the development of an independent environmental audit and the preparation, in collaboration with the company, of a three-year environmental plan. Over the first year, if the goals set out in this plan are met, the municipality certifies the company. The company is then able to use the Eco-Lighthouse logo and benefits from, in addition to the clear energy and other savings, this certification in sales and marketing of its product and services. For companies not selected in this first tier, but wishing to participate nonetheless, the city pays 50 percent of the costs of the audits and three-year plan. So far, the program has been quite successful, with more than 430 companies participating nationally. Industry environmental standards are established through this process, and sustainability is given greater visibility in these companies. The financial incentives provided have proven to be a significant inducement.

A new politics of place can also benefit from new creative political alliances and coalitions. Encouraging interest groups and disparate factions to, in a sense, extend the vision of their respective groups would help. Examples include the strong involvement of unions over the last year—the federation of grocery workers, in particular—in opposition to the expansion of Wal-Mart in Southern California. And, as the American population continues to age, the lobbying power of the elderly and groups like AARP to positively influence the design and planning of communities (e.g., more and better public transit, public spaces, and pedestrian facilities) will increase.

New collaborations are also important, as noted earlier, between local public agencies and departments and various private groups and organizations in the community. Tremendous promise exists to reshape our places when these groups and agencies work together to achieve common goals. As shown in such initiatives as Cool Schools (see Chapter 10) in Los Angeles, a collaborative effort between the L.A. Unified School District, the L.A. Department of Water and Power, and private nonprofit groups, notably, TreePeople, much can be achieved. The experiences of forward-looking local agencies like the L.A. Department of Water and Power and Seattle's Public Utility, moreover, demonstrate the potential value of thinking "outside the box," of recognizing that their missions extend beyond narrow engineering and service provision and must encompass a broader mix of place-building and community-building issues, including public art, energy conservation, urban greening, and neighborhood building, areas perhaps not usually viewed within their bailiwick.

The new politics is one that nurtures transparency and openness, which can take many different forms. One dimension of transparency is public knowledge about current environmental and social conditions. Such information can serve to motivate and propel citizens and citizen groups, as well as government actors and offices. There are a number of good examples of tools and mechanisms that document and educate about current state of affairs in a community.

In the early 1990s, Sundsvall, Sweden, began preparing an annual environmental balance sheet that shows progress made during the year as well as ways in which it may have declined. Copies of the report are widely distributed, and its findings are presented by the local media. The present chief executive officer for the municipality feels that the reports have reduced confrontation and conflict and have resulted in greater levels of community consensus (Union of Baltic Cities, 2001).

In the Finnish city of Turku, creative use is similarly being made of an annual environmental accounting report. Among other things, it shows how the city is doing in terms of major environmental indicators—CO_2 emissions, air quality, even the calculation of the city's ecological footprint. The report compares these indicators with other municipalities in Finland. Perhaps most important, it contains future goals and targets put forth by different departments of the local government. The report is widely circulated, and has had the effect of broadening the conception of environment to one that views it not as an isolated "box" but one that recognizes the relevance to all city departments.

Other cities in the United States and Europe have similarly used such tools. Many communities, such as Seattle, Washington, and Den Haag, the Netherlands, have developed and extensively used community sustainability indicators to assess progress (or lack thereof) at reaching environmental and social goals. Sustainable Pittsburgh, Ohio, has recently prepared its own excellent set of regional indicators, and other civic and nonprofit organizations have prepared similar state-of-the-city or indicator reports that help build awareness and shape local debate.

Part of the change in local politics is one that recognizes and rewards actions that strengthen places and make them more sustainable. A number of cities, including Sundsvall, Sweden, give yearly awards that recognize sustainability accomplishments not by local governments, but by private organizations seeking to extend and support good practice. In Cleveland, Ohio, for instance, the private group Eco-City Cleveland's annual Bioregional Hero awards, whereby the group recognizes businesses and individuals who have made special contributions to the city and region, is a creative example of this.

A Politics Built around the Special Qualities of Place

A new politics of place must acknowledge, understand, and build upon the special physical and cultural features of place. It is a politics and a political agenda that thinks first about preserving the best of the history, traditions, flavor, and unique ecology of a city or town or region. It understands that these are the building blocks of a meaningful life, as well as a sustainable and responsible existence.

A politics of the local is as much about an attitude of appreciating these local things as it is about shifting priorities from the sameness and bigness that typifies much of contemporary mass society and commerce. More specifically, it means such things as supporting local businesses, encouraging expressions of local creativity in all its forms, and nurturing many and distinct voices (in music, architecture, literature, community practices and traditions), preserving local landscapes and historic buildings, documenting local history and traditions, and supporting every chance to celebrate and come together as a community to support place.

One model for such a new political outlook comes, as many of our most fruitful ideas have, from Italy. Slow Food, a movement born in the 1990s in response to the perceived intrusion of globalized sameness of fast food (and specifically a proposal to build a McDonald's near the Spanish Steps in

Rome), gave rise to new efforts throughout the world to appreciate and enjoy the unique culinary offerings of home—and in the process to slow down and enjoy each other and our communities. In 1999, *Città Slow* (slow city) was formed as an offshoot of Slow Food by Paolo Saturnini, mayor of the small city of Greve in Chianti. Extending the underlying philosophy of Slow Food to cities, while sometimes suffering from a certain degree of vagueness and imprecision, offers a fresh new perspective on local politics and governance, one that elevates the unique and special qualities of place—not just its food, but its environment, its landscape, it special industries and crafts, its people and their likes and traditions—and in a variety of uniquely local ways works to protect and nurture them.

Città Slow has some sixty different criteria or standards that cities (or towns) must satisfy if they wish to be certified as a "slow city." A city must reach or satisfy at least half of these criteria, and demonstrate that it is on the road to reaching the others. Once certified, cities can display the Città Slow logo—a townscape riding on the back of a snail. They can use it on their official stationery, in their tourism advertising, and on signs along the main roads leading into town. Every couple of years the community is revisited to ensure that the Città Slow criteria are still being met. Nonetheless, as Mayor

Figure 12.3 | Paolo Saturnini (center), mayor of Greve in Chianti, Italy, and founder of Città Slow, or Slow City.

Saturnini notes, it is less about reaching some end point ("We are now a slow city") and more about the ongoing process: thinking through a slow lens about the many local issues, controversies, and decisions that necessarily arise. So far, about fifty Italian cities are participating in Città Slow and the number is growing.

When I recently visited Mayor Saturnini in Greve, the potential impacts of the movement were clearly evident. In the case of Greve in Chianti, the goals are to protect the charm and flavors of the town, to strengthen small hotels that accommodate modest and locally respectful tourism, to incorporate education about local foods and cuisine in schools, and to work in many other ways to save the heritage of this town and region and to resist sameness wherever it might rear its ugly head. And Greve itself is a living showcase of these local specialties and unique aspects of place—with a charming, walkable, arcaded town center offering a variety of small shops. There are no chain stores here.

Other Città Slow cities have emphasized various topics. Some see the importance of slowing traffic and expanding pedestrian areas; others have sought to protect and restore historic buildings; still others are planning to feature special local festivals, celebrations, and cultural events. In San Daniele del Friuli, Italy, another Slow City that I visited, the agenda was different still. It included efforts to strengthen markets for special varieties of locally produced wine, continued appreciation and support for unique local products (including its famous *prosciutto*), support for local crafts (e.g., weaving) produced by mentally handicapped residents, and the continued operation of one of the last remaining schools of mosaic art in the world— the Spilimbergo School for Mosaic Making. In many respects, this school embodies the Città Slow spirit: a unique and special local institution imparting skills and techniques from Roman and Byzantine eras, and in the end resulting in tremendous beauty. There is palpable local pride in this school and a belief in the need to support it strongly in whatever way necessary, including financial, to ensure its continued operation.

The "slow city" philosophy is certainly also about the possibilities of reducing the harried pace of our lives, and imagining how our communities and landscapes can both help in this regard and benefit from it. I am intrigued by what the implications might be of a slow-city form of politics.

Might we imagine more time to discuss collectively the local (and global) issues of today; more time to register one's opinion about such issues, perhaps by writing a letter to the editor, attending a public hearing, organizing a protest, or for that matter even just voting? Would we as residents of a slower city, in the midst of a slower form of politics, be expected to better understand a variety of practical challenges facing livable and sustainable places, from that proposed highway bypass to the tipping fees at the landfill, to the gradual destruction of local and regional landscapes, to development? More of us might be tempted to run for office or serve on a local board or become involved in the activities of our neighborhood association.

In places like Greve, precise action plans or programs are absent; rather, it is a matter of looking for opportunities to make the right political choices and policy moves when they (inevitably) arise; looking for ways that can give expression to the Città Slow philosophy. Mayor Saturnini described a pending proposal to build a large 150-room hotel in his town, as an example. Thinking out loud, he says he thinks he is inclined not to support such a thing—to him it seems inconsistent with the smaller-scale nature of the hotels and villas already in the area. Others might come to a different conclusion, but the thought process is useful indeed.

A politics of place need not just be about the old, and preserving rigidly the status quo. Mayor Saturnini does believe it is possible to combine the "modern" and the "slow," and he contends that Città Slow is not about resisting new ideas or technology. One facility that the mayor points to as an example of this fusion of the slow and the modern is the Encarta, a wine tasting facility and wine information center in Greve. It reflects the Città Slow emphasis on the old and the local—educating about and heralding wines and foods from the region, housed in a recycled older building, but tackling its business mission in modern ways. Encarta provides a bank of computers that visitors can use to look up specific information about wines or food or special recipes or ways of preparing food.

A slow cities philosophy and politics—one that celebrates unique people, histories, culture, and economy—might apply to any community, regardless of size, though in Italy it is an initiative of smaller towns. When asked whether Città Slow, in its present restriction to cities of 50,000 or less, is anticity, Mayor Saturnini appears to leave much room, saying "bigger cities can be slow in something." Large cities, he seems to accept, can equally find ways to express the philosophy of Città Slow. Mayor Saturnini speaks approvingly of the recent action by the mayor of Paris to create a new public beach along the River Seine. While the towns in Città Slow are pursuing a variety of different goals, what unites them, what they have in common, is a desire to protect the unique and distinctive aspects of their communities.

New Forms of Place Leadership

In his own way, the mayor of Greve, Italy, demonstrates the importance of political leadership in building and sustaining places. This is a common theme in explaining many of the innovative practices described in earlier chapters. Much can be explained by the work of place leaders such as Mayor Ken Livingstone in London, or Mayor Richard Daley in Chicago, or Mayor Joan Clos in Barcelona.

Indeed, much of Chicago's innovation and green progress can be explained by the active advocacy of these issues by Mayor Daley. His hands-on style of city governance, and commitment to Chicago's move in the direction of sustainability (he is an avid bicyclist, so much of this commitment is at a personal level) has resulted in Chicago emerging as a leader in sustainability. Staff reportedly received personal handwritten notes complaining about dilapidated buildings or brownfield sites needing cleanup. This is essentially how the city's efforts at recycling and redeveloping sites of abandoned gasoline stations began. Daley personally noticed these stations, and saw them as the first signs of neighborhood decline. Better to address these neighborhood eyesores through active city intervention as early as possible, he thought.

Daley's style is also one of encouraging collaboration among departments and branches of the city government as well as organizations and businesses throughout the city. So many of the city's successful initiatives, from green streets to brownfield redevelopment to green homes, are a direct result of different agencies and actors working together to bring about a common project. Brownfields, for instance, are seen not just as a real estate or legal issue,

Figure 12.4 | The City of Chicago has taken many actions in recent years to move itself in the direction of becoming a green city, including holding a design competition to promote green design and financially underwriting the construction of five model green homes (one shown here).

but one requiring input and participation by a number of different disciplines and perspectives.

Daley, moreover, is credited for his dogged follow-through on many urban sustainability issues. An enforcement action is followed by cleanup and active redevelopment. And most impressive, Daley recognizes the connections between creating a green and sustainable Chicago, and enhanced livability and quality of life. A green, energy-efficient city will be a place where new companies, and their employees and CEOs alike, want to live and be.

Chicago has very effectively, as we have seen, made use of pilot projects and initiatives in which smaller funds are used to demonstrate and educate and in turn to leverage modest public investments into more extensive longer-term private-sector monies. Many good examples of this were discussed in earlier chapters, including the Chicago Historic Bungalow Initiative and the Green Homes for Chicago initiative (see Chapter 3).

Global-Local Communities

Strengthening the local realm doesn't, however, mean disconnecting from the rest of the world and our new place politics must acknowledge global duties. A truly sustainable community and a genuine place is one that takes responsibility for the extralocal—indeed, often global—impacts of the consumption and lifestyle choices made locally. Yet, local myopia makes it difficult to muster up any concern about, for instance, carbon dioxide emissions or the other very serious environmental impacts associated with fossil fuel dependence. This is, I have argued earlier, part of the American backdrop that sustainability must acknowledge and work within. Instilling a sense of local concern about and responsibility for the global impacts of local actions remains a major impediment to achieving a vision of community sustainability.

A recent Pew Research Center study of foreign policy attitudes offers some insight into the ways in which the American public views the world. In this survey, conducted before September 11, 2001, more than half of the general public respondents indicated they felt the world was a more dangerous place than ten years earlier. Low interest in international affairs can be discerned in several of the results. Knowledge of major world leaders, and key issues they are confronting, is one proxy. Only 23 percent of the survey respondents were able to identify Vladimir Putin as the president of Russia, for example. Nearly 70 percent of the respondents agreed with the statement: "We should not think so much in international terms but concentrate more on our own national problems and building up our strength and prosperity here at home." (Pew Research Center 2001.)

There is a common perception that where Americans are interested in other parts of the world, it is essentially for selfish or self-interested reasons. The Pew results seem to bear this out. When asked which subjects should be given top priority in long-range foreign policy, 74 percent indicated "insuring adequate energy supplies for the U.S." and 77 percent indicated "protecting the jobs of American workers." In contrast, a low 25 percent indicated that "helping improve the living standards in developing nations" should be a top priority, and only 49 percent believed that "protecting groups or nations that are threatened with genocide" should be a top priority. This is perhaps understandable human nature, but it seems to show a pattern of viewing the primary global responsibility as one of securing and advancing the direct interests of Americans only (see Pew Research Center, 2001).

In surveys following September 11, more Americans appear to support a strong U.S. leadership role in the world, but they see that role, not surprisingly, as a necessary response to the threat of terrorism. Terrorism is the dominant international concern of Americans today. Moreover, the new concerns about terrorism appear to be diminishing and squeezing out even further the concerns about addressing the spread of AIDS, world hunger, and global warming (Pew Research Center, 2002).

What needs to be discussed and fleshed out is another essential element of a new politics of place, and a new model of local governance, one that acknowledges global interconnections and interdependencies, and appreciates its potential role in improving the living conditions in other places and advancing sustainability outside its borders. Whether we call this *global localities* or *global-local places*, the emphasis is placed on *local* initiatives, actions, and changes that acknowledge respect for communities and cultures beyond narrow local borders and those affected by local consumption and development decisions.

One area where tangible global action could be taken by localities is in directly connecting with, and collaborating and assisting, other localities in other parts of the world. The concept of an *ecological* or *sustainable sister cities* initiative is especially intriguing, both for making global connections and connectedness tangible and visceral to local residents, and for making a difference in improving the lives and living conditions of others in the world. There has already been considerable experience and work by Western European cities in building such relationships with cities in the developing world. First World and Third World communities in Europe. The latter visit the former to learn needed technical skills and to share their cultures, wisdom, and knowledge. The former send volunteer labor, technical skills and knowledge, as well as money and resources needed to address the unique environmental and other problems facing those specific communities. Ecological sister cities have the potential for cross-cultural sharing, but are an especially promising outlet for expressions of responsibility for the less advantaged in the global community, and of responsibility for helping communities in Developing Nations solve environmental problems at least partly created by opulent lifestyles and consumption patterns in the developed north.

Since 1997, USAID has sponsored a program called "resource cities" (directed by ICMA, International City Management Association) aimed at developing partnerships between cities to solve environmental problems. To date, more than thirty partnerships, involving more than sixty cities, have been formed. Cities such as Dayton, Ohio, and Lusaka, Zambia, and Houston, Texas, and Johannesburg, South Africa, have been linked to help each other on solid waste management and recycling issues, and to share respective innovations (Porter, 2000). More recently, Sister City International has started an international sustainable sister cities network that represents a major new avenue through which American communities might give meaning to global responsibilities (Honey, 2002).

The possibilities of sponsoring projects in (other) less affluent cities and countries might be seen in the ongoing development of the Midrand Eco-City in Johannesburg, a project I had the great pleasure of visiting in 2002. In the area of a large informal settlement, Ivory Park, this new community project is a shining, uplifting bit of positive in a community of much poverty. This bustling, grassroots effort at building a sustainable community village is exemplary, albeit small, evidence of the potential. Here, a zero-energy community center is under construction, as well as a series of other ecological homes and buildings that will eventually provide a model of creating healthy community and home to people who are now living on the edge, at the same time pointing the way to a more sustainable future. Other elements of this project include the operation of an agricultural (growers) cooperation, a bicycle repair cooperative, and the creation of some 300 jobs (U.N. Habitat, 2002). Training for eco-guides and eco-tourism industry is another element. Partners have included the Danish government, but also local organizations like London-based BioRegional. Similar inspirational, life-changing initiatives could be undertaken or helped along throughout the world by U.S. cities.

Another way local governments can express their global environmental responsibilities is to design, build, and operate their building stock in the most energy-efficient and least ecologically damaging ways. A growing number of cities are adopting policies that either mandate or strongly encourage green building measures when new municipal or local buildings are needed.

A number of places are now keying these policies to the U.S. Green Building Council's LEED (Leadership in Energy and Environmental Design) rating system. The City of Seattle, Washington, for instance, has adopted a policy that all future new construction or remodeling of public buildings, those over 5,000 square feet in size, must reach at least the minimum silver rating under the LEED system. Reaching higher ratings is encouraged. The stated purposes of this policy are to "demonstrate the City's commitment to environmental, economic, and social stewardship, to yield cost savings to the City's taxpayers through reduced operating costs, to provide healthy work environments for staff and visitors, and to contribute to the City's goals of protecting, conserving, and enhancing the region's environmental resources." The intent is to, as well, help "to set a community standard of sustainable building" (City of Seattle, undated).

Seattle already has fourteen green public buildings in some stage of design or construction. One completed example is the new Seattle Justice Center, which houses the municipal courts and the police department. The building incorporates a number of green features, but its most prominent feature is the glass façade on its west side. A double layer of glass, with a 30-inch air buffer, provides extensive daylight to the interior spaces as well as significant energy savings. Louvers open automatically to pull out hot air on hot days, and close on cold days to maximize the building's insulation. Light shelves on each floor further diffuse and bounce around the incoming daylight. Other features include a green rooftop, a flexible design that easily allows reconfiguration and reuse of the spaces, and a system for collecting rooftop rainwater (Thieme, 2002; Zieve, 2002; Laughlin and Dedyo, 2002).

Similarly, many cities are now rethinking public buildings like libraries. The City of Chicago is also now designing and building new libraries to be certified under LEED. The new West Englewood library is a beautiful and green addition to a highly distressed neighborhood. The building incorporates a number of environmental features: extensive use of daylight and an energy efficient design overall, sustainable wood used in book cases, and more than 50 percent of the materials came from within a 500 miles radius (Kessler, Jackson, and Saville, undated). And, as with many new libraries in Chicago, there is little parking as residents are expected to arrive by walking or public transit.

Other recent examples of local governments expressing global concerns include requirements that vendors doing business with communities pay a living wage and satisfy anti-sweatshop procurement provisions. New York City, for instance, passed in March 2001 an Anti-Sweatshop Procurement Bill (some thirty American cities have enacted such laws). Under the bill, contracts for city purchases of textiles (e.g., for city uniforms) must show that the manufacturer of these products provides a fair wage and safe and healthy working conditions for their employees. The potential power exerted here is tremendous when the extent of apparels and textiles purchased by a city of this stage is realized. New York City is the second-largest government purchaser in the United States, mostly for city uniforms (LeBlanc, 2001).

That local governments can collectively make a real difference on global environmental issues like climate change is absolutely clear. The Cities for Climate Protection Campaign, of the International Council for Local Environmental Initiatives (ICLEI), is an excellent example. More than 500 cities are now participating—cities that have made tangible commitments to reducing their energy consumption and carbon emissions, and have developed long-term strategies for reaching those reduction goals (Yienger et al., 2002). Usually, as shown in earlier chapters, reducing energy consumption and minimizing pollution will have other community benefits and is often quite cost-effective. With a little assistance and encouragement from organizations like ICLEI, as well as from peer networks of cities and local jurisdiction, local governments can do much to advance global sustainability.

The Swedish City of Växjö is one of several cities participating in a program sponsored by the Swedish Society for Nature Conservation, called Challenging Communities. They have set what to many will appear an almost unimaginable goal (by American perspectives) of becoming a fossil-fuel-free city (see Växjö Kommun, 2003). How is this city of 75,000 doing this? Through many means, including biofueled cogeneration plants, installation of rooftop solar panels, energy-efficient improvements to public buildings, increasing use of environmental-fuel vehicles (half the city's buses run on RME, rape-methyl-ester fuels), promoting walking and bicycle use in the city (pedestrianizing much of its city center), and a bicycle campaign for city employees.

The city has already made considerable progress toward becoming fossil-fuel-free, though the transport sector and rising car usage remains a problem. The share of renewable fuels used in the city has risen sharply (now more than 30 percent) and carbon emissions have seen a significant reduction. Obviously, the city has far to go, but making this kind of commitment to the planet and to the future is impressive, to say the least.

San Francisco, San Diego, and Chicago have each taken significant steps to actively promote renewable energy in their cities. In San Francisco, voters passed a pair of ballot measures in 2001 that allow the city to float up to $100 million in bonds to finance solar power. The city aspires under this initiative to provide all of its municipal energy from local renewable sources, and adding some 10 megawatts of solar power each year. The installation of 60,000 square feet of photovoltaic panels to the rooftop of the Moscone Convention Center is a dramatic first step (and together with the energy efficiency improvements made to the structure, providing enough energy for an estimated 8,500 homes!) (Solar Energy News Center, 2004; Blum, 2004).

Barcelona, Spain, has been leading southern Europe in similarly moving toward a renewable energy city. It has developed an exemplary comprehensive energy plan (Barcelona Plan for Energy Improvement), identifying fifty-five projects it intends to undertake through the year 2010. The city has already taken impressive actions, including installing photovoltaics on the rooftop of city hall and enacting a unique Municipal Solar Ordinance. Under the ordinance, modeled after a similar proposal in Berlin, all newly constructed buildings and those undergoing substantial renovation must provide, at a minimum, 60 percent of their hot water (sanitary) needs from solar. A number of buildings in the city have already satisfied the ordinance, including the Guinardo sports hall (with 45 thermal collectors, covering 76 square meters along the side of the structure) and several hundred housing units (Energie-Cities, 2000; Puig, 2002).

The following are some of the more promising additional ideas of *global localism* or *global-local places*:

- *Adopt an Earth Charter or sustainable resource agreement* (or other similar expression of global environmental and social commitments). Some communities have expressed their global commitments through adoption of the Earth Charter, a comprehensive ethical statement that has been debated and endorsed by many individuals and organizations around the world. Burlington, Vermont, for instance, adopted the charter in 2001, and more than thirty other Vermont communities have adopted it (see www.earthcharter.org).

- *Purchase renewable energy and other green goods.* Cities such as Chicago, Illinois, and Santa Monica, California, have sought to purchase green power. Santa Monica now acquires 100 percent of the energy it needs for municipal buildings and facilities from green sources.

- *Local support for fair trade.* Municipalities in Europe commonly buy fair trade coffees and other goods. Some localities provide free public space for fair trade businesses or otherwise support fair trade products. The Town of Garstang, in the United Kingdom, has become the first town in the world to be certified as a Fairtrade Town by the Fairtrade Foundation. To be certified requires meeting certain minimum criteria, including a minimum number of stores and shops that stock fair trade goods. Already some 65 other localities in the United Kingdom have followed Garstang's lead, including larger cities and towns such as London, and are working towards becoming Fairtrade communities.

- *Extralocal treaties in support of global resources and protection of global commons.* Large cities especially can affect global or regional resources and biodiversity in significant ways. The City of Chicago has now entered into a Migratory Bird Treaty that commits it to taking actions to protect and conserve the amazing number of migratory birds passing through its jurisdiction.

- *Protection of globally significant resources and local initiatives and efforts to protect resources beyond their borders.* Communities might acknowledge the impact of local energy and resource consumption on distant places and ecosystems, and take tangible steps to mitigate or reduce these impacts. A city might financially support habitat restoration or reforestation efforts in another country to compensate for such effects.

- *Community-to-community arrangements or agreements.* Cities can pair with other cities to help them in solving local environmental problems and in sharing technical expertise. In pursuit of this idea, Sister

Cities International has recently initiated a kind of "ecological sister cities" program.

- *Locally based global education.* Each city or community could promote greater awareness of global problems and the impact of local lifestyles and actions on global ecology through a variety of educational programs, from high school classes on sustainable lifestyles to model U.N. programs that explicitly address cross-boundary and global environmental issues.

- *Eco-tourism and ethical tourism programs (for local residents).* Residents of Northern and Western nations travel a great deal and spend a considerable amount of money on vacations and tourism. This tourism could be steered in the direction of ethical or eco-tourism. Initiatives include pre-trip educational programs to foster greater knowledge about a country's ecology and culture, and tangible steps (such as a ticket surcharge to compensate for the carbon emissions emitted through the travel) to directly assume responsibility for the impacts of travel and tourism.

Global-local communities are concerned with the importance of their energy usage and carbon emissions, the impacts of their purchasing decisions, and the extent and quality of local habitat for migratory birds and wildlife. They recognize and support the need to be engaged globally, and look for opportunities to share knowledge and technologies and to help improve the conditions and environment and quality of life in other places. Global-local communities at heart recognize that their place duties extend beyond their meager borders and that creating uplifting sustainable places is a global imperative.

A New Kind of Citizen

As the third anniversary of September 11 passes, it is appropriate and timely to reassess what it means to be a good citizen. This is surely an important part of any new politics of place. Citizenship is typically defined in fairly conventional and fairly narrow ways. To be a good citizen usually means to vote, to pay taxes, to obey the law. These are valid and important aspects of citizenship, and to be sure, we have difficulty even with these. Yet, this is a modest form of citizenship and not one especially demanding of Americans. Today we need a more expansive notion of citizenship. We need a new kind of citizen.

As Daniel Kemmis, the former mayor of Missoula, Montana, and others have argued, what is needed is a movement at the individual level, a new or at least rehabilitated form of citizenship and citizen duties, an outlook largely absent in much of our local politics. (See Kemmis, 1990, 1995.) Thinking outside of and beyond short-term personal self-interest, and acknowledging duties to a broader public interest, are important elements of this citizenship.

Our notion of citizenship is one that begins to expand what philosophers describe as the moral community—that group of people or things to which we have duties and responsibilities. Most of us view this community in terms of our immediate families, our street, our neighborhood. Yet, in fundamental ways we are embedded in a broader ecological and social system to which we owe allegiance as well. We are members of a larger community of life and as such ought to aspire, in real and genuine ways, to become, as Aldo Leopold eloquently says, "plain members and citizens" of this larger community.

Whether or not these other forms of life and the environment in general hold inherent worth—that is, worth beyond the narrow instrumental and economic value we place as humans—is a major question in environmental ethics today. My own answer is that they do, and that those more than 120 species of dragonflies and damselflies native to this part of the world are indeed part of the community of life to which I personally have some duty of respect.

We need to expand our community of concern in other ways as well. Increasingly, we recognize that actions today will over time affect future generations who will live in this place on Earth. The kind of community we create, the health of the landscapes and places we inhabit, the quality of life we leave residents 100 years or perhaps even 500 years from now must be a matter of present citizenship.

What, more specifically, does this expanded citizenship demand of us? One of our first duties is to be better and more fully informed about the material flows and environmental implications of our daily lives and lifestyles. Where does the water, energy, and food come from that sustains us; where does the waste and garbage that we produce on a daily basis end up and to what environmental effect? Conventional citizenship says little about these things.

Expanded citizenship, moreover, demands that we actively educate ourselves and learn about this broader biological community of which we are a part. It is distressing that today place-specific knowledge appears on the decline. Although kids (and adults) can recognize with tremendous accuracy the logo for Target or Wal-Mart, their ability to recognize an Eastern forktail dragonfly or a chimney swift is woefully limited. Without intimate knowledge of place and community, commitment is unlikely to follow. It is our duty of citizenship to become intimately acquainted with our fellow ecological citizens.

Writer Kirkpatrick Sale argues compellingly for our personal duty to learn about places (Sale, 1985):

> We must try to understand ourselves as participants in, not masters over [the] biotic community . . . but to become dwellers in the land, the crucial and perhaps only and all-encompassing task is to understand place, the immediate specific place where we live . . . the limits of its resources; the carrying capacities of its lands and waters; the places where it must not be stressed . . . and the cultures of the people, of the populations native to the land and of those who have grown up with it, the human social and economic arrangements shaped by and adapted to the geomorphic ones, in both urban and rural settings—these are the things that must be appreciated.

But knowledge and awareness are not enough; they must be accompanied by personal action and commitment. A guiding principle of the new citizenship, then, is commitment to others and the commons—a duty to think and act beyond one's own narrow self-interest and work, and to act in ways that take the interests of the community into account.

Expanded citizenship holds that there are important duties and responsibilities that correspond to the traditional rights we are so quick to claim, and that these require personal action. Our right to reliable, potable water implies a corresponding duty to use that resource sparingly and carefully. Our perceived right to be free of toxic substances in our food and water implies a responsibility to avoid using theses substances.

At the core of expanded citizenship is the fundamental recognition that local choices have a string of consequences that cannot be ignored and for which personal accountability must be taken. Our local consumption of energy, mostly coal-generated, cannot be disconnected from the ravaged landscapes and communities of Appalachia. Our consumption of wood cannot be disconnected from the impacts of deforestation on biodiversity and water quality. This means understanding, as well, the ways in which our auto-dependence and our fossil-fuel addiction wreak havoc on environments and cultures many thousands of miles away.

We must reconceive and redefine many of our traditional actions, decisions, and choices through the lens of citizenship. The decisions we make at the grocery store—what products to buy, whether or not to purchase locally grown foods, whether we avoid seafood from depleted fisheries—are all very much about citizenship. The transportation decisions we make are also citizenship choices. I ride a bicycle as often as I am able in part because I feel a duty to reduce my own personal carbon footprint, to minimize my environmental impacts, both local and global. But I am also saving money, of course, and am healthier as a result of the daily exercise.

Household management choices are equally about citizenship. Being a good citizen means avoiding the use of pesticides, herbicides, fertilizers, and other harmful lawn-care products, where we can, and taking positive actions to enhance habitat for birds and wildlife. The Virginia Department of Environmental Quality recently released its annual stream quality assessment—very alarming but perhaps not surprising, 40 percent of Virginia's stream segments are not suitable for fishing or swimming. Is the culprit big business? No, it is mostly the stormwater runoff from fields and lawns and parking lots. The famous quote from the comic strip Pogo, "I have met the enemy and it is us," comes to mind.

Some of our biggest life choices entail some of the biggest opportunities to be good citizens: where we choose to live, the kind of home we purchase or build, the kinds of vehicles we drive (or, ideally, avoid driving). Now, I am not suggesting that other variables are not important to take into account—convenience, fashion, cost—but equally important to factor into the moral equation is the impact of these decisions on community and place, broadly defined.

Those fortunate enough to own forest or farmland have special citizenship duties. Working to protect native habitat, to conserve soil and water, to maintain the sustainable bounties of these lands and to use them cautiously and sparingly are all demands of good citizenship. Our new citizen recognizes that along with the rights and privileges of landownership go significant corresponding duties—duties to sustain or protect the inherent public values and services of that land.

One of the most pressing new duties of citizenship is to take a hard look at the sheer quantity of our consumption, and the impacts of that consumption on the planet. The ecological footprint of the average American is an astounding 25 acres—that is, it takes about this much land area to produce the food, energy, and materials needed to support our opulent existence. This is about five times the global average, and about twice the average for a western European nation such as France.

And this consumption is not without its ramifications. A recent study by the Worldwide Fund for Nature found that global consumption already exceeds the regenerative capacity of the earth by some 20 percent. By 2050, it will require 1.8 to 2.2 planet Earths to support our consumption levels, and this assumes a modest level of global population growth. As global citizens, we are questionable global citizens—5 percent of the world's population consuming one-third of the world's resources (World Wide Fund for Nature, 2002).

Reducing our ecological footprint would result in a more sustainable existence at both local and global levels and as I have argued throughout this book stronger places. And, there would be many other benefits as well. Because I ride my bicycle, I am getting to know my neighbors and my place on this earth in a way not possible in a car. I still vote and pay my taxes, but I am a new kind of citizen now.

Conclusions

Politics continues to be a pejorative word to many. Too often it is primarily about promoting narrow interests or protecting individual homeowners or neighborhoods from some perceived threat, whether in the form of a group home or a multifamily housing project or a business expansion. While such impulses are understandable, what is needed is a new politics of place, or more accurately a *renewed* politics of place. The qualities and attributes of such a politics include widespread participation and inclusiveness, a rich number and variety of grassroots groups that are able, under this new political sensibility, to collaborate and come together in support of place strengthening. Enlightened, forward-looking leadership by elected officials is also essential. And politics can be profoundly driven by the unique cultures, landscapes, and qualities of place, at the same time that respect for other cultures, people, and places is acknowledged. Reviving notions of citizenship and individual responsibility, and instilling new place duties, is a piece of local political reform. Politics should be viewed as a noble undertaking, and local politics the noblest of all.

Renewing Our Place Commitments

Americans, it can be said, function in parallel worlds. One world is the very local, the viscerally physical and personal. We walk out of our doors in the morning to the extremely particular weather, climate, and topography and the particular spaces of the built environments in which we live. We see and meet and talk with very specific people—members of our family, our friends and co-workers, even people we pass on the street whose faces we recognize but whose specific names and identities may not be known to us. In this way, our lives and existences are inherently (and reassuringly) particular and local.

Yet, at the same time we operate, increasingly it seems, in a more globalized, more ephemeral universe, in which particular and local qualities seem irrelevant or of lesser importance and value. One neighborhood, one community, one city becomes indistinguishable from another. Particular place-based knowledge is replaced with generic and universal knowledge. A child in Nebraska grows up knowing perhaps quite a lot about tigers or elephants or dolphins, but little or nothing about the flora and fauna native to that special spot on Earth. Broad caricatures and stereotypes replace understanding of the specific history, culture, and ecology.

There is a kind of distressing anonymity that comes about as a result, and with some serious consequences for what we care about, if we care about much at all. It seems sensible to assume that if we do not directly know and understand (and see and touch) the other specific members of our community, we will tend not to care about them (we will tend not to care that there are families living in poverty, that species and ecosystems are being lost, that local businesses are folding, etc.). There is, then, a kind of growing *place numbness*, a sort of amnesic *place fog* that eschews the deeper, lasting place relationships that I believe we need. For these and other reasons, we are close, I believe, to reaching a *crisis* of place, if we are not there already; a point at which the ramifications of reckless, placeless living begin to cascade in many ways, some of them understood, others less so. Many of our specific and precious places are threatened because we now know so little about them. The richness of the biodiversity and unique natural heritage of our communities is badly understood and consequently undervalued. Commitment to the broader public realm is in decline, and the continuing replacement of the public realm with excessive private spheres threatens the very fabric and foundation of a civil, caring society, and the important sense of our being interdependent and mutually dependent creatures. Sterile, placeless planning and development leaves us with little to cherish, little to be excited about, and much to discourage us. Placeless living has many, many other ramifications, as shown earlier, from declining public health (rising rates of obesity) to continued resource depletion (in the United States, ever greater dependence on oil, much of it from foreign sources), to loss of irreplaceable natural landscapes and biodiversity, to the emergence of a socially detached, passive, and disconnected citizenry.

In many important ways the trend toward homogenized places, and the growing disconnect between people and their local and regional environments, carries a steep price. Our mental health, our happiness, and our ability not just to survive but to lead richly rewarding lives requires these elements of real places.

At some level, though, many Americans recognize that genuine place connections are, in the end, quite essential, quite necessary for our long-term health and happiness and to a meaningful existence. Internet Web browsing will take us only so far; real lives must be lived in real places. There is considerable evidence that many Americans seek new connections with other people, broader communities, and the natural environment. In the immediate aftermath of September 11, 2001, the need to be with others, to be in public spaces, to reaffirm interpersonal goodness and our instincts to help each other came to the fore, and reminded us that our broader community and real places remain essential. There are positive signs that Americans see the value of place and are prepared to undertake and support actions to protect and nurture distinctive place qualities. While these impulses have diminished somewhat, there are reasons to be optimistic and signs that we are now in a period of unusual opportunity for rebuilding community and recommitting to place.

This book is a hopeful one in that it documents, describes, and evaluates a rich variety of strategies and ideas that can help to move us (back) closer to our place roots and provide some guidance about how we can recommit to place. These include strategies such as the following:

- Containing sprawl, promoting compact, infill development that strengthens existing places and conserves land and resources.
- Stimulating diverse and creative architecture and urban design.
- Rebuilding walkable communities and encouraging a walking culture.
- Recognizing and building onto the historical assets that every community has, including its historic buildings, housing stock, and industrial landscapes, and making that history as visible as possible through such techniques as urban trails, murals, and public education.
- Supporting smaller, locally owned, community-invested businesses and commerce; encouraging local consumption, as much as possible; supporting such ideas as community supported agriculture (CSA) and food cooperatives and use of local wood and timber.
- Protecting, restoring, and designing-in nature and the natural environment, wherever possible, and looking for every opportunity—from bridges to streets to the façades of buildings—to integrate nature into our communities.
- Organizing celebrations of place, and artistic expressions throughout the community that enhance its uniqueness and help to solidify place commitments.

- Promoting greater awareness among homeowners and citizens about the ecology, heritage, and resources needed to sustain our places; as well as the duty to minimize impacts on people and communities far away, and the overall health and condition of planet Earth.
- Underwriting and supporting local cultural life—local artists, craftsmen, community theater—and every manner of local artistic expression that can help strengthen unique place.
- Promoting place-based renewable energy that strengthens local economy, reduces environmental impacts, and further builds on and strengthens unique place attributes.

There are indeed many ways in which such recommitments to place can happen, and many methods through which a return to place can occur. From adaptive reuse of historic buildings and industrial landscapes, to greening streets, bridges, and rooftops, to finding creative ways of injecting art throughout our communities, much can be done and indeed is being done.

An important point made throughout this book is that place making, community building, and sustainability are strongly reinforcing endeavors and dovetail in many significant ways. As noted throughout, many things can help to make a community fundamentally more sustainable and at the same time enhance sense of place, commitments to place, and the building of stronger community and social ties.

There are a number of tensions left unresolved in this place-making agenda. One has to do with the power of physical form and the impact of housing and community design on the ability to both create a unique feeling and sense of place and commit to others and the broader community. How far the physical design can take us is undoubtedly still an open question, but at a fundamental level I do believe the physical form and configuration of neighborhoods has a significant impact on community. I also believe that having the spaces for a community and public life is essential—pedestrian spaces, community gardens, community forests, and the like will provide opportunities for building relationships, interpersonal connections, and direct experiences of places that are difficult otherwise.

But it is folly, of course, to ignore the many other factors that have an undeniable influence. We can provide fantastic pedestrian environments, marvelous spaces for people to enjoy nature and their fellow citizens, but if there is little time during the day to partake of the civic realm, such spaces will have been provided for naught. The inevitable conclusion is that more than spaces will be needed. It means providing various structures and opportunities for meaningful participation in the life of a community, it means reemphasizing the essential need (obligation?) of community volunteering and community and political engagement generally. Harder still, it will mean making some steps toward redefining progress and the cultural standards we use to assess what it means to live a good and meaningful life. It will mean, ideally, a cultural reassessment of work, both the kinds of work we do and the ways in which it is valued and rewarded, and the amount of our lives consumed by work to the exclusion of community and environment. Slowing down, participating in the evening stroll, spending as much time getting to know the sounds and sights and nuances of one's immediate natural environment, are difficult things to achieve, to be sure, in our harried material world, but equally important to any reordering of the physical spaces in our communities. As this book has pointed out, movements like Slow Food, and now Slow City, help to change the perception of "slow" as a pejorative word, and might, if embraced in the United States, reprioritize our time and energies of community and place.

Equally true, if we expect to evolve toward communities and places where higher degrees of sharing occur, it will require more than new devices or processes for sharing—it will probably demand the nurturing of a sharing ethic or attitude. It is difficult to know precisely how and in what ways such new place sensibilities can be fostered (through education, community dialogue, mentoring, reflection, etc.), but we should accept that such a task is as essential as the more programmatic or technical steps we might take.

Much of this agenda involves reconceptualizing our present notions of *home*. Indeed, I have argued that a fundamentally new approach to conceiving of and thinking about home is an essential part of any long-term vision of sustainable communities and place strengthening. One's home, in today's society, is viewed in very narrow ways—it is primarily and essentially real estate, a set of interior spaces and rooms for conducting daily life (i.e., where we sleep), a very limited perception of outdoor spaces (a lawn and backyard in which the kids can play), and increasingly important, a wealth-amassing investment. We need, consequently, a fundamentally expanded notion of home that recognizes that each individual house and point on a subdivision map is situated in a broader ecological sphere, and that responsibilities flow from such knowledge. Place learning and place commitments should be equally as important to us as wealth accumulation and opulent interior spaces. Returning to place requires new knowledge, a new consciousness about the impact of personal (and collective) choices, but it also requires direct participation and affirmation of the beauty and value of the places in which we live.

So, the challenges before us are serious, to be sure. Becoming a people and culture genuinely *native* to the places in which we live, in the face of the seemingly unrelenting forces of sameness and generality, may well be the most daunting and difficult issue facing our planet today. Any dramatic shift in the direction of new commitments to place will be difficult in the short run. But communities (and individuals) should do what they can, taking even small steps, that move, perhaps ever so incrementally in the direction of better knowing, appreciating, and strengthening commitments to real place. Adopting a set of design guidelines to moderate the otherwise stultifying effects of big box retail, requiring at least a small percentage of our new homes and businesses to be energy-efficient and carbon-neutral, taking small steps to celebrate place and place victories, and incorporating a natural history component in the local school system would be accomplishments. Whatever can be done should be viewed as good progress, on the longer journey to becoming *native to somewhere.*

References

10,000 Friends of Pennsylvania. Undated. *The Costs of Sprawl in Pennsylvanina.*

Adams, Gerald. 2002. "Single Purpose New Neighborhood Group Aims to Save Marina Movie House from Walgreens," *San Francisco Chronicle*, May 29.

Abdur-Rahman, Sufiya. 2003. "A Tomato Grows in Chicago, and Beets," *Chicago Tribune*, August 26.

Akbari, Bretz, Kurn, and Hanford. 1997. "Peak Power and Cooling Energy Savings of High-Albedo Roofs," *Energy and Buildings,* Vol. 25, pp. 116–126.

Alberta Education. 1992. "A Study into the Effects of Light on Children of Elementary School-Age—A Case of Daylight Robbery," Policy and Planning Branch, Planning and Information Service Division, Government of Alberta, Canada, January.

Alford, Roger. 2001. "Coal Slurry Darkens Streams: Pipe Break Spills Out 135,000 Gallons," *Associated Press,* April 11.

Alexander, Christopher, Sara Ishikawa, and Murray Silverstein. 1977. *A Pattern Language.* New York, NY: Oxford University Press.

Altman, Irwin and Setha M. Low, eds. *Place Attachment.* New York: Plenum Press, 1992.

Amaza, Cornell. 2000. "SPU Takes a Leadership Role in Salmon Habitat Recovery," *Seattle Daily Journal of Commerce,* http://www.djc.com.

American Forests. 2002. *Urban Ecosystem Analysis for the Washington, D.C., Metropolitan Area.* Washington, D.C.: American Forests.

American Planning Association (APA). 2002. "Nine Mile Run Stewardship Model," City Parks Forum, www.planning.org.

America Walks. 2002. "A Pedestrian Agenda for GREEN TEA." Portland, OR: America Walks.

Anderson, Tom. 2001. "Dunedin Embraces Elder-Ready Status," *St. Petersburg Times,* January 29.Guest column, State Edition, p. 2.

Apple, Lauri, and Mike Clark-Madison. 2003. "Borders Backs Out," *Austin Chronicle,* April 25. Vol.22, No. 34, http://www.austinchronicle.com.

Arcade Journal. 1998. "An Aesthetic Utility: Interview with Diana Gale," http://www.arcadejournal.com.

Arnesen, John, Tracy Chollak, and Shane Dewald. 2001. "Street Edge Alternative (S.E.A. Streets)," in Puget Sound Water Quality Action Team, *Low-Impact Development in Puget Sound: Abstracts and Biographies,* June 5–6.

Arts Education Partnership. 1999. "Champions of Change: The Impact of the Arts on Learning," http://aep-arts.org.

Autich, Anthony, Harvey R. Gobas, and Jag Salgaonkas. 2003. "The Santa Monica Urban Recycling Facility and the Sustainable Environment," *Stormwater,* http://www.forester.net/sw.html.

Baker, Beth. 2002. "Happy by Nature: Fondness for Plants and Animals May Be Hard-Wired," *Washington Post,* June 4. Health Tab, p. F-01.

Balfour, J. L., and G. A. Kaplan. 2002. "Neighborhood Environment and Loss of Physical Function in Older Adults," *American Journal of Epidemiology* 155: 507–515.

Basel Action Network (BAN). 2002. *Exporting Harm: The High Tech Trashing Of Asia,* February 25. Seattle, WA: Basel Action Network.

BBC News. 2002. "Devon Dung Plant 'first of many,'" May 17.

Beach, Virginia. 1998. "Going Green: Environmentally Friendly Businesses Thrive in the Low Country," *Charleston Regional Business Journal,* http://www.crbj.com.

Beatley, Timothy. 1994. *Ethical Land Use: Principles of Policy and Planning.* Baltimore, MD: Johns Hopkins University Press.

Beatley, Timothy. 2000. *Green Urbanism: Learning from European Cities.* Washington, D.C.: Island Press.

Beatley, Timothy, and Richard Collins. 2002. "Americanizing Sustainability: Place-based Approaches to the Global Challenge," *William and Mary Environmental Law and Policy Review.* Vol. 27, No. 1, fall, pp.195–229.

Beatley, Timothy, and Richard Collins. 2000. "Smart Growth and Beyond: Transitioning to a Sustainable Society," *Virginia Environmental Law Journal,* Vol. 19, No. 3, pp. 287–322.

Beatley, Timothy, and Kristy Manning. 1997. *The Ecology of Place.* Washington, D.C.: Island Press.

Beaumont, Constance. 1988. "Debunking the Myth of Sprawl's Inevitability," remarks made to Washington Trust for Historic Preservation and Washington chapter of the American Planning Association, Sept. 24.

Benotto, Catherine. 2002. "Greenbacks in the Greenery: Never Forget the Economic Value of Trees, Park and Open Spaces," *Landscape Northwest,* April 18, http://www.djc.com/special/landscape02/.

Benyus, Janine. 1998. *Biomimicry: Innovation Inspired by Nature.* New York: HarperCollins Books.

Best Foot Forward, Ltd. 2002. *City Limits*. London: Best Foot Forward Ltd.

Berkman, Lisa F. 1995. "The Role of Social Relations in Health Promotion," *Psychosom Medicine*, Vol. 57(3).

Bernstein, Scott, 2002. "Planning As If People And Places Matter: Surface Transportation Research Needs and Performance for The Next Century." Testimony before the Committee on Environment and Public Works, March 15, http://www.cnt.org/congressional-testimony/bernstein-15mar02.html.

Bhatty, Ayesha. 2004. "How Small Potatoes is Saving the Planet," Nationwide News Service, January 18, http://www.nationwidenews.ca/archives/000031.html.

BioRegional. Undated. "Beddington Zero Energy Development." London: BioRegional.

Blum, Andres. 2004. "Solar Power Goes Urban at San Francisco's Moscone Center," *Metropolis*, http://www.metropolismag.com/html/sustainable/case/Moscone CenterSolar.html.

Brummett, B. H., J. C. Barefoot, I. C. Siegler, N. E. Clapp-Channing, B. L. Lytle, H. B. Bosworth, R. B. Williams, Jr., and D. B. Mark. 2001. "Characteristics of socially isolated patients with coronary artery disease who are at elevated risk for mortality," *Psychosom Medicine*, Vol. 63, pp. 267–72.

Bryant, Elizabeth. 2003. "Heat Wave Sparks Elder Reform Debate," *United Press International*, August 28.

Breen, Tim. 2002. "Transit: Study Says Boosting Ridership May Be Only Real Way of Cutting Fuel Pollution," Greenwire News Service, Vol. 10, No. 9, July 18. http://www.eenews.net/greenwire.php.

Brookings Institution Center for Urban and Metropolitan Policy. 1999. *A Region Divided: The State of Growth in Greater Washington, DC*. Washington, D.C.: Brookings Institution.

Brower, Sidney. 1990. *Good Neighborhoods: A Study of In-Town and Suburban Residential Environments*. Westport, CT: Praeger.

Buchanan, Rosemarie. 2001. "The Greening of Chicago: 5 Architecture Firms Meet City's Challenge: Design Efficient, Affordable Homes," *Chicago Tribune*, January 13, new homes section, p. 1.

Buck, Genevieve. 1999. "Rural Retreat: Tryon Farm, in Northern Indiana, Breaks New Ground for New Home Development," *Chicago Tribune*, Nov. 27, pp. C1–C4.

Buntin, John. 2001. "Dead End Revolt," *Governing Magazine*, November.

Busby and Associates. Undated. "Telus/William Farrell Building Revitalization," http://www.busby.ca/9805telus/index.htm.

Businesses for a Sustainable Tomorrow. 2003. "Hot Lips Awarded for Energy Efficiency," case study series, City of Portland, Oregon.

Business Week, online. 2002. "See Europe—at 217 miles an hour," Oct. 31, http://www.businessweek.com/bwdaily/dnflash/oct2002/nf20021031_8250.htm.

Bushy & Associates Architects. Undated. "2001 Professional First Place Award," http://www.designresource.org.

Cabiskey, Olivia. 2001. "Art Expression on Expressway." *Streetwise*, Feb. 4, p. 6.

California Integrated Waste Management Board. 2003. "Urban Ore," case studies, http://www.ciwmb.ca.gov.

Canada, Mortgage and Housing Corporation. Undated. "Pelgromhof: Sustainable and Energy-Efficient Living in the Netherlands," http://www.cmhc-schl.gc.ca/en/imquaf/himu/buin_014.cfm.

Canedy, Dana. 2002. "Florida Redoubles Effort to Accommodate Aged," *New York Times,* May 5. Section 1, p. 39.

Casey, Caroline. 2000. "'Walking School Buses' Curtail Traffic, Increase Safety," http://ap.hwdsb.on.ca/transport/articles/010612_5asp.

Cass, Connie. 2002. "Only in Washington: Summer Art Sparks Political Disputes," *Washington Post,* Aug. 29.

Center for Urban Policy Research. 1999. *Eastward Ho! Development Futures: Paths to More Efficient Growth in Southeast Florida.* New Brunswick, NJ: Rutgers University.

Centers for Disease Control. 2003. "Physical Activity and Good Nutrition: Essential Elements to Prevent chronic Diseases and Obesity, 2003." Atlanta, GA: CDC.

Cervero, Robert, 1998. *The Transit Metropolis: A Global Inquiry,* Washington, D.C.: Island Press.

Chemainus Festival of Murals. 1993. *The Chemainus Murals.* Chemainus, British Columbia.

Chicago Department of Cultural Affairs. Undated. "Riverwalk Gateway," http://www.cityofchicago.org.

"Chicago Goes Green." June 20, 2001, http://climateark.org/articles/2001/2nd/chgogree.htm.

Chicago Public Schools. 2002. "CPS New Community Schools to Offer Education Programs, Activities to the Community," press release, Sept. 19.

Chicago Tribune. 2002. "Dimming Lights Saves Birds, Study Says." *Chicago Tribune,* May 9, Section 1.

Chicago Wilderness. 2000. *An Atlas of Biodiversity,* Chicago.

Chittum, Ryan. 2003. "Sprawl Opponents Applaud 'Smarter' Redevelopment," *Wall Street Journal,* March 17, http://homes.wsj.com/propertyreport/propertyreport/20030317-chittum.html.

Christian Science Monitor. 2003. "Curbing City Drivers," Feb. 23, http://www.csmonitor.com.

City of Columbus. Undated. *The Urban Commercial Overlay: Promoting Pedestrian-Oriented Development in the City of Columbus, Ohio.* Department of Planning, Planning Division.

City of Davis (California). 1998. "An Ordinance Amending Chapter 6 of the Davis Municipal Code Pertaining to Outdoor Lighting Control."

City of Ft. Collins (Colorado). 1995. "Design Standards and Guidelines for Large Retail Establishments."

City of Helsinki. 2002. "Viikki: A University District and Science Park for the 2000s," Town Planning Division.

City of Seattle. Undated. "Sustainable Building Policy."

City of Toronto. 2002. "Toronto Pedestrian Charter," http://www.city.toronto.on.ca/pedestrian/index.htm.

———. 2002. Undated. "Toronto Pedestrian Charter Background," http://www.city.toronto.on.ca/pedestrian/background.htm.

City of Vancouver. 1994. "Public Art Policies and Guidelines," Land Use and Development Policies and Guidelines, adopted June 23 and November 22.

———. 1999. "Heritage Policies and Guidelines," Land Use and Development Policies and Guidelines, amended September 10.

Civic Economics. 2002. *Economic Impact Analysis: A Case Study, Local Merchants vs. Chain Retailers.* Complete Report, prepared for Livable City, December, Austin, Texas.

Cleeland, Nancy, and Abigail Goldman. 2002. "Wal-Mart Blocked by Union Lobbying," *Los Angeles Times,* Oct. 25. Business Section, p. C-1.

Coalition for Community Schools. 2002. "Chicago Public Schools Announce Major Community Schools Initiative," *Community Schools Online,* October 11, Vol. II, No. 13, http://www.communityschools.org.

Cohn, D'Vera. 2003. "Creeping Toward Danger: Area's Box Turtle, an Easy Target, Feared to Be on Its Last Legs," *Washington Post,* Sept. 7, p. C-1.

Commerzbank. Undated (a). "The New Commerzbank Headquarters in Frankfurt: Landscape Planning," Frankfurt, Germany.

———. Undated (b). "Architecture."

Community Resources. 2000. "Exploring the Value of Urban Non-Timber Products," working paper. Baltimore, MD.

Congress for the New Urbanism (CNU). 1998. "Charter of the New Urbanism," http://www.cnu.org.

Cooper-Marcus, C., 2000. "Site Planning, Building Design and a Sense of Community: An Analysis of Six Cohousing Schemes in Denmark, Sweden and the Netherlands," *Journal of Architecture and Planning Research,* Vol. 17, No. 2, Summer, pp. 146–163.

Cooper-Marcus, C., and M. Barnes. 1995. *Gardens in Healthcare Facilities: Uses, Therapeutic Benefits and Design Recommendations.* Martinez, CA: The Center for Health Design.

———. 1999. *Healing Gardens: Therapeutic Benefits and Design Recommendations.* New York, NY: John Wiley.

Crawford, J.H. 2002. *Carfree Cities,* Amsterdam, the Netherlands: International Books.

Dagger, Richard. 2003. "Stopping Sprawl for the Good of All: The Case for Civic Environmentalism," *Journal of Social Philosophy,* Vol. 34, No. 1, spring, pp. 28–42.

Dahl, L. 2002. "Health and Greening the City: Relation of Urban Planning and Health," *Journal of Epidemiology and Community Health,* Vol. 56, p. 897.

Davey, Monica. 2003. "A Garden Flourishes Amid Chicago's Projects," *New York Times,* Aug. 25. Section A, p.8.

Delatiner, Barbara. 2001. "The Commuters May Rush, But the Art Is There to Stay," *New York Times,* Dec. 2, Section 1LI, p. 28.

DeMaio, Paul J. 2003. "Smart Bikes: Public Transportation for the 21st Century," *Transportation Quarterly,* Vol. 57, No. 1, winter, pp. 9–11.

Desai, Pooran, and Sue Riddlestone. 2002. *Bioregional Solutions for Living on One Planet.* London, England: Green Books for the Schumacher Society.

Determan, William. 2003. Personal communication, February 21, Columeet Environmental Resource Center.

Dietz, Diane. 2003. "New Law for Motorists Gives Pedestrians a Break," *Eugene Register Guard,* June 17. http://www.registerguard.com/.

Diffily, Ann. 1998. "Riverfront Renaissance: After Providence Reinvented Its Waterways, a Brown Alumnus Gave People a Compelling Reason to Come," *Brown Alumni Magazine,* March. www.brownalumnimagazine.com/storydetail.cfm?Id=1265.

Dresser, Michael. 2003. "Ehrlich's Smart Growth Plan Praised by National Advocate: Ideas Change Emphasis of Glendenings Policies," *Baltimore Sun,* Oct. 11, p. B1.

Dreiseitl, Herbert, Dieter Grau, and Karl H.C. Ludwig, eds. 2001. *Waterscapes: Planning, Building and Designing with Water.* Basel, Germany: Birkhauser.

EcoCity Columbus. 2001. *EcoCity Columbus Plan,* final report, Ohio State University, http://facweb.knowlton.ohio-state.edu/mconroy/ecocitycolumbus/final report.htm.

EcoStaden. Undated. "Echoes of Tomorrow," history and description of Augustenburg eco-neighborhood redevelopment project.

Elias, Marilyn. 2001. "Friends May Make Breast Cancer More Survivable," *USA Today,* March 7. Life Section, p. D-01.

Elliott, Scott. 2002. "10-Year Plan Focuses on Neighborhoods," *Dayton Daily News,* Oct. 29, p. 1-A.

Emery, Marla R. 2001. "Non-Timber Forest Products," Fact Sheet No. 6, Virginia Tech, Blacksburg, VA.

Eng, Patricia M., Eric Rimm, Garrett Fizmaurice, and Ichiro Kawachi. 2002. "Social Ties and Changes in Social Ties in Relation to Subsequent Total and Cause-Specific Mortality and Coronary Heart Disease Incidence in Men," *American Journal of Epidemiology,* Vol. 155, No. 8, pp. 700–709.

Energie-Cites. 2000. "Solar Thermal Energy: Barcelona." Barcelona, Spain.

Enoch, Marcus. 2002. "Supporting Car Share Clubs: A Worldwide Review," presented at 3rd MOSES ESG meeting, Feb., London, England.

Entwicklungsgesellschaft Mont-Cenis (EMC), 1998. *Mont-Cenis,* September, Herne, Germany: EMC.

Ewing, Reid, Rolf Pendall, and Don Chen. 2002. *Measuring Sprawl and its Impact.* Washington, D.C.: Smart Growth America.

European Academy for the Urban Environment. Undated. "Malmö: BoO1, City of Tomorrow: European Building Exhibition and Sustainable District," Berlin, Germany.

Fairfax County, VA. Undated. "Gum Springs Glen: A New Retirement Community for Active Seniors with Moderate Incomes," http://www.co.fairfax.va.us.

Fairtrade Foundation, "Fairtrade Towns," http://www.fairtrade.org.uk/get_involved_fairtrade_towns.htm.

Fieldworks. 2000. "Shared Space Benefits Young and Old," *Fieldworks,* Sept./Oct., http://www.huduser.org.

Fleming, Peyton. 2003. "Commentary: Big-Box Stores vs. N.E. Downtowns," *Providence Journal-Bulletin,* April 11, p. B-06.

Florida, Richard, 2002. *The Rise of the Creative Class: And How It's Transforming Work, Leisure, Community and Everyday Life.* New York, New York: Basic Books.

Food Alliance. 2003. "Food Alliance Helps Bring Northwest Grown, Eco-Friendly Flour to Portland Pizzeria," news release, Portland, OR: Food Alliance.

FoodShare. Undated. "What is the Good Food Box." http://www.foodshare.net/good foodbox01.htm.

Fortner, Brian. 2001. "Glass Art," *Civil Engineering,* January, pp. 47–51.

Fox, Colin. 2002. "A Festival That's for the People," *The Scotsman,* Aug. 14, p. 10.

Frasure-Smith, N. et al. 2000. "Social Support, depression, and mortality during the first year after myocardial infarction," *Circulation,* 101: 1919–24.

Friedman, E., and S. A. Thomas. 1995. "Pet Ownership, Social Support, and One-Year Survival after Acute Myocardial Infraction in the Cardiac Arrythmia Suppression Trial (CAST)," *American Journal of Cardiology,* Vol. 77, pp. 1213–77.

Froelich, Janis D. 2003. "Panel Wants 'Landmark' on Former Cigar Factories," *Tampa Tribune,* December 10, p. 4.

Frontera Farmer Foundation. Undated. "Frontera Farmer Foundation Announces the Avilability of 2004 Grant Applications." Chicago, IL. http://www.frontera kitchens.com/restaurants/foundation/fff_grant_app.html.

Frost, Joe L., and Paul J. Jacobs. 1995. "Play Deprivation: A Factor in Juvenile Violence," *Dimensions of Early Childhood,* spring, Vol. 23, No. 3, pp. 14–39.

Frumkin, Howard. 2001. "Beyond Toxicity: Human Health and the Natural Environment," *American Journal of Preventive Medicine,* Vol. 20, No. 3, pp. 234–240.

Gallery 37. 2001. "Annual Review, 2001." Chicago, IL: Gallery 37.

Gallery 37. Undated. "Gallery 37: Learning, Working, Connecting through the Arts." Chicago, IL: Gallery 37.

Gao, Helen. 2002. "New Model Fuels School Site Hunt," *Los Angeles Daily News,* Nov. 25. http://www.nsbn.org/articles/item.php?id=60.

Garman, David K. 2000. "Statement of David K. Garman, Assistant Secretary, Energy Efficiency and Receivable Energy, Before the Committee on House Energy and Commerce Subcommittee on Oversight and Investigations," June 6, Lexus-Nexis.

Garreau, Joel. 1992. *Edge City: Life on the New Frontier.* New York, New York: Anchor Books.

Gaynor, Pamela. 2001. "To Market, to Market—But Where Are the Farmer's Markets?" *Pittsburgh Post-Gazette,* Sunday, Aug. 19. Business News, http://www.post-gazette.com/businessnews/20010819markets0819bnp3.asp.

Gilderbloom, J. I., and J. P. Markham. 1998. "Housing Quality Among the Elderly: A Decade of Changes," *International Journal of Aging and Human Development* 46(1), pp. 1589–1607.

Gill, Michael. 2003. "Whiskey Island's Future," Cleveland Free Times, June 11. http://www.ClevelandFreetimes.com.

Glynn, T. 1981. "Psychological Sense of Community: Measurement and Application," *Human Relations* Vol. 34 Pp. 789–818.

Goldberger, Paul. 2003. "Disconnected Urbanism," *Metropolis.* November.

Goodman, Peter S. 2003. "China Serves as Dump Site for Computers: Unsafe Recycling Practice Grows Despite Import Ban," *Washington Post,* Feb. 24, p. A1.

Great River Earth Institute. Undated. "Bioregionalism," http://www.greatriv.org/.

Greater London Authority (GLA). 2002. *The Draft London Plan: A Summary.* London, England: GLA.

———. 2003. "Valuing Greenness: Green Spaces, Housing Prices and Landowners' Priorities." London, England: GLA, June.

Green Zone. Undated. "A Road to Sustainability," Carstedts Ford, Umeå, Sweden.

Greene, Jan. 2000. "Prescribing a Healthy Social Life: A Robust Social Network is Important in Healing-And Staying Well," *Hippocrates,* August, Vol. 14, No. 8.

Greenstein, Joe. 2002. "West Side Story: The Rise and Fall of Manhattan's High Line," *Trains,* March, pp. 56–61.

Grossman, Kate N. 2002. "20 Schools to Become Community Centers," *Chicago Sun-Times,* Oct. 15, p.18.

Hackett, Regina. 2001. "Buster Simpson Cultivates Art with Help from Mother Nature," *Seattle Post-Intelligencer,* June 9, Arts and Entertainment section. http://seattlepi.nwsource.com/visualart/26679_buster09q.shtml.

Hahn, Peter and Stephen Kellert. 2002. *Children and Nature: Sociocultural, and Evolutionary Investigations.* Cambridge, MA: MIT Press.

Hartig, T., Mang, M., and G.W. Evans, 1991. "Restorative effects of natural environment experience," *Environment and Behavior,* pp. 3–26.

Hartline, Jack. 1998. "Outdoor Murals Saved Tiny B.C. Community," *Ottawa Citizen,* Feb. 21, p. L8.

Hartman-Stein, P., and E. Potkanowicz. 2003. "Behavioral Determinants of Healthy Aging: Good News for the Baby Boomer Generation" *Online Journal of Issues in Nursing.* Vol. #8 No. #2, Manuscript 5. www.nursingworld.org/ojin/topic21/tpc21_5.htm.

Hiss, Tony. 1990. *The Experience of Place.* New York, NY: Random House.

Historic Chicago Bungalow Association. Undated. "Design Guidelines," Chicago, IL: HCBA.

Hodskins, Liza G. 2003. "A Stampede of Local Color," *Washington Post,* Dec. 2, p. C10.

Hollander, Sarah. 2000. "Choice of Site for Hullets is expected by years end," *Cleveland Plain Dealer,* Oct. 5, p. B7.

Honey, Tim, 2002. "New Challenges and New Models for Sustainable Urban Development," Urbanicity, http://www.urbanicity.org/Topic2.asp?TopID=1&ConTyID 1&ConID=44.

Horizon Solutions. 2003. "Downtown Redevelopment: The Denver Dry Building," May 2, www.solutions-site.org/artman/publish/printer_113.shtml.

House, J. S., et al. 1988. "Social Relationships and Health," *Science* 241: 540–545.

Huang, Yolanda. 1999. "Collaboration Between Willard Greening Project & BOSS," Progress Report, January. http:www.sarep.ucdavis.edu/grants/Reports/Huang/huang97-28.htm.

Hummon, David M. 1992. "Community Attachment: Local Sentiment and Sense of Place," in Irwin Altman and Setha Low eds., *Place Attachment*. New York, NY: Plenum Press.

Hunt, Steve. 2003. "Bringing Together Seniors and Youngsters at Gum Springs Glen," *Mt. Vernon Voice*, June 26, p. 10.

Ivey, Mike. 2002. "The Economic Argument Against Big Box," *Capital Times,* Madison, WI, June 11, p. D8.

Innovative Design. Undated. "Sustainable School Guidelines," http://www.innovativedesign.net/guidelines.htm.

International City Management Association. 2001. "Westergasfabriek: Collaboration of Local Government and Community," an International Brownfields Case Study.

Insurance Institute for Highway Safety. 2000 (a). "Roundabouts: They Sharply Reduce Crashes, Study Finds," *Status Report,* Vol. 35, No. 5, May 13.

———. 2000 (b). "In Pedestrian Crashes, It's Vehicle Speed That Matters Most," *Status Report,* Vol. 35, No. 5, May 13. Pp. 4–5.

———. 2001. "Roundabouts Reduce Traffic Backups." *Status Report,* Vol. 37, No. 7, July 28. 7 pp.

Jackson, Richard. 2003. "Editorial: The Impact of the Built Environment on Health: An Emerging Field," *American Journal of Public Health*, September, Vol 93, No. 9, pp. 1382–1384.

Jackson, Richard J., and Chris Kochtitzky. 2002. *Creating a Healthy Environment: The Impact of the Built Environment on Public Health*. Washington, D.C.: Sprawl Watch Clearinghouse.

Jacobs, Jane. 1961. *The Death and Life of Great American Cities*, New York, NY: Penguin Books.

Jahnige, P. 2002. "The Hidden Bounty of the Urban Forest," in E. T. Jones, R. J. McLain, and J. Weigand eds., *NonTimber Forest Products of the United States*. Pp. 96–107. Lawrence, KS: University Press of Kansas.

Janssen, Ben and Theo Keultjes. 2000. *Pelgromhof Zevenaar*, Amsterdam, the Netherlands: Fagus.

John, DeWitt. 1994. *Civic Environmentalism: Alternatives to Regulation in States and Communities*. Washington, D.C.: CQ Press.

Jones, Andrew. 2001. "Geographic Launches Project to Promote Protection of US

Rivers," *National Geographic News*, http://news.nationalgeographic.com/news/2001/06/0627_georiveraction.html.

Kaiser Family Foundation. 1999. "New Study Finds Kids Spend Equivalent of Full Work Week Using Media," November 17, http://www.kff.org.

Kaplan, Rachel. 1973. "Some Psychological Benefits of Gardening," *Environment and Behavior*, Vol. 5, No. 2, June, pp. 145–162.

———. 1983. "The Role of Nature in the Urban Context," in I. A. Altman and J. F. Wahlwill eds., *Behavior and the Natural Environment*. New York, NY: Plenum Press. Pp. 127–161.

Kaplan, Stephen. 1995. "The restorative benefits of nature: Toward an integrative framework," *Journal of Environmental Psychology*, 15, pp. 169–182.

Katcher, A., H. Segal, and A. Beck. 1984. "Comparison of Contemplation and Hypnosis for the Reduction of Anxiety and Discomfort During Dental Surgery," *American Journal of Clinical Hypnosis*, Vol. 27, pp. 14–21.

Kats, G. 2003. "The Costs and Financial Benefits of Green Buildings," A Report to California's Sustainable Building Task Force, October.

Katz, Peter. 1994. *The New Urbanism: Toward an Architecture of Community*, New York, NY: McGraw-Hill.

Kawachi, I., G. A. Colditz, A., Ascherio, E. B. Rimm, E. Giovannucci, M. J. Stampfer, and W. C. Willett. 1996. "A Prospective Study of Social Networks in Relation to Total Mortality and Cardiovascular Disease in Men in the USA," *Journal of Epidemiology and Community Health*, Vol. 50, pp. 245–251.

Kellert, S. R. ed. 2002. *Children and Nature: Psychological, Sociocultural and Evolutionary Investigations*. Cambridge, MA: MIT Press.

Kellert, Steven, and E.O. Wilson. 1995. *The Biophilia Hypothesis*, Washington, D.C.: Island Press.

Kemmis, Daniel. 1990. *Community and the Politics of Place*. Norman, OK: University of Oklahoma Press.

Kemmis, Daniel, 1995. *The Good City and the Good Life*, Boston, MA: Houghton-Mifflin Co.

Kennedy, Bob. 2003. "Towering Bronze Sculpture by World-Renowed Haida Carver," Turtle Island Native Network, http://www.turtleisland.org.

Kilborn, Peter T. 2002. "Slow down, You Move Too Fast: Bulbs, Knobs and Circles," *New York Times*, Dec. 22, Section 1, p. 26.

Killingsworth, Richard E., and Jean Lamming. "Development and Public Health; Could Our Development Patterns be Affecting Our Personal Health?" *Urban Land*, Urban Land Institute, July, pp. 12–17.

Klatt, Mary Beth. 2003. "It's Easy Being Green: Chicago Restores Four Vacant Houses as "Green Bungalows," *Preservation Online*, Jan. 3, http://www.preservationonline.org.

Klein, Alec. 2002. "Pampered at the Wheel: High-Tech Vehicles Act as Nannys to Drivers on the Road," *Washington Post*, January 21. Section A, p. A01.

Klein, Alvin. 2002. "An Arts Festival with Many Sites, but a Keen Sense of Place," *New York Times*, June 9, Section 14CN, p. 19.

Klepeis, Neil E., W.C. Nelson, W.R. Ott, J.P. Robinson, A.M. Tsang, P. Switzer, J.V. Behar, S.C. Hern, and W.H. Engelmann. 2001. *The National Human Activity Pattern Survey (NHAPS): A Resource for Assessing Exposure to Environmental Pollutants*. Berkeley, CA: Lawrence Berkeley National Laboratory.

Kloppenburg, Jack Jr., John Hendrickson, and G.W. Stevenson. 1995. "Coming in to the Foodshed." Forthcoming in William Vitek and Wes Jackson eds. *Home Territories: Essays on Community and the Land*. New Haven, CT: Yale University Press.

Konopacki, S., and H. Akbari. 2001. "Measured Energy Savings and Demand Reduction from a Reflective Roof Membrane on a Larger Retail Store in Austin," Berkeley, CA: Lawrence Berkeley National Laboratory.

Kunkle, Frederick. 2002. "Mapping a Run through History," *Washington Post,* Sept. 29, metro, p. co1- [see also the website of Fairfax Trails and Streams, http://www.fairfax.trails.org].

Kuo, Frances E., and William E. Sullivan. 2001. "Aggression and Violence in the Inner City: Effects of Environment Via Mental Fatigue," *Environment and Behavior,* Vol. 33, No. 4, July, pp. 543–571.

Lahaie, Therese. 2003. "Emeryville Youth Create Nation's First Solar-Powered Mural," *The Spartan Speaks,* Oct. 23, http://www.thereselahaie.com.

Langholtz, Eileen. Undated. "Young People Examine Their Communities," http://www.planning.org.

Laughlin, Robin, and Paul Dedyo. 2002. "Sustainability Comes With a View," *Seattle Daily Journal of Commerce,* October 31, http://www.djc.com.

Lavorel, Jennifer. 2003. "The Chicago Effort," *Urban Land,* January, pp. 39–43.

Lawrence, Barbara Kent, et al. 2002. *Dollars and Sense: The Cost Effectiveness of Small Schools*. Cincinnati, OH: Knowledgeworks Foundation.

Lawrence Berkeley National Laboratory and Philips Lighting Company. Undated. "The Philips Lighting Formula: An Energy Blueprint for the Nation."

Leather, Phil, Mike Pyrgas, Di Beale, and Claire Lawrence. 1998. "Windows in the Workplace: Sunlight, View, and Occupational Stress," *Environment and Behavior,* Vol. 30, No. 6, November, pp. 739–762.

Lehner, Peter H., George P. Aponte-Clark, Diane M. Caneron, and Andrew G. Frank. 1999. *Stormwater Strategies: Community Response to Runoff Pollution*. New York, NY: Natural Resources Defense Council.

Leserman, J., J.M. Petitto, R.N. Golden, B.N. Gaynes, H. Gu, J.D. Folds, D.L. Evans, D.O. Perkins, and S.G. Silva. 2000, "Impact of stressful life events, depression, social support, coping, and cortisol levels on progression to AIDS," *American Journal of Psychiatry,* Vol. 157, No. 8, pp. 1121–1228.

Leopold, Aldo. 1947. *A Sand County Almanac*. London, England: Oxford University Press.

Levine, Leslie. 1998. *Will This Place Ever Feel Like Home? Simple Advice for Settling in After You Move*. Chicago, IL: Real Estate Education Company.

Light, Andrew. 2000. "Resotration, the Value of Participation, and the Risks of Professionalization," in Paul Gobster and R. Bruce Hull eds., *Restoring Nature: Per-*

spectives from the Social Sciences and Humanities. Pp. 163–181. Washington, D.C.: Island Press.

Lister, Sam. 2003. "Home Office Builders Use 'Illegal' Timber From Indonesia," *The Times* (London), June 5, home news, p. 8.

Los Angeles Department of Water and Power (LADWP). 2001. "Nationally Acclaimed LADWP Cool Schools II Tree-Planting and Energy Efficiency Program Begins," press release, Feb. 2, http://www.ladwp/cms/ladwp004046.jsp.

Los Angeles Department of Water and Power. Undated. "Cool Schools Program," http://www.ladwp.com/ladwp/cms/ladwp001087.jsp.

London, Scott. 1995. "The Politics of Place: An Interview with Terry Tempest Williams," http://www.scottlondon.com/insight/scripts/ttw.html.

Low, Setha. 1992. "Symbolic Ties That Bind: Place Attachment in the Plaza," in Irwin Altman and Setha M. Low, eds. *Place Attachment,* pp. 165–187. New York, NY: Plenum Press.

Low, Setha M., and Irwin Altman. 1992. "Place Attachment: A Conceptual Inquiry," in Irwin Altman and Setha M. Low, eds. *Place Attachment,* pp. 1–12. New York, NY: Plenum Press.

Lucy, William H. 2002. *Charlottesville's Downtown Revitalization.* Charlottesville, VA: City of Charlottesville.

Lucy, William, and David Phillips. 2000. *Confronting Suburban Decline.* Washington, D.C.: Island Press.

Lyall, Sarah. 2000. "Go Ahead, Drive Into London. That Will Be £5, Please," *New York Times,* Sept. 5, http://www.nytimes.com.

Lynch, Kevin. 1960. *Image of the City.* Cambridge, MA: MIT Press.

Lynch, Kevin. 1972. *What Time is this Place?* Cambridge, MA: MIT Press.

MacJohnson, Rod. 2003. "'Blood Diamonds' Initiative a Mixed Success in War-Scarred Sierra Leone," *Agence France Presse,* May 18.

Mann, Denise. 2001. "Friendship Good for What Ails You," *WebMD,* http://content.health.msn.com/content/article/31/1728_75265.htm.

Martin, Frank Edgerton. 1995. "Riverside Revisited?" *Landscape Architecture,* August. Pp. 1–3.

McQuillen, Daniel M. 1998. "The U.S. Answers the Green Building Challenge," *Environmental Design and Construction,* Sept/Oct, pp. 43–50.

Mesch, Gustavo S., and Orit Manor. 1998. "Local Social Ties, Residential Satisfaction and Community Attachment." *Environment and Behavior.* Vol. 30, No. 4, pp. 504–519.

Metropolitan Water District (MWD). 2003. "Metropolitan Begins Transforming Region's Public Spaces Into Water Efficient Heritage Landscapes," press release, May 21, http://www.mwdh2o.com/mwdh2o/pages/news/press–releases/2003-05/city_makeover.htm.

Meyer, Caroline E. 2003. "Nurturing Brand Loyalty." *Washington Post,* Oct. 12, F-1.

Miles, Gray. 1999. "When Lost Souls Become a Parade," *Thunderbird: UBC Journalism Review,* December, http://www.journalism.ubc.ca/thunderbird.

Miles, Irene, William C. Sullivan, and Frances E. Kuo. 1998. "Ecological Restoration Volunteers: The Benefits of Participation," *Urban Ecosystems*, Vol. 2, pp. 27–41.

Miller, Coral Poh. 1972. "Cleveland's Huletts Still Standing Tall," Society of Industrial Archeology Newsletter, Vol. 26, No. 4, winter, pp. 1–3.

Millett, Katherine. 2004. "Birds on a cool green roof," *Chicago Wilderness Magazine*, Summer.

Mitchell, Stacy. 2003. "Big Box Stores Drain City Revenue, Study Finds," *The Home Team Advantage Bulletin*, February.

Moe, Richard, and Carter Wilkie. 1997. *Changing Places: Rebuilding Community in the Age of Sprawl*. New York, New York: Henry Holt.

Montgomery, John. 1995. "The Story of Temple Bar: Creating Dublin's Cultural Quarter," *Planning Practice and Research*, Vol. 10, No. 2, pp. 135–172.

Morris, Hugh. 2002. *Trails and Greenways: Advancing the Smart Growth Agenda*. Washington, D.C.: Rails-to-Trails Conservancy.

Nabhan, Gary Paul, and Stephen Trimble. 1995. *The Geography of Childhood*, Beacon Press.

Nacka Kommun. 2001. "Nacka Nature School and Ecopedogogic Centre," in *Report from an Environment Pedogogic Centre Seminar in Nacka, Sweden, on February 22–23, 2001*. City of Nacka, Sweden.

Nash, Roderick. 1989. *The Rights of Nature: A History of Environmental Ethics*, Madison, WI: University of Wisconsin Press.

Nasser, Haya El. 2002. "Gated Communities More Popular, and Not Just for the Rich," *USA Today*, Dec. 15.

National Low Income Housing Coalition. 2002. *Out of Reach 2002*. Washington, D.C.

National Trust for Historic Preservation. 2000. "Denver Public Schools Ensure the Future by Teaching the Past," press release, October 18, www.nationaltrust.org/news/docs/20001018_award_denver.html.

National Trust for Historic Preservation. 2002. *Rebuilding Community: A Best Practices Tool Kit for Historic Preservation and Redevelopment*. Washington, D.C.: NTHP.

Nau, John L. III, 2002. "Preservation is One Key to Salvation for Cities and History," *Cleveland Plain Dealer*, October 9.

New Economics Foundation. 2003. "New Survey Launched at Localism Conference Shows Britons in Favor of Local Produce and Concerned at the Power of Supermarkets," http://www.neweconomics.org.

Newberg, Sam. 2003. "The Bungalow Belt," *Urban Land*, January, pp. 65–66.

Newman, Peter, and Jeff Kenworthy. 1999. *Sustainability and Cities: Overcoming Automobile Dependence*, Washington, D.C.: Island Press.

Nicklas, Michael, and Gary Bailey. 1996a. "Energy Performance of Daylit Schools in North Carolina," Unpublished papers, Raleigh, NC: Innovative Design, Inc.

Nicklas, Michael, and Gary Bailey. 1996b. "Analysis of Performance of Students in Dayit Schools," Unpublished paper, Raleigh, NC: Innovative Design, Inc.

Northwest Energy Efficiency Alliance. 2002. "Hot Lips Pizza: Efficient Oven with Heat Recovery," *Betterbricks,* http://www.BetterBricks.com.

Oakrock, Barbara. 2002. "The Street Becomes a Stage: New Roles for Roads," *Landscape Northwest,* April 18.

Office of the Governor, State of Maryland. 2003. "Governor Ehrlich Establishes Priority Places Strategy Executive Order," Oct. 9, http://www.maryland.gov.

Office of the Mayor, City of Chicago. 2001. "City Selects ComEd to Provide Clean Power," press release, June 6, Chicago, IL.

Pappano, Laura, 2002. "Energy Efficient Schools Grasp Green Incentives," *Boston Globe,* July 15, Metro/Region, p.A-1.

Paquette, Carole. 2002. "School Projects Are Designed for Use by the Public," *New York Times,* Nov. 16. Section 11, p. 9.

Parker, D., and K. Sheinkopf. 1999. "Cool Home Features Bring Peak Energy Savings," *Home Energy,* Vol. 16, pp. 22–27.

Parker, D., J. Sherwin, and J. Sonne. 1998. "Measured Performance of a Reflective Roofing System in a Florida Commercial Building," *American Society of Heating, Refrigerating, and Air-Conditioning Engineers (ASHRAE) Technical Data Bulletin,* Vol. 14, No. 2.

Patron, Eugene J. 2002. "Taking a Different Task: An Old Railroad Line Offers a New Perspective on New York," *Designer/Builder,* May/June, pp. 10–17.

Peabody Trust. 2002. *Annual Review 2002.* London.

Peck, Steven, and Monica Kuhn. Undated, "Design Guidelines for Green Roofs," Toronto: CMHC.

Peñalosa, Enrique. 2001. "Parks for Livable Cities: Lessons from a Radical Mayor," Project for Public Spaces, remarks found at: http://www.pps.org/topics/whyneed/newvisions/penalosa_speech_2001.

Perez, Luis. 2004. "Architects offer 'visions' for High Line," New York Newsday, July16.

Perry/Affordable Housing Development Company. Undated. "Highlands' Garden Village: Old Elitch Gardens Amusement Park Redeveloped," *Colorado Best Practices,* http://www.sustainablecolorado.org/Best_Practices/Highlands/highlands.html.

Pew Research Center. 2001. *America's New Internationalist Point of View.* Washington, D.C.: The Pew Research Center for the People and the Press.

Pew Rsearch Center. 2002. *What the World Thinks in 2002: How Global Publics View Their Lives, Their Countries, The World, America.* Washington, D.C.: The Pew Research Center for the People and the Press.

Phelps Deily, Mary-Ellen. 2002. "Steering Clear of Trouble: Senior Drivers' Ed Programs Aim to Make the Road Safer," *Washington Post,* January 29, pp. F-1, F-5.

Porter, Charlene. 2000. "It takes Us All, It Takes Forever," *Green Cities,* http://usinfo.state.gov/journals/itgic/0300/ijge/gj-08.htm.

Portland Office of Sustainability. 2002. "Hot Lips Awarded for Energy Efficiency," Businesses for an Environmentally Sustainable Tomorrow, Portland, OR.

Powell, Kenneth. 1999. "Architecture: How Green Was My Allen?" *The Independent,* July 19, Arts section, p. 10.

Puget Sound Action Team. 2003. "Current PIE Projects," *Sound Waves*, Vol. 17, No. 1, winter.

Puig, Josep. 2002, "The Barcelona Solar Ordinance," http://www.eurosolar.org/solarzeitalter/solarzeit_3_01-3.html.

Putnam, Robert D. 2001. *Bowling Alone: The Collapse and Revival of American Community*. New York, NY: Simon and Schuster.

Putnam, Robert D., and Lewis Feldstein. 2003. *Better Together: Restoring the American Community*. New York, NY: Simon and Schuster.

Rails-to-Trails Conservancy. 2002. *Trails and Greenways: Advancing the Smart Growth Agenda*. Washington, D.C.: Rails-to-Trails Conservancy.

Redefining Progress. Undated. "Consuming Kids," Genuine Progress Indicator (GPI) Case Study no. 2, http://www.rprogress.org/publications/gpi1999/consuming_kids.html.

———. Undated. "Food for Thought," GPI Case Study No. 1, http://www.rprogress.org/publications/gpi1999/food_for_thought.html.

Regan, Margaret. 2003. "Simon Donovan: One of Tucson's Best-Known Artists Is a Renowned Joker—but He's Serious about His Art," *Tucson Weekly*, Feb. 6, http://www.tucsonweekly.com/gbase/currents/Content?oid=oid:46549

Reger-Nash, Bill, Kenneth J. Simon, Linda Cooper, and Adrian Bauman. Undated. "Wheeling Walks: A Media-Based Intervention to Increase Walking," unpublished paper, West Virginia University.

Renewable Energy World. 2001. "Large-scale Biogas Plant," *Renewable Energy World*, November–December 2001.

Ritsch, Massie. 1998. "Work Begins on History-Themed Murals in Santa Paula," *Los Angeles Times*, September 10, p. B1.

Rivers West. 2000. "Greenway on the Red: Forum Proceedings," Red River Corridor Association, June 15 and 16.

Rose, Ruth. 2003. "Wal-Mart Wars." *San Francisco Chronicle*, June 26. p. A-23.

Rushton, Betty. 2001. "Low Impact Parking Lot Design Reduces Runoff and Pollutant Loads," *Journal of Water Resources Planning and Management*, Vol. 127, No. 3, May/June, pp. 172–179.

Rysavy, Tracy. 2000. "TreePeople," *Yes* magazine. winter issue, http://63.135.115.158/article.asp?ID=318.

Saguaro Seminar. Undated. "Social Capital Community Benchmark Survey: Executive Summary," http://www.ksg.harvard.edu/saguaro/communitysurvey/results.html.

Sagoff, Mark, and David Wasserman. Undated. "Ecological Restoration and Concept of Place," Maryland Sea Grant program, http://www.mdsg.umd.edu/CB/sop/index.htm.

Sale, Kirkpatrick. 1985. *Dwellers in the Land: The Bioregional Vision*. San Francisco, CA: Sierra Club Books.

Salvesen, David, and Phillip Hervey. 2003. *Good Schools—Good Neighborhoods*, Chapel Hill, NC: University of North Carolina Center for Urban and Regional Studies.

Scharf, Kathryn. Undated. "The Good Food Box: A Case Study of an Alternative Non-Profit System for Fresh Fruit and Vegetable Distribution," in Mustafa Koc, Rod MacRae and Jennifer Welsh, *Toward Hungerproof Cities*, IDRC.

Schneider, Keith. 2001. "Conservation-Minded Housing in Indiana," *New York Times*, Nov. 25, p. 513.

Schor, Juliet. 1999. *The Overspent American: Why We Want What We Don't Need.* New York, New York: Basic Books.

Schor, Juliet. 1993. *The Overworked American: The Unexpected Decline of Leisure*, New York, New York: Basic Books.

Schukoske, Jane E. 2000. "Community Development Through Gardening: State and Local Politics Transforming Urban Open Space," *Legislation and Public Policy* Vol. 3, pp. 351–392.

Schwartz, John, and Geraldine Fabrikant. 2003. "War Puts Media Giant on the Defense," *New York Times*, March 31, p. C1.

Seattle Public Utility. 2001. "SEA Streets," http://www.cityofseattle.gov/util/About_SPU/Drainage_&_Sewer_System/Natural_Drainage_Systems/Street_Edge_Alternatives/index.asp.

Shanabruck, Charles. 2003. Personal interview. February 21, Executive Director, Historic Chicago Bungalow Association.

Sheldon, Kennon M., Andrew J. Elliot, Youngnee Kim, and Tim Kasser. 2000. "What Is Satisfying about Satisfying Events? Testing 10 Candidate Psychological Needs," *Journal of Personality and Social Psychology*, Vol. 80, No. 2, pp. 325–339.

Shukovsky, Paul. 2003. "NW Ports Are Link in Threat to Imperiled Apes: Orangutan Habitat Is Being Destroyed by Export-Driven Logging," *The Seattle Post-Intelligencer*, July 5, p. A1.

Shutkin, William A. 2000. *The Land that Could Be: Environmentalism and Democracy in the Twenty-First Century*, Cambridge, MA: MIT Press.

Sierra Club, 2000. *Sprawl Costs Us All*, San Francisco: Sierra Club.

Skogsberg, Kjell, and Bo Nordell. 2001. "The Sundsvall Hospital Snow Storage," *Cold Regions Science and Technology*, Vol. 32, pp. 63–70.

Smith, Doug. 2002. "Why Green Buildings Favor the Bottom Line," *Seattle Daily Journal of Commerce*, May 2, http://www.djc.com.

Snyder, Gary. 1974. *Turtle Island*, New York, NY: New Directions.

Snyder, Gary. 1990. *The Practice of the Wild*, San Francisco, CA: North Point.

Society for the Preservation of New York Manhole Covers. http://www.nycmanhole covers.org/index.html.

Solid Waste Authority of Central Ohio. 2001. "'My House' at the Columbus Zoo," http://www.swaco.org/education/myhouse.htm.

Spector, Rebecca. 2000. "Regaining Connections Between Farmers and Consumers," in Andrew Kimbrell ed. *The Fatal Harvest Reader: The Tragedy of Industrial Agriculture* Washington, D.C.: Island Press.

Steinglass, Matt. 2000. "The Machine in the Garden" *Metropolis*, October, pp. 126–131, 166–167.

Steinhouer, Jennifer. 2003. "New York Facing Epidemic of Diabetes, Health Officials Say," *New York Times,* Jan. 25, p. A18.

Stepp, Laura Sessions. 2003. "Boomer Bust: A Generation Learns That The World Doesn't Revolve Around It After All," *Washington Post,* June 10, C1–C2.

Stevens, Mark R., and Samina Raja. 2001. "What's Eating You About What You Eat," Madison Food System project Working paper, Madison, WI.

Still, Mike. 2003. "Sustainable Timber Sale Effort Is Given a Marketing Boost," *Bristol Herald-Courier,* June 23, p. A-9.

Surface Transportation Policy Project. 2002. *Mean Streets 2002.* Washington, D.C.: STPP.

Sustainable Building. 2001. "Telus: Revitalization of an Office Building." Issue 02–2002.

Society of American Florists. Undated. *The Impact of Flowers and Plants on Workplace Productivity,* press release and research summary, http://www.aboutflowers.com/workplace/research.htm.

Taylor, Andrea Faber, Angela Wiley, Frances E. Know, and William C. Sullivan. 1998. "Growing Up in the Inner City: Green Spaces as Places to Grow," *Environment and Behavior,* Vol. 30, No. 1, January, pp. 3–27.

Thayer, Robert L. 2003. *LifePlace: Bioregional Thought and Practice.* Berkeley, CA: University of California Press.

Thieme, Duncan. 2002. "A Model for Sustainable Design," *Seattle Daily Journal of Commerce,* October 31, http://www.djc.com.

Thompson, J. William. 1996. "From Blight to Bounty," *Landscape Architecture,* July. pp. 44–49.

Thorncroft, Tony. 2002. "Festivals That Bring Cities Fringe Benefits," *Financial Times,* June 1, Summer Arts Guide, p. 1.

Trafford, Abigail. 2000. "The Healing Power of Friendship," *Washington Post,* Oct. 3, health section, p. 5.

TreePeople. 2002. "Broadus Elementary School Demonstration Project," *Watershed Best Management Practices,* newsletter produced by TreePeople, Los Angeles, CA.

Trivedi, Bijal. 2002. "Survey Reveals Geographic Illiteracy." *National Geographic Today,* Nov. 20, http://news.nationalgeographic.com/news/2002/11/1126_021120_TVGeoRoperSurvey.html.

Tuan, Yi-Fu. 1977. *Space and Place: The Perspective of Experience.* Minneapolis, MN: University of Minnesota Press.

Tucson Weekly. 2002. "Best Public Art," http://www.tucsonweekly.com.

Turner, Robyne S., and Margaret S. Murray. 2001. "Managing Growth in a Climate of Urban Diversity: South Florida's Eastward Ho! Initiative," *Journal of Planning Education and Research,* Vol. 20, pp. 308–328.

Ulrich, Roger S. 1984. "View Through A Window May Influence Recovery From Surgery," *Science,* Vol. 224, pp. 420-421.

———. 2002. "Health Benefits of Gardens in Hospitals," paper prepared for conference, Plants for People. International Exhibition Floriade, the Netherlands.

Union of Baltic Cities. 2001. "Heading Towards A Sustainable Society by 2020: Sundsvall Used to Be Known for Its Burdening Environmental Problems," *Local Agenda 21 Good Practice Revice,* Turku, Finland: UBC.

University of California Sustainable Agriculture Research and Education Program. 1999. "Collaboration Between Willard Greening Project and Boss," program report, January 1999, http://www.sarep.ucdavis.edu.

U.N. Habitat. Undated. "Eco-City, Johannesburg," Best Practices Database, http://www.bestpractices.org.

U.S. Conference of Mayors. 2002. "In Burlington, Youngest and Oldest Residents Share Multi-Generational Center," U.S. Mayors Best Practice, http://www.usmayors.org.

U.S. Environmental Protection Agency. 2002. *U.S. Climate Action Report—2002.* Washington, D.C.: USEPA.

———. Undated. "Waterfront Regeneration Trust: Integrating Ecosystem Management with Brownfields Redevelopment and Local Land Use Planning," an International Brownfields case study. Washington, D.C.: USEPA.

USEPA and ICMA. 19. "Westergasfabriek: Collaboration of Local Government and Community," an international brownfields case study.

USEPA. 1998. "Parking Lot at Florida Aquarium Becomes Laboratory," *Nonpoint Source News-Notes,* November 1998, Issue 54.

Van den Berg, Leo and Peter Pol. 1998. *The European High Speed Train and Urban Development.* Aldershot, United Kingdom: Ashgate.

Van Siclen, Bill. 2002. "Burning Bright," *Providence Journal-Bulletin,* May 2, Live This Weekend Section, p. L-25.

———. 2003. "Waterfire Struggles to Keep Burning," *Providence Journal-Bulletin,* May 23. News Section, p. A-01.

Venezia Commune, 1996. *Venezia Il Nuovo Piano Urbanistico,* Venice, Italy: Gius, Laterza and Figli.

Växjö, Kommun. 2003. "Fossil Fuel Free Växjö," http://www.Växjö.se/english/sustainable.htm#fossulfree.

Victoria Population Health Survey. 2001. "We Do Better Health Facts," http://www.togetherwedobetter.vic.gov.au.

Villarosa, Linda. 2003. "Prevention Can Start Young, Studies Suggest; but How?" *New York Times,* December 2. p. F-1.

Vogel, Lucie. 1998. "Charlottesville, VA: Collaborative Planning for Infill Development," *Planners Casebook,* no. 27, Summer, Chicago. American Institute of Certified Planners.

Vuong, Mary. 2003. "Mike Peringer: Finding Creative Solution to Blight," *Seattle Post Intelligencer,* March 6, p. A10.

Wackernagel, Mathis, and William Rees. 1995. *Our Ecological Footprint: Reducing Human Impact on the Earth.* Gabriola Island, British Columbia: New Society Publishers.

Waters, Alice. Undated. "Making Good the Educational Priority," remarks for the

American Institute of Wine and Food (AIWF) Conference: Children's Education: Feeding Our Future, http://www.edibleschoolyard.org.

Weihs, Karen. 2001. "Press Release: Study Shows Breast Cancer Patients Live Longer the Larger Their Support Network," http://www.psychosomatic.org.

Weiss, Jonathan D. 2002. "Local Sustainability Efforts in the United States: The Progress Since Rio," Environmental Law Review, News and Analysis, 32 ELR 10667.

Wells, Nancy M. 2000. "At Home with Nature: Effects of 'Greenness' on Children's Cognitive Functioning," *Environment and Behavior,* Vol. 32, No. 6, November, pp. 775–795.

Whyte, William H. 1980. *The Social Life of Small Urban Spaces.* Washington, D.C.: Conservation Foundation.

Wilson, Craig. 1999. "Nights too bright to See Stars' Lights. No Longer in the Dark, Town Directs Efforts to Clear Sky," *USA Today,* August 30. Life Section, p. D-07.

Wilson, E. O. 1984. *Biophilia: The Human Bond with Other Species.* Cambridge, MA: Harvard University Press.

Winikoff, Tamara, ed. 1995. *Places Not Spaces: Placemaking in Australia.* Sidney: Environbook.

Wolch, Jennifer, John P. Wilson, and Jed Fehrenbach. 2002. "Parks and Park Funding in Los Angeles: An Equity Mapping Analysis." Los Angeles: University of Southern California Sustainable Cities Program.

World Wildlife Fund (WWF), 2002. *The Living Planet Report, 2002,* Gland, Switzerland: WWF International.

Yencken, David. 1995. "Collaboration in Placemaking," in Tamara Winikoff, ed. *Places Not Spaces, Placemaking in Australia.* Sidney: Environbook. Pp. 11–13.

Yienger, James, Lizbeth Brown, and Nancy Skinner. 2002. "Experiences of ICLEI's Cities for Climate Change Protection Campaign (CCP): A focus on Asia," Proceedings of IGES/APN Mega-City Project, January 2002. Kitakyushu, Japan.

Zieve, Rick. 2002. "Architecture Odd Couple Is Bound by Public Spirit," *Seattle Daily Journal of Commerce,* October 31, http://www.djc.com.

Ziner, Karen Lee. 2002. "Waterfire Still Glowing, Growing," *Providence Journal-Bulletin,* November 3. Local News Section, p. B-01.

Index